More advance praise for
Empress of the East

"Leslie Peirce, one of the world's foremost historians of the Ottoman empire, has created a brilliant, absorbing, and profoundly insightful account of one of the most enigmatically interesting figures of the sixteenth century: Roxelana, the captive slave who ultimately reigned alongside Sultan Suleiman the Magnificent. Peirce is rightly celebrated for her expertise on the fascinating subject of the Ottoman harem, and there is no one better qualified to help us understand how Roxelana emerged from the sultan's harem to become one of the most powerful political figures of her times. This is a book that should be read by anyone interested in understanding the deep history of Turkey, the Ottoman empire, and the Muslim Middle East."

—Larry Wolff, author of *The Singing Turk*

EMPRESS
OF THE
EAST

HOW A EUROPEAN SLAVE GIRL BECAME
QUEEN OF THE OTTOMAN EMPIRE

LESLIE PEIRCE

BASIC BOOKS

New York

Basic Books
Hachette Book Group
1290 Avenue of the Americas, New York, NY 10104
www.basicbooks.com

Printed in the United States of America
First edition: September 2017
Published by Basic Books, an imprint of Perseus Books, LLC, a subsidiary of Hachette Book Group, Inc.

The Hachette Speakers Bureau provides a wide range of authors for speaking events. To find out more, go to www.hachettespeakersbureau.com or call (866) 376-6591.

The publisher is not responsible for websites (or their content) that are not owned by the publisher.

Print Book Interior Design by Amy Quinn

The Library of Congress has cataloged the hardcover edition as follows:
Names: Peirce, Leslie P., author.
Title: Empress of the east : how a European slave girl became queen of the Ottoman Empire / Leslie Peirce.
Description: New York : Basic Books, 2017. | Includes bibliographical references and index.
Identifiers: LCCN 2017003912 (print) | LCCN 2017006112 (e-book) | ISBN 9780465032518 (hardback) | ISBN 9780465093090 (e-book)
Subjects: LCSH: Hurrem, consort of Sèuleyman I, Sultan of the Turks, approximately 1504–1558? | Queens—Turkey—Biography. | Turkey—Kings and rulers—Biography. | Sèuleyman I, Sultan of the Turks, 1494 or 1495–1566—Marriage. | Slaves—Turkey—Biography. | Mistresses—Turkey—Biography. | Ukrainians—Turkey—Biography. | Turkey—History—Sèuleyman I, 1520–1566. | BISAC: HISTORY / Modern / 16th Century. | BIOGRAPHY & AUTOBIOGRAPHY / Royalty. | BIOGRAPHY & A UTOBIOGRAPHY / Women. | HISTORY / Middle East / Turkey & Ottoman Empire. | BIOGRAPHY & AUTOBIOGRAPHY / Historical.
Classification: LCC DR509.H87 P47 2017 (print) | LCC DR509.H87 (e-book) | DDC 956/.015092 [B]—dc23
LC record available at https://lccn.loc.gov/2017003912

ISBNs: 978-0-465-03251-8 (hardcover); 978-0-465-09309-0 (e-book)

LSC-C

10 9 8 7 6 5 4 3 2 1

For Joanne, Lynda, Nancy, Linda,
and the memory of Jude

This woman, of late a slave, but now become the greatest empresse of the East, flowing in all worldly felicitie, attended upon with all the pleasures that her heart could desire, wanted nothing she could wish but how to find means that the Turkish empire might after the death of Solyman be brought to some one of her owne sons.

—Richard Knolles, *The Generall Historie of the Turkes* (1603)

Contents

Map   *viii*

BEGINNINGS

1 The Russian Concubine   3

2 Abduction   14

3 In the Old Palace   27

4 The Politics of Motherhood   51

5 Lovers and Parents   69

CHALLENGES

6 Roxelana's Rival   82

7 Coming of Age   100

8 A Queen for the New Palace   121

9 The Two Favorites   145

10 Building a Reputation   170

POLITICS

11 Family Matters   196

12 Home and Abroad   214

13 Recovery   235

14 Showdown   257

15 Last Years   280

Epilogue   304

Acknowledgments   *318*

Who's Who and What's What   *321*

List of Illustrations and Credits   *325*

Notes   *327*

Bibliography   *339*

Index   *346*

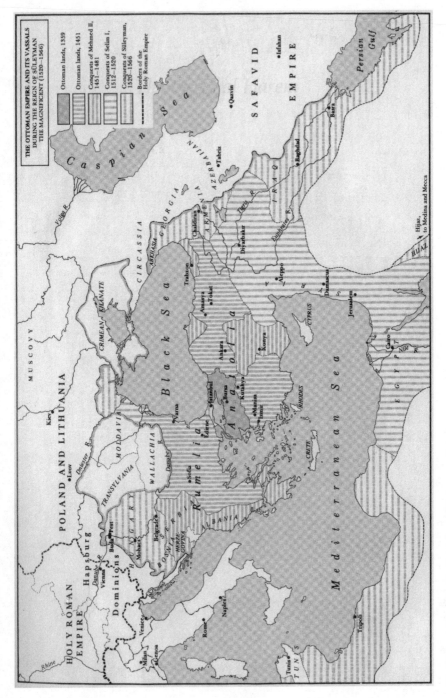

The Ottoman empire in the reign of Suleyman I.

BEGINNINGS

1

THE RUSSIAN CONCUBINE

This week there has occurred in this city a most extraordinary event, one absolutely unprecedented in the history of the Sultans. The Grand Signior Suleiman has taken to himself as his Empress a slave woman from Russia. . . . There is great talk about the marriage and none can say what it means.

—Dispatch from the Genoese Bank of Saint George,
Istanbul representative[1]

THE RUSSIAN SLAVE had been the concubine of Suleyman I, "the Magnificent," for fifteen years when the royal wedding celebration took place in 1536. Like all concubines of the Ottoman sultans, she was neither Turkish nor Muslim by birth. Abducted from her homeland, the young girl proved herself adaptable and quick-witted, mastering the rules, the graces, and the politics that propelled her from obscurity to the sultan's bed. She rapidly became Suleyman's favorite, astounding both his court and his public. Sultans of the Ottoman empire did not make demonstrable favorites of their consorts, however much they came to care for them. But Suleyman and Roxelana became the parents of six children in quick succession, five of them sons. Some thought Roxelana used seductive powers, even potions, to induce the love Suleyman appeared to bear her. They called her witch.

Together the royal couple overturned one assumption after another. Roxelana was the first Ottoman concubine ever to marry the sultan who was her master. She was also the first to cut an overtly conspicuous figure. It was Roxelana who transformed the imperial harem from a residence for women of the dynasty into an institution that wielded political influence. Royal women following in her footsteps crafted powerful roles in Ottoman politics while serving as advisers to their sons and, in the seventeenth century, ruling as regents. When Roxelana died in 1558, she also left as a tangible part of her legacy numerous charitable foundations in the Ottoman capital of Istanbul and across the empire—another break with tradition.

While there was no formal office of queen among the Ottomans, Roxelana filled this role in all but title, a formidable match for the great female rulers and consorts of Europe who shared the sixteenth century with her. But the radical nature of what can only be called the reign of Suleyman and Roxelana—a ruling partnership never repeated by the Ottomans—made her a controversial figure in her own time. The debate over her place in Ottoman history persists today.

Roxelana's given name is not known. Nor are we certain of her exact birthplace, the date of her birth, or the names of her parents. But historical hearsay is plausible in her case because of the fascination she held for watchers of the Ottomans like the Genoese banker. Contemporary consensus held that she came from Ruthenia, "old Russia"—today a broad region in Ukraine—then governed by the Polish king. Europeans interested in her origins called her Roxelana, "the maiden from Ruthenia."

The Ottoman name given to the young captive was Hurrem, a Persian word meaning "joyful" or "laughing." Though she lived with this name for the rest of her life, she was rarely called it, except by Suleyman. Powerful people were known by their titles. To his subjects, Suleyman was "the Padishah," the sovereign. As the monarch's exclusive consort, Roxelana acquired the title "Haseki," the favorite. When Suleyman made her a free woman and married her, she became the "Haseki Sultan" (the addition of "sultan" to a woman's name or title indicated her membership in the dynastic family). This book calls her Roxelana, the name by which those outside the Ottoman world knew her and many still remember her.

Some Ottomans later came to believe that Roxelana was the daughter of an Orthodox priest—or so they told a Polish ambassador who came to Istanbul in the 1620s. But the only absolute certainty about the young captive is that her natal family was Christian. From the early fifteenth century onward, the sultans fathered all their children with

Christian-born females taken from the empire's borderlands or beyond. These captive females were converted to Islam and assimilated into Ottoman culture before they were chosen as royal mothers. Concubines offered the advantage of having no ties to Ottoman families who might challenge the dynasty's dominance.

Roxelana had the good fortune to be chosen within a few months of Suleyman's enthronement in September 1520 as the empire's tenth sultan. He was twenty-six; she was seventeen or so. Suleyman had had other concubines before his accession, but Roxelana was the first partner of his long reign, and she succeeded in keeping herself the only one.

ROXELANA WAS A survivor. It was no small achievement that the young girl overcame the violence of her capture. She persevered through the perilous trek from her homeland to the distant Ottoman capital, where she embarked on the bewildering next phase of her life. The Ottoman name chosen for her suggests that she managed to put a congenial face on her fate. Roxelana's aptitude for survival would soon lift her above the common servitude that was the destiny of most female slaves. She rapidly became adept at reading the political and sexual dynamics of the

Portrait of the young Roxelana, titled "Roxelana, wife of Suleyman." Venetian School, sixteenth–seventeenth century.

imperial harem—that private world of the sultan's female relatives, concubines, children, and their many attendants. It was Roxelana's charm combined with her savvy that enabled her to best the competition within the harem and to achieve the hitherto unknown roles of favorite and then wife and queen.

Roxelana and Suleyman shattered tradition by creating a nuclear family in a polygynous world. Until then, royal concubines had a single, well-defined responsibility. Once a concubine bore a male child to an Ottoman prince or sultan, her sole duty was to work toward the boy's future political success. No conflict would arise here because the birth of a son terminated his mother's sexual connection with her master. It did not matter if their relationship was one of passion, for tradition dictated that she bear him no more children. He would move on to a fresh concubine, while she remained with her son, her duty to raise him and accompany him to whatever provincial post he was assigned as prince.

These reproductive practices made uninhibited or prolonged relationships nearly impossible. Only if a concubine first gave birth to one or more daughters could her master continue to indulge any affection for her, at least until she bore a son. Hollywood stereotypes of lascivious sultans and their bevies of languid, sex-obsessed slaves only rarely held true for the Ottomans. Sex for males of the dynasty was a political duty as much as it was a pleasure. As with all hereditary dynasties, survival depended on the production of talented princes eligible to rule. As for the concubine, she was a sexual being for only a phase of her career but a mother for the rest of her life. Roxelana was both.

A royal concubine had to be physically appealing, for the arousal of desire was critical. (At one point in the seventeenth century, the newly enthroned sultan's aversion to females temporarily imperiled the survival of the Ottoman state.) But the concubine also had to possess a keen mind and a capacity for political intelligence in order to successfully promote her son in a dangerously competitive world. Daughters also needed astute mothers who could raise them to be princesses worthy of the dynasty and loyal allies of their brother. The Ottomans believed that all princes, except those who were physically or mentally disabled, were born with the right to succeed their father. Here they differed from their European rivals, who practiced primogeniture, assigning only the eldest the right to rule. In the Ottoman view, competition among princes identified the successor best able to govern, defend the empire, and conquer new lands.

The birth of her first child, Mehmed, in the fall of 1521 thrust Roxelana into this sometimes fierce world. The contest for the throne demanded that the sultan's sons be prepared to compete to the death, and so princes were bred to the honor of sacrificing themselves to the future glory of an empire painstakingly assembled by their ancestors. In theory, this intradynastic violence was institutionalized and limited to interregnums. Conflict was to be confined within the royal family, sparing the populace at large chronic civil strife such as the Wars of the Roses among claimants for the English throne. The formula worked, for fraternal rivalry had produced a chain of exceptionally talented sovereigns. But the violence sometimes spilled over into the public.

It was left to the mothers of slain princes to bear the burden of lifelong grief produced by this fratricidal system. The sultanate could not impose such a fate on a woman of distinguished pedigree. A slave concubine, on the other hand, could be enlisted in the precarious, if ennobling, career of mother to a prince. If Roxelana did not succeed in protecting her princes, she would carry the burden of more than one son's death. As mother to a princess, she would not be banished from Istanbul in political exile, but she would suffer the disgrace of another woman's elevation to the lofty position of queen mother of the Ottoman empire. By the time Mehmed arrived, Roxelana was certainly aware of her duty to succeed, but it is unlikely that she anticipated the lengths to which it would take her.

LIKE FOREIGN DIPLOMATS, the sultan's subjects were confused by the peculiarities of Roxelana's maverick career. She not only continued to live intimately with the sultan, but she also had more than one son to tutor for success. The public was used to the old traditions. (Among the Ottomans the vocabularies of tradition and law overlapped.) It was not surprising that many favored Suleyman's oldest son Mustafa and the boy's mother Mahidevran. Mustafa had arrived when his father was still a prince abiding by the accepted rules of reproduction. Now, as sultan,

Suleyman had broken those rules. People focused their suspicions on Roxelana, for it would not do to doubt the mighty monarch. The slave had no family and no pedigree to protect her.

Across the globe, the times were ripe for blaming queens. In 1536, the year Roxelana celebrated her wedding, the Tudor king Henry VIII executed his wife Anne Boleyn, whom he accused of bewitching him— tricking him, that is, into falling in love with her.[2] Suleyman never accused Roxelana of such trickery; nor did he share Henry's failure to get a male heir from his favorite. Nevertheless, Roxelana could sympathize with Anne's dilemma, for the public would compare her unfavorably to Mahidevran, her predecessor as royal consort, as England's subjects compared Anne to Henry's first, divorced wife, Catherine of Aragon. The extravagant devotion of powerful men, it seemed, had to be the fault of their female lovers. Even Cleopatra, last of the Ptolemaic pharaohs of Egypt, has been popularly remembered for the talent of beguiling great Roman generals.

History has treated Roxelana cavalierly, for no one has yet told the story of her remarkable life from the perspective of a concubine. No one who wrote about her ever met her, except for Suleyman. He composed copious love poetry for his favorite, but none of his letters to her, written during his long absences at war, survive. Though the sultan's subjects could be vocal about royal consorts, Ottoman chroniclers and commentators stayed silent on the subject, for social protocol frowned on speaking of the women of another man's household, most of all the monarch's. For the same reason, we do not know what Roxelana really looked like, although painters imagined her more than once. On the other hand, European observers of the Ottomans—ambassadors, merchants, travelers, and former captives—wrote extensive descriptions of the sultan, his palaces, his children, and their mothers. Their interest in the females of the dynasty, however, was confined to politics and power (including sexual power). Almost never did they mention the efforts that may have won Roxelana more admirers at home than detractors—her many philanthropic projects across the empire, for example.

The life of this elusive woman contains many blank spaces. This book cannot hope to fill them all, although it can and does suggest probabilities and imagine possibilities. Fortunately, Roxelana provided something of a record of herself. Although only a small number of the letters she wrote to Suleyman survive, they span four decades, from the 1520s, when she had gained enough familiarity with the Turkish language to muster a communication, to the 1550s, by which time she had become a master of politics. Her prose, lively and affectionate, helps us see why she acquired a name meaning "joyful." Roxelana would prove tough-minded and ambitious, but she never seemed to lose her playful side.

We can also glimpse Roxelana's character in the charter deeds she drew up for her charitable foundations. While not as intimate as her letters, they reveal her personal understanding of the Islamic mandate to give. She repeatedly insisted that the staffs of her foundations be just as dedicated to treating the needy with kindness and consideration as they were to dispensing relief to them. Her special benevolence toward slaves suggests that she never forgot her past.

Elevated to the position of the sultan's wife, Roxelana recognized that she must give on a conspicuous scale. The Ottoman empire was populated almost exclusively by followers of the three great monotheistic religions originating in the Near East—Judaism, Christianity, and Islam—each of which held charitable giving as a core tenet and obligation. Roxelana appears to have embraced the obligation wholeheartedly. But she was also canny enough to appreciate that displaying generosity toward ordinary people was the most effective strategy for gaining the esteem and gratitude that could offset any negative repercussions of her unconventional career.

Over the course of her life, Roxelana endowed mosques, schools, soup kitchens, hostels for travelers and pilgrims, sufi lodges, shrines for saintly figures, public baths, and a hospital modern for its day. Mothers of princes and princesses had erected notable philanthropic foundations before her, but Roxelana's work far surpassed that of any previous Ottoman woman in volume and geographic reach. It set a model for future females of the dynasty that would trickle down through elite circles and out to women in the thousands of Ottoman cities and towns. Several of Roxelana's monuments still stand today, and so do many of the monuments that her work inspired.

THE RUTHENIAN MAIDEN began her career as a hapless young girl forcibly drafted into the complex politics of the Ottoman dynastic house. Having lost her natal family, she spent the rest of her life in a perpetual quest to preserve and protect her new Ottoman family. But making a haven of domestic life was not easy when royal motherhood demanded partisan involvement in the treacherous politics of the throne. Protecting her sons was bound to pit her against Mustafa and his mother Mahidevran. Six years older than Mehmed, Mustafa had a head start. By the age of twelve, he was already popular among soldiers. The Ottoman army, especially the famous Janissary infantry corps, sometimes threatened to exert its will on politics.

When Roxelana came into Suleyman's life, he had just inherited an empire that commanded the eastern Mediterranean seas, the Black Sea and its shores, southeastern Europe, and much of today's Middle East. His great-grandfather Mehmed II stamped his coins with the phrase "Sultan of the two seas, Khan of the two lands." Known among the Turks as "the Conqueror," Mehmed had put an end to the millennium-old Christian empire of the Byzantines and made ancient Constantinople his capital. While Suleyman's grandfather Bayezid II was more a statesman than a warrior, his father Selim I threatened east and west. In two long wars, Selim pushed back the rising new power in Iran and demolished the venerable Mamluk sultanate in Cairo. From the latter he took Egypt and the Levant, as well as the prestigious title of "servitor of the two Noble Sanctuaries," the holy cities of Mecca and Medina. Selim was preparing to invade Europe when he died suddenly in 1520. The pope and several kings were said to be relieved when Suleyman ascended the Ottoman throne, for they considered him a novice at fighting wars. He would soon prove them wrong.

Starting with the wresting of Belgrade from Hungarian control in 1521 and the island of Rhodes from the Knights of St. John in 1522, Suleyman pushed the empire further into Europe and Asia and, within a decade, laid claim to the mantle of the Roman empire. Of the thirty-seven years Suleyman lived with Roxelana, he spent a total of ten apart from her on twelve different military campaigns. She missed him terribly, as her letters demonstrate, but there was much to keep her busy in his absence. The raising of their several children was an enormous responsibility. When her sons left home to embark on their public careers, she worried about them, and so she went long distances to visit them. In Istanbul, she had the company of her only daughter Mihrumah, who was famously devoted to her parents and equally treasured by them. Tutored by her mother in the dynastic responsibilities of royal females, Mihrumah would become the greatest of Ottoman princess philanthropists. She would also learn from her mother that corresponding with foreign royalty could sometimes benefit the empire in ways that diplomacy among men did not.

As queen, Roxelana kept herself occupied as mistress of the female court, receiving visitors and organizing celebrations to mark religious and social holidays. She had the palace harem household and its cadres of attendants and servants to oversee, though the principal responsibility for order and discipline lay with the palace staff of female administrators and eunuchs. It was Roxelana who ensured that talented harem women graduated from palace service to marriage with a deserving partner, generally an esteemed member of Suleyman's government. She also managed the staff of male agents who worked for her outside the palace. The business of her far-flung charitable endowments in particular took up an increasing amount of her and their time. And as she acquired political acuity, she became Suleyman's eyes and ears in the capital when he was away. Developing networks of contact and gathering intelligence became critical, including information that could be gleaned from female agents and female visitors to the palace. Following the death in 1534 of Suleyman's mother Hafsa, Roxelana became Suleyman's most loyal informant.

It was the demise of Hafsa, beloved by her son and a venerable figure, that made possible Roxelana's marriage to Suleyman. Not that Hafsa necessarily opposed the union (there is, unfortunately, little to tell us what she thought of her son's extraordinary relationship), but the politics of the court would not permit a concubine to rise above the status of the queen mother. Then Roxelana's nuptials in 1536 literally opened the door to the New Palace, Suleyman's own domicile, which welcomed her with an elegant suite of rooms adjacent to his. A cadre of attendants and servants accompanied her from the Old Palace, longtime home of the royal harem. Roxelana retained chambers in the Old Palace, however, for

Hafsa's death meant that she, as the top-ranking female of the dynastic family, was now responsible for the harem's welfare.

Roxelana's change in residence ushered in what was to be her greatest legacy: the transformation of the royal harem into a political force. Known today as the Topkapı Palace, the New Palace was a vast complex of structures built by Mehmed the Conqueror when his first royal residence in Istanbul (now the Old Palace) proved too small to house both his royal presence and the major offices of his government. Under Roxelana's tutelage, the New Palace harem would expand rapidly and become, by the end of the century, a regularized institution in Ottoman government. The upper echelon of royal women now lived and labored at the political heart of the empire, while the Old Palace retained its stature as a training institution and home for retired harem women. Working from the New Palace, senior women developed networks that connected them with political allies on the outside, including foreign emissaries. Despite periodic outbursts of antipathy to female "meddling," the harem's practice of politics had become normalized, and so it remained throughout the life of the empire.

Roxelana died in 1558, leaving Suleyman without her for eight years until his death in 1566. She died with the comfort of knowing that one of her sons would succeed his father but also with the fear that the contest between them would be bloody. She would not live to know that the idea of a reigning couple—a sultan and his queen—proved too controversial for the Ottomans to repeat. After her, the New Palace harem whose rise she sparked would be headed by the queen mother. Nor did Roxelana know that she would gain both fame and notoriety in the centuries after her death through her depiction in European literature and opera and even through a modern Turkish television drama with an avid worldwide following.

Roxelana may have anticipated correctly, however, that the nature of politics at the heart of the empire would change. In fact, her career was proof that change had already begun. Even if there never was another queen, she and Suleyman set precedents that were still at work in their children's and grandchildren's generations. A more peaceable system of identifying the next sultan began to emerge from transformations in the practice of succession-by-combat that began with her. Roxelana helped to move the Ottoman empire into modern times, where treaty negotiations became as challenging and significant as victory in battle and domestic well-being occupied as much of the government's attention as conquest. Bolstered by the reforms she introduced, the Ottoman sultanate would sustain itself for another three and a half centuries. All this was generated along with the Ottoman empire's greatest love story.

2

ABDUCTION

ROXELANA'S CACHET WAS such that more than one nation would lay claim to her. It was said, for instance, that she was Italian by origin, from Siena. Or perhaps she was abducted from Castel Collecchio in Parma in 1525 (when she was already the mother of three Ottoman children).[1] The French never called Roxelana their own, but a popular belief held that the kings of France enjoyed a blood relationship with the Ottoman sultans. A French princess of the fifteenth century had allegedly given birth to Mehmed II, the conqueror of Byzantine Constantinople—or perhaps it was to his father Murad II.

The notion that a French princess was mother to an Ottoman son may have been far-fetched, but it was not entirely implausible in the fifteenth century. Ottoman princes were still making marriage alliances with foreign dynasties into the reign of Murad II (who died in 1451). The assertion of a blood tie perhaps looked quite appealing in the sixteenth century, when Suleyman and the French king Francis I began to cultivate a political alliance against their mutual rivals, Spain and the Holy Roman Empire. But the suggestion that the Ottoman harem once housed a princess from France seems to have run its course by the late eighteenth century, when the French ambassador to Istanbul blamed Roxelana for propagating it.[2] He found the idea that a princess could go missing absurd. It is surely a measure of Roxelana's posthumous fame that she bore the blame for deeds that may never have crossed her mind.

More plausible assertions of Roxelana's own origin came—and still come—from Ukraine and Poland. Neither claim negates the other, for she is widely thought to have been abducted into the slave trade from Ruthenia, a broad area that today encompasses western Ukraine but was then under the rule of the Polish king.[3] Recently, with Ukraine's achievement of independence from the Soviet Union in 1991, the new nation has embraced heroic figures from the past. In 1999, the town of Rohatyn, popularly alleged to be Roxelana's birthplace, erected a lofty bronze statue of her atop a pedestal.[4] (Rohatyn today is a town of close to 9,000 located some forty-five miles southeast of the historic city of Lviv.) Until more concrete proof surfaces, however, the assumption that Roxelana was taken from Rohatyn remains uncertain. But she is perhaps fortunate to have her memory localized and enshrined. Other well-known Ottoman concubine mothers seem fated to lack communities that might celebrate them.

While Roxelana's Ruthenian origins seem reasonably certain, rumors about her birthplace gained traction because the precise origins of royal concubines were largely uncertain. The reason was that they were irrelevant. Natal loyalties had to be erased so that Christian captives could be turned into devoted servants of the Ottoman sultanate. And so slaves recruited to the service of the dynasty underwent a regime of intense instruction. Its goal was to render them speakers of Turkish, followers of Islam, and exemplars of Ottoman ritual and duty. Palace staff and teachers brought in from outside drilled Roxelana and her fellow recruits. Female slaves who would attend high-ranking women received more advanced instruction in dynastic etiquette. Especially well educated were candidates deemed eligible for the role of concubine, for their principal responsibility as future mothers would be to school their children to lead the empire.

The assertion of Roxelana's Ruthenian roots came early in her career. In 1526, six years after she first became Suleyman's concubine but before she was a widely recognized figure, diplomatic circles were informed that Suleyman now preferred a woman from Ruthenia. Pietro Bragadin, the Venetian Republic's resident ambassador in Istanbul, described her as *di nazion russa*—of Russian origin—the word *Rus* then connoting Ruthenia.[5] Bragadin was unlikely to report this fact without reliable confirmation by either someone serving in the imperial palace (perhaps a slave of Venetian origin?) or a trusted member of the embassy compound.

Because Venetian ambassadorial reports were consumed in Europe as models of diplomatic prose, the news of the sultan's favorite would spread.[6] When other Europeans in Istanbul began to notice and write home about her, they remarked on her "Russian" roots. The name Roxelana caught on when Austrian ambassador Ogier Ghiselin de Busbecq called her *Roxolana*, "the maiden from Ruthenia."[7] His *Turkish Letters*, published in Latin in 1589, were widely read across Europe.

THE FATE OF the maiden from Ruthenia was entangled in the histories of several nations. Not only did the Ottoman sultanate figure in Roxelana's destiny but so did the kingdom of Poland (from whose territory she was captured) and the Crimean Khanate (which did the capturing). More distantly, the ways of the Mongols and even the medieval empire of the Seljuk Turks before them echoed in Ottoman royal culture and a concubine's place within it. Roxelana was only one of an enormous number of captives who passed through multiple hands in multiple lands, but her very journey seems to have catalyzed an innate sense of survival. The harsh conditions of the slave trade would teach her to fasten onto whatever element in the political repertoires of the region came to hand.

The line between raiding as an economic staple and the common practice of taking prisoners in warfare had always been a thin one among peoples of the Eurasian steppe. From the late fifteenth century onward, Ruthenia was among the regions ravaged by slave raids. The chief perpetrators of these sometimes massive expeditions were the Tatars of the Crimean Khanate. They were hardly the first to profit from the slave trade, a feature of the Black Sea region from ancient times. Rome and the Byzantine heirs to its eastern domains were major consumers, as was the famed Abbasid caliphate centered in Baghdad. The preponderance of Slavic-speaking peoples among the victims has given us the word "slave."

In late medieval times, much of the Black Sea slave trade had been controlled by the colonies of two Italian maritime states, Venice and especially Genoa. Their near monopoly came to an end when Mehmed the Conqueror pushed them out around 1475 in his drive to establish control over maritime trade. The sultan also made a vassal of the khan of the Giray Tatars, who had recently established themselves in the Crimean peninsula, long an international crossroads, and its northern reaches. It was no coincidence that the seizure and marketing of captives became a staple of the khanate's economy only a short time after the Ottomans imposed their semi-suzerainty. Istanbul was the single-largest market for the lucrative commodity, and its appetite for slave labor only grew over the course of the sixteenth century. In all likelihood, it was Tatar slave raiders who seized Roxelana from her home and family and cast her into an unknown future.

The Giray Tatars' role in Ottoman history was disproportionate to their numbers. It was less their mastery of the slave trade, however, that gave them prestige in Ottoman eyes than their claim to descent from Chinggis (Genghis) Khan. This Mongol pedigree endowed the House of Giray with a lineage distinguished across the lands once ruled by the great khan and his progeny. Indeed, the prestige enjoyed by the Giray Tatars, who were Muslim, was such that it was believed they would inherit sovereignty over the Ottoman domain if its dynastic house ever died out.

Like the Tatars, the Ottoman sultans also looked to Central Asia as a source for political legitimation. They traced their genealogy not to Chinggis Khan, however, but to the quasi-legendary Oghuz, great khan of a large Turkic tribal confederacy. The Ottomans were not the first Turkish-speaking sovereigns to claim descent from Oghuz. So did the family of one Seljuk, who migrated in the late tenth century from Oghuz Khan's home territory (in today's Uzbekistan) to the Caspian shore in northeastern Iran. It was the Seljuks who introduced Turkish rule to the Middle East.

Moving westward into Iran and Iraq, the descendants of Seljuk carved out a domain that at its zenith in the late eleventh century stretched from today's Uzbekistan to eastern Anatolia, from the Caspian Sea to the Persian Gulf to (off and on) the eastern shores of the Mediterranean. Although the Seljuk empire broke apart within 150 years, its several successor states perpetuated the formula that had helped to make Turkish rule acceptable in the heart of the Middle East. This was a region that had only known Arab sovereigns claiming descent from the clan of the Prophet Muhammad or Persian sovereigns who could draw on an ancient and glorified tradition of Iranian kingship. The Seljuks, like the Ottomans after them, had neither resource to validate their rule. As Turks, the Seljuks were outsiders, and while Muslim, they came from later converts to the religion.

And so the Seljuks adjusted the playbook. Their rulership would derive legitimacy from defense of the land and the religion. Military and governing authority would be theirs. They called themselves "sultan," a title that connoted power, not heritage. For guidance and expertise in administration, they looked to the sophisticated cadres of native Persian political advisers, religious authorities, and treasury and chancery specialists. They also learned to be great patrons of the arts, religious learning, and the welfare of their subjects.

All this enabled the Seljuks to blend Turkish ideals of sovereignty with the classic kingly virtues of heroism, justice, and magnanimity celebrated in the region since antiquity. When, two centuries later, the Mongols entered Iran (one of the four sectors of Chinggis Khan's empire), they too eventually made the same accommodation between sovereign authority and indigenous heritage. The Ottomans would do the same, cherry-picking elements of the Roman and Byzantine imperial pasts to add to the playbook they inherited from the east. As for Roxelana, she would manage her career with a quintessentially Ottoman approach, utilizing now this, now that tradition.

THE OTTOMAN STYLE of governing owed a particular debt to Seljuk history. Popular tales of the dynasty's beginnings recounted the arrival in northeastern Anatolia of one Ertuğrul, a Turkish nomad chieftain who had come from the east along with "four hundred tents" under his command.[8] Ertuğrul would go on to be remembered as the progenitor of the long-lived Ottoman ruling house. His son Osman, a local warlord who died in 1324, is counted as the first of thirty-seven sultans, the last of whose career ended with the demise of the empire in 1922.

Ertuğrul's mythic journey took him all the way to northwestern Anatolia, not far from either the Aegean Sea or Constantinople, capital of the Byzantine empire. This meant passing through the lands of the Seljuks of Anatolia, a branch of the original Seljuk dynasty who had moved westward into the extensive Anatolian peninsula and there established a kingdom that outlived its parent state. A popular variant of the story recounting Ertuğrul's arrival in what would become the Ottoman homeland features a direct tie between the Anatolian Seljuks and the birth of the empire: Ertuğrul joins the service of the Anatolian Seljuk sultan and receives as a reward the small domain from which his descendants would build a world empire.

Regardless of whether or not this particular legend—a story of migration—is true, large numbers of Turks did move westward, from the late eleventh century onward, rendering Anatolia increasingly Turkish and Muslim. The tale of Ertuğrul and the four hundred families is suggestive of the surge of many thousands who fled from the onslaught of the Mongols into the Middle East in the mid-thirteenth century.

One aspect of the Ottomans' heritage, however, probably owed more to these newcomers from the east than to the Seljuks, who over time had assimilated to the sedate social habits of the Middle East. This was the public prominence of women. When the famous Moroccan world traveler Ibn Battuta visited the several new Turkish principalities springing up in western Anatolia, he remarked that women as well as men came out to hail him as he entered their towns and cities. This was clearly a habit he had not observed as he traveled in the old Muslim lands, from Morocco across North Africa to Egypt and then northward through the Levant.

Ibn Battuta provides us with a touchstone for the long and shifting history of Ottoman royal consorts and Roxelana's pivotal place within it. He would learn firsthand in his northern travels that high-ranking women among the Turks and the Tatars might command public authority. When in 1331 he reached Nicea, a formerly Byzantine city recently conquered by Osman's son Orhan, it was one of the latter's wives, Nilufer, who welcomed the distinguished traveler. She was in charge of the soldiers stationed in Nicea while Orhan, whom Ibn Battuta called the richest of the Turkish leaders, was away on a tour of his fortresses. Of his audience with Nilufer, whom Ibn Battuta describes as "a pious and excellent woman," he says, "she treated me honorably, gave me hospitality, and sent gifts."[9] Likewise, when the traveler continued on across the Black Sea to the lands of the Golden Horde Mongols, royal women, some of whom commanded their own encampments, entertained him lavishly.

Over time, however, the Ottomans, like the Seljuks, adopted more conservative social habits. Females of notable families began to mark their status by restricting their movements in public and employing servants to do their bidding. Men too practiced a studied aloofness, albeit to a lesser degree than their wives, with the prominent and the wealthy dispatching underlings to manage their affairs and receiving petitioners in their residences. First among Ottoman householders, the dynasty took the lead in this practice, with the effect that the sultan's select appearances—attending Friday prayers, marching out of the capital on campaign—drew crowds of onlookers. The Ottomans were becoming expert at exploiting the politics of spatial manipulation.

These developments had consequences when it came to choosing ideal mothers of princes. During the first century, when the nascent Ottoman enterprise needed allies, princesses of neighboring dynasties, some of them Christian, made good wives and mothers. But when the sultans began to send their sons, and with them their mothers, to train in the provinces, foreign princesses were unlikely to relish leaving the Ottoman capital for distant and less cosmopolitan towns. It was also becoming clear, as the Ottomans became more of a threat to their neighbors, that a foreign princess's loyalty might rest more with her natal family than with her Ottoman son. So by 1400 or thereabouts, the sultans began to look to slave concubines to assume the risky job of political motherhood.

It took the Ottoman populace a long while to discard the assumption that the mothers of princes and princesses were all royally born. This reluctance, present even today, helps to explain why legend has long claimed Suleyman's mother Hafsa to be a Giray Tatar princess. Hafsa may well have hailed from the northern Black Sea region or even been a gift of the Tatar khan to the Ottoman court, but she was in fact a captive convert of modest origins, like virtually every woman in the imperial harem at the time when she entered it, probably the early 1490s.[10]

The tenacious story of Hafsa's royal Tatar pedigree probably has something at least to do with a different sort of association she enjoyed with the Crimean Khanate. Hafsa accompanied Suleyman on his first political assignment as prince when in 1509 he was appointed, at the age of fifteen, to serve as governor of Caffa. The city was capital of a ribbon of territory running along the southeastern shores of the Crimean peninsula that constituted a province under direct Ottoman rule. In Caffa, Suleyman and his mother doubtless had contact with the Tatar authorities, perhaps with the khan himself.

DURING THEIR FOUR years in Caffa, both Suleyman and Hafsa would become familiar with the slave trade. Tatar slave trains were generally marched to the Crimean peninsula, and slaves were loaded mainly at Caffa onto vessels that would transport them to Istanbul. Caffa generated handsome tax revenues for the Ottoman sultanate, and it would be Suleyman's duty as governor to make sure that revenue was safely channeled into the imperial treasury in the capital. The sums were staggering: in 1520, the year of Suleyman's accession, Caffa's slave tax amounted to roughly 10,000 gold ducats; combined with Caffa's customs duties, this constituted the largest source of the treasury's income (21,000 ducats).[11] By 1527, when Suleyman and Roxelana had been together for six years, the slave taxes from Caffa and Kilia, another Black Sea center of the trade in captives, totaled 50,000 ducats.[12]

The captive Roxelana may well have followed the route from Ruthenia to Caffa. The first major Tatar raid into what is now western Ukraine occurred in 1468, when some 18,000 men, women, and children were taken prisoner. After that date, Tatar forays into either Polish or Muscovite territory continued on a near-annual basis, some reaping enormous numbers of captives.[13] In 1498, thirty years after the first expedition, the region allegedly lost an unimaginable (and likely exaggerated) 100,000 to the raiders.

It is possible that Roxelana fell victim to an expedition mounted in 1516. Estimates of its captives range from 5,000 to 40,000 to an even larger, undetermined number.[14] While the girl may very well have been abducted on a smaller raid in a different year (a Polish historian has suggested 1509, when her supposed birthplace Rohatyn was the target of Tatar raids[15]), the date 1516 is not implausible. Roxelana was probably no younger than seventeen when she became Suleyman's concubine in the winter of 1520–1521 and thus around thirteen at the time of this raid. She would have been just old enough to manage survival on her own should she lose any relatives or neighbors captured with her.

The tactics of the Tatar slavers were described in 1578 by the Polish ambassador to the Crimean court, Marcin Broniewski. The raiding season was typically winter, when the freezing over of rivers and otherwise soggy terrain facilitated swifter advance. The Tatars moved quickly, noted Broniewski, laying waste to what they didn't plunder. Prisoners were typically poorly fed and marched on foot, in chains. They risked physical abuse by their captors, while relatives who tried to ransom them along the way risked extortion.

To make it all the way to the Ottoman capital from Ruthenia was no small accomplishment for a young girl like Roxelana. Even surviving the long trek to Caffa was a hard-won trial. Evliya Çelebi, an Ottoman courtier famous for his extensive travelogue, witnessed a train of captives on their way to the city in the mid-seventeenth century. It was a wonder, he wrote, that any of them survived the march to the slave markets, so badly were they treated along the way.[16]

The trauma of the raids and of the multiple stages of captivity became enshrined in folklore. A Ukrainian folk song spoke of the devastation of the countryside:

> *The fires are burning behind the river*
> *The Tatars are dividing their captives*
> *Our village is burnt and our property plundered*
> *Old mother is sabred and my dear is taken into captivity.*[17]

A Kazakh proverb records the different fates that awaited young males and young females—"the son went as hostage, the daughter to the Crimea"—she to certain slavery, he to an uncertain future.[18] And the physical journey from captivity to slavery is remembered despairingly in a Polish proverb: "O how much better to lie on one's bier, than to be a captive on the way to Tatary."[19]

The immediate destination for captives varied. Those taken from Polish lands might be marched to Ochakiv, a fortified city on the western Black Sea coast, from where most were shipped to Caffa. Many would be sold at the city's slave markets, while others might be kept by their captors or sold directly, without the aid of dealers. The calculation probably took into account the fluctuating price of slaves—low, ironically, when a successful foray glutted the market with its harvest. Not all captives of the Tatars were for sale, for the khan was owed one captive in ten.

Once in Caffa, captives destined for sale would likely find themselves in the large complex that constituted the slave market. Some parts of the market dated from the era of the Italian traders (the thirteenth to the mid-fifteenth centuries), while new facilities were added as the slave trade grew over the sixteenth and seventeenth centuries. The slave dealers were primarily Jews, Greeks, Armenians, and some Italians—in other words, non-Muslims (the Tatars saw themselves as warriors and captors, not middlemen). Dealers typically purchased their merchandise in large lots and then separated the slaves by age, sex, and aptitude for resale, either locally or to other dealers for transport elsewhere.

This sorting process in Caffa probably resembled practices at the Tatars' own large slave emporium in Karasubazar (black water market), located near the border between the khanate and Ottoman Caffa. Describing it, Evliya Çelebi wrote, "A man who has not seen this market has seen nothing in this world. There a mother is severed from her son and daughter, a son from his father and brother, and they are sold among lamentations, cries of help, weeping, and sorrow."[20] Of the Caffa slave market a European observer remarked in the mid-sixteenth century, "Herds of these unfortunate folks sold into slavery are driven onto the boats in Kaffa. Because of this practice the city of Kaffa may well be classed a heathen giant who feeds on our blood."[21]

Roxelana was likely one of those unfortunates traveling across the Black Sea to Istanbul. If so, we cannot know if she made the arduous journey alone or had the good fortune to be accompanied by others taken from her community. Nor do we know if she was purchased directly by imperial agents in Caffa for palace service or merely shipped to the Istanbul slave market as a common commodity. If the former, she was no doubt protected during the approximately ten-day journey to the Ottoman capital, for other royal agents would likely have been on board in addition to palace slave recruiters. Merchants were frequently dispatched by the imperial treasury to the northern Black Sea region to acquire luxury items purveyed by Muscovy. These included high-quality leather and especially furs, with sable taking pride of place among the Ottomans. In 1529, for example, Suleyman allotted some 6,000 ducats for the purchase of furs.[22] Goods for the sultan, material and human alike, were precious commodities.

EUROPEANS RAILED AGAINST the Tatar slavers. Their place was hell—the Tartarus of Greek mythology, the abyss below Hades where the wicked were imprisoned. The play with Tatar was obvious. But these critics were typically less concerned with the horrors of servitude than with the prospect of Christian captives converting to the "infidel" faith.[23] Slavery was no stranger to them, for they had not hesitated to purchase human wares from the Black Sea purveyed by the Genoese and others. Only those Christians bound for Muslim lands seemed to give them pause.

Tirades against the Tatars were sometimes merely recited by rote, as is apparent in a treatise titled *On the Customs of Tatars, Lithuanians and Muscovites*, composed for the Polish king Sigismund I. Its author, writing under the name Michalon Lituanus (Michael the Lithuanian), repeatedly detailed the abuse of Christian slaves by their Tatar owners.[24] Of slaves working Tatar estates, he wrote, "The best of these unfortunates, if they are not castrated, are branded on the forehead and on the cheeks and are tormented by day at work and by night in dungeons. Their life is worse than a dog's."[25] Elsewhere, however, Lituanus noted that the Tatars treated their captives with consideration and freed them after seven years.

The author of the treatise is worth remembering, for this same Lituanus figures in Roxelana's story. He was one of the first to publicize the belief that she was a captive from Polish-ruled territory. "The beloved wife of the Turkish emperor, mother of his eldest son and heir," he reported, "was some time ago kidnapped from our land."[26] (The king of Poland was also the grand duke of Lithuania, hence the Lithuanian's claim to "our" land.) The man behind the pen name Michael the Lithuanian is uncertain, but he may have been Vaclav Mykolaevyć, who served Sigismund as ambassador to both the Crimean and Ottoman courts.[27] If so, "Lituanus" probably encountered this information regarding Roxelana when he traveled to Istanbul in 1538 with gifts for Suleyman.

The Venetian ambassador had already asserted Roxelana's Ruthenian roots twelve years earlier. By the Lithuanian's time, however, she was acquiring recognition as an influential figure in the capital, adding stature to her reputation as the concubine who had seduced the mighty sultan. Moreover, she was now married to him, her influence at court secured. With affirmation by their own envoy of this rising star's origins, Polish authorities could envision scenarios in which Roxelana might be useful in keeping peace between Sigismund and Suleyman. For Sigismund had a delicate diplomatic balance to maintain.

On the one hand, the Tatars ravaged his lands. Adding insult to injury, they also demanded payment of an annual tribute, as they did from Muscovy. Not to pay was to risk the loss of greater numbers of countrymen and women to the slavers (Ivan IV, "the Terrible," ruler of Muscovy, was so strapped for funds to ransom captives that in 1535 he asked monasteries to donate their silver to the cause).[28] On the other hand, peace on the Polish-Ottoman frontier was a sine qua non for Sigismund. Even though the Ottomans regarded the Crimean Khanate as their ally, it was ultimately less risky for Poland to channel moral outrage at the Tatars. After all, the Ottomans merely consumed slaves—the Tatars manufactured them.

It is undeniable, though, that the sultans were wholly complicit in the slave trade. They openly backed the Tatar khanate of the Crimean, whose trade in captive bodies brought them revenue, and they routinely indulged their insatiable appetite for slave labor. Those same Europeans who castigated the Tatars for the suffering of Christian captives were also complicit, at least when it came to the Ottomans. What fascinated them, what they publicized, was not the dubious fate of Christian slave converts working for the sultans but rather the careers of those who rose to the top echelons of power. And so the legend of Roxelana would grow. The more famous she became, it seemed, the richer a backstory she warranted.

Almost immediately, Roxelana's life became embroidered with fiction, for the simple reason that there was little fact to go on. In regions north of the empire, for example, the notion circulated that she was the key to the long peace that prevailed between Suleyman and Poland-Lithuania, as it was assumed to be her natal land. Ivan Novosiltsov, ambassador of Ivan the Terrible to Istanbul, claimed in 1570 that when her son Selim was born, Roxelana pleaded with Suleyman not to go to war with Lithuania because she had been born there (the story favors Selim because he was sultan during Novosiltsov's visit).[29]

Roxelana was even more consequential in the telling of Samuel Twardowski, who composed a long poem describing the Polish embassy to Istanbul of 1622, of which he was a member. Published in Latin in 1633, the poem depicts Suleyman defending himself against the accusation of succumbing to Roxelana's charms in maintaining his warm relations with the Polish king. Suleyman declares that his cordial dealings with the Polish king are not due to Roxelana's allure but rather because she was herself of that royal lineage.[30]

Twardowski was also instrumental in propagating the story that Roxelana came from the town of Rohatyn and that her father was an Orthodox priest. Turks allegedly told him as much during his stay in Istanbul. Twardowski appears to have added on his own, however, that the priest was wicked,[31] perhaps a reflection of his Polish and Catholic prejudice toward Orthodox Ruthenians.[32] The notion that Roxelana's original name was Anastasia Lisowska, another fixture in the lore surrounding her, appears to have originated in Ukrainian legend and folk song. (The name Aleksandra, also attributed to her, allegedly belonged to Anastasia's mother Leksandra.)[33]

The most recent incarnation of Roxelana, in the Turkish historical television series *Muhteşem Yüzyıl* [Magnificent Century], originally broadcast from 2011 to 2014, casts her as Aleksandra, daughter of a good priest, all of whose family is slain by her Tatar captors. And so she is likely to be remembered for now, for an estimated 150 million viewers worldwide have followed the series in dozens of languages. That Roxelana was and remains an object of such fascination is a testament to her extraordinary life.

3

IN THE OLD PALACE

OXELANA'S RISE TO prominence and power began in the grand
residence that housed the women and children of the Ottoman dynasty. The Old Palace was a world of females and eunuchs. It was there
that Roxelana began to learn the ways of the Ottomans. She would live
in the Old Palace for some fifteen years, until she married Suleyman and
began to occupy elegant chambers in the New Palace. Even then, she
kept close ties with her original Ottoman home and continued to maintain quarters there.

Located in the bustling center of the imperial city, the Old Palace
served as home for the sultan's family—his mother, his concubines, and
his children. Widowed or unmarried princesses of the dynasty might
also live there. In much larger numbers, the Old Palace housed select
female slaves in training, a sizeable administrative staff, and the legions
of female servants who ministered to the women of privilege. As a new
arrival, Roxelana would encounter a bewildering array of women of different ages, statuses, and origins.

The Old Palace was a well-protected bastion. A Venetian map published ca. 1530 shows a large parklike expanse in the middle of the city
surrounded by a strong circular wall.[1] Within it lay the "seraglio vec-
chio," the Old Palace, its own enclosing wall reinforced with a double
watchtower. Gardens and lawns filled unoccupied spaces, relieving
the fortresslike feel of the whole complex—it had originally been designed as a well-defended residence for Mehmed II after the conquest of
Constantinople.

One of Roxelana's first tasks as a novice in the Old Palace was to
sort out the who's who of its hierarchy. Mehmed's division of the Ottoman royal household into two palaces, males in the New and females in

"Byzantium or Constantinople." Giovanni Andreas di Vavassore, ca. 1530. The Old Palace is located in the center, surrounded by angled walls; the New Palace is in the lower right. European communities resided principally in Galata (Pera), to the right, separated from Istanbul proper by the Golden Horn.

the Old, opened up new opportunities for women to develop positions of influence. At the top of the Old Palace hierarchy was the mother of the reigning sultan, female elder of the Ottoman dynastic house. Second in command was the Lady Steward, mistress of palace operations and monitor of etiquette and ceremony. Experienced staff ran the day-to-day life of the palace, enforcing its rules of conduct and managing its finances. Some participated in the instruction and disciplining of new slaves. Trainees who showed aptitude were assigned to dress, coif, and sometimes entertain their royal mistresses. Those of lesser talent, grace, or good looks became domestic servants who fetched trays of food, stoked the fires that heated water for the hamams, tended wardrobes, and did the laundry and cleaning.

Because men were not permitted in this establishment of women, eunuchs acted as its residents' guardians as well as their intermediaries with the outside world. Eunuchs had a long history as special servants

to imperial regimes, from the Chinese to the Byzantine empires. The Old Palace eunuchs supervised the female teachers who came daily to provide instruction. The eunuchs were also enforcers, monitoring the female denizens of the palace, escorting them when they ventured beyond its walls, and helping to discipline those who stepped out of line. Senior eunuchs were repositories of imperial protocol, versed in the history of the women's domain that they helped to govern. The all-male New Palace had its own substantial eunuch corps, similarly tasked with guarding as well as supervising its residents.

The Old Palace was home to all who lived within it and school to the lucky ones marked for advancement. In this world Roxelana acquired the polish she needed to attract the sultan's attention. Catch his eye she must, for Suleyman came to the Old Palace only on occasional visits. He lived in and governed from the New Palace.

Surrounded by extensive lawns and gardens and fortified walls, the sprawling pastoral complex of the sultan's palace occupied the old Byzantine acropolis. The promontory was a majestic setting for the seat of an expanding empire. It commanded the confluence of the city's three great waters: the Bosphorus, gateway to the Black Sea; the Golden Horn, an estuary whose natural harbor sheltered the imperial shipyards; and the Sea of Marmara, which led through the Aegean to the Mediterranean. From the very edge of Europe, the sultan could gaze upon the shores of Asia.

The New Palace was resolutely a world of men. This royal capital in miniature housed not only the sultan and his large personal suite but also the various offices of government. These included two treasuries (public and royal), bureaucratic offices, and the Divan, the council hall where the most important matters of state were deliberated. The sultan's own private chambers occupied one corner of the innermost of the palace's three courtyards. An academy for training the most promising of young male recruits to Ottoman service took up much of the rest. Their quarters formed a perimeter around the tree- and flower-studded lawn that blanketed the courtyard's interior space. Like the most promising Old Palace trainees, these youths were instructed and disciplined by both resident eunuchs and teachers brought in from outside. The most advanced served the sultan personally and, if fortunate, might subsequently rise to high office, even to become grand vizier.

When sultans visited the Old Palace, they did so to enjoy the company of their senior concubines, to pay their respects to their mothers, and to monitor the progress of their children. Sometimes they neglected their filial duties, or so thought Gulbahar, Suleyman's great-grandmother. She wrote plaintively to her son Bayezid II, "My fortune, I miss you. Even if you don't miss me, I miss you. . . . Come and let me see you. It's been forty days since I last saw you."[2]

Suleyman, by contrast, was a more frequent visitor, at least in the very first years of his reign. No doubt he sought the counsel of his mother Hafsa, whom he had come to rely on during the years of his princely apprenticeship. But at the Old Palace he also sought new women to bed. The Venetian ambassador Marco Minio reported in 1522, two years after Suleyman's succession, that the young sultan was "very lustful" and went frequently to "the palace of the women."[3] The Venetians avidly tracked the sultan's love life because knowledge of who was who in royal politics—who was the mother of which prince, for instance—was vital intelligence.

A story repeatedly told by Europeans described the method by which a sultan chose a new concubine: he would stroll down a lineup of females and drop his handkerchief in front of the one he found desirable. This may have happened on occasion, but the tale seems a poor fit with imperial etiquette and the well-crafted dignity of the sultan. It missed the point that a potential concubine needed opportunity to display the fruits of her training as well as her allure. The Old Palace devised suitable opportunities accordingly.

During a sultan's visit, his mother or a resident sister would organize refreshment and entertainment. These receptions offered him opportunity to survey attractive young women who served fruit-flavored sherbets or offered a music-and-dance interlude. For her part, an aspiring concubine was ready and eager to display grace and accomplishment. The bolder among them perhaps engaged in guarded flirtation. Did Roxelana beguile Suleyman with the laugh or the smile for which she presumably earned her Ottoman name, Hurrem?

ROXELANA WAS NO raw recruit when she and Suleyman first cast eyes upon one another. Somewhere along the line, between her abduction from Ruthenia and her arrival at the Old Palace, the slave girl must have demonstrated to discerning observers her fitness for more than menial employment. If not directly acquired in Caffa either by a palace agent or a dealer who appraised her as promising material for private resale, she was most likely sold in one of Istanbul's slave markets.

The principal slave market was located in the commercial heart of the city adjacent to the great Covered Market, which in turn was not very far from the Old Palace. In Roxelana's day, when the sale of slaves was less centrally controlled, smaller markets could be found in other city districts like the town of Üsküdar on the Asian shore of the Bosphorus. Auctions could be loud affairs as dealers touted their wares. In fact, residents of one Üsküdar village found the din created by brokers and bidders so objectionable that they took court action.[4]

For slaves, memory of the market could be indelible, especially as they were liable to physical examination to establish value, with potential concubines subject to a virginity check. The lot of slaves, especially those with aptitude, varied with the socioeconomic status of their male or female buyers. Since slavery among the Ottomans consisted predominantly of household (rather than agricultural) service, slaves' duties tended to match their owners' lifestyles. Wealthier households trained slaves in a range of positions—cook, groom, scribe, even entertainer. A slave's appearance varied accordingly, to the point that a runaway male might go unnoticed because he wore his master's cast-off clothing.[5] "They treated their servants better than we do," noted Theodore Spandouginos, a Greek of noble descent who knew both Istanbul and Turkish. The reason was that "Mahomet [the Prophet Muhammad] decreed that no one should keep a slave for more than seven years."[6] In fact, emancipation after a term of service was common, at least among the wealthier Ottomans. It was one factor in their unceasing demand for slave labor.[7]

Perhaps a speculator in female slaves, most likely a woman, perceived promise in Roxelana and bought her at market. She would wager on turning a smart profit by training and then reselling the girl at a price commensurate with her enhanced value. Perhaps a prominent Istanbul household acquired the Russian girl and soon discovered her to be talented and adaptable. Especially if Roxelana was purchased at some point by a high-ranking government official—or his wife, for rich women had their own money and their own slaves—the opportunity to curry favor by grooming and presenting her to a member of the dynasty would be obvious.

Claims that Roxelana was a gift to Suleyman circulated among both Ottomans and foreign envoys. If that was the case, she likely came to him as a congratulatory offering on the occasion of his accession in September 1520. One account held that a married sister of the new monarch secretly trained the girl and gave her as a present to her mother Hafsa, who in turn introduced the slave to her son.[8] More than one account, however, held that it was Ibrahim, Suleyman's male favorite, who gave Roxelana to him.[9] Originally a fisherman's son captured from the Adriatic coast, Ibrahim would be raised by Suleyman in 1523 to the highest state office, the grand vizierate. In any event, the young sultan certainly lost no time in bedding his new concubine, for their first child, Mehmed, was born within at most thirteen months of his enthronement.

Whether Roxelana was a high-value gift or merely a promising slave matters to our appreciation of her unprecedented success. A gift slave came ready with sophisticated training. Her donor's best hope was that she would become an intimate of the sultan. If Suleyman chose not to make her a concubine or even to take her to his bed for one night, her value would at least protect her from menial status. If, however, Roxelana was merely one among the many purchased at market who were working their way up the Old Palace ranks, she had only her wits and guts and whatever innate physical appeal she possessed to propel her.

What had Roxelana's sellers, buyers, mistresses, and masters seen in the Russian slave girl that motivated them to take her so far? Pietro Bragadin, Venetian ambassador during the early years of Suleyman's reign, reported that the sultan's new favorite was "young but not beautiful, although graceful and petite."[10] Physical attractiveness combined with a certain sexual guile was necessary in a royal concubine, but beauty was not the sole requisite. A healthy body was critical in someone whose mandate was to propagate the dynasty. Virginity, an essential condition, meant that Roxelana had remained unmolested during her passage from Ruthenia to the royal palace. But these physical attributes were worth little without intelligence. The real job of royal concubines, once they had aroused their master's sexual interest, was to bear and then to raise royal children. A sharp mind along with a savvy instinct for political survival was a sine qua non in a culture that trusted the mother of a potential heir to prepare him for the sultanate. Roxelana had to demonstrate that she was a quick learner.

Like most slaves who entered Muslim households, Roxelana was converted to Islam at some point in her training. Along with her new religion, she received a new name, her former identity symbolically erased. As a new Muslim, she was taught to repeat the core Islamic creed—"There is no god but Allah, Muhammad is the messenger of Allah"—and to perform her daily prayers. She probably also learned to recite the Fatiha, the short opening chapter of the Qur'an, considered by many Muslims to express its essence. But Roxelana could not have made much, if any, headway with Islamic scriptures because their language was Arabic. Her first linguistic challenge was to acquire facility with Turkish, the tongue of the Ottoman dynasty and the lingua franca of cosmopolitan Istanbul. Turkish, written in the Arabic script, may also have been her first written language, although, if truly the daughter of a priest, she could perhaps recognize and even write her Cyrillic letters.

Roxelana would also need to master the body language and courtly poise appropriate to the Ottoman palace. The would-be concubine must learn how to carry herself and how to dress. She must know when to lower her gaze, when to bow, and whose hand to kiss and then touch to her forehead as a sign of respect. She must glean the etiquette of palace discourse: to whom she might speak, on what occasions, in what words—and, perhaps most important, when to remain silent.

Roxelana needed to demonstrate that she was not only astute but also loyal. Advancing to the threshold of the royal concubine's career—presentation to the sultan—required the backing of patrons as well as personal skill. If Roxelana was the gift of a high-ranking individual, she already had a patron, but if she came to the Old Palace as a slave-market purchase, her own initiative in attracting support from her superiors was crucial. Because a successful concubine had the sultan's ear, various individuals in the royal household would acquire a stake in her progress, helping her along the way in exchange for future favors. Roxelana's advocates could point out how to balance deference with displays of intelligence and how to recognize the moment when a spark of flair could catch the notice of a key superior—or perhaps of the sultan himself.

WHEN ROXELANA ARRIVED in the Old Palace, she encountered an array of imposing women. First and foremost among them was Suleyman's be- loved mother Hafsa, apparently a favorite concubine of his father Selim. In his 1526 report to the Venetian Senate, Bragadin noted that she was "a very beautiful woman of forty-eight, for whom he bears great reverence and love."[11] During Suleyman's European military campaign in the same year, he wrote personally to tell his mother the momentous news of his army's rout of the Hungarian forces on the plain of Mohacs.

Contrary to the popular legend that claims Hafsa to be the daugh- ter of a Crimean Tatar khan, she, like all concubines of the era, was almost surely an enslaved and converted Christian of unknown origin. However, as legends often do, this one may encapsulate a truth within its error, namely, that the girl who became Hafsa may have been ab- ducted from the northern Black Sea region. Whatever Hafsa's story, it was doubtless whispered to new recruits in Old Palace service. For these young women, she was surely a celebrity, what with her great beauty, her enormous success as a slave convert, and the aura that was begin- ning to surround her as mother to a "magnificent" son.

When Suleyman was sent out in 1509 to begin his princely appren- ticeship, Hafsa was the dynastic elder at her son's court at Caffa, capital of the Ottoman province that stretched along the northern Black Sea coast. (His father Selim remained in his own princely post on the sea's southeastern coast at Trabzon.) Suleyman was fifteen when he became governor of Caffa, where the hierarchy of his harem began to take shape. Hafsa presided over her son's domestic household for four years in Caffa and then, after Selim won the contest for his father's throne in 1512, in the western Anatolian city of Manisa.

Salary registers dating from Suleyman's tenure in Manisa signal Hafsa's esteemed status. Her monthly stipend—6,000 silver aspers— was the highest figure on the princely payroll and triple the personal income of the prince himself.[12] Suleyman was still a junior member of the dynasty, despite the fact that he was his father's only surviving son and heir and was already producing heirs of his own. When Selim died suddenly in 1520 and Suleyman became sultan, Hafsa simply adapted her role to the new scale of imperial life in Istanbul, acquiring greater status as queen mother. She was now a free woman under Islamic law, which provided protections for the concubine mother: she could not be sold or given away during her master's lifetime, and upon his death she was automatically freed. This regard for the slave who bore a child to a free Muslim man stemmed in part from the fact that the law recognized the child as freeborn.

As Roxelana grew in prominence, she likely also came into direct contact with the Lady Steward, one of whose principal responsibilities was to supervise the select group who served the queen mother and, during his visits, the sultan. While this office was an old one, little is known about it before the late sixteenth century, when prominent members of the New Palace harem established by Roxelana became figures of political interest. The steward during Roxelana's tenure, or at least part of it, may have been a woman called Gulfem, whom Roxelana mentions often in her letters to Suleyman. Steward or not, Gulfem was clearly helpful and supportive of the young concubine. In one letter, Gulfem appended a note explaining to the sultan how she had solved a budget problem for his favorite. Some have claimed, without evidence, that Gulfem was a former concubine of Suleyman whose offspring had died; if true, it appears that at some point he rewarded her for her talent and service with the stewardship.

Second in rank only to Hafsa among royal women were the concubine mothers of Suleyman's children. They were likely the objects of Roxelana's keenest interest, for she surely hoped to join their number. One of the duties—and pleasures—of a prince was to populate a new dynastic generation. When Suleyman first encountered Roxelana, he already had four children. Mahmud was eight years old at his father's accession, Mustafa was five, and their brother Murad an infant. They also had a sister, whose birth date and name (perhaps Raziye) are uncertain.[13] With the possible exception of Mahmud, they and any others who had not survived infancy were born to Suleyman in Manisa.

Mahmud, Mustafa, and Murad each had a different mother, as the Ottoman politics of reproduction demanded. The rationale was that each heir presumptive deserved his mother's undivided attention as coach and partisan in his future candidacy for the throne. As for Suleyman's daughter, she may have shared a mother with one of the boys, since there was no limit to the number of female children a concubine might bear before the birth of a son put an end to her sexual relationship with the sultan.

If princes were the lifeblood of the Ottoman sultanate, princesses were loved specially. Unlike their brothers, they could never rival their father for popularity and prestige. And like their counterparts around the world, they were useful for the political alliances their marriages consolidated. A vigorous producer of sons, Suleyman may well have wished for more daughters, for only one, Mihrumah, would survive to adulthood. Later in life the sultan seemed to compensate by devoting a great deal of attention to his granddaughters' engagements and weddings.

The concubine mothers of the four children were already acquainted with one another from their time in Manisa. A government in miniature, Suleyman's princely household included family, servants, teachers, cooks, courtiers, bookkeepers, soldiers and officers, and the myriad other personnel who composed the entourage of an heir to the throne. Except for a basic staff and military guard that remained in the Manisa palace, his court moved with him to the capital. Once in Istanbul, the sexes separated, men to the New Palace, women to the Old Palace, eunuchs to both. There their numbers expanded, as new slaves arrived to fill out the two royal residences. The mothers of Suleyman's children doubtless wondered which, if any, of the new female recruits might rise to their own status.

Among this small elite was Mahidevran, who had traveled from Manisa with her son Mustafa. When tragedy struck in October 1521, taking the toddler Murad and then Mahmud and his sister, apparently the victims of an epidemic, Mahidevran's stature rose. Only Hafsa outranked her. But with the birth of a new baby boy of her own in the fall of 1521, Roxelana became Mahidevran's rival for the sultan's attention. At least for the moment—there was the possibility, even the likelihood, that Suleyman would answer the sudden need to produce more princes with new concubines.

As ROXELANA'S FORTUNES rose from slave to concubine to royal mother, she almost certainly encountered one or more of the sultan's six sisters. By the time she arrived in the Old Palace, all the sisters had been married. Since the reign of Suleyman's grandfather, it had been Ottoman practice to give princesses in marriage to the sultan's top statesmen. These were the pashas who served alternately as military commanders and governors of Ottoman provinces and ultimately, if their work was exemplary, as viziers and members of the Imperial Council through which the sultan ran his empire. These royal sons-in-law were nearly all products of the New Palace training regime or its smaller-scale replica in a prince's household. Most had begun their career as a personal attendant to the sultan or one of his sons.

The rich households formed by the union of a princess and a statesman functioned as satellites of the great dynastic establishment in the capital. A princess could live at quite a distance from Istanbul if her husband were dispatched to govern a frontier region. His periodic summons to the capital, however, provided opportunity for his wife to visit home and show off her children. The festive receptions that greeted her were doubtless welcome breaks in the daily routine of the palace. To the Old Palace family, princesses were beloved daughters, sisters, and aunts. They were also surely objects of pride and affection for the female staff and eunuchs who had helped raise them.

Less joyful were the reunions that took place when a widowed princess returned with her children to the Old Palace. Widowhood was a stark liability of marriage to a pasha, who might be considerably older than his bride. Moreover, he ran the risk of death in battle. But a widow's stay in the Old Palace might be short-lived if she was still of marriageable age, for she could be given to another pasha, subjecting her all over again to the same uncertainties. A second marriage could work out well though, as it did for Suleyman's granddaughter Shah Sultan. After the death of her first husband, she married one Zal Mahmud at the age of thirty. So suited were husband and wife, it was said, that they fell ill simultaneously, lay together in their deathbed, and expired at the very same moment.

The gravest risk for a princess was that her husband might be found guilty of violating the empire's laws, which was tantamount to betraying his monarch. Execution was the punishment, the sentence of death the sultan's to give. Suleyman's sister Beyhan was so outraged when he ordered the beheading of her husband Ferhad Pasha that she not only refused to remarry but chose to live in self-exile away from Istanbul. Accused of rapacious and bloody conduct as a governor in eastern Anatolia, Ferhad had already received a second chance through Hafsa's and Beyhan's pleas. Reports of repeated abuses in his new post on the Danube, however, sealed his fate.[14]

The Venetian ambassador Bragadin reported that Hafsa was greatly grieved by the execution, no doubt out of concern for Beyhan and her children.[15] Thought by some to have been Beyhan's mother, Hafsa was surely torn between the princess's anguish and a queen mother's recognition of the need for justice, lest her son be perceived as weak or negligent. A reality of Ottoman rule—that policy and security trumped family bonds—was no less brutal for being shared with other sixteenth-century monarchies, such as that of England's Henry VIII or Muscovy's Ivan IV, "the Terrible."

Roxelana was doubtless privy to the news of Ferhad's demise and perhaps witness to Beyhan's angry grief. By 1524, the year Ferhad was executed, she had become a figure of importance in the Old Palace. Once Suleyman had bedded his new concubine, sometime in the first half year of his reign, she became *gözde*, "in the eye of the sultan," someone of account. Her presence at the various receptions and entertainments sponsored by ranking women of the palace was now expected, and soon she would be responsible for providing such amenities in her own suite of rooms for her growing circle of attendants and allies.

News from Istanbul and beyond passed from ear to ear in the Old Palace, as did local harem gossip, but formal gatherings were venues where certain kinds of information—the Ottoman victory over the Hungarians, the rupture between Beyhan and Suleyman—could be relayed to those who needed to know. As she rose from *gözde* to concubine mother of one, two, and then more children, Roxelana rapidly became one of the "need to know" elite. The Old Palace was hardly sealed off from politics, as modern stereotypes of royal harems so often presume. It *was* politics, and it taught politics. Foreign envoys were wholly correct to consider the harem a vital object of diplomatic intelligence, for it generated its own news and even its own scandals.

Life in the Old Palace was not all parties and policy, however. Instruction took up much of the daily routine, especially for new personnel. The teaching was supervised by the Lady Steward. This powerful majordomo and her staff organized training protocols that sorted out new recruits: promising girls with the talent to join the suites of high-ranking women, others who showed a flair for administration, and the rest, whose lesser aptitude or beauty suggested lesser modes of service.

No one was exempt from instruction, however. Giovanni Maria Angiolello, a Venetian captive who served in the household of a son of Mehmed II, described the training regime to which all were subject but at which only some excelled: "The most senior [women], who are accomplished, teach the new and unrefined to speak and read, and instruct them in the Muhammadan law, and also teach them to sew and embroider, and to play the harp and to sing. They instruct them in all their ceremonies and customs, to the degree that [these girls] have the inclination to learn."[16]

The arts of the needle were a universal talent of women in the sixteenth century.[17] For the women of the Old Palace, needlework was, if nothing else, a means of survival. Should they fall on hard times—having been expelled from the royal home for misconduct, say, or retired when the reign of the sultan they served ended—they had a marketable skill to fall back on. Ottaviano Bon, Venetian ambassador in the early seventeenth century, noted that retired palace women could generate income by selling their handiwork to Jewish tradeswomen.[18] These female entrepreneurs were valuable intermediaries between the outside world and palace women. The well connected among them could even act as political liaisons for high-ranking women—for example, the woman Strongila, who served Hafsa in this capacity and whose services Roxelana inherited following Hafsa's death.

Needlework instruction was taken with utmost seriousness. According to Giovanni Antonio Menavino, a Genoese who served Suleyman's father and grandfather, ten teachers of embroidery came every morning to the Old Palace. Writing in the mid-sixteenth century, Guillaume Postel, French diplomat and scholar of languages, claimed that instruction was restricted to the bulk of recruits who, for "lack of beauty and grace," would not rise to higher status. These women were nevertheless trained with such care, he observed, that one would think they were the sultan's own daughters.[19] Postel was not entirely correct in presuming that only the less talented received instruction. Roxelana herself would acquire sufficient expertise with a needle to send richly embroidered gifts to the king of Poland.

WHY WERE ITALIAN and French audiences hearing about palace women's devotion to needlework? Was the emphasis on industriousness and sobriety in these European writings an effort to counteract popular European stereotypes of harem wantonness? The question is significant since it was European observers and writers, not the Ottomans themselves, who helped to shape their contemporaries' ideas of Roxelana by reporting openly about life behind palace walls. Always an object of great curiosity, the sultan's "seraglio" and its women sold books and generated translations of best sellers from one language to another. Later, in the seventeenth century, when Ottoman armies had proved stoppable and Europeans could feel superior, the theme of the sultan's lasciviousness and the decadence of empire grew popular.

When Angiolello, Menavino, and Postel were writing, however, the fascination with the Ottomans was more innocent and more comprehensive. The panoptic title of Menavino's publication *Five Books on the Laws, Religion, and Way of Life of the Turks, on the Court, and on Some Wars of the Grand Turk* reflected the thirst for knowledge of all things Ottoman. It was a time of both curiosity about and dread of the Ottoman military machine. The conquest of Constantinople in 1453 was not that far in the past; nor was the Ottoman threat that far away. In 1480, Mehmed the Conqueror's forces had briefly occupied Otranto, on the heel of Italy's boot, a short sail from Ottoman-controlled territory on the Adriatic. Only his death nine months later muted fears that the empire was bent on a quest for Rome, the "golden apple" of Ottoman legend.

At least in Roxelana's time, European fascination with the court of the "Grand Turk" and the lives of its females probably owed less to a lurid interest in the sultan's sex life and more to a shared appreciation that palaces and the monarchs who lived in them were the heart of the matter of sovereignty. Suleyman's contemporary Francis I replaced the crumbling structures within the medieval fortress of the Louvre with a splendid Renaissance palace, installing there the foundations of what would become the French monarchy's great art collection. The founder of England's celebrated Tudor dynasty, Henry VII, spent lavishly on his new Richmond Palace, its finishing touches applied just in time for display at the event that crowned his foreign policy—the marriage of his oldest son Arthur to the Spanish princess Catherine of Aragon. Europeans also took for granted the elaborate separate quarters in which royal women presided over their own courts. In this light, their scrutiny of the domestic education of Old Palace women was not so remarkable. And until Roxelana's rise to power and notoriety, news of the mundane was probably the best harem news that observers could muster.

For its time, the Old Palace was a veritable institution of higher learning for women. It was the one place in the empire that offered a systematic education for large numbers of females. And it was international in its makeup, commingling individuals from Asia, Europe, and Africa. A new resident need not search far in this Tower of Babel to find another who could speak or at least understand her language. Everyone, of course, had to acquire fluency in Turkish, but other tongues were doubtless spoken in private. Friendships and alliances could be struck through shared vernaculars. Mothers, governesses, and wet nurses, especially young ones with imperfect Turkish, perhaps soothed royal infants with their own childhood lullabies. With a mother and a grandmother whose native tongue was not Turkish, a royal child might acquire a smattering of another language or two.

The Old Palace was, in today's terminology, a multiethnic and multilingual institution where all were dedicated to mastering a new, shared culture of refinement. It was not wholly unlike European courts that attracted the daughters of ambitious noble families or even royalty. Such was the court of the Archduchess Margaret of Austria, where Roxelana's contemporary Anne Boleyn began to acquire her sophistication, or the French court, where Anne continued as lady-in-waiting in the queen's household and Mary Stuart, widow to a French king and queen of Scotland, received a Renaissance education. The difference was that the Old Palace did not provide an education for women of notable Ottoman families. Rather, it created an educated female elite from a population of slaves, albeit a highly select one.

While the Old Palace regime provided its female pupils with the training as well as the opportunity to advance in royal service, its goal was equally to inculcate total allegiance to the empire that had torn them from their homes. Was this careful attention to nurture aimed at uprooting their native cultures as well? Certainly it was imperative to steep recruits, male and female alike, in the religion, etiquette, and political ideology they would now represent. But though it may seem counterintuitive, it was by deliberate design that it was the youth of Christian towns and villages who were drafted into high Ottoman service rather than the seemingly more culturally compatible children of Muslims.

TO BE SURE, the choice to surround the royal family with skilled converts was influenced by the teaching that a Muslim cannot enslave another Muslim. But the Ottoman sultanate did not hesitate to ignore the parallel teaching that a Muslim (monarchs included) cannot enslave a Christian or a Jew living under a Muslim government. While large numbers of imperial slaves came through legally approved sources—prisoners of war, purchased slaves of non-Ottoman origin—others came from the sultan's own territories, particularly from frontier provinces. Such slaves were a kind of human tax levied on the empire's Christian subjects.

The rationale most historians have offered for building the sultanic household with converted Christian slaves is that it bred loyalty. Severed from their homelands, the dynasty's slaves were completely dependent on its largesse. In turn, they could expect reward for devoted service, especially the talented among them. Exceptional service garnered exceptional reward—riches, influence, and a fancy household of one's own, all worlds apart from what was imaginable in one's homeland. Flawed service like that of Ferhad, on the other hand, was rewarded with exile or execution. Under this system it was less risky for an Ottoman ruler to punish an uprooted slave than it was for kings and emperors elsewhere to discipline their noble servants without alienating powerful families.

The sultans had learned from their own struggles with aristocrats. The troubled early fifteenth century taught them about the unreliability of foreign vassal princes and, more dangerous, the dubious loyalties of native Turkish princes who had submitted to Ottoman rule. The nascent empire was nearly wiped out in 1402 when these presumed allies fled the battlefield at Ankara in the disastrous confrontation between Bayezid I and the Central Asian conqueror Timur (Tamerlane). It took over a decade of violence for one of the dead sultan's sons, Mehmed I, to reunite the Ottoman territories.

For Mehmed II, the real architect of government by slave converts, this was all recent history. Born in 1432, "the Conqueror" grew up with knowledge of Bayezid I's humiliating defeat and the subsequent rise of pretenders who rallied discontented Ottoman subjects to their banners, challenging his grandfather's and then his father's hold on the newly recovered throne. Mehmed diluted this troublesome structure by making convert Christians the backbone of his administration. As one element in this policy, foreign princesses were no longer taken as wives by Ottoman sultans and princes.

But the critical importance of loyalty to the dynasty still does not explain why the slave pool was so international. What the Ottomans were looking for—a broad knowledge base—could not be supplied by seeking slaves only from the empire's own heartlands or from its immediate frontiers. As a state propelled by conquest, at least through the greater part of Suleyman's reign, the empire kept adding new territories and, with them, new ways of life—languages, economies, modes of worship, cultural traditions. It also kept coming up against new rival powers across advancing frontiers. In such a kaleidoscopic world, it was politically expedient to assemble polyglot cadres who could literally speak with inhabitants of the provinces they might be sent to govern or negotiate with governments the Ottomans might want to trade or make peace with. In the case of the New Palace training school, the underlying principle seemed to be that a mélange of borderland recruits with a richly diverse talent pool would make for good military strategy and good foreign policy. In the case of the female harem of the Old Palace, the assumption seemed to be that a diverse gene pool through which the dynasty continually hybridized the world around it made for monarchs adept at managing an empire on three continents.

Did Roxelana feel torn between two worlds? If a royal concubine ever saw her family again, we do not hear of it. This is not to say that Roxelana and her fellow harem residents forgot their native lands or never spoke of them. The polyglot universe of the Ottoman ruling class probably encouraged new recruits to gravitate toward others who spoke their language. It was an obvious survival tactic to seek solidarity, protection, or guidance in making one's way in this astonishing new world. On the other hand, memories of home might recede, especially for those who were children at the time of their capture. Occasions to reminisce, if any, were probably privately shared moments.

If longing for home and worry over the fate of her family clouded Roxelana's efforts to adapt, if she feared that her diligence as a new Muslim betrayed her childhood faith, if memory of her abduction dogged her determination to keep that smiling countenance, she could draw some consolation from the fact that she was not alone in the struggle. Everyone was a convert, everyone learned a new tongue, everyone strove to please, and everyone had to forget. The rigor of the Old Palace educational program was surely a blessing in disguise. It organized new recruits into groups, and it kept them busy. The training system into which Roxelana was thrust was a meritocracy where the capacity to compete was what spelled success. Its encouragement of talent focused the more ambitious on advancement—on the future, not the past.

ROXELANA'S SUMMONS TO Suleyman's chamber was a tribute to her success. The ultimate test, however, was whether he called her back and continued to do so until she became pregnant. As the Venetian Luigi Bassano, resident in Istanbul in the 1530s, explained the process to his readers, "The Grand Turk has a palace of women at quite a distance from his own. There he keeps a great number of young Christian slave girls. . . . From these the Grand Turk chooses whoever pleases him the most, and keeps her separate for two months, and amuses himself with her as he pleases. If she becomes pregnant, he takes her as his consort."[20]

Roxelana had been groomed and guided to the point of selection by Old Palace women and eunuchs, whose job it was to produce solid choices for the sultan. Any of a number of individuals could have brought her to the sultan's attention: Hafsa, a sister, a patron who had presented her to the court. Or perhaps Roxelana devised her own strategy to make herself noteworthy. But it was the sovereign who had the last say in a slave's future.

Suleyman's choice launched Roxelana on the career track that led to royal motherhood. No matter how she regarded her forced sexual submission to the monarch whose empire had enslaved her, she would understand that motherhood was the fastest route to a secure future in the competitive world of Ottoman royal politics. His summons exempted her from the career alternatives of continuing service in the Old Palace, perhaps culminating in the office of head stewardess, or, more likely, promotion from the palace as wife to a well-trained statesman with whom she would form another one of those satellite households.

Where did Suleyman "keep Roxelana separate"? He could conceivably have lodged her in an apartment retained for the sultan in the Old Palace (Menavino reported that Suleyman's grandfather Bayezid II stayed there periodically for three or four days). But he almost certainly kept her in the New Palace, where he might more conveniently "amuse himself as he pleased." The New Palace contained quarters for females known as the Hall of the Maidens, a small and confining offshoot of the inner courtyard, perhaps deliberately out of alignment with the strictly linear layout of the all-male palace structure.[21] Its rooms functioned primarily to house the sultan's current favorites and the staff who served them.

In one of the earliest accounts of Mehmed II's new palace that mention this small harem, the Genoese merchant Iacopo di Promontorio described the residents of this "second seraglio of damsels," as he put it, as "the most splendid, well-kept, and beautiful women that could be found in the world."[22] Estimates of female numbers varied: Promontorio thought there were 150 in 1475, while Venetian envoy Alvise Sagundino reported only 10 in the late 1490s.[23] Promontorio was probably misinformed, or else he exaggerated for effect, but numbers may have fluctuated naturally, depending on the age and sexual activity of the sultan. Sagundino was envoy to the court of Bayezid II, who was in his early fifties at the time and appears to have fathered the last of his many children in the 1470s. In any event, most of these women were staff members, not concubines.

Istanbulites were used to a constant flow of traffic between the New and Old Palaces. In addition to the sultan himself, officials, messengers, couriers, and servants went back and forth. So did princes as they got older—they lived in the Old Palace but acquired their education in part with their father's apprentices in the New Palace. Some of those who traveled back and forth went on horseback, some by carriage, and some on foot, some singly and some with an accompanying retinue. Today it is more or less a half-hour walk from the Topkapı Palace to Istanbul University, which occupies the heart of the former Old Palace grounds. The lively if congested thoroughfare one follows has a long history. It served as the Byzantine Mese (middle way), the principal thoroughfare of Constantinople, while in Ottoman times (and still today) it was called Divan Yolu—Avenue of the Divan, the grand hall in the New Palace where the council of viziers met. This was the route Roxelana would follow on her journey to meet the sultan.

Roxelana would make her way down the Avenue of the Divan in a curtained carriage, maintaining the seclusion from the public gaze that was the duty and prerogative of women of status. According to the Frenchman Postel, a newly chosen concubine was transported to the sultan's residence in a richly caparisoned carriage, accompanied by four or five eunuchs.[24] Whether or not Roxelana traveled in such splendor, she certainly went with attendants and probably a small armed guard. She would not need all her Old Palace trainers with her, for the Hall of the Maidens had its own staff adept at preparing girls for presentation to the sultan. Later, as Roxelana's prestige grew, her trips between the two imperial residences would become more elaborate affairs.

OVER TIME ROXELANA would become a connoisseur of Istanbul's built landscape, of both its Byzantine monuments and the Ottoman rebuilding and remodeling that had burgeoned since the conquest. She would also become a great patron of the capital, leaving her own mark on the city's face. It is tempting, then, to imagine her initial exposure to its imperial core. What would she have seen on her first trip "in state," peeking guardedly from the windows of her vehicle?

The small procession turned out of the Old Palace gates onto the Avenue of the Divan. Soon it would pass by the mosque of Bayezid II, Suleyman's grandfather, an imposing structure situated on the square that in Byzantine times had been the forum of the emperor Theodosius I. The mosque anchored a whole foundation that included a madrasa (a college that taught Islamic law and other religious sciences), a primary school, a caravanserai cum hospice, a large public bath, and the tomb of its founder.[25]

Bayezid's complex was not as large as the mammoth one endowed by his father Mehmed II. Befitting the founder of Ottoman Istanbul, the Conqueror's foundation included, in addition to the features present in his son's, a hospital and a library. Its eight madrasas and eight preparatory madrasas would jump-start the production of a new class of Ottoman jurists, judges, teachers, and experts on matters of religion. One of the goals of these large imperial foundations, with the services they provided and employment they offered, was the stimulation of urban development. It was critical in the war-devastated city the Ottomans needed urgently to rebuild.

If Roxelana were traveling near one of the five daily prayer times, she would see people making their way toward, or leaving, the precincts of Bayezid's mosque. The streets were probably already congested with pedestrian traffic, as the city's grand Covered Market was located adjacent to the mosque. Perhaps the colorful wares of peddlers working outside the bazaar walls caught her eye. Bayezid may have chosen the location of his mosque with the old bazaar in mind. It served the religious needs of Muslim shop owners, employees, and shoppers, while some of the foundation's other services were presumably open to their Jewish and Christian counterparts as well.

As the carriage moved along the Avenue of the Divan, Roxelana would encounter one of the oldest public baths in the Ottoman city. It had been donated in 1475 by Gedik Ahmed Pasha, a man of Serbian origin, one of Mehmed's grand viziers. Top-ranking statesmen followed their monarch's example in endowing urban amenities whose neighborhoods sometimes went on to acquire the donor's name—to the point that one-fifth of Istanbul neighborhoods in 1990 bore the name of an Ottoman pasha.[26] The next monument along Roxelana's route was the small mosque of Atik Ali Pasha, a eunuch originally from a village near Sarajevo who served as grand vizier to Bayezid II. Commissioned in 1496, the pasha's endowment, with its college, soup kitchen, and lodge for dervishes, straddled both sides of the Avenue.

Visible ahead, dwarfing the minaret of Atik Ali's mosque, was the ancient Column of Constantine. It was known to the Ottomans as the "hooped column" because of the iron bands that held together its six porphyry drums. The column stood in what had been the Forum of Constantine the Great, marking the foundation of Constantinople in the year 330 as the capital of the Roman empire. The splendor of the Byzantine square, with its imposing civic buildings and houses of worship, had long since vanished. But soon the elegant small mosque of another of Bayezid's eunuch officials, the chief treasurer Firuz Agha, slipped behind the carriage as the greatest of all Byzantine monuments loomed ahead in its majestic immensity.

The Church of the Holy Wisdom—Hagia Sophia—was the work of the emperor Justinian the Great. Its doors opened to worshipers in 537. Procopius, Justinian's contemporary and the principal historian of his long reign, wrote of it, "The church presents a most glorious spectacle, extraordinary to those who behold it and altogether incredible to those who are told of it. In height it rises to the very heavens and overtops the neighboring houses like a ship anchored among them, appearing above the city which it adorns."[27] The enormous basilica was allegedly the first destination of Mehmed II when he entered his new capital, only hours after the last emperor, Constantine XI, gave his life defending what had been for more than a millennium the capital of the now defunct Byzantine empire.

It was said that Mehmed immediately called for an imam to recite the call to prayer inside Hagia Sophia, an act that reconsecrated the church as a mosque. The victor's sentiments were not all triumphal, however. Tursun Beg, secretary to Mehmed's council, biographer of "the Conqueror," and participant in the conquest, recorded the twenty-one-year-old sultan's reaction. Observing that the outer buildings of the church had fallen into decay in the empire's twilight years, he "thought of the impermanence and instability of this world, and of its ultimate destruction."

One can only imagine Roxelana's own musings as her carriage made its way past the edifice that had been forcibly converted from Christianity to Islam, as she herself had been. She probably had only a vague grasp of the glories of Byzantium, but as a young child she had doubtless heard tell of the tragic fall of the Constantinople Patriarchate into the hands of the infidel Turks. It stood to the Eastern Orthodox Christian Church, the heart of her family's faith, as the Vatican stood to the Roman

Catholic Church. But rather than destroy the greatest symbol of Byzantium's Christian faith, Mehmed and his successors kept Hagia Sophia as the premier mosque of the Ottomans, the greatest symbol of the empire's Muslim faith. (Turkish still calls it Aya Sofya.) As Angiolello put it, "The Turks have chosen [it] for their cathedral, and they worship there according to their laws."[28] There was nothing especially Ottoman in this reverence for sacralized space: the first great mosque built by a Muslim monarch, the Umayyad mosque of Damascus, lay atop a succession of former houses of worship—an ancient Aramaic temple dedicated to the god Hadad, a Roman temple to Jupiter, and lastly a cathedral to St. John.

The first courtyard of the New Palace (later Topkapı Palace). Janissaries guard the outer entrance; Hagia Eirene is to the left immediately inside the gate, and the Middle Gate is at the top right. Seyyid Lokman, *Hünernâme.*

This much history Roxelana did not know, at least not at that early moment in her career. But during the considerable time it took to circumnavigate Hagia Sophia, perhaps she reflected on the sights she had just seen. She probably recognized that three of the four Ottoman endowments she had passed were sponsored by converts like herself (for one thing, their scale was obviously smaller than that of Bayezid's mosque). Living in the Old Palace, she learned that the most successful graduates of imperial training were expected to endow a mosque and, funds permitting, additional public service institutions. Hafsa's own big project under construction in Manisa demonstrated that gender was no bar to this expectation. Did Roxelana already have a glimmer of what she herself might undertake if her encounter with Suleyman turned out successfully?

The great basilica-mosque may have consumed the whole of Roxelana's attention, but if she shifted her gaze to the right, she would see the old Byzantine Hippodrome. The surviving fragments of its coliseum-like grandstands were perhaps too distant to see from the carriage. But she could glimpse three monuments that still stood at its center, two of them ancient: an Egyptian obelisk, a bronze serpent column from Delphi, and a Byzantine obelisk. This vast open space, whose name the Ottomans retained—the square of the horses—would soon begin to function as the main arena for public spectacles and celebrations sponsored by the dynasty. Later in her life, Roxelana would watch the festivities from the enclosed balcony of a new mansion that would soon go up on the Hippodrome square, Suleyman's gift to his grand vizier Ibrahim Pasha.

Finally, as Roxelana and her escort moved beyond Hagia Sophia, they would arrive at the great outer walls of the New Palace. As the carriage passed through the gatehouse arch, guarded by members of the Janissary infantry corps, there appeared Hagia Eirene, former Church of Holy Peace. Now incorporated into the first public courtyard of the New Palace precincts, it served the Janissaries as an arsenal. The imposing "Middle Gate," entrance to the palace proper, stood only a few minutes away.

4

THE POLITICS OF
MOTHERHOOD

Roxelana was well prepared for her presentation to Suleyman. A royal concubine had more than the usual coaching of a virgin on the eve of her first sexual experience, for not offending her master was crucial for her survival. Rehearsing her introduction to the sultan was perhaps the final piece of a first-time concubine's training. Roxelana would learn the protocols for approaching him and the formulas for addressing him when it was time to do so. Memorizing the right words may have been a reassuring exercise, especially if her Turkish was still hesitant.

It would fall to Roxelana alone, however, to master any conflicting emotions she felt about the coming encounter. She recognized that to be chosen was an honor, the ultimate measure of her success. She also understood that by stimulating the sultan's desire and holding onto it long enough to become pregnant she could ensure her future security among the Ottomans. But that did not necessarily mean that the young woman welcomed the prospect of sexual thralldom to the ruler of the empire that had made her a slave.

In the Hall of the Maidens, Roxelana would be washed and dressed. If she had a patron in the Old Palace, a modestly alluring gown may have been provided for her. A small retinue of eunuchs would lead her to Suleyman's private quarters. As she approached the Privy Chamber, eyes downcast, Roxelana would encounter the privileged male slaves who guarded its threshold. Her retinue would protect her from distraction, keeping her focused on the man she was about to be alone with.

WHEN SULEYMAN GAVE the order to summon Roxelana to his bed chamber, he was no stranger to initiating a virgin slave into her role as concubine. He had had his own harem from the time he was seventeen or so, when he was serving in Caffa. It was not large, though, as befitted Suleyman's status as an apprentice governor. An expense register from 1511, a year before his first son Mahmud was born, lists ten female slaves, while a later, undated one from the prince's time in Manisa, a more significant post, listed seventeen.[1] Not all of these women were his bedmates.

What did Suleyman expect from his encounter with Roxelana? He was not duty bound to make the new girl a mother, though he probably hoped for a satisfying night with her. If he found her wanting, he could dismiss her after a polite reception. Even so, Suleyman came to this meeting prepared. He was head of the dynastic family, after all, and the new concubine could conceivably become an important part of it. He would know something of her—her Ottoman name, Hurrem, and where she came from. He may well have spoken a bit of her language, especially if his mother Hafsa had come from the same region.

Sex for males of the Ottoman sultanate, as for any scion of a hereditary dynasty, was not always pleasure driven, for it was laden with political consequence. European fantasies about the libertine sensuality of Ottoman sultans were misplaced, at least with regard to Suleyman. The pressure to perform—to produce heirs to the throne—was inescapable. As his father Selim's only surviving son, Suleyman's task, as soon as he matured, was to provide children to perpetuate the dynastic line. But by the time he called for Roxelana, he had done his duty. He could afford to indulge himself—he had only one daughter, but he was the father of three sons. If Suleyman was pleased with his new choice, he would call her back. If she became pregnant, so much the better. Another son was dynastic insurance, and another daughter a delight.

Whatever transpired that first night in the royal bedroom, Roxelana must have acquitted herself well. She conceived sometime within five months of Suleyman's accession to the throne. (The timing of her pregnancy depends on the child's birth date, for which only the year is recorded: 927 in the Islamic calendar, which ended on November 30, 1521.) Suleyman and Roxelana's son Mehmed likely arrived sometime during his father's absence at war—the sultan and his army left Istanbul in May of that year and returned in late October. With Suleyman gone, it is uncertain who gave the baby boy his name. Perhaps it was his grandmother Hafsa, the family's head in her son's absence. Or perhaps Suleyman indicated his preferences before departing—at that point it would have been obvious that his new concubine was with child. Whether Roxelana had any say in Mehmed's naming we do not know.

Even with Suleyman away from Istanbul, cannons would sound to announce the royal birth. While not his first son, Mehmed was the first child of Suleyman's sultanate. He was also the first son of a sultan to be born in the capital in some forty-five years. It must have been a thrilling moment for the people of Istanbul, proud that their young ruler was both militarily and sexually dynamic. As if celebrating the first anniversary of his ascension, Suleyman presented them with a new prince and a stunning victory. The first military campaign of his reign culminated in spectacular success with the capture of Belgrade, capital city of Serbia.

Alas, sorrow tinged the joy of Mehmed's birth. In mid-October, during the army's victory march back to Istanbul, Suleyman's small son Murad died. The tragedy was horribly compounded when Murad's sister, Suleyman's only daughter, died two days before her father's entry into the capital. On October 29, ten days after the sultan's return, his oldest son, the nine-year-old Mahmud, succumbed to the epidemic, perhaps plague.[2] The waves of devastating news surely called out large throngs of mourners to honor the funeral cortege as it wended its way on foot over Istanbul's hills. Led by the empire's viziers, the procession arrived at the cemetery where the children's grandfather Selim lay in his tomb. If Mehmed's was the city's first royal birth in decades, the spectacle of three small coffins provided unaccustomed evidence of the all-too-human vulnerability of the royal family, the pivot of the empire's existence.

As it mourned, the Old Palace was no doubt on medical alert. Any contagious disease could spread rapidly in its confined quarters. Roxelana had presumably been living in the Old Palace since the early stages of her pregnancy, since its team of female doctors could better care for her than could the skeletal staff in the Hall of the Maidens. Now, precautionary medical measures may have required that a demonstrably healthy wet nurse and governess temporarily care for the infant.

Everything we know about Roxelana suggests she was a person of determination and self-control, but she could certainly be forgiven any turbulent emotions in the aftermath of Mehmed's birth. Relief and happiness that she and the child had emerged from the epidemic healthy were natural. Moreover, Roxelana had rapidly accomplished her purpose—producing a child for the dynasty. In turn, Mehmed garnered for her what she presumably desired—a secure position within the royal household. The slave girl who had lost her natal family now had a new one: through her son she now had blood ties to his father and grandmother.

Mehmed's birth introduced a legal shift in Roxelana's status. Islamic law recognized and protected the concubine's role as mother: unlike an ordinary slave, she could not be sold or given away, and she would automatically be freed upon the death of her master. Her new status under the law as *umm al-walad* (mother of a child) signaled these rights and her identity. The Ottoman dynasty was not always faithful to the letter of the law, but in this case it capitalized on the legal category by charging royal concubines with dedicating themselves to their children's welfare and upbringing.

There were limits to Roxelana's prerogatives as mother, however. Mehmed was her son, but he was primarily a child of the dynasty. The House of Osman, as historians of the time called it, was a venerable lineage, now entering its third century of rule. As son of the reigning sultan and a potential ruler of the empire, Mehmed carried with him the investment of the entire imperial family. Now the alarming death of two princes within a matter of weeks raised both Mehmed's and his mother's value, something Roxelana was bound to appreciate. The heightened health measures that would be instituted may have kept mother and child isolated from one another.

The tragic deaths of Mahmud and Murad within a matter of weeks sharpened awareness of the hazards of an empire based on hereditary rule. Were the House of Osman to die out, the empire would dissolve, and a new state under the aegis of a new dynasty would inevitably come into being. If the new mother's emotions were mixed, Suleyman carried the heavy weight of political as well as personal distress. His biographers have paid scant if any attention to the wrenching loss of three children and the grief that inevitably ensued. They focus instead on the affairs of state into which the sultan was plunged on his return from Belgrade. To be sure, Suleyman was probably fortunate to have the distraction of envoys who arrived one after the other from Venice, the merchant state of Ragusa, and the Grand Duchy of Moscow. They came to convey congratulations on his recent victory and to request favors of his government. But the security of the royal family was also a political matter.

As if the loss of three children was not devastating enough, the young father would feel concern over the well-being of the living ones— of Mustafa, now the oldest at six, and the newborn Mehmed, the only other Ottoman prince. Suleyman clearly needed more sons. For her part, Roxelana had presumably mastered something of the politics of concubinage during her training and understood the future that was in store for her. Her career as mother of a son was laid out carefully, including the rule that she was no longer eligible for the sultan's bed. She was mother of a prince now; her work as concubine was complete. If Roxelana had come to depend on the father of her son or learned to care for him in the months they were together, she would need to rein in those feelings.

THE BIRTH OF Mehmed introduced changes into Roxelana's life. As her status and value rose within the imperial household, so did her material circumstances. "When one of the maidens becomes pregnant by the Monarch, her salary is increased and she is honored and elevated above the others, and is served as a Lady," observed the Venetian Giovanni Maria Angiolello, usually our best informant on the career of the concubine.[3] In the detailed palace account books that recorded the stipends of imperial household members, Roxelana would now be listed not by name but by the honorific title "the mother of Prince Mehmed." Her son had catapulted her into the handsomely rewarded elite of palace women, the mothers of royal offspring.

Roxelana could now begin to spend—indeed her position demanded that she do so, generously but prudently. (All palace women of status received a daily stipend and a separate "kitchen" budget.)[4] Apart from seeing to the sundry daily needs of her suite, protocol required that she reward with tips and gifts those who served her or the baby. As the health crisis passed and Roxelana emerged from the rituals of postpartum confinement, she would embark on the privilege of receiving visitors and the duty of providing refreshments to palace women who came to call on the little prince and his mother. Suleyman now also had a reason to visit, rather than to summon.

A new mother's spatial location within the palace served as a public announcement of her elevated rank. Once she returned to the Old Palace from her interlude with Suleyman, Roxelana graduated from the dormitory quarters of the trainees to private chambers befitting a full-fledged concubine carrying the sultan's child. Mehmed's birth perhaps earned her an even larger and more lavishly appointed suite. Additional attendants would be assigned to serve Roxelana, organizing meals, supervising her visits to the bath, looking after her wardrobe, and conveying messages. Mehmed too would acquire a small retinue. Foremost among the women assigned to care of the infant was his *daye*, the governess assigned to him for life. Unfortunately, her identity is unknown, since she too was recognized by her title.

While the interior of Roxelana's rooms was visible only to her mentors, guests, and servants, she herself was an ambulatory messenger of her rank to all who might encounter her during the day. Her person required more elegant adornment, and so her wardrobe expanded.

Headband and handkerchief belonging to Roxelana, preserved in her tomb.

Roxelana's new income would enable her to select fabrics for her gowns from the array of rare and expensive textiles produced around the empire and imported from abroad.

Jewels came to Roxelana as congratulatory childbirth gifts. The most treasured of her ornaments almost certainly came from Suleyman. Every sultan cultivated a manual skill, and his was the art of goldsmithing. He had allegedly learned his craft from a Greek master in Trabzon, the city where he was born and educated. Known as Trebizond among the Byzantines, it was the last outpost of Greek civilization to fall to the Ottomans, in 1461. By 1526, the Venetian ambassador Pietro Bragadin could report that Suleyman had bestowed 100,000 ducats' worth of jewels on his favorite.[5] Even if rumor aggrandized the sum, the jewels were apparently a news item worthy of international note.

The daily routine of the young mother was now a busy one. Although much of Mehmed's care was in the hands of his *daye* and his wet nurse, Roxelana was not deprived of opportunity for intimacy with her infant. A prince's mother was to be his lifelong mentor. His father by contrast was frequently absent, either on military campaign or deep in council deliberations. Even when present in Istanbul, the sultan lived apart from his children. Angiolello underlined the parental responsibility of the concubine mother: "If she gives birth to a son, the boy is raised by his mother until the age of ten or eleven; then the Grand Turk gives him a province and sends his mother with him. . . . And if a girl is born, she is raised by her mother until the time she is married."[6] By Suleyman's day, the age at which princes and their mothers took up provincial service was rising—he himself had been fifteen when sent with Hafsa to Caffa. Mustafa would graduate to public life at eighteen and Mehmed at twenty.

As a new mother, possibly as young as seventeen, Roxelana needed guidance in the Ottoman approach to raising royal children. She could learn from Mehmed's caregivers, who were available and also accountable if anything went wrong with the little boy's development. If she had the opportunity to observe Mustafa and Mahidevran together, the senior concubine's conduct could serve as a useful referent for the future—to emulate, improve upon, or perhaps disregard. Hafsa surely kept a grandmother's eye on Mehmed and presumably asked her staff to monitor

Roxelana's well-being. At the same time, the culture of child raising in the Old Palace allowed a modicum of freedom for new mothers to follow the ways of their ancestors. After all, one reason for perpetuating the dynasty with slave concubines of varied origin was to exploit their very foreignness.

The nursery was not the only locus of Roxelana's days. Her education continued and in fact accelerated. Her Turkish skills would advance, most likely with the help of a tutor, and her knowledge of Islam would deepen, perhaps with the guidance of a spiritually inclined palace elder. Improving her penmanship would free her from reliance on a harem scribe if she wanted to communicate privately. All of this activity, with its focus on the new little prince and the preparation of his mother as his future counselor, had another effect: it helped the concubine leave behind the intense interlude with the sultan who had gotten her pregnant. Her transformation required that she adjust her expectations and desires to her new destiny. Her gratification would now derive from her child and his successes.

UNEXPECTED THEN WAS Suleyman's call for Roxelana to return to his bed. She conceived again sometime within four months of his return from Belgrade in October 1521. Suleyman was again away at war for most of Roxelana's second pregnancy and also for the birth of their daughter Mihrumah in the fall of 1522. The following February, he returned to his capital with a stunning new victory: the capture of the Mediterranean island of Rhodes from the formidable crusader order of the Knights Hospitaller. Once again a conquest was paired with a new addition to the dynastic family. And once again, victory was followed by a return to the bedchamber with the concubine who had clearly become his favorite.

Over the next few years, Roxelana and Suleyman produced three more boys: Selim, Abdullah, and Bayezid. All were presumably planned, or at least welcome. Islamic law sanctioned forms of birth control, and the Old Palace had ways of dealing with unwanted conceptions.[7] No children were born to Suleyman with any other concubine during his entire reign. If he slept with any during his long absences from Istanbul or during Roxelana's pregnancies, care was taken that no child issued from these encounters. Five children with one concubine in seven years and none with any other was a revolutionary break with tradition. An Ottoman sultan had become monogamous. What the consequences might be, no one could yet say.

Roxelana's rise to favorite did not go unremarked. Public announcements of the royal births conveyed news of the couple's fecundity and, by implication, the lovers' presumed pleasures. Istanbulites may not have known the favorite's name at first, but they could not escape a dawning awareness of the sultan's maverick sexual habits. Venetian ambassadors, Europe's keenest eyes and ears in Istanbul, tracked Suleyman's growing attachment to Roxelana. In the space of a few years, the sultan's amorous profile shifted in their reports from keen interest in his harem to constancy to one woman. Marco Minio had noted in 1522 that Suleyman was "very lustful," but Pietro Zen, a longtime intimate of the Ottoman court, wrote to the Venetian Senate in 1524 that "the Seigneur is not lustful" and was devoted to a single woman.[8] By 1526, Pietro Bragadin could assert that the sultan no longer paid attention to the mother of his eldest son Mustafa, "a woman from Montenegro," but gave all his affection to "another woman, of the Russian nation."[9]

Although both Europeans and the Istanbul public were beginning to recognize Roxelana's monopoly in the royal bedchamber, the old ways died hard in people's minds. Even foreign observers appeared flummoxed by the idea of a monogamous sultan. Some fifteen years after Roxelana's emergence as sole consort, Luigi Bassano was still relaying the standard story that sultans traded one concubine for another.[10] The rumors that would later plague Roxelana—of her sorcery and Suleyman's lovesickness—may well have germinated around this time, as people became aware of her seemingly permanent place in his life. The force of public opinion in the Ottoman capital was considerable, and Istanbulites had been known to censure their monarch when provoked.

For one thing, the public disapproved if the sultan appeared to overindulge in pleasure. His duty, they believed, was the defense of the empire from the several enemies threatening its borders. Even Mehmed the Conqueror had faced a challenge from his soldiers when he sent his grand vizier to command the army while he stayed home. When, in 1525, Janissaries in Istanbul rose up in protest against Suleyman's prolonged absence—he had taken a long winter sojourn in Thrace to hunt—the rebels would pillage the customs house, the Jewish quarter where it was located, and the palaces of two viziers and the head treasurer.[11] One was the sumptuous residence of Ibrahim, Suleyman's boon companion who was now grand vizier.

Subjects of the Ottoman empire understood and honored the political logic of serial concubinage—rotation out of the sultan's bed of each new mother of a son. They grasped the point that a prince should not share his mother with another prince, that his mother was both his ally and the sultan's check on his son's loyalty. The contest among princes was expected to be even, and each needed and deserved his mother's exclusive devotion and counsel. Heir to political traditions shared by Mongols and Central Asian Turks, the Ottomans believed that all physically sound sons of the sovereign had an equally legitimate claim to power. The widespread European practice of primogeniture—the automatic succession of the king's eldest son—no doubt seemed to them both unjust and unwise. First there was the spiritual belief that sovereignty was god given and man should not interfere, and then there was the mundane rationale that casting sons of the reigning monarch as rivals would demonstrate who was best able to rally a loyal following and win the backing of the military, thus the best candidate to succeed his father. To the public, it must have seemed dangerous to tamper with a formula that had yielded a stellar succession of strong monarchs.

But the times were dangerous. It was immediately after he threw down the gauntlet to Europe at Belgrade that Suleyman lost three children. In 1522, the ambassador Minio commented that the empire would be in great confusion should the sultan happen to die leaving only infant heirs.[12] A crisis in the life of the dynastic family was a crisis in the state, and Europe had used such moments in the past to assemble crusading coalitions against the Ottomans. The famous Battle of Varna in 1444 was a case in point. When Murad II gave up the throne for a life of contemplation, turning it over to his twelve-year-old son Mehmed (the future "Conqueror"), a coalition of several kings and princes blessed by the pope saw an opportunity to advance. Fortunately for the Ottomans,

Murad returned at the grand vizier's summons and vanquished the crusaders.

Although Suleyman could do nothing about the tender age of his offspring, he clearly had to father more as insurance against the myriad hazards of childhood in the sixteenth century. His viziers would have impressed this upon him in guarded, respectful terms, his mother more emphatically. Suleyman was not alone in his dilemma, for the quest for heirs bedeviled other monarchs in these years. In 1525, Basil III, grand prince of Moscow, confined his wife to a convent after twenty years of a childless marriage; four years later, in a second union, he finally got his son, the future Ivan IV. The Tudor kings of England were stymied in their efforts to establish a new dynasty in the aftermath of the internecine slaughter that had been the Wars of the Roses. The first Tudor ruler, Henry VII, lost his eldest son, Crown Prince Arthur, when the boy was fifteen. Henry VIII, Arthur's younger brother and successor, waited twenty-eight years for his own male heir.

Henry VIII was notorious for the lengths he went to get a son—a divorce that precipitated a rupture with the pope in Rome in 1533, the execution in 1536 of an alleged adulteress who had only produced a girl. If Basil and Henry knew of the Ottoman monarch's plight, he must have looked lucky to them: he did not have to rid himself of his consorts to obtain the sons who brought dynastic security.

WHAT PERSUADED SULEYMAN to answer his own reproductive crisis by reuniting with Roxelana? Of all our uncertainties about Suleyman and Roxelana's relationship, this is the most vexing. Returning the mother of a prince to the role of concubine violated his ancestors' long-standing practice. It was an act that would reset the course of Roxelana's life and forever change the face of Ottoman politics.

What part, if any, Roxelana played in stimulating her reunion with Suleyman is also unclear. She may well have been loath to see another woman in Suleyman's bed now that she had a son whose future she must protect. A new concubine could mean a new son for the sultan and a competitor for her Mehmed. And if Roxelana had become emotionally attached to Suleyman, she had all the more reason to resist a rival. On the other hand, perhaps she was content simply to focus on Mehmed and their future together.

What was Suleyman thinking when he shared his bed again with Roxelana? Was he heedlessly following his heart, as his critics would later claim? Was it simply easier for him, in the midst of personal grief and the relentless press of politics, to turn to a woman now familiar to him than to initiate a barely known and inexperienced virgin? Ottoman politics of reproduction exacted a price from a male dynast, who by convention had to relinquish a concubine he might have come to care for. Whatever the case, the pressure for more sons was certainly a factor in Suleyman's decision to bend the rules for a woman who had conceived quickly and produced a healthy boy.

Still, as the young sultan well knew, to flout imperial custom was a hazardous move. Abandoning the practice of rotating concubines would disrupt delicate power balances worked out over two centuries. The Old Palace prided itself on providing sultans with multiple partners worthy of companionship and motherhood, and resentment of Suleyman's return to Roxelana would naturally arise in some quarters. His pashas and viziers must have worried that the unprecedented devotion to a single woman—especially a young and politically inexperienced one—would interfere with his political judgment. Even more consequential, compelling Roxelana's sons to share the political asset that was their mother threatened to give the competitive advantage to Mustafa. As ambassadors noted, his mother Mahidevran was wholly focused on his success. On the other hand, a son of Suleyman's favorite might be unfairly favored in the game of rivalry for the throne.

It matters why Suleyman ignored long-established custom when he returned to Roxelana after Mehmed's birth, for this decision would turn out to be the first in a chain of events that ultimately altered the manner of succession to the throne and the very nature of the Ottoman sultanate. Even before becoming sultan, Suleyman had legitimate reason for thinking that his ancestors' methods of perpetuating the dynasty called for reconsideration. During the eight years of his princely apprenticeship, he had had a good deal of time to both experience the vagaries of imperial politics and reflect on them. His father's path to the Ottoman throne had been a whirlwind of violence and victory.

Selim I's tenure as sultan began in 1512 with the forcible over-throw of his father Bayezid II. The allegation that Selim had the sultan poisoned—Bayezid perished on his way to forced retirement—has been neither proved nor disproved. Selim then proceeded to battle his two older brothers, both of whom, like himself, had connived for the throne. After defeating and executing both, Selim had his agents hunt down and kill their sons. He then ordered the execution of the male offspring of other brothers previously deceased. There were many, since Bayezid had numerous children, eight of whom were male. Moreover, Bayezid had lived long enough to give his own sons plenty of time to reproduce—he was sixty-eight by the Islamic calendar when he died. By the spring of 1513, Selim had eliminated all branches of the dynastic family except his own. As for Suleyman, he was indirectly his father's accomplice in the bloodbath, as Selim appointed him deputy ruler in the capital while he pursued his rival relatives.

Selim was no monster, however. It was his grandfather Mehmed the Conqueror who had sanctioned internecine violence with his so-called law of fratricide, approved by religious authorities (possibly under duress). Sovereignty must be indivisible and the sovereign unchallenged. As history had cautioned, empires that embraced the principle that all male dynasts had a right to rule—the Seljuks, the Mongols—could fragment into feuding factions, fatally weakened by incessant combat among royal brothers, cousins, and uncles. The House of Osman itself had struggled from the beginning with the ill-matched principles of unitary sovereignty and competitive succession. It took Mehmed's authority to push through a legislated solution. Still, if legitimate by law and tradition, Selim's contest with his brothers was the most violent on record since the long civil war of 1402 to 1412 had threatened partition of the state among Ottoman princes.

Suleyman was fortunate not to face the same lethal rivalry upon his father's death, for he was the only son of Selim to reach adulthood. But we should not content ourselves, as almost all historians have done, with the assumption that Selim had only a single son, as he and his concubines produced at least six daughters. Rather, the man whose epithet *Yavuz* meant both resolute and ferocious appears to have "disappeared" his other male offspring in order to render Suleyman his unchallenged successor.[13] (Whether he ordered them eliminated or hidden in the strictest anonymity is a matter of speculation.)[14]

With the stock of male dynasts now reduced to two, Selim relied on Suleyman, the only Ottoman prince left standing, to replenish it. As a consequence, however, Suleyman's sons and their mothers could not escape reenacting the pattern that Selim had spared his own son: rivalry among the brothers and their mothers. Then the deaths of Mahmud and Murad reduced the number of Suleyman's heirs to two—a six-year-old and a newborn—and reminded people of the fragility of childhood. Suleyman had to father more males, but in doing so, must he honor the tradition that a concubine mother should have only one? Selim had broken a cardinal rule on the grounds that the empire was at risk. Burdened with the same challenge, might Suleyman now break another? Though he may have strongly desired to return to Roxelana, he almost certainly came to the decision to do so after serious deliberation.

The only person with the moral and political right to dissuade—or encourage—Suleyman was his mother Hafsa. Frustratingly, because it was a private discussion, we cannot know what they said to one another. Hafsa's responsibilities and concerns differed from Suleyman's. As the family elder, she would consider the welfare of the whole dynastic enterprise in wider scope than her son sometimes could, charged as he was with the immediate exigencies of rule. Hafsa may have approved the idea of redefining the role of the concubine mother, an inevitable outcome if Roxelana should produce another son. Having spent most of her life tied to Selim's fortunes, she might welcome an end to the violence that appeared unavoidable in the Ottoman system of succession. But she would doubtless pose the question just how introducing a new family configuration with Roxelana would effectively get around the problem of fratricide. Suleyman already had two sons who were half brothers, but calling Roxelana back to his bed could ultimately pit two full brothers against each other. Suleyman himself may not yet have had an answer, but he was clearly ready to set change in motion.

OVER TIME ROXELANA would come to know Suleyman's history more fully and to grasp the degree to which his father's experiences determined his own choices as sultan. In fact, she had a compelling interest in that history since it intertwined with her own and her sons' fates.

Selim had had a long and difficult career as prince. Frustrated with his post in distant Trabzon on the eastern Black Sea coast, he complained to his father Bayezid II of its wretched state: "Poverty and shortages are ever present, any governor would be weak and helpless [here]. . . . I don't even have the wherewithal to build my own boat."[15] The closer a prince's assignment to Istanbul, it was thought, the faster he could race to the capital at his father's death to literally occupy the throne. But Selim's petition for a nearer site foundered when his older brother Ahmed objected. He did manage, however, to persuade Bayezid to assign Suleyman to Caffa in 1509 (but only after Ahmed had opposed two proposed sites in central Anatolia, claiming them as his sphere of influence).

Selim's backwater assignment in eastern Anatolia gave him additional reason to angle for the empire's throne. From his post he could observe at close quarters the mounting threat posed by the newly established and rapidly expanding Safavid state in Iran. Its charismatic young shah, Ismail, was winning the hearts of many Anatolians, nominal subjects of the sultan. Safavid propagandizing contained a mix of messianism and political promise. To Selim, Bayezid and his other sons seemed insufficiently concerned with the menace on their eastern frontier.

Selim proceeded to use Suleyman and Hafsa's presence in Caffa as a springboard to the throne. He took refuge there in 1510 as he made his way toward the capital and the confrontation that culminated in his unseating of his father.[16] Selim then enlisted the help of the Crimean khan Mengli Giray to transport Hafsa and Suleyman to Istanbul, where he could better protect them. Selim then left Suleyman to guard the capital as his deputy when he set off to fight his brothers. Suleyman was nineteen when he got his first taste of what it meant to hold an empire together. Only when his throne was secured did Selim in 1513 permit his son to take up a new provincial assignment in Anatolia, the theater of the brothers' brief but vicious civil war.

At first, Manisa was not an easy post for Suleyman. The third of the three rival brothers, Korkud, had been stationed in this western Anatolian provincial capital, and Selim had personally hunted him down with a large army. Now Suleyman confronted a province whose public order had been shattered. He appealed to his father for instructions, and Selim responded with a compilation of regulations. It detailed the penalties Suleyman should mete out to curb rampant theft and banditry, and it advised him to publicize his disciplinary measures in the towns and villages of the region before judges began implementing them.[17] Suleyman was in the midst of guiding Manisa's recovery, applying tax and property reforms Selim had devised, when he was summoned to Istanbul in 1514 to serve again as his deputy. There he would remain for two years during Selim's extended campaign against Shah Ismail, the brilliant young ruler who had reunited a fragmented Iran under the banner of the Safavid dynasty.

Selim was a great warrior, and his son would inherit a much-enlarged empire from him. The juggernaut that was his army doubled the extent of the Ottoman domains. After pushing back the Iranians and annexing eastern Anatolia, Selim led another long offensive, this one aimed at the famed Mamluk sultanate. (Suleyman was again his father's stand-in, stationed this time in Adrianople in Thrace, to face down any opportunistic European advance.) Selim first subdued Greater Syria (today's Syria, Jordan, Lebanon, Palestine, and Israel) and then, in January 1517, took Cairo, seat of the Mamluk sultans, and Egypt with it.

This two-year campaign won for the Ottomans the coveted title "servitor of the two Noble Sanctuaries," signifying the right and privilege of protecting the holy cities of Mecca and Medina. With the shores of the eastern Mediterranean, from Greece to Egypt, united for the first time since the seventh century, Selim had resurrected the eastern Roman empire. But it was at great cost that he won his dazzling reputation as *sahib qıran* (master of the celestial conjunction)—in other words, a man destined to world conquest.

Suleyman is often said to have come to the throne with no experience. Because he had not fought in his father's campaigns, as previous Ottomans princes often had, his European and Iranian competitors could assume he lacked Selim's brilliance as a military strategist. It was partly for this reason that he undertook two major offensives in the first two years of his reign. But Suleyman did not lack an education under fire in the politics of dynastic rule. In the space of two years, he had lost his grandfather, two uncles, and many cousins so that his father could clinch his hold on power. Suleyman's first son was born in 1513, in the midst of the violence. His delight with Mahmud's mother perhaps drew his thoughts to all the other mothers, daughters, and sisters left stranded by his father's triumph.

On the other hand, Selim had identified Suleyman as his successor, saving him and his sons from the very fate he visited on his brothers and their sons. He had carefully tutored Suleyman in the delicate balance between governing justly and enforcing order. Selim had also provided his heir with three opportunities as deputy ruler to hone his skills. And he left an impressive record of conquest and expansion. Some Ottoman pundits would later call Selim's reign a golden age. Upon his death in 1520, his legacy presented Suleyman with much to live up to and much to live down.

Suleyman's initial acts as sultan suggest that he had used his apprenticeship to consider the kind of a ruler he wanted to be. His first deeds were obligatory. On his second day in the capital, he was formally invested as sultan with the traditional oath of allegiance pledged by religious and political leaders. He then left the palace and crossed the city to receive his father's funeral train, just arrived from Thrace. Once the late sultan's burial was accomplished, Suleyman ordered the construction of a mosque, a madrasa, and a tomb to honor his resting place. On the third day, Suleyman opened the seals of the imperial treasury (locked at his father's death) and distributed the customary accession bonus awarded to the empire's soldiers. He filled top government offices, confirming his father's appointees in some, including the grand vizierate, and placing his own men in others.

Official duties behind him, Suleyman began to impose his own imprint on the sultanate. Selim's son would be merciful and munificent. He freed six hundred Egyptians whom his father had taken prisoner in 1517. Then he ordered the payment of 1 million silver aspers as compensation to Persian silk merchants whose goods Selim had confiscated when he banned trade with Iran (much to the chagrin of his advisers, some of whom argued that hostilities should not stand in the way of lucrative international commerce). The new sultan then turned to domestic affairs, demonstrating that he would not tolerate misgovernment. After calling for an investigation into accusations against the royal admiral Cafer Beg, Suleyman condemned him to hang when judges delivered a guilty verdict. He dismissed one of his leading military officials, the *agha* of armaments, because his troops had violated protocol, and then he executed the five responsible parties.

In the words of Joseph von Hammer, author of the first exhaustive history of the Ottomans in a European language, the hallmark of these acts was a combination of "rigorous justice and generous clemency."[18] A young official in the Austrian embassy in Istanbul in the 1790s and a contemporary of the great statesman and diplomat Klemens von Metternich, von Hammer understood the importance of symbolic acts that ensured political continuity but signaled a new era.

Personality differences between father and son began to reveal themselves. Bartolomeo Contarini, Venetian ambassador dispatched to convey congratulations on the 1517 victory in Egypt, wrote of Selim, "He reflects constantly; no one dares to say anything, not even the pashas who are there with him; he governs alone, on the basis of his own thinking."[19] By contrast, Suleyman would develop numerous collaborative relationships over the course of his reign, the closest and most enduring of them with Roxelana. At his accession, the current ambassador described him as "friendly and in good humor. Rumor has it that Suleyman is aptly named, enjoys reading, is knowledgeable, and shows good judgment."[20] (Suleyman, the Ottoman rendering of Solomon, was, in other words, thought to be wise.) Later in his reign, the epithet Kanuni (the lawgiver or, more loosely, the just) was bestowed on him.

It was in the midst of establishing his own brand of rule in these initial months that Suleyman took Roxelana as the first and only concubine of his reign. As sultan, Suleyman had the power to change the rules. He had already shown signs that he intended to do some things differently than his father had. For her part, Roxelana was learning about Suleyman's past, perhaps from Hafsa, who had lived through it alongside him, or possibly from a loyal retainer concerned to apprise the mother of a baby prince of what might lie ahead. She, in other words, understood something of what was at stake in both his life and her own. Then the palace epidemic of 1521 rewrote facts on the ground. If ever there was a time to consider innovation in the politics of reproduction, this was it. Roxelana was the right woman in the right place at the right time.

5

LOVERS AND PARENTS

A S THE YEAR 1521 came to a close, Roxelana found herself safely situated as mother of a new baby prince. Still, she could not yet rest assured of a lasting place in Suleyman's affections. Following the loss of two sons, the bereaved sultan would likely need to take on a new concubine to replenish the supply of potential heirs—and perhaps to soothe his grief. Roxelana did not make a habit of simply waiting for events to happen, however. A dramatic incident reported in 1526 by Pietro Bragadin, Venetian ambassador to Istanbul, reveals her instinct for survival in the charged atmosphere of the harem.

Venice's ambassadors to the Ottomans occupied the top post in the island republic's diplomatic service. Envoys sent regular dispatches home, but upon returning from their tenure abroad, they delivered a comprehensive oral assessment of affairs to members of the Venetian government. Bragadin's report, the first to broadcast the rise of the Russian favorite, was made to the assembled dignitaries in June. Roxelana had by then become significant enough for the Venetian elite to keep tabs on, and we may think of this moment as her international debut.

Among the ambassador's various accounts of the sultan's domains, the dignitaries listened to a story that revealed the young concubine's determination to advance. As Bragadin reported, "The sultan was given two beautiful Russian maidens by a provincial governor, one for his mother and one for him. When they arrived in the palace, his second wife [*sic*], whom he esteems at present, became extremely unhappy and flung herself to the ground weeping." The ambassador then noted the reactions of Hafsa, Suleyman's mother, and the sultan himself, as they attempted to mollify the distraught Roxelana. "The mother, who had given her maiden to the sultan, was sorry about what she had done, took her back, and sent her to one of the governors as wife, and the sultan agreed

"The house and garden of the Venetian ambassadors in Constantinople." Seventeenth-century European drawing of the Venetian ambassadorial compound.

to send his to another governor, because his wife would have perished from sorrow if these maidens, or even one of them, had remained in the palace."[1]

Bragadin's report revealed that Suleyman was still receiving gifts of fresh female slaves, and from his mother no less. No wonder Roxelana could not feel confident of his constancy. She knew by now that not every gift slave turned into a bedmate—some would be employed as attendants and others regifted to high-level servants of the dynasty, like the two Russian women. Apparently, though, she considered it too risky to assume such outcomes. Her histrionics seemed to be a clever ploy to shield her emerging status as favorite.

Roxelana was hardly unreasonable in fearing that Suleyman might consider a new partner. In the years when the drama took place (well before Bragadin reported it in 1526), Roxelana was more often than not pregnant or in confinement with an infant, unavailable to share Suleyman's bed. A new partner for the sultan could lead to a new son or daughter—and even a new favorite. Perhaps the fact that the two beauties had origins like her own aroused a particular jealousy.

The most remarkable feature of Bragadin's account, however, was Suleyman and Hafsa's willingness to accommodate Roxelana's sentiments. It seems the concubine's bold presumption of rank did not offend the sultan and queen mother. Indeed, Hafsa appears to have been remorseful. Suleyman and especially his mother, herself a former slave consort, would understand the young concubine's determination to protect herself and her son at all costs. If Roxelana acted out of pure jealousy, hers was likely not the first such display to occur in the harem. It would not be surprising if she had developed a deepening attachment to Suleyman. Her bond with him was the only intimate adult relationship she would experience in her captivity among the Ottomans.

IF A GENUINE passion had indeed taken root, it is not entirely obvious how often or where Suleyman and Roxelana found time alone together. He was literally one of the busiest men in the world. And they lived apart, he in the New Palace, she and the children in the Old Palace, an arrangement not conducive to daily interaction. Perhaps Suleyman organized interludes for them from time to time in the New Palace. But after two long stretches when he was at war, the couple could finally enjoy something of a honeymoon.

The three years from winter 1523 to spring 1526 were one of Suleyman's rare breaks from campaigning—a period of "military inaction," as one historian has called it.[2] The sultan had plenty of reason to remain in the capital. His victories in Belgrade and Rhodes required a reorganization of diplomatic and military strategy, and he needed to better integrate the defunct kingdom of Serbia into Ottoman provincial administration. Internal problems like the Ferhad Pasha affair called for attention. More troublesome was a revolt in Egypt in 1524. Suleyman sent Ibrahim, his old friend and grand vizier, to impose order and reorganize this strategic and economic bastion, incorporated into the empire by Selim only seven years earlier. At home, the capital needed attention, what with the rapidly expanding population and the ongoing project of Ottomanizing the city. From a war-wasted population of roughly 30,000 at the Byzantine collapse in 1453, Istanbul would grow to some 100,000 by 1535 and triple that by the 1570s.[3]

But Suleyman was clearly preoccupied in these years with his favorite and her children. If Mehmed and Mihrumah were conceived in the interstices between campaigns, Selim and Abdullah, their next children, were honeymoon babies. Selim was born in May 1524 and Abdullah probably sometime in 1525 or early 1526 (his precise birth date is not known). Roxelana had given Suleyman four children in five years. Upon his return in November 1526 from fighting in Europe, she conceived another son, Bayezid, giving birth probably in 1527. A final boy, Cihangir, would arrive in 1531. Roxelana and Suleyman were carving out space for a traditional family—father, mother, children—within an imperial structure that did not prize the nuclear domestic unit. Together they were living in uncharted emotional territory.

As parents, Roxelana and Suleyman began to experience the trials as well as the joys of raising children. Abdullah died as a toddler, Roxelana's first loss and yet another grief for Suleyman, the third of his sons to perish in childhood.[4] The couple was tested again when Cihangir was born with what appears to have been a deformity of his shoulder. This accumulated wealth of shared experience doubtless led over the years to a certain familiarity and comfort between Suleyman and Roxelana. Time allowed the couple a deepening acquaintance. As Roxelana's Turkish improved, she most likely learned more about Suleyman's childhood, and he about hers. It is tempting to wonder if he inquired about the circumstances of her abduction, an intimate aspect of the slave trade he could only know if his slave servants dared to tell him. Much later in her life, the ambassador Bernardo Navagero would comment, in accounting for Roxelana's hold over the sultan, that "she understands his nature very well."[5]

Honeymoons come to an end, but the foundations of a lifelong partnership were laid down during these three years of relative domesticity. In the spring of 1526, Suleyman departed Istanbul with the aim of taking Buda, capital of the kingdom of Hungary. On September 11, the victorious sultan entered the city at the head of his army. The battle of Mohacs—alleged to have lasted a mere two hours—had been fought in the marshes of southern Hungary, where King Louis II drowned while fleeing. It was the end of the historic kingdom of Hungary.

Although unable to hold Buda—disturbances in central Anatolia demanded his return—Suleyman had made the Ottomans a player in the politics of central Europe. His empire now came face to face with the House of Hapsburg, the only other European power that could match Ottoman military resources. Competition and confrontation on land and on sea with the Hapsburg brothers—King Charles V of Spain and his designated successor, Archduke Ferdinand I of Austria—persisted throughout Suleyman's reign. He would die at the age of seventy-four (by the Islamic calendar) defending his empire on the Ottoman-Hungarian frontier.

The victory at Mohacs triggered a century and a half of rivalry and conflict between Hapsburgs and Ottomans. Buda did not come under direct Ottoman control for another fifteen years, and Ferdinand never abandoned a tenacious duel for Hungary. The struggle for tactical superiority would be matched by a contest for ideological supremacy when Charles resuscitated the notion of the Holy Roman Empire as a universal monarchy—with himself at its head.[6] Suleyman would counter with the Ottomans' own claim to the Roman legacy. With the stronghold of Buda in central Europe and the gradual advance of Ottoman naval forces in the Mediterranean, Suleyman, like his father Selim, was reviving the eastern Roman empire with its capital at Constantinople.

WHILE SULEYMAN WAS occupied in 1526 with one of the most momentous campaigns of his long reign, the anxieties that Roxelana had been spared for the previous three years must have taken hold. He could be injured or even killed and her life thrust into uncertainty, even chaos. If disaster struck, Suleyman's eldest son Mustafa, now twelve and already popular with the Janissaries, would be a safer choice to succeed his father than her Mehmed, seven years younger. It was a nightmare worse, perhaps, than the loss of her natal family. The one thing Roxelana could do to reassure herself, besides keeping abreast of news from the front and praying, was to write to Suleyman.

Roxelana composed the first of her surviving letters during the Hungarian campaign. The emotion-filled missive was designed to arouse reciprocal feelings of longing in Suleyman and to keep him mindful of his family. "My sultan, there is no limit to the burning anguish of separation," she wrote in conclusion. "Now spare this miserable one and do not withhold your noble letters. Let my soul gain at least some comfort."

The letter's constant stress on the pain of being apart probably owed something to Suleyman. He had apparently chided Roxelana gently for not reading his letters thoroughly enough. Otherwise, he pointed out, "you would have written more of your longing to see me."[7]

Roxelana replied with spirit that it was too painful to do so because both she and his two elder children missed him excessively: "Now my sultan, this is enough, my soul is too affected [to write more]—especially as your servant and son Mir Mehmed and your slave and daughter Mihrumah weep and wail from missing you when your noble letters are read. Their weeping has driven me mad, it is as if we were in mourning. My sultan, your son Mir Mehmed and your daughter Mihrumah and Selim Khan and Abdullah send you many greetings." The pain of separation was a familiar Ottoman trope, especially among the mystics, who filled their poetry with yearning for union with the divine. Roxelana's letter reworked the theme vividly.

Roxelana probably did not pen the long letter herself. Nor did she likely dictate it, perhaps even the more informal fragment above, for her Turkish was not yet up to the task. The letter's exquisite penmanship confirms that it was composed by a harem scribe. The scribe's professional training would make her adept at employing the elaborate locutions characteristic of formal chancery style, likewise the intricate metaphors of the suffering lover and the references to the Qur'an, which were a familiar feature of Ottoman correspondence. But it is not hard to imagine Roxelana instructing the scribe on what to emphasize in the letter and to say it with feeling. Her personal note to Suleyman at the letter's end reveals a certain playfulness, no doubt intentional. It also suggests that she was learning to speak the poetic language of love.

Perhaps it was Roxelana's idea to include mention in the letter of Yusuf, the Joseph of biblical tradition and a prophet in Islam (the only one to have a chapter of the Qur'an devoted to his history). Over time Muslims came also to think of Yusuf as a paragon of beauty, and some, perhaps including Roxelana, would know the allegorical tale of Zeliha (the wife of Potiphar in the biblical account), whose carnal love for Yusuf was transformed into the mystic's love for God. Roxelana's letter hails Suleyman—"O you with the face of Yusuf and words sweet as candy." Later she comments that one has to read the chapter on Yusuf to fully

Talismanic shirt made for
Prince Selim in 1564–1565.

understand the state of someone (like her) in the throes of separation.
(The disappearance of his son caused Yakub—Jacob, the biblical patriarch and father of Joseph—to go blind with weeping.)[8]

Another letter that Roxelana dispatched to Suleyman during the
1526 campaign suggests that she was already acting as conduit for messages and gifts from well-wishers. In this case, she was forwarding to
Suleyman a talismanic shirt that had been brought to Istanbul by "one
of God's holy men, from Mecca."[9] Such garments were intended to protect the wearer, especially in battle. The shirts were typically covered
with minutely inscribed verses from the Qur'an, prayers, magic numbers, and, as with the Meccan's gift, the "beautiful names of God."[10]
The donor had apparently searched the city for the right channel to Suleyman. "He investigated the city and finally he brought it to Emre Koja
[presumably an individual known to or working in the palace], and Emre
Koja sent it to me, so now I'm sending it to you," wrote Roxelana. The
Meccan wanted Suleyman to wear it in battle, and so did she. "For the
love of God and reverence for the Prophet, don't do anything unless you
have put it on!"[11]

This same letter reveals something of Roxelana's life in the harem.
We hear these details not in her own words, however, but from a postscript added by Gulfem, a fellow resident of the Old Palace. Despite her
obvious prominence during Suleyman's reign, Gulfem's identity remains

frustratingly uncertain. She is usually assumed to have been one of Suleyman's earlier concubines and the mother of a son who did not survive
childhood; however, palace documents suggest that she was a high-level
harem administrator, most likely the Lady Steward.[12] The two roles are
not strictly incompatible if Gulfem requested a change of position from
consort to supervisor after the death of her child. Such a shift would give
her continued status within the Old Palace and perhaps new meaning to
her life.

In Roxelana's letters to Suleyman during his future absences from
Istanbul, Gulfem was the one person whose greetings she relayed in addition to her own and the children's. The two women seemingly developed a close and trusting relationship. Roxelana could certainly use a
friend and mentor, one she might look to as an older sister. (If Gulfem
was indeed a former concubine mother, she was at most in her early
thirties in 1526.) In addition to providing advice on managing the household, Gulfem might share with Roxelana many other kinds of beneficial
experience and intelligence—how to navigate Old Palace politics and
protocol, how to attract support for herself and the children, how to be
a gracious hostess of harem entertainments, and maybe how to write a
letter to Suleyman.

Whatever her relationship with the sultan, Gulfem knew him well
enough to speak openly and candidly in her postscript to Roxelana's letter. It seems he had extracted from her a promise to keep an eye on his
favorite. He apparently had some concern about Roxelana's ability to
manage the finances of her growing household. As Gulfem explained,
when she approached Roxelana directly for an account of her monies,
keeping her vow to the sultan, she met with silence. She then consulted
a certain Enver (possibly an Old Palace eunuch) and learned that the
concubine had "five hundred gold pieces remaining," presumably from
funds Suleyman had allocated to her before setting off for Hungary.
Gulfem also wanted him to be aware that Roxelana knew nothing of her
conversation with Enver.[13]

Gulfem's chatty tone lets us see that while protocols of status governed the personal lives of members of the dynasty, they could at the
same time enjoy the familiar banter of an ordinary family. Perhaps that
is exactly what Suleyman wanted to hear while he endured the rigors

of military life. Gulfem's postscript begins with a story of drunkenness. Among the souvenir gifts Suleyman sent from the road was some cologne for her. She apparently mistook it for a beverage, and regaled Suleyman with an account of the results: "I drank the cologne right away, you should have seen the state I was in. There were guests, I have no idea what I said, I dozed the whole long day. . . . You made a complete buffoon out of me! God-willing, when we see each other again, we can talk about it."

GULFEM'S CHECK ON Roxelana's finances provides a rare insight into the domestic world that dominated the favorite's life for some fifteen years. Not until the mid-1530s would she emerge as a public figure and object of widespread scrutiny. (The Venetians were ahead of the game in the 1520s.) This does not mean that Roxelana lacked political awareness or had no influence during these years. Among the Ottoman ruling class, the domestic was inherently political. The New Palace, with the sultan's personal quarters at its heart, was at the same time the seat of Ottoman government. Among the numerous structures of the vast compound were the imperial treasury, the hall of the Imperial Council, the royal audience chamber, and the training school for future statesmen, generals, and viziers. The royal harem housed in the Old Palace was likewise inherently political. One developed one's career by keeping abreast of events, important actors, and potential trouble spots. Old Palace networks, both internal and external, kept leading figures up to date.

Suleyman's expectation that Roxelana learn to manage her monies for herself underlines the degree of responsibility invested in a concubine mother. The goal of her training was mastery of the skills she would need when she graduated to provincial service with her son. There she would act as mistress of the domestic wing of the newly established princely household. If royal consorts around the world were often domiciled separately from their monarch spouses, the Ottomans had inherited particular twists to this practice from the past.

The sultans' concubines benefited from Turkish and Mongol imperial precedents. When the khans took their families to war, senior women might command their own encampments. Among the Ottomans, whose women did not typically go on campaign, this practice translated into senior women "commanding" a tutelary authority in the provinces. The mother of the prince who won the contest for succession would then move on to command the Old Palace hierarchy. Islamic law provided additional support for women's own management of their households. The Muslim male's right to polygyny (up to four wives) entailed the concomitant right of each wife to her own "door," that is, to a separate residence or suite of rooms equal to those of her fellow consorts. Although a royal concubine was not married to her sultan master (Roxelana was the famous exception), her equal status with his other concubines conformed in spirit to this legal precept. (Perhaps the infrequency of polygynous marriage among Ottoman upper classes stemmed in part at least from this mandated financial outlay.)

When Bragadin first brought Roxelana to attention in 1526, her quotidian responsibilities revolved around her four children. While an experienced staff provided hands-on care, she was answerable for the health, welfare, and education of her daughter and sons. At five the eldest, Mehmed was beginning instruction with a tutor, possibly Suleyman's own childhood preceptor Hayreddin. Later, the boys would receive a portion of their training together with Suleyman's pages in the New Palace. As for their mother, she too was continuing her education. Although Roxelana presumably had a tutor of her own in these early years, to advance her Turkish if nothing else, she no doubt progressed along with her older children as they studied their first lessons in Islamic scripture and in the glorious history of their ancestors.

What private education Roxelana imparted to her children herself is impossible to know, but there was apparently no ban on teaching them something of what she had learned as a child. The real question is what she remembered. In this Ottoman Tower of Babel, where virtually everyone came with a childhood culture and language different from that purveyed by the Old Palace, there must have been room for songs and folk tales and the vocabulary they taught. How much of her childhood faith Roxelana might have imparted is difficult to gauge, but in any event Christianity and Islam shared numerous patriarchs and matriarchs whose stories could be told.

Among the skills Roxelana was perfecting were the arts of the needle. She was apparently becoming adept at embroidery and sewing and taking pride in her accomplishments, for she would later make gifts of her work to the king of Poland. So would Mihrumah, who followed her mother along several of the paths that Roxelana would forge for royal women. Mihrumah, who spent her whole life in Istanbul, would always be her mother's pupil and companion. But perhaps the most consuming and private of Roxelana's preoccupations was her correspondence with Suleyman. We can imagine her unfurling his letters from the cylindrical case in which they arrived, reading and rereading them, and planning what news to impart to him in return.

Roxelana was not the only one who anticipated letters from Suleyman. As his army marched toward Buda in early September 1526, he wrote to his mother (a fact noted by the Venetian statesman and historian Marino Sanuto).[14] The letter doubtless informed Hafsa of the August 29 victory at Mohacs. She would share this news with others in the Old Palace, perhaps in a celebratory gathering to offer thanks to God and prayers for the continued safety of the sultan and his men.

It was the queen mother's prerogative and duty to initiate and preside over such occasions in the Old Palace. At them, Roxelana was bound to encounter the other royal consort, Mahidevran. Otherwise, the structure of the Old Palace and its daily habits would not thrust them together on a regular basis. But the future would cast them as rivals, and rumor would depict Roxelana as the confirmed enemy of her concubine predecessor. There is little evidence, however, to suggest an overt tension between the two, at least at this point in their lives. They could, however, be expected to keep a close eye on one another, given the presumption that both were dedicated to the ultimate success of their sons. It fell to Hafsa to enforce a discreet balance among Suleyman's two families.

In 1526, Roxelana had been Suleyman's concubine for six years. They were the parents of four children. Her maverick stature as his favorite was becoming recognized in Europe. If Mahidevran could take pride as the mother of the sultan's eldest son, Roxelana was developing a different claim to eminence.

CHALLENGES

6

ROXELANA'S RIVAL

A T THE END of a letter Roxelana wrote to Suleyman during the
Hungarian campaign, she added a postscript: "If you send greetings to Sultan Mustafa, send him my note too." Apparently she had included a separate letter to Suleyman's eldest son in the scroll cylinder
that carried her own to the sultan. The future would cloud Roxelana's
relations with Mustafa and his mother Mahidevran, but in 1526 there
appeared to be harmony, or at least an effort on Roxelana's part to keep
up communication.

Mustafa was twelve years old when his father captured Buda, capital city of Hungary. He had spent his early years among his siblings
in the western Anatolian city of Manisa, traditionally a seat of prince-
governors like his father. But it was in the imperial capital, under the
tutelage of a father who was now the monarch of a vast empire, that
Mustafa began his formal education. The little prince probably tagged
along with his half brother Mahmud, two years his senior, at least to
some of their tutors. But less than a year after their arrival in Istanbul,
the epidemic of 1521 took all three of Mustafa's siblings by Suleyman's
previous concubines, including Mahmud. Now he would presumably be
the model for Roxelana's children, who were joining the royal family in
rapid succession.

In the year that Roxelana dispatched her note, Mustafa was lavishly
praised in the pages of Pietro Bragadin's report to the Venetian Senate.
"He has extraordinary talent, he will be a warrior, is much loved by the
Janissaries, and performs great feats," the ambassador wrote.[1] That the
prince managed, at such a tender age, to garner such a reputation, even if
exaggerated, suggests that some of his training was already taking place
outside the Old Palace, among his father's men. Suleyman may well have
engaged leading Janissary officers to introduce his son to the arts of war.

The Janissaries, infantry legions who formed the core of the Ottoman standing army, were prone to strong partisan loyalties (and disloyalties).

The child Mustafa was clearly demonstrating aptitude for the job his ancestors had worked at with such diligence. The bravura performance of Suleyman's first years on the throne no doubt rubbed off on the prince, and one can imagine his father proudly showing him off on public occasions. Roxelana's note suggests that Mustafa was not in Istanbul during the Hungarian campaign, or at least not in his usual quarters in the Old Palace. Perhaps he was assigned during his father's absence to Adrianople, the Thracian second capital of the empire. Twelve was a young age to charge a prince with acting as deputy to a sultan at war, but then Mehmed the Conqueror had only been twelve when his father attempted to abdicate in his favor.

Wherever he was, Mustafa was accompanied by his mother Mahidevran. Like Roxelana and countless others, Mahidevran had begun her career in enslavement and conversion to Islam. Her Ottoman name meant "moon of good fortune." But unlike Roxelana, whose Ruthenian origins were a matter of consensus, Mahidevran's roots were less certain. She was variously said to be from Albania, Montenegro, Circassia, or the Crimea. Perhaps opportunistically, Venetian ambassadors in the 1520s asserted her Albanian and Montenegrin identities, with the implication that she had been abducted from Venetian-controlled territory on the eastern Adriatic coast (it could be useful if an ex-national rose to the top ranks of power). But in the 1550s, consensus on Mahidevran's origins would shift to the Black Sea region. The Hapsburg ambassador Ogier Ghiselin de Busbecq reported that she was Crimean and the Venetian Bernardo Navagero that she was Circassian.

Mustafa must have been Mahidevran's first (and only) child, for she appears to have had no daughters. "Her whole pleasure is this [child]," commented Bragadin in his brief mention of her.[2] When Mustafa, having come of age, took up his apprenticeship in the provinces in 1533, Mahidevran would continue to win praise, now as a wise counselor to her son. Roxelana's precedent-shattering parenthood to five boys stood in stark contrast to the classical Ottoman unit—the team, really—of the prince and his mother, so neatly exemplified by Mustafa and Mahidevran. From this perspective, the great privilege that Suleyman bestowed on Roxelana robbed her of the protective garb of customary protocol. Mahidevran was well versed in what she needed to do, but Roxelana had to cut a new path through the dense thicket of dynastic politics.

IF ROXELANA WAS a creature of the imperial capital, Mahidevran learned her trade in the world of the provinces. Royal concubine mothers of sons had traditionally made their careers in one of the Anatolian capitals that served as princely governing posts, among them Amasya, Manisa, and Konya. As former capitals of states and principalities conquered by the Ottomans, these cities carried a prestigious pedigree. In them mothers came of age along with their sons. The prince was the charismatic focus of the entire provincial enterprise and obviously its political raison d'être, but his mother outranked him as the head of his domestic household.

The hierarchy of the princely household is mapped for us in imperial account books from Suleyman's years in Manisa. Essentially salary registers, they list palace residents and their daily or monthly stipends, from the prince and his mother on down to the laundry staff. Stipends were a symbolic as well as a practical measure of status. In the earliest such account book, from 1511, Hafsa received a monthly 1,000 silver aspers to Suleyman's 600; a few years later, Suleyman's stipend had grown to 2,000 aspers, but his mother's to 6,000.[3] Hafsa's greater proportional increase was probably a recognition of her status as the empire's top-ranking female once Selim became sultan in 1512 (his own mother had predeceased him).

A prince-governor's mother was not his only counselor. To instruct him in policy matters, the sultan assigned a trusted official to his son's suite. Addressed as *lala* (tutor) by his royal pupil, the official was charged with overseeing the prince's management of the provincial sultanate-in-miniature. The *lala* was the sultan's man as well as the prince's, acting as the father's check on the son's conduct. Often a leading statesman, he had his own career to look out for. *Lalas* in the past had been known to desert their pupil if the latter's prospects faded. The prince's mother too was her master's rein on their son, but as his most loyal partisan—for the obvious reason that her political survival was linked to his—her eye had also to be on the tutor, lest he lead the prince into ruin.

Suleyman's unfortunate uncle Alemshah was one such unhappy prince. An apparent alcoholic, Alemshah had been the cause—or perhaps the victim—of sharp tensions in his princely household at Manisa. His mother Gulruh blamed Alemshah's deficiencies on seven members of his suite, especially his tutor, who allegedly lured the prince into excessive drink so that he would endorse proposals "against the law of Islam and the law of the sultan," as she put it. In a plaintive letter detailing twisted plots against the prince and herself, Gulruh urged Alemshah's father Bayezid II to dismiss the pernicious cabal: "My fortune-favored sultan, heed my cry for help. . . . Rid us of [my son's] tutor, teacher and doctor. They are masters of corruption. . . . [O]ur situation has been pitiful since these persons arrived. They have deprived me of my mother's rights. If these seven do not go, they will utterly destroy the household of my son, your servant." Gulruh's final letter to the sultan informed him of Alemshah's death in 1510.[4]

When princes died, it fell to the reigning sultan and his mother to care for the females they left behind. The Venetian Giovanni Maria Angiolello, who served in the household of Mehmed II's second son Mustafa, described the aftermath of the prince's death in 1474 from natural causes. Having accompanied the funeral cortege to Mustafa's burial site in Bursa, the first Ottoman capital, Angiolello recorded Mehmed's disposition of his son's female survivors: "The Grand Turk sent word that the Most Esteemed Lady—that is, the mother of Mustafa—should remain in Bursa . . . and he had good provision made for her that she might live there honorably." Mustafa's daughter and her mother, however, were to come to Istanbul, along with the women of his harem. "The women were lodged in the palace where the Grand Turk's other women and maidens stay," reported Angiolello, "and after several days the maidens were married to courtiers and others."[5] The princess was married to her cousin, Bayezid's son Abdullah.[6]

During Suleyman's reign, Hafsa would attend to members of the royal family who had fallen upon hard times. When she heard news of the death of Alemshah's mother Gulruh from the young women who had been in her care, she petitioned her son to make provision for them. Such protective largesse could extend to nonblood members of the greater dynastic household: when the widow of the faithful pasha whom Selim had appointed to govern Egypt wrote to Hafsa to say she was all alone in Cairo, the queen mother thereupon requested funds to bring the woman to Istanbul, where she intended to look after her.[7]

Seven of Bayezid II's sons would die in the field, some like Alemshah of illness, two—Ahmed and Korkud—victims of the bloody contest for the throne. But their mothers' work did not cease with their demise. For one thing, the bereaved parent continued to protect her son's household by acting as an intermediary with Istanbul. Husnushah, mother of Bayezid's son Shehinshah, wrote to the victorious sibling Selim to request a post for one Pir Ahmed "the gentleman," a scholar at her son's court who had been overlooked when new jobs were found for its male staff. The principal responsibility of a deceased prince's mother, however, was to recoup her son's honor by constructing a tomb to memorialize him and endowing a fund for its upkeep. Bulbul (nightingale), mother of Selim's fiercest rival brother Ahmed, built a tomb for him in the beautiful royal cemetery in Bursa, the city where she and her fellow concubine mothers settled in retirement. There Bulbul might hope to

The Family of Bayezid II

MEHMED II, "the Conqueror" 1451–1481

BAYEZID II 1481–1512 *Gulbahar*	Mustafa d. 1474	Cem d. 1495

Shehinshah d. 1511 *Husnushah*	Ahmed ex. 1513 *Bulbul*	Alemshah d. 1510 *Gulruh*	Abdullah d. 1483	Korkud ex. 1513	SELIM I 1512–1520 *Gulbahar*	Mehmed d. 1504 (07?)	Mahmud d. 1507

Notes: Mothers mentioned in this book appear in italics under the name of their son. Bayezid's thirteen daughters are omitted.

ex.= executed; d.= died of natural causes.

find her own final rest, beside the son to whom Ottoman politics had inextricably bound her destiny.

The burial site in Bursa of Murad II, father of Mehmed the Conqueror, was fast becoming the principal cemetery for the royal dead. By 1520, nearly a century after Murad ordered the construction of his own tomb, the cemetery had grown to contain the tombs of five princes, five royal mothers, the midwife who delivered Mehmed II, and the women of Murad's harem. Rare was the tomb that did not also house numerous caskets belonging to relatives who, for whatever reason, had not acquired a resting place of their own. Several denizens of the Muradiye cemetery were Suleyman's uncles and their mothers, members of Bayezid's large family. Here they were reconciled in death as they had been divided in life. It was said that when the Qur'an was recited at the grave of Mehmed II's son Mustafa, it could be heard at the gravesides of Bayezid's sons.

Bayezid's reproductive plenitude undeniably caused a larger than usual number of individual tragedies. At the same time, however, this sultan made a point of elevating the profile of his sons' mothers. Even today, their status is visibly evident in their philanthropy—the schools, mosques, soup kitchens, hospitals, and the like that they commissioned and funded. Until Bayezid's reign, the most conspicuous female patrons had been princesses, and he certainly had plenty of daughters to carry out the dynasty's altruistic mission, but it was his consorts who took the lead.

Granting concubine mothers the financial means to take a leading philanthropic role was probably related to another policy pursued by Bayezid—restoring status and jobs to the religious establishment. Its members had lost both when Mehmed the Conqueror expropriated their properties to finance his expansionist military program. In the communities that were chosen for their locations, imperial foundations also brought employment to many besides men of religion, from ground breaking for construction to daily maintenance of the finished premises. Bayezid located his own foundations in "royal" cities—Amasya, where he was stationed for twenty-seven years as prince-governor, Adrianople, and Istanbul.

Bayezid's consorts on the other hand covered a broad swath of Anatolia with their works. Gulruh, mother of the wayward Alemshah, commissioned mosques in two provincial cities and a village. In four additional cities, she either bought or built shops, hamams, caravanserais, and large commercial centers known as hans. The revenues from these enterprises would go to upkeep of the mosques. When Hafsa undertook her principal philanthropic endeavor—a substantial foundation for Manisa, begun during Suleyman's apprenticeship—the city already boasted a remarkably large complex built and endowed by Husnushah, mother of Shehinshah. Begun in 1490, it consisted of a mosque, a madrasa, a soup kitchen, and a hospital. A few years later, Husnushah constructed a hamam and a caravanserai to provide income to her foundation. Her work may have inspired Hafsa, mother of the heir apparent, to fund an even more elaborate foundation in Manisa.

It was Bayezid's consorts who broke ground for Roxelana's extraordinary career as endower of charitable foundations. Suleyman's consort would stand out in this long tradition of public works by constructing her first foundation in the imperial capital, where no royal concubine before her had been permitted to build.

IN MANISA, MAHIDEVRAN would trace the progress of Hafsa's mosque as it began to go up. She had joined Suleyman's household sometime before 1515, the year her son was born. Nothing is known of Mahidevran's relationship with Suleyman or her status within his harem, except that she was the mother of his second son. Where she began her palace service is also uncertain—perhaps in Manisa or in Istanbul, where Suleyman served eighteen months as his father's deputy during Selim's long campaign against the Iranians.

This anonymity is typical of virtually all slave concubines. They entered history only when their sons began to make names for themselves or they themselves acquired reputations as philanthropists. Even Roxelana, who became Suleyman's consort at a moment when international attention was riveted on the dynamic new sultan, was a relatively obscure figure until 1526 or so, by which time she was already the mother of four children. Fortunately, we can imagine something of Mahidevran's place in Suleyman's harem thanks to an account book detailing the members of his princely household. If Ottoman culture maintained a strict taboo on gazing at royal females or even mentioning them by name, its obsession with bookkeeping threw open the gates of royal palaces. These records guide us from the well-guarded inner quarters to the workshops and stables on the palace periphery.

In this undated list of names and stipends, Mahidevran appears among seventeen females in the document's initial section, labeled "the Ladies of the Imperial Palace, may Allah, whose name is exalted, preserve them."[8] One of four women with a daily wage of four silver aspers, Mahidevran was outranked by Yasemin, Hubeh, and Server, who received five aspers a day. What separated her from these three may be that she was not yet a mother when the list was drawn up; that she figured in the second of five harem wage ranks may indicate that Suleyman had taken her as concubine. Among the less well remunerated of the harem personnel were two unnamed laundresses and a servant.

What is striking about the stipends of harem women is how low they were, given that they presumably included at least one mother of a royal child. Even the lowest-paid male scribe in the Manisa palace received six aspers a day. The range of harem stipends more closely paralleled that of the staff of craftsmen—the bow maker at three aspers a day, the halberd and boot makers at five, and the maker of the conical caps worn by the Janissaries at six. The women's stipends also matched those of the rank and file of various military divisions, the tent masters for example, who had charge of the elaborate structures in which the prince and his chief officers worked and slept on campaign—their stipends ranged from two to five aspers. The one group with stipends consistently lower than the women's (averaging slightly more than two aspers a day) was the division of fifty-six pages in Suleyman's inner household, those select Christian converts who were being trained to aspire to the highest offices of the empire. In the everyday world, two aspers was the standard daily allowance for the upkeep of an orphan child, a runaway slave in detention, or a stray animal waiting to be claimed by its owner.[9]

Why the two pools of potential power brokers, female and male, were compensated so modestly is suggested by the name of the pages' division—*Gulam-i Enderun* (male slaves of the interior). The rationale would seem to be that the members of the two "interior" divisions, female and male, were not yet public figures. Although they enjoyed the privilege of physical proximity to the prince, they were creatures of the inner palace who had not yet "graduated out," to approximate the Ottoman term, to an official appointment in state service. In this, they somewhat resembled Suleyman's status in relation to his mother. In Manisa, Hafsa was fully graduated, so to speak, with a commensurate stipend, while Suleyman was only partly so, still in training but now in the field with his *lala*, Kasim, a distinguished statesman with experience in the imperial treasury office.[10]

However modest their stipends as trainees, the cream of the inner-palace slaves could rise with startling rapidity. The 1521 epidemic would suddenly make Mahidevran, now mother of Suleyman's eldest son, the top-ranking royal female after Hafsa. Fate could also take the form of the sultan's will. The fifth *Enderun* slave in the stipend list, one "Ibrahim, Albanian, 3 aspers," was almost certainly the Ibrahim who would become grand vizier in less than a decade, jumping rank at Suleyman's command. Ibrahim was from Parga, a seaside town in Epirus that had passed from Venetian rule into Ottoman-controlled Albania during the reign of Mehmed the Conqueror.

The Manisa harem was smaller and more intimate than the imperial establishment Roxelana would enter in Istanbul. But did it enjoy a greater sense of community? Until Mustafa's birth, Mahidevran spent most of her days in the company of other young women, and perhaps the nights as well if sleeping quarters had a dormitory configuration. Companionship and perhaps even camaraderie were available. In unsupervised moments, the women likely discussed the Lady Steward who monitored their conduct and training, and maybe, when occasion warranted, the skills of the Lady Doctor. Perhaps they even dared to talk about Suleyman. Jealousy, if not outright competition, doubtless flared up from time to time. It was Hafsa's job to tamp down any disruption her charges might provoke in the surface calm of the harem.

While the account book suggests the contours of Mahidevran's life in the Manisa harem, it does not help us fathom her state of mind. It surely shifted as she passed through the successive stages of apprenticeship, "in the prince's eye" (his bed), pregnancy, the birth of a son, and, finally, sexual retirement as Suleyman moved on to the next *gözde* and the next royal child. It is entirely possible that there were concubines who regarded the whole project of bearing a child for the dynasty that had enslaved them as a repugnant obligation. (Even Roxelana cannot be assumed to have initially embraced her fate as a concubine with no say in the matter.) For such women, the construction of their essential identity as mothers was a saving grace. So were the rewards they could expect if they mothered well. If, on the other hand, Mahidevran was a willing partner to Suleyman, their emotional relationship was bound to be asymmetrical: if they developed a strong bond, he would of necessity move on, and she would channel celibacy into maternal devotion. This may all have been harder since Suleyman was apparently a prince easy to love.

Whatever the women's attitude toward Ottoman politics of reproduction, there were compensations that Mahidevran and her cohort must at least have weighed in the balance. An emotionally and sexually fulfilling marriage had not necessarily been in store for them in their hometowns and villages. The common practice of arranged marriage could saddle them with husbands who were unattractive, considerably older, or even brutal. Mostly peasants, they were more likely than not destined for a life of daily toil and perhaps poverty and early death. The dynastic family to which they now belonged at least kept them in luxurious comfort and good health.

Thankfully for all, the city of Manisa provided diversion, perhaps a particular boon to females whose lives were guardedly private. The province's fertile plain supplied ample playground for the children and opportunities for their mothers to make excursions. Manisa had its own gardens that provided easy access for leisurely enjoyment. Perhaps Mustafa and Mahidevran were also fond of the large park named for its patron, Ali Beg, which encompassed running waters, flower gardens, and an arboretum-like area with fruit-bearing trees. We can imagine royal outings organized for the women and children, with the team of tent masters providing shelter and harem-like privacy and the kitchen staff a suitably elaborate picnic. When Hafsa purchased a section of the Ali Beg park for her mosque complex, the children could watch builders at work, perhaps meet the architect, and indirectly receive a lesson in dynastic beneficence.[11]

Such occasions were useful opportunities for building family solidarity. The recent war for the throne, which ended only two years before

Mustafa's birth, was a stark reminder that the little prince and his older brother Mahmud might one day challenge each other as their grandfather Selim had his older brother Korkud, right there in Manisa. The children were surely protected from the unsavory details of the face-off—that Selim, with a force of some 10,000, had surrounded the palace in an attempt to force Korkud into surrender. The doomed prince escaped in disguise, his beard dyed white, and hid for three weeks in a cave until a farmer gave him away.[12]

If the mothers of Suleyman's children were visibly anxious about the future, it was up to Hafsa to encourage them to put trepidation aside. Hafsa was also the individual best equipped to foster ties of affection among the half siblings. She was the grandmother who could love them all—the two boys, the sister whose name is lost to history, and the baby Murad who arrived in 1519. One of Suleyman's sisters, likely an unmarried daughter of Hafsa, had joined the Manisa household around 1513; she too possessed the stature to smooth over any tensions that might erupt.

The rhythm of the seasons probably also helped to foster an esprit de corps among the members of Suleyman's household. Manisa's hot summers were offset by the presence of temperate mountain pastures near enough to permit family sojourns at royal camps. Mustafa apparently had a special love for these visits, for local legend would later claim that he built a summer palace on Mount Manisa when he took up his own post in the city in 1533. During these summer idylls, palace protocol that enforced rank and separated females from males was perhaps relaxed a bit.

Did the two singers in Suleyman's musical ensemble entertain the whole family? Was Ibrahim (if the *Enderun* slave was indeed he) called upon by his master to play the violin, a talent he famously cultivated? Especially in Suleyman's last two years in Manisa, uninterrupted by summons to act as Selim's deputy, the seasonal retreats were occasion to instruct his sons in the leisurely arts of sovereignty, especially perhaps the hunt. Suleyman's exemplary corps of huntsmen could develop the young boys' skill with the bow and stage small-scale forays for them. With the Ottomans, as with royalty from China to England, the hunt was both the sport of kings and a school for war.

These two years may have prompted Suleyman to recall his own childhood in Trabzon, at the side of his father. Twenty-four when

Suleyman was born, Selim was a steady presence in the boy's childhood due to the tight rein Bayezid II kept on his sons' mobility. In fact
it was Suleyman who first departed the city when his grandfather appointed him governor of Caffa in 1509. For the prince, fifteen when he
parted from his father, continuity with his Trabzon years did not rest in
his mother Hafsa's hands alone. Suleyman's preceptor, Hayreddin, was
at his side throughout the eight years of his apprenticeship. In Manisa,
Hayreddin was rewarded with a stipend of 1,800 aspers a month, the
highest remuneration after Hafsa's 6,000 and Suleyman's own 2,000 and
more than Suleyman's sister's 1,200 aspers. The venerable teacher was
likely charged with the next generation's introduction to study of the
Qur'an. Mustafa was just old enough to begin his lessons.

WHEN SULEYMAN RECEIVED the news that his father had died suddenly,
he left Manisa at top speed and arrived in Istanbul on September 30,
1520, just two weeks after Selim's demise. Haste was imperative, since
custom dictated that news of a sultan's death be concealed until his heir
reached the capital. The purpose of this enforced secrecy was to fore-
stall any outbreak of disorder. But the new sultan's extended family was
under no such pressure to move as quickly. The Venetian ambassador in
Corfu reported on December 18 that "the mother, who was previously in
Gallipoli, has arrived in Constantinople."[13] Even at this late date, Hafsa
may well have come ahead of the rest of the family to resume her role as
counselor to Suleyman in those first critical months and to oversee the
preparation of the Old Palace quarters for the arrival of his family.

When Mahidevran finally arrived in Istanbul, she may not have
taken immediate note of Roxelana. Her priority was to settle herself into
the Old Palace so that she could help Mustafa adjust to the new and un-
familiar environment. There were of course many familiar faces from
Manisa, but the Old Palace presented them with new routines as well as
a maze of rooms and corridors to master. No doubt there were also many
questions about the configuration of the city and how to keep the children
entertained so they would not miss Manisa. There they might see their
father daily, but now he was engrossed in matters of state and moreover
living in another palace that required planning and arrangements to visit.

By the time Mustafa found his footing in Istanbul, preparations for Suleyman's first military campaign were under way. What the little boy knew of war likely came from stories of his ancestors' victories, a thrilling history lesson graphically illustrated in the empire's capital: the mammoth Byzantine walls breached by his great-grandfather Mehmed, for instance, or the great Christian basilica-turned-mosque of Hagia Sophia, in which Mustafa perhaps attended communal prayer alongside his father. Fortunately there were few stories of military defeat to conceal from the children, although Mahmud, eight years old when the army paraded out of Istanbul some months after their arrival, probably understood better than his younger brother that not all the soldiers would return.

During the quiet months of the summer of 1521, with Suleyman gone, Mahidevran had time to take stock of Roxelana. It was probably no surprise to the women of the Manisa harem that the young sultan had not slept alone during the gap between his and their arrival in the capital. The presence of a pregnant concubine was probably not wholly unexpected, especially since Suleyman's reproductive output had been relatively modest for someone entrusted with repopulating the dynasty. But then in the fall came the sudden death of all the Manisa siblings save Mustafa and the near simultaneous birth of Mehmed. If tempted to dwell on the latter event, Mahidevran was surely distracted by the need to comfort the bereaved mothers as well as her son. The loss of his sister and brothers must have terrified Mustafa and rendered him understandably fearful of his own death. Mehmed was perhaps a godsend in this regard, a tiny boy whom his big brother could be encouraged to love and to protect.

What turned the future into a tale of two concubines was not the birth of Mehmed but rather of that of Mihrumah and then Selim, very real proof of Suleyman's astonishing relationship with Roxelana. Breaking all tradition, she had remained in Suleyman's bed rather than retiring from it to raise her precious son as Mahidevran had done. Roxelana's rise in status now threatened Mahidevran's newfound precedence in the harem. If Mahidevran turned to Hafsa for answers, she was likely told to remember who she was, a very high-ranking member of the imperial family who must maintain a standard of conduct for other women to emulate. Hafsa herself now faced a shifting constellation of favor and hierarchy in the harem, even though it was perhaps she who had introduced the new star to her son. If Mahidevran needed distraction, her circle of supporters presumably urged her to concentrate on the obvious, Mustafa's education. If her son was not already her "whole pleasure," as Bragadin put it, he necessarily became so in those first years when she and Roxelana were living under the same roof.

We see and hear Mustafa for the first time in Bragadin's 1526 oral report to the Venetian Senate, when the ambassador related two stories that reveal the maturing prince's keen sense of his stature. Mustafa had apparently also acquired sensitivity to the complicated dynamics of a royal court that intermingled slaves and princes. The first incident concerned the boy's jealousy of Suleyman's intimacy with Ibrahim, his longtime protégé who became grand vizier in 1523. One day, when Ibrahim had gone to dine with Suleyman, Mustafa entered the room. "His father rose to show him respect and seated him at the table, bringing three wooden spoons as customary," related Bragadin's virtual eyewitness narrative. Suleyman gave one spoon to Ibrahim, and the two began to eat, but Mustafa did not. So his father held out a spoon to him and said, "Now, Mustafa, eat," whereupon the boy broke the spoon in pieces and threw it aside. "Signor Mustafa," said Ibrahim, "you did that because the sultan gave a spoon to me first. Do you not know that I am the sultan's slave, and yours too?" "I don't know what a slave is," retorted Mustafa. "You eat every day at my father's palace and have your spoon before I do."[14]

Bragadin's second story also underlined Ibrahim's sympathetic patience with the proud child, whose sense of entitlement was apparently both acute and insecure. "The sultan sent Ibrahim a beautiful saddle for his horse with jewels and other ornaments; and Mustafa, aware of this, sent word to Ibrahim to have one like it made for him. [Ibrahim] understood this and sent him the saddle, and said to him, 'Hide it! If the sultan learns of this, he will make you send it back.'"[15] These two incidents may simply reflect a jealousy on Mustafa's part of anyone close to his father. But perhaps the prince had a sense that his father's generosity to Ibrahim was excessive, demonstrating a degree of indulgence of his male favorite that far surpassed a grand vizier's rightful expectations from his master.

By the time Bragadin deemed Mustafa worthy of the Senate's attention, the boy had been exposed to the world of politics. He had recently lived through the Janissary rampage of March 1525 and may well have picked up on currents of discontent among the troops. Suleyman had not taken his soldiers to war for three years, depriving them of both the opportunity to exercise their skills and the plunder that they regarded as their due. The spark that ignited their mounting discontent was the sultan's extended hunting sojourn in Adrianople during the winter months. Mustafa experienced the incident in one of two ways: either he had accompanied his father to Adrianople and witnessed the hasty royal return to the capital, or he waited out the violence in Istanbul, no doubt aware of his elders' fears that the rebels would attack. They had already sacked the elaborate palace Suleyman had given Ibrahim as a wedding gift (the grand vizier was absent in Cairo, putting down the revolt of its governor).

The Janissary revolt was quelled, Ibrahim was recalled from Egypt, and planning for the Hungarian campaign of 1526 soon began. Strategic factors were uppermost in the preparations for war, but rallying the troops with the promise of booty was an obvious consideration. If Mustafa longed to march beside his father, who was once again master of his army, the boy's consolation was apparently a safe defensive assignment, or so Roxelana's forwarded letter suggested.

ACUTE OBSERVER OF the Ottoman court though he was, Bragadin still got some facts wrong in his report. For example, he gave an incorrect birth order for Roxelana's sons (he ignored her daughter Mihrumah): "The first son by her is named Selim, five years old; the second Morat, three years old; the third Mamet is about one, born after the arrival of the pasha Embraim from Cairo."[16] (Mehmed was nearly five at the time, Mihrumah three, Selim one, and Abdullah either a newborn or imminently expected; Murad [not Roxelana's son] had perished in 1521.) Details about small children were probably not the kind of information that regularly leaked from the harem to the curious public (the eunuchs being the most obvious but not the only interlocutors). News of Roxelana, on the other hand, was obviously in demand. Bragadin informed the outside world that the Ruthenian was small and graceful though not beautiful and that Suleyman now concentrated all his affection on her and had given her jewels worth 100,000 ducats. Herein lay a potential problem for Roxelana's sons: she was the story, not her little princes. Mahidevran's Mustafa, by contrast, was the protagonist of their story.

It took nearly three decades for a rare beam of light to fall directly onto the relationship between Mahidevran and Roxelana. Bernardo Navagero, Venice's ambassador in the first years of the 1550s, recounted at considerable length an apparent showdown between the two royal mothers, at least from Mahidevran's perspective. The incident certainly occurred before 1533, when Mahidevran left Istanbul to accompany Mustafa back to Manisa as governor; it probably happened sometime in the 1520s. Here is Navagero's account:

> The sultan has two highly cherished women, one a Circassian, the mother of Mustafa the firstborn, the other . . . a Russian, so loved by his majesty that there has never been in the Ottoman house a woman who has enjoyed greater authority. The way in which she entered into the favor of the sultan I understand to have been the following. The Circassian, naturally proud and beautiful, and who already had a son, Mustafa, understood that [the other] had pleased the sultan, wherefore she insulted her with injurious words, and, words escalating to deeds, scratched her all over her face and mussed her clothing, saying, . . . "Traitor, sold meat! You want to compete with me?"
>
> It happened that a few days later the sultan had this Russian summoned for his pleasure. She did not let this opportunity pass, and angrily told the eunuch *agha* who had come to fetch her that she was not worthy to come into the presence of the sultan because, being sold meat and having her face completely spoiled and being almost bald, she recognized that she would offend the majesty of such a sultan by coming before him. These words were related to the sultan and induced in him an even greater desire to have her come to him, and he commanded again that she come. He wanted to understand why she would not come and why she had sent him such a message. The woman related to him what had happened with Mustafa's mother, accompanying her words with tears and showing the sultan her face, which still bore the scratches, and how her hair had been pulled out.
>
> The angry sultan sent for the Circassian and asked her if what the other woman had said was true. She responded that it was, and that she had done no less to her than she deserved. She believed that all the

women should yield to her and recognize her as mistress since she had
been in the service of his majesty first. These words inflamed the sultan
even more, for the reason that he no longer wanted her, and he gave all
his love to this other.[17]

It is difficult to evaluate an incident relayed as much as three decades after it happened, although the story of the fight probably circulated in Istanbul earlier. Why it was not reported earlier is a puzzle, for
Roxelana's extraordinary influence was evident by the mid-1530s at the
latest. Bragadin had not hesitated in 1526 to air the news of her hyster-
ics over Suleyman's acquisition of two gift slave women, so it was not
a sense of propriety that kept the Venetians from telling intimate tales
of the harem. But the alleged brawl had acquired relevance at the time
Navagero related news of it. In the years the ambassador was resident in
Istanbul, political gossip revolved around the looming contest to succeed
the aging sultan (by the Islamic calendar, Suleyman was sixty in 1553,
old by sixteenth-century standards). Enormously popular, Mustafa was
a particular focus of the conversation, and the fate of Roxelana's sons
formed an obvious corollary of his apparent advantage. Interest in the
two mothers was doubtless heightened.

Navagero's report shows us Roxelana once again demonstrating the
kind of clever histrionics that had caused Suleyman and Hafsa to dispose of the two Russian slaves. In exposing Mahidevran's assault, Roxelana appeared to be playing both the eunuch and the sultan. It should
be no surprise that the training of royal mothers prepared them to be as-
tutely manipulative. Mahidevran's own arsenal contained verbal rapiers.
The insult "sold meat" implied that Roxelana had been bought directly
off the slave market, while Mahidevran had presumably arrived in the
Ottoman palace by some more refined route.

But can we trust Navagero's story? It matters because Venice's ambassadorial reports were read and valued in European capitals. They
functioned as an index of intelligence as well as local public opinion
that contributed, for better or worse, to Roxelana's reputation. Tension
between the two royal consorts was not unexpected, although the story
of the brawl had perhaps been embroidered over time. Whether Mahidevran had an irascible personality or was prone to violence is hard

to say; all other references to her in Venetian reports are exemplary. But the tale is not preposterous, and her self-defense to the sultan—the assault on her rank as senior concubine—is wholly plausible.

Mahidevran had nothing left to lose but her rank once Suleyman focused his favors so lavishly on Roxelana. The sultan was upsetting the careful balance among consorts that the politics of reproduction demanded, and Mahidevran apparently took it on herself to right it. She was a product of the old world of separate but equal family constellations, a system that imbued the role of mother to a prince with considerable honor and dignity. The monopoly by a favorite with multiple sons inevitably stole a portion of that stature. The mothers of the dead princes Mahmud and Murad were there to share the indignity, but Mahidevran was the only mother of a prince left standing to resist further erosion of her small family's fortunes. If her audacious assertion of rank cost her the sultan's favor, it may have won her sympathy and support, and even admiration, in other quarters.

Mahidevran and Roxelana were together in the Old Palace for thirteen years. It is possible they got along during much of that time or at least maintained a cordial distance. They were probably rarely alone together, given the large number of women who lived alongside them. Hafsa, widowed princesses, high-ranking staff, retired concubine mothers including those of Selim's several daughters—all were women of account in the harem who presumably had a stake in preventing ruptures. The strict decorum of the Old Palace was designed to head off incidents such as Navagero described. In a polity where the royal household was the government, disorder in the harem could provoke disorder in the state.

7

COMING OF AGE

LITTLE IS KNOWN of Roxelana's life between Pietro Bragadin's report of 1526, which introduced her to the European diplomatic world, and the 1534 report of a subsequent Venetian envoy. Daniello de'Ludovici delivered the arresting news that Suleyman and Roxelana were now wedded. Earlier dispatches from Istanbul had continued to remark that the Russian was still the sultan's favorite, but this was a startling new development. The marriage would prove only the first step in Roxelana's entrance onto the stage of wealth and power. Within a few years, the public measure of her radical new status would appear in the form of an elegant charitable foundation she sponsored in Istanbul, the first by an Ottoman woman in the imperial capital.

"Neither [this sultan] nor any of his ancestors has ever taken a wife," commented Giovanni Antonio Menavino, a Genoese familiar with Istanbul. While this statement was not wholly accurate (Ottoman rulers made marital alliances until the mid-fifteenth century), it was true that no sultan had been married to the mother of his successor, with the apparent exception of Osman, the founder of the dynastic line.[1] As Menavino informed his European audience, a sultan contented himself with concubines and avoided taking a wife because, if he did so, "it would then be necessary that she be treated as Queen, just as he is the King."[2] Roxelana would soon prove the accuracy of this statement, upending generations of Ottoman precedent. Could Suleyman's subjects learn to accept an Ottoman queen? The sultan was certainly filling the political ideal of valiant warrior and just ruler, but at the same time, he was appearing increasingly iconoclastic when it came to family politics.

The lack of news on the diplomatic circuit between 1526 and 1534 does not mean that Roxelana's role as royal consort was uneventful. As she groomed her maturing children—her sons to take up active service to the empire and Mihrumah, the only princess of her generation, to uphold the traditions of the two-hundred-year-old state—Roxelana too grew in knowledge and stature. Professionalizing the next royal generation was no mere domestic task but rather a core preoccupation of the whole dynastic regime. Luckily Suleyman was a consistent presence in the children's and their mother's lives in this period. Only one military campaign took him away between his triumphal return from Hungary in November 1526 and May 1532, when he set out again for central Europe.

These years must also have advanced Roxelana's political acumen. No correspondence with Suleyman survives from this time, but Roxelana was certainly acquainted with the circumstances of his daring 1529 campaign into central Europe, which ended in an aborted siege of Vienna, capital of the Hapsburg Ferdinand's domains. The interim between Vienna and the so-called German confrontation of 1532 was far from calm as the rivalry between the two greatest powers in Europe— the Hapsburgs and the Ottomans—was heating up. How actively Suleyman tutored Roxelana in the intricacies of war and diplomacy is not clear, but it was her mandate as a potential queen mother to stay abreast of current affairs. This need to master the geopolitics of empire must have spurred Roxelana's language facility, and one wonders when Suleyman might have begun to seek her views—perhaps less about strategy than about the individuals he relied on most closely.

Suleyman was occasionally away from Roxelana in these interim years, spending some of his winters in the palace at Adrianople. No more than a few days' march northwest from Istanbul, this second capital of the empire was the staging ground for land operations in Europe. From there, the sultan could be ready if need be to take off rapidly with his soldiers. How often Roxelana and the children or Mustafa and Mahidevran joined Suleyman in Adrianople is not known, but he likely wished his older sons and their mothers to become familiar with the palace and the troops stationed there. He himself had been assigned to Adrianople for more than a year, acting as his father's deputy to face down any potential threat from Europe while Selim was battling the Iranians in the east.

If Roxelana was not much discussed on the international news circuit in the years preceding her marriage, neither was Mahidevran. Only in 1533, when Mustafa came of age and graduated to his first post as prince-governor, did her small family emerge onto the political field. Mahidevran was presumably occupied in these quieter times with Mustafa's preparation for his career. Although Suleyman had apparently spurned her in anger, we should not assume that he and his senior consort did not collaborate on important issues. Mustafa's inauguration as governor was certainly a significant matter. As for the two mothers, whether they managed a cordial relationship we don't know, but they would be united in 1530 in a ritual occasion that was the public debut of Mustafa, Mehmed, and Selim, Suleyman's three oldest sons.

SPECTACLE HAD BEEN a feature of life in Constantinople for more than a millennium, and Suleyman was a connoisseur of its political uses. Istanbulites were avid consumers of royal panoply, as were soldiers of the standing army housed in a large center-city barracks complex. Foreign ambassadors were honored guests at public occasions, for they would spread the word of Ottoman wealth and splendor. In 1530, Suleyman made the circumcision of his three eldest sons a pretext to orchestrate the most lavish celebration that the Ottoman world had seen. Fifty years had passed since the festival marking the circumcision of seven grandsons of Mehmed the Conqueror was held in the Old Palace.[3]

Historians have commented that the 1530 festivities were a mask for Suleyman's first military failure at Vienna in 1529. This is no doubt true, in part at least, but sooner or later Suleyman would have staged the magnificence for which he would become so famous. He had already begun in 1524 with the spectacular festivities organized to celebrate the marriage of his grand vizier and friend Ibrahim.[4]

Had it not been for the times, the sums of money expended on behalf of Mustafa, Mehmed, and Selim would seem prodigal. The sixteenth century was an age of royal exhibitionism, and Suleyman's contemporaries had gotten a head start. In 1520, the year of his accession, the French and English kings—Francis I, like Suleyman aged twenty-four, and Henry VIII, three years older—met with their respective courts near Calais on the so-called Field of the Cloth of Gold. The eighteen-day extravaganza included a two-day tournament featuring both kings. The purpose of the event was to cement treaties between France and England

and to project both courts' splendor to the rest of Europe. The principal target of the Anglo-French alliance, Charles V, Europe's most powerful monarch, would soon become Suleyman's principal rival as well. In a majestic ceremony in Bologna that took place four months before the Ottoman princes' circumcision, the pope placed the crown of the Holy Roman Empire on the thirty-year-old Charles's head. Perhaps the circumcision festival represented Suleyman's response to the ostentation of the Bologna coronation. If so, it would not be his last competitive act.

Other monarchs celebrated their coronations and their children's marriages. Ottoman accessions were comparatively subdued occasions, however, with little panoply and no crown. New sultans were acknowledged in the private interior of the palace, their enthronement sealed by the sober oath of allegiance of leading dignitaries. And by the mid-fifteenth century, Ottoman sultans were no longer marrying foreign princesses, thereby depriving thousands of the opportunity to view the elaborate entourages that in the past guided brides from their fathers' lands to the Ottoman capital. What the sultans did celebrate publicly were their sons' circumcisions and their daughters' marriages, both of which signified entrance into adulthood.

The timing of the 1530 occasion was probably determined in part by the fact that Mustafa was by then fifteen, the age at which his father had taken up his first post, at Caffa. Suleyman may have wanted his eldest son to be ready should his presence in the provinces became strategically necessary. As for Mehmed and Selim, it was common to group brothers together for the circumcision ritual. But there were perhaps additional reasons for the triple celebration. Suleyman may have seen political value in presenting his three sons as a set, a small phalanx representing the imperial future.[5] And perhaps it seemed only fair to award the nine-year-old Mehmed some public recognition. Even more likely was pressure from Roxelana to ensure that at least one of her sons shared the limelight with Mustafa (Selim, aged six, was just old enough to conduct himself with appropriate gravity). In any case, both Mahidevran and Roxelana could take deserved pride in their princes. Both were presumably absorbed in preparing them for the ceremonies.

Parades, private banquets for political and religious leaders, and lavish entertainments for the public filled the three-week celebration. The opening day, June 27, made clear that a principal goal of the festivities was to display the empire's military power, riches, and human capital.[6] Escorted by two pashas, the second vizier Ayas and the third vizier Kasim, Suleyman paraded from the New Palace on horseback to the old Byzantine Hippodrome, the central venue for the occasion. A cordon of leading officials then escorted the sultan to the splendid throne that awaited him. Standing on columns of lapis lazuli, it was crowned by a canopy of gold with rich fabrics flying from its pinnacle.

Symbols of Ottoman victory surrounded this dazzling structure— the tents of the revered Akkoyunlu sultan Hasan (defeated by Mehmed II) and the Mamluk sultan al-Ghawri (defeated by Selim), as well as the three bronze statues of Apollo, Diana, and Hercules taken by Ibrahim Pasha from the palace of the Hungarian king Louis II (defeated by Suleyman). Arriving at this replica of a military encampment, the sultan dismounted his horse and then, to fanfare played by the famed Ottoman military band, he mounted his throne. From this moment on, however, Suleyman did not engage in events but rather presided over them. His was a magisterial presence, his function to marshal, exhibit, and reward the agents of his power.

In this, Suleyman differed from his European counterparts, for whom festival occasions were an opportunity to show off martial skill and daring. Suleyman's own martial talents needed no demonstration, it was presumed, for he repeatedly reaffirmed them in battle, to Europe's chagrin. But for a monarch like Henry VIII, who took his soldiers to war less frequently, tournaments provided a stage to display his excellence as a jouster and his mastery of chivalric virtues.[7] Another reason for Suleyman's physical reticence at his sons' circumcision was the studied modesty before God of Muslim monarchs. They allowed no statues of themselves or portraits on coins, no ostentatious coronations, no displays of personal bravery for the entertainment of a crowd. Pomp and valor were appropriate in the service of God—pomp in the procession to Friday prayers, valor on the battlefield. The princes' circumcision, a religious obligation, could rationalize the panoply of the 1530 event, although Suleyman's "magnificence" in the first decades of his reign would eventually find its critics. In the later decades of his rule, the sultan himself would famously shun the flaunting of his majesty that was earlier so visible.

Arrival of the princes at the Hippodrome, circumcision festival of 1530. Two princes, Mustafa and Mehmed, appear at the right (Selim was perhaps too young to participate in this occasion); the grand vizier Ibrahim Pasha, on horseback, awaits them on the left. Seyyid Lokman, *Hünernâme*.

Despite being the object of the whole celebration, the princes appeared for the first time only on the fourteenth day of the three-week event. An escort of court officials and army officers ushered them from the Old Palace to the Hippodrome. Venetian envoy Pietro Zen thought they looked like angels.[8] The princes' steeds were probably as lavishly outfitted as they were themselves. The horses' trappings, like the robes and turbans worn by Ottoman royalty and the thrones and tents they occupied, created a living tapestry of imperial splendor. To the crowds along the way, for whom a parade of princes was a very rare occasion, it must have been a thrilling sight. Once arrived at the Hippodrome, the brothers were received by the assembled viziers, who approached them on foot, a sign of deference, and led them to their father's tent. It was a replica of the recently refurbished hall of the Divan, where the sultan made the great decisions of state with his Imperial Council. Privileged guests of Suleyman had a rare opportunity to view a simulacrum of the impenetrable inner reaches of the New Palace.

But where were the mothers and the better-known queen mother? Hafsa, Mahidevran, and Roxelana were almost certainly in attendance on the day of the princes' presentation and perhaps on other days as well. The three women were invisibly visible, so to speak—they most likely viewed the events from ringside seats within a screened balcony attached to the palace of the grand vizier. Their presence there would be no secret. Fronting the Hippodrome, the elegant structure had been a gift from Suleyman to Ibrahim (today it is the Turkish and Islamic Arts Museum). All three women, as well as the princes' governesses, were surely present in Ibrahim's palace on the eighteenth day, when the circumcision ritual finally took place. They would not participate in the actual ceremony, but they could be ready to attend to the princes later.

If the festival was the princes' public debut, it was also a coming out for their mothers, tangible proof of their success in raising and grooming their sons. For Mahidevran especially, it was a long-awaited moment. The parade of princes doubtless prompted the crowd to debate who was the mother of each and to compare rumors of their accomplishments. While the great majority of spectators were male, Ottoman miniature paintings of the period occasionally show ordinary women at the edges of crowds that lined the parade routes and gathered for the entertainments. Old Palace watchers would be on the lookout for the procession of the royal women's carriages to and from the grand vizier's palace.

THE RUN-UP TO the main event had been a carefully orchestrated sequence of feasting and entertainment. It was all meant to build up anticipation for the princes' arrival and, more pointedly, to demonstrate Suleyman's munificence, a universal desideratum of monarchs. The first days were occupied with reception of the guests, each of whom kissed the sultan's hand in fealty, and then with formal reception banquets for prominent government figures, past and present, and foreign emissaries, among whom the Venetians dominated. Lavish gifts to the sultan piled up at the foot of his throne (grand vizier Ibrahim's presents alone were allegedly worth 50,000 gold ducats). On the fifth day, the games and amusements began, punctuated by fireworks displays at night.

Entertainers included clowns, jugglers, magicians, acrobats, and Chinese shadow-theater masters.

A mock battle between the Ottomans and Mamluks, graced with Suleyman's presence, enabled ordinary Istanbulites to experience vicariously Selim I's conquest of Egypt thirteen years earlier. The battle ended in a stalemate with the torching of each side's fort, to the accompaniment of fireworks. (The Mamluk general was authentic, one Inal Beg, a former Circassian Mamluk now in Suleyman's service.) The stalemate was only a teaser, it turned out, for overnight, two new forts were assembled. The next day's victory, obviously an Ottoman one, culminated with a number of young males and females emerging from the fort of the vanquished as booty for the victors. (Did the royal mothers, or their sons on their behalf, react dubiously to this display of captive taking?) The eighth and ninth days featured music and dance (by males dressed as females), while army and navy recruits vied to retrieve prizes that were suspended from greased poles known as "circumcision candles."

In the days between their appearance at the Hippodrome and their circumcision, Mustafa, Mehmed, and perhaps even Selim most likely attended some events, seated beside their father in his splendid tent. It would be their formal introduction to the constitution of the empire's government, with its two fundamental elements, *din ve devlet* (religion and state). The fifteenth day belonged to the *devlet*—a banquet for numerous men of state, including current and former viziers, the governors of the original two Ottoman provinces of Anatolia and Rumelia (the Balkan region), the military judges of the same two honored provinces, and Suleyman's old preceptor Hayreddin.

Present also were the son of the vassal Crimean khan and scions of three eastern dynasties—the Akkoyunlu, Mamluk, and Dulkadir—defeated by Mehmed the Conqueror, Selim, and Suleyman, respectively. Though apparently invited guests, were these princes, hostages to the past, meant to serve as symbolic minions to Suleyman's sons? If so, the banquet also made clear that these Muslim princes were descended from worthy if defunct royal lineages. Scorn was reserved in these years for the shi`i Safavid empire of Iran. Heretics in Ottoman eyes, the rival Safavids were conspicuously excluded in this festival from the family of Muslim rulers.

The sixteenth day was given over to *din*, religion, in the form of discussion among prominent Muslim scholars. With the chief mufti and Hayreddin as their escorts and Suleyman himself the presiding referee, the scholars engaged in debate on a topic posed by the sultan: the Fatiha, first chapter of the Qur'an. The less able "drowned in the sea of their sweat," as Ibrahim Peçevi, a seventeenth-century historian, put it.[9] One gentleman, mortified by his sudden loss of words, suffered an attack of apoplexy and expired upon reaching home. This story became a staple of future Ottoman historians' accounts of the grand celebration of 1530.

There were at least two lessons for Roxelana's and Mahidevran's sons to take away from their public initiation. First, they must learn to reign as well as govern, to conduct themselves as effectively in a Hippodrome festival as in a council meeting or in war. The celebration had demonstrated Suleyman's mastery of the visual and the spatial aspects of managing one's "presence"—the selective exhibition of the royal body. The princes were surely aware of the magnetism exerted by their own display.

The second lesson could be summed up as liberality for loyalty. A sovereign could not expect his subjects, high or low, to trust and serve him if he did not share the fruits of empire. The circumcision festivities were merely a more conspicuous example of this ancient principle of sound government. By making the Hippodrome the stage for the gift of his family's presence and the revelry that accompanied it, Suleyman revived a long-standing tradition in the imperial city. Originally built as a circus arena by the Roman emperor Septimus Severus at the end of the second century C.E., the Hippodrome had been the Byzantines' venue for chariot races, the public proclamation of new emperors, and the "triumphs" that celebrated their military victories. As Suleyman reinvigorated the practice of entertaining the populace of the great capital city, he broadcast a distinctly Ottoman style.

Mustafa was now poised to take these lessons to the provinces, but Suleyman did not award him a governorship for three more years. Not until the winter of 1533 did the prince and his mother depart for Manisa, when it made political sense for Mustafa to graduate to a provincial post. Suleyman had just concluded negotiations for a peace treaty with the Hapsburgs and was now free to plan his first eastern venture, a major campaign against the Safavids. With the western front quiet for the moment and the twelve-year-old prince Mehmed his father's deputy in the capital, Mustafa's presence in Anatolia would help to keep that chronically fractious region under control as the Ottoman army marched toward distant Iran. For his part, the prince was doubtless eager to begin his public career.

In the popular version of Roxelana's history that would come to depict her as ruthlessly determined to eliminate all rivals in her path, she engineers Mahidevran's banishment from Istanbul to Manisa. The two women may well have been eager to put distance between themselves, but it was political tradition, not scheming on Roxelana's part, that sent Mahidevran into the field as mother to a provincial governor. Once in Manisa, Mustafa and Mahidevran would take up residence in their old home, together with their newly assembled entourages. For her part, Mahidevran was no doubt delighted that her son was finally head of his own household and she now in charge of its female court. As Hafsa had monitored Mahidevran in her early years at Suleyman's consort, she would look after the young women in Mustafa's harem. One of his charges was to assume the responsibility of bringing more Ottoman princes and princesses into the world.

Shortly before leaving Istanbul, Mustafa was again the object of public attention—this time on the occasion of his investiture as governor. The ceremony, which took place on February 9, was the first occasion when Mustafa stood alone to represent the public face of the Ottoman dynasty. The Venetian Pietro Zen, seasoned envoy to Istanbul and currently vice ambassador, happened to be in the New Palace that day. Mustafa was received in an assembly of the full Imperial Council, where his father awaited him, wrote Zen in his dispatch. The prince was escorted there by "the whole world"—the head "guard of the gate," top official in the New Palace, and all the inner-palace functionaries.[10]

Mustafa then proceeded to demonstrate his fealty by kissing his father's hand, whereupon the grand vizier Ibrahim placed a robe of honor on his shoulders. To the second vizier Ayas Pasha belonged the privilege of holding Mustafa's stirrup as he mounted the horse on which he would exit the imperial palace. These actions underlined the point that

the sultan's most important advisers now also served this potential heir
to the throne. On the other hand, it was a limited degree of political authority that the New Palace ceremony transferred to Mustafa. Subordi-
nate, like all Ottoman governors, to the sultan's authority, the prince had
an additional check on his autonomy in the *lala* appointed by Suleyman
to tutor his son in statecraft.

If the investment formalities were a closed political affair, Mustafa's
progress to and from his father's palace was not. Unless his mother Mahidevran had already departed for Manisa, she would travel with him as
their train wound its way across the capital and paraded out through one
of the several gates in the monumental city walls. The Ottoman public
now had a new royal generation to follow.

MUSTAFA'S DEPARTURE WITH his mother for Manisa removed one of the
three top-ranking royal women from the capital. With Mahidevran gone,
Roxelana became the second most significant woman in the Old Palace
(Hafsa continued to preside over the large household). In this "seraglio
of the women," noted de'Ludovici, "[there] reside both the female slaves
of the Gran Signore and his unmarried female relatives." His report put
their numbers at "perhaps six hundred."[11] A fair portion of that number
was devoted to the care of Roxelana and her five children. Their suite of
apartments and its small army of servants, minders, and teachers occupied ample physical space as well as budgetary volume.

When the eighteen-year-old Mustafa left Istanbul, his younger half
siblings ranged in age from twelve to two. Mehmed, Suleyman and Roxelana's firstborn, was too young for a provincial post, but he was nearing
the age when Ottoman princes had sometimes been thrust into the political arena. The boy perhaps had mixed feelings about his older brother's
graduation to the world of politics—he might miss Mustafa, but now he,
Mehmed, would step into the position of oldest prince in the capital and
perhaps become a new favorite of the Janissaries. Mihrumah, approaching her eleventh birthday, was the only little princess in the palace. She
must have been its darling, although perhaps the toughness she would
exhibit in later years was beginning to show. Selim, soon to be nine, no
doubt had a sense of his own status as prince, having been included in

the 1530 celebration. He would be easy to spot among the siblings because of the reddish hair that he perhaps inherited from his Ruthenian grandparents.

The death of Roxelana's fourth child, Abdullah (the precise date is unknown), left a gap between the oldest three, so close in age, and their two younger brothers, Bayezid and Cihangir. Six or seven years old at Mustafa's departure (his birth date is also unclear), Bayezid would understand something of the reason for his oldest brother's elevation. Cihangir, a mere toddler, probably had not yet sorted out the complexities of just who Mustafa was.

Cihangir would be the last of Suleyman's children. The sultan turned forty in August 1533, five months after he placed Mustafa in the field. The timing of the prince's political inauguration was not coincidental. Forty was a number replete with religious, mythical, and historical significance for the Ottomans. For men, it was universally thought to be the threshold of full maturity. In Islamic tradition, the Prophet Muhammad was forty when he received the first of the revelations brought to him by the archangel Gabriel. In premodern times, the realities of the average person's life span meant that a forty-year-old man was probably head of an extended family in which he and his wife were counting their own children's children. Suleyman's age was easy for his subjects to calculate if they remembered the year of his birth, 900, in the Islamic calendar. The beginning of a new Islamic century was thought to be a moment when a great leader might emerge.

Roxelana herself was still relatively young in 1533, probably in her late twenties at Cihangir's birth two years earlier, almost certainly no more than thirty. But it would not be seemly to make a man who could now anticipate his first grandchild a father all over again. If decorum brought an end to her childbearing career, Roxelana may not have regretted leaving behind a phase of her life during almost half of which she had been pregnant. With five royal children to prepare for adulthood, she had her hands more than full. The end of childbearing did not spell the end of a sexual relationship between Roxelana and Suleyman, however. The sultan had apparently been unable to stay away from his favorite, and nothing suggests that their intimacy did not continue. And now it would be freed of the physical encumbrance of pregnancy.

But how did the couple keep from conceiving more children? It is fair to say that without the practice of birth control, the Ottoman sultanate could not have evolved the highly engineered politics of reproduction that it sustained. In the opinion of the majority of Muslim jurists, abortion in the first trimester was acceptable if the birth of a child would bring physical harm to the mother or hardship to the family.[12] The Old Palace midwives and female doctors were doubtless experts not only in conception and childbirth but also in forms of birth control that were compatible with the needs of the imperial household.

A variety of abortifacients and contraceptive techniques were known and had been catalogued already in medieval times. Use of suppositories and tampons by females predominated. Among the prescriptions of Al-Razi were five for intravaginal suppositories that used oil from cabbage flowers, pepper, juice of peppermint, leaves of pennyroyal, and dill.[13] Known to western tradition as Rhazes, the great Persian philosopher was also head of the Baghdad hospital, cutting-edge for its time, and a practicing physician. Roxelana herself was by now probably familiar with the palace's recommended techniques, or so her slower rate of childbirth from 1526 on suggests.

Dynastic family planning was political planning. The personal decision of how many children to have and when was fraught with political consequence in the Ottoman dynastic family. Too many sons was a liability, as Suleyman had observed all too closely in the bitter rivalry between his uncles and his father. Even before their deadly showdown, he had watched Selim chafing at his confinement in Trabzon while his seven brothers and then their sons gained princely posts closer to the capital.

In 1533, Suleyman had four sons eligible to succeed him: Mustafa, Mehmed, Selim, and Bayezid. We can safely presume that Suleyman and Roxelana deliberated the question of whether or not to have more children. Both would recognize that the birth of yet another boy would only add more grief to the spectacle of their sons combating one another, let alone Mustafa. Four healthy sons was sufficient dynastic insurance, one more than Mehmed the Conqueror had provided. The public introduction of the three eldest princes at the 1530 circumcision celebration may have been intended in part to signal that the sultan considered his reproductive obligation to the empire fulfilled. A late baby, Cihangir was perhaps unanticipated or an afterthought—the result of a decision by Roxelana and Suleyman to have one last child.

THE FIRST IN a series of tectonic shifts in imperial politics occurred in the spring of 1534. On March 19, Suleyman's beloved mother passed away. Hafsa was probably in her early sixties when she died, older than Bragadin's report of 1526 suggested ("a very beautiful woman of forty-eight, for whom [Suleyman] bears great reverence and love"[14]). While Ottoman writers generally avoided mention of women, the prominence of the sultan's mother called for a memorial salute. A long tribute was paid by Suleyman's private secretary and chancellor Celalzade Mustafa in his panegyric history of his sultan's reign.

In the florid prose then employed by men of the pen, Celalzade wrote of the torrents of tears that poured forth when people learned of Hafsa's death. (He gave facts as well—that Hafsa was buried next to the tomb of Selim I, that a tomb of her own was constructed over her grave, and that Qur'an reciters were posted within it.)[15] In his early seventeenth-century history, Ibrahim Peçevi paid the ultimate tribute of likening Hafsa to the Prophet Muhammad's daughter Fatima and his beloved wife Aisha: "The mother of the monarch, refuge of the world, the great woman whose whole work was piety, the [pure] woman whose every thought was good, the Fatima of the time, the Aisha of the age."[16]

Hafsa was the ideal model of a royal concubine and mother. She had labored for the empire for nearly forty years, apparently with dignity and determination. Freed by Islamic law on the death of her master, Selim I, Hafsa raised the position of queen mother to new prominence and may have been the first addressed with the title *Valide Sultan* (royal mother). The mosque she built in Manisa made visible her special status. It was the first commissioned by a woman of the dynastic family to have two minarets, and the charitable complex it anchored acquired a lofty appellation—Sultaniye (the imperial). Hafsa's duties included staying apprised of political developments within and beyond the empire, for which she maintained her own network of informers. For instance, when Suleyman was fighting in southern Austria in 1532, she dispatched her *kira*—a Jewish woman traditionally employed as an intermediary by harem women—to get the latest news on troop movements from the Venetian ambassador.[17]

As Selim's concubine and Suleyman's mother, Hafsa came to know a good deal of the empire. She lived in Trabzon, Caffa, Manisa, Adrianople, and Istanbul and traveled vast stretches of the territory that lay along the routes among these far-flung cities. Probably from the northern Black Sea region, Hafsa was later rumored to be royalty, daughter of the Crimean khan, but she was almost certainly an ordinary if beautiful girl who entered history as an imperial slave. Hafsa became a wealthy woman, but the privileged luxury she enjoyed had come at the cost of many lives as Selim defeated his internal and external foes. Out of compassion or duty, she cared for the progeny of at least one of her unsuccessful counterparts, Gulruh, mother of a failed prince. Perhaps the people of Istanbul who mourned her passing understood something of the trauma and triumph that had fueled her career.

Hafsa's death marked the end of the old regime, although it was not immediately apparent to all. Within two months of her passing, Roxelana and Suleyman were married. Addressing the Venetian Senate on June 3, 1534, de'Ludovici delivered the news that "the Gran-Signore has married [the Russian], as his wife."[18] Given that the return journey from Istanbul to Venice could take a month or more, the marriage had likely taken place by early May.

Roxelana had apparently gained her freedom at some point before becoming Suleyman's spouse. Then, following her marriage to the sultan, she gradually took up residence in the New Palace, the first royal woman ever to do so. Manumission, marriage, the opening of harem quarters in the previously all-male palace—each development was a radical move, each shattered Ottoman precedent. A whole new position was coming into being in the Ottoman empire that can only be called the office of queen.

One might expect Ottoman pundits to recognize these major transformations at the imperial center and mark them with clear dates. Instead, the puzzling silence of the historical record raises questions. Why did the marriage happen at that time? Had Roxelana pushed for the alteration in her status? Why did the marriage not become public immediately? When could it be said that Roxelana actually lived in the New Palace? Did the children move with her from the Old Palace? And could it be that the mystery regarding dates was in fact intentional?

Sultans had made marriages before—more commonly, they had arranged marriages for their sons and daughters—but these had been diplomatic gestures between the Ottomans and Christian as well as Muslim regional powers. Through such unions, the early Ottoman rulers sought to gain allies or, as their power and territory expanded, to seal the allegiance of vassals. By the early fifteenth century, however, they had learned the danger posed by foreign uncles who could intervene militarily on behalf of an Ottoman nephew. Although marital accords with foreign princesses continued for a couple more generations, they became childless unions, while slave concubines became the favored vehicle for propagating the dynasty.

By 1534, it seems that even the memory of royal marriage had faded, or so Menavino's comment that the sultans never took wives would suggest. Suleyman's audacity in breaking with tradition made it imperative that he move judiciously. He must accomplish each of the three steps that made Roxelana a married woman of high status— the grant of freedom, the contract of marriage, and the settlement of a dower—in concordance with members of the Ottoman religious establishment. Since this was the sultan's marriage, the presiding officiant was most likely one of its three highest-ranking jurist-scholars, the chief mufti and the two military judges of Anatolia (Asia) and Rumelia (Europe). All this demanded imperial gravity and adherence to the requisite religious propriety.

Matrimony in Islamic practice was a legal matter, a contractual agreement that conformed to Sharia law. It is probable, in fact, that Roxelana and Suleyman were not even present at the signing of their contract but rather represented by proxies. This was a typical procedure, with distinguished figures standing in for both groom and bride—in this case, most likely viziers or high-ranked palace personnel. This is not to say that the royal marriage was clandestine but rather that it was a private legal transaction, not a public affair. It was a momentous occasion, to be sure, and one that Suleyman may well have wanted to oversee personally, even if he did not participate in the official proceedings.

Among ordinary Muslims, a wedding celebration often followed the contractual marriage, although it might not take place for a while, usually to allow time for establishing the conjugal household in preparation for the marriage's consummation. Suleyman and Roxelana had long since consummated their relationship. But in their case too, the wedding festivities waited—for almost two years. The gap was probably not intentional but rather necessitated by Suleyman's sudden departure from Istanbul on June 13, when he set out to join the great campaign against the Safavids of Iran. It was already in progress under the command of the grand vizier Ibrahim.

PLANS FOR THE sultan's first campaign to the east had been afoot for some time. Challenging the Safavid armies on the long frontier separating Ottoman and Iranian territory, from Iraq to Azerbaijan, called for a far longer campaign season than did the march into Europe and back. Appointed *serasker* (commander in chief), Ibrahim had left Istanbul in late October 1533. It was an unusual summons from Ibrahim that precipitated Suleyman's departure for the east. Apparently the soldiers, "dispirited and tense," were protesting his absence. Without their sultan's leadership, they refused to push further into the territory of the Safavid shah, Tahmasp, who was advancing from eastern Iran toward Tabriz. "A king requires a king," they rumbled. "If the shah comes, who will stand up to him, what will be the fate of the soldiers of Islam?"[19]

Like his father, Suleyman had marched out of Istanbul with his army in every campaign of his reign. His lag in heading out to join this one perhaps stemmed from an obvious decline in Hafsa's health and then, after her death, the requisite obsequies and arrangements for her tomb—to say nothing of his personal bereavement. But Suleyman may also have delayed in order to arrange the marriage. The conjunction of these two events in the spring of 1534—Hafsa's demise and Suleyman's urgent need to go east—is the most likely explanation for the timing of the marriage.

Several factors were apparently at play, the most obvious being that Hafsa's death made wedding Roxelana feasible. Elevating a concubine through marriage would have dishonored the queen mother by diminishing her well-deserved and hard-earned status as the ranking female of the Ottoman dynasty. Hafsa was the family elder, the only person in whose presence her son was said to rise to his feet. Nor was the marriage likely to happen while Mahidevran still lived in the Old Palace, but that issue had resolved itself a year earlier.

There were other pressing reasons for securing Roxelana's status. As always, when grand vizier and sultan were both absent, a loyal and dependable deputy governor was assigned to administer and supervise Istanbul. But with his mother gone, his confidant Ibrahim on the frontier, and his only adult son assigned to monitor all Anatolia, Suleyman was in want of a trusted intimate in the capital. Given the duration of an Iranian campaign, the need was especially urgent (Suleyman in fact did not return to Istanbul until December 1535). The only person who could act as the sultan's eyes and ears was Roxelana, by now a seasoned denizen of imperial Istanbul.

For her part, Roxelana had every reason to urge Suleyman toward an immediate marriage. Paramount no doubt was security for herself and her children. The Iranian campaign would bring renewed fears for the sultan's safety and therefore for her own and her children's futures. In contrast to the European frontier, the borderlands with Iran were relatively unknown. The Ottomans had fought only a single war with the Safavids. Though Selim had been victorious in 1514, the east still evoked unsettling memories. In 1402, the Turko-Mongol conqueror Timur had swept into Anatolia from Iran, provoked by Bayezid I's expansion eastward. Taken prisoner by Timur, Bayezid died in captivity, according to legend by suicide, while his Serbian princess-wife was humiliatingly reduced to servitude.

It was, moreover, almost in spite of his army that Selim had won a resounding victory over Tahmasp's father Ismail at Chaldiran in eastern Anatolia. Selim's soldiers were exhausted by the long march across Anatolia, coping with a shortfall in provisions, and doubtful that it was right to fight against other Muslims. Before the battle was engaged, the Janissaries even fired at the sultan's tent and afterward refused to pursue the retreating shah, forcing Selim to end the campaign and withdraw to Amasya, an Anatolian provincial capital, for the winter.[20] Suleyman's Janissaries were criticizing him before he even left home.

Passion and politics inevitably intertwined Roxelana and Suleyman's lives. While strategic considerations certainly played a role in
their decision to marry, personal feelings were undoubtedly at work as
well. It had long been obvious that Roxelana was more than an ordinary
childbearing slave of the dynasty. Her career as the sultan's favorite was
unique in the history of the Ottoman dynasty, or at least in contemporary memory. Suleyman had broken several precedents for his favorite,
and he had certainly not hidden his devotion to her. What the marriage
accomplished was to legitimate this concubine's maverick position as
the mother of all the children of Suleyman's sultanate and to imbue her
stature with an aura of majesty.

It would be a mistake, however, to assume that the initiative in instigating the marriage was all Suleyman's. Roxelana may well have
deemed it just reward for her extraordinary responsibilities. By 1534, she
had some fourteen years of service at the very heart of Ottoman politics.
She had the children and the jewels to prove Suleyman's esteem. So it
was wholly reasonable that her pride and ambition might demand official
validation of her station through elevation as Suleyman's wife—which
she already was in all but name. Roxelana had not hesitated to display
audacity in the defense of her privilege before, when she dramatically
resisted Suleyman's acceptance of the two newly gifted slave women
or Mahidevran's aggressive assertion of superior status. If Roxelana re-
frained during Hafsa's lifetime from pressing for public recognition of
her exceptional status, she could now hope for its realization.

In fact, it is entirely possible that Roxelana actively fought for her
freedom, or so stories circulating in Istanbul suggested. Norms of
propriety did not permit Ottoman writers to speculate about the royal
marriage publicly, but European observers were freer to do so. Ogier
Ghiselin de Busbecq, ambassador of the Hapsburg emperor in the mid-
1550s, was one diplomat who repeated the story that Roxelana had refused to sleep with Suleyman unless he married her. "[Concubines] earn
their freedom . . . if they bear children," he wrote (in error). "Advantage
was taken of this privilege by Roxolana, Soleiman's wife, when she had
borne him a son while she was still a slave. Having thus obtained her
freedom and become her own mistress, she refused to have anything

more to do with Soleiman, who was deeply in love with her, unless he made her his lawful wife."[21]

Busbecq was wrong about the emancipation of concubine mothers. Motherhood brought them a protected status—they could not be sold or given away—but they were not released into freedom until their master's death. Perhaps the ambassador confused this fact with the legal rule that to free a slave and sleep with her without marrying her was to commit the grave crime of adultery. As for the story of Roxelana's resistance, it may have been pure rumor. But it has a certain plausible logic—the holdout of an unusually powerful concubine—that apparently allowed it to persist throughout Roxelana's lifetime. Busbecq was correct, however, that she received the dower that the law required a bride be given as part of matrimonial negotiations. Roxelana's was reputed to equal 100,000 gold ducats, or so later Venetian reports would allege.[22]

How widely known the marriage was when it took place is hard to say, but the Venetian de'Ludovici was certainly aware of it and its significance. Key individuals in both the Old and New Palaces would be apprised of Roxelana's new status, as perhaps would the governor placed in charge of the capital city when the sultan was at war. Where Roxelana spent the nineteen months of Suleyman's absence is not clear, but she may have stayed at the New Palace for at least some of the time. The old Hall of the Maidens had been refurbished and expanded in the mid-1520s, rendering it appropriate lodgings for the new queen. Mehmed too most likely spent time at the New Palace, for at thirteen he was old enough to serve as his father's titular deputy. He would write Suleyman at least one letter during the campaign with news of Istanbul.

We can only imagine what went on between Roxelana and Suleyman as they made ready for his departure. She had watched him leave on five campaigns, but this one would be the longest and had the least predictable outcome, presumably increasing her trepidation. War had not always proven healthy for Suleyman's forbearers. His father Selim and his great-grandfather Mehmed the Conqueror had died of sickness shortly after setting out on campaign. More ominous, his grandfather Bayezid II was overthrown and possibly murdered by Selim, who was impatient to take up arms against the Safavid advance into Anatolia.

Roxelana had to reconcile herself to Suleyman's duty to his empire; indeed she may have been in favor of the Iranian campaign in principle. But it is not hard to imagine her arguing that Ibrahim could manage, that it would hardly be the first time a sultan had delegated command to his grand vizier (Mehmed the Conqueror had done so).

If Roxelana feared losing the man she had come to depend on and apparently to love, her political mind must also have been at work. It was her duty, as the mother of three potential heirs to the Ottoman throne, to anticipate the worst-case scenario. Suleyman might never return to Istanbul, taken prisoner like Bayezid I; he might not return alive; or he might return incapacitated and unable to govern. A struggle for the succession would inevitably ensue. Mahidevran would be entertaining similar thoughts and, moreover, taking proactive measures on her son's behalf. Mustafa had troops already at his disposal in Manisa. The prince might conceivably be called upon to take command of his father's army (he had been popular with the Janissaries since his childhood, and the soldiers had already demonstrated their hesitation to follow Ibrahim). In the heat of war, so far from the capital, might not the army even proclaim Mustafa the new sultan?

Roxelana's advantage as Suleyman's favorite, and any edge it could gain her sons, might count for little in the eastern reaches of the empire; her security in the capital would depend on the loyalty of its commanders and their troops. In this regard, the loss of Hafsa may have genuinely alarmed Roxelana. Who would take her place as mistress of the Old Palace? Presumably not the slave Roxelana, even if she were the most politically informed and adept of its residents. Rather, it could well be the most senior princess, perhaps a sister of Suleyman, who might favor Mustafa and Mahidevran. To Roxelana, and to Suleyman as well, marriage presented itself as the best way to shore up both her stature and her competence as his ally in Istanbul.

8

A Queen for the New Palace

L UIGI BASSANO TITLED Chapter 13 of his book on the customs of the Turks "Of the seraglio of the Grand Turk, and of the Sultana his wife." Writing in the late 1530s, the Venetian informed his audience that "the palace of the Sultana is within that of the Grand Turk, and one can go through secret rooms from the one to the other."[1] Some fifteen years later, the ambassador Bernardo Navagero supplied further details: "In the middle [of the magnificent garden] are the rooms of the Grand Signor and of the Signora Sultana, whose room is separate; to go from one to the other, one must pass through a small walled garden belonging to the Grand Signor, and thence to another garden belonging to the Sultana, which is also walled."[2] Sultan and sultana, signor and signora— Suleyman and Roxelana were a king and queen united in the imagination by a garden gate.

It has often been assumed that Roxelana and her entourage moved to the New Palace only after a fire in 1541 destroyed much of the Old Palace. However, the Hall of the Maidens, which housed Roxelana in the New Palace during her initial interlude with Suleyman, had been revamped in 1527 and 1528, quite possibly with Suleyman's favorite in mind. It was these refurbished and expanded quarters that Bassano and Navagero described. The ambiguity regarding Roxelana's change in residence doubtless stems from the fact that it did not happen in one fell swoop. The more plausible reality is that Roxelana remained a significant figure in both royal palaces, moving back and forth between them but gradually making the New Palace her primary residence following her marriage.

Suleyman would have special reason to want Roxelana in the New Palace during his absence on the long Iranian campaign, for which he set out in early June 1534. Not only would she be closer to the pulse of politics, but so would Mehmed, who was just turning thirteen. Given the custom of stationing a prince of the blood in Istanbul during a prolonged absence of his father, this was Suleyman's opportunity to launch the youth's apprenticeship. Observers who understood the logic of preparing a prince and his mother for their potential roles as sultan and queen mother might wonder if Roxelana and her eldest son were beginning to create in Istanbul a version of Mustafa and Mahidevran's tenure in Manisa.

Bassano provided details of Roxelana's quarters in the New Palace. "Like those of the Gran Signore, the chambers of the Sultana are most splendid," he wrote, "with chapels, baths, gardens, and other amenities, not only for herself, but for her damsels as well, of which she keeps as many as one hundred." This was a far cry from the Hall of the Maidens. Bassano's European readers could now imagine the former concubine in a setting not unlike that of their own queens.

Account books detailed the work that Suleyman and Ibrahim had ordered.[3] Built-in cupboards, storage trunks, seats, and wooden flooring were added to the quarters of "the maidens," apparently with the aim of accommodating a larger, more permanent female presence. A new kitchen was constructed, and the water supply for the upgraded bath was improved. In addition to this remodeling, the "splendid chambers" described by Bassano appeared—a residence, a small pavilion, a fountain, and a pool. A wall enclosed this elegant ensemble, its purpose presumably to ensure its privacy and set it off from the dormitory quarters. An iron gate in the wall opened onto the private gardens of the sultan.

With their completion, the renovations of the mid-1520s had turned a female annex to the New Palace into a permanent wing for women, with Roxelana as its presiding resident. By the end of the century, its population would grow to 275 (including numerous staff and servants).[4] What would be called the "imperial harem" also grew in size, as new halls and apartments were built to accommodate its expanding numbers. This important shift in the gender demographics at the very heart of the empire—from all male to male and female—was the physical manifestation of a new model of governance, built step by step by Roxelana, that would give political stature and voice to royal women.

The improvements to the women's section were no doubt overdue. Suleyman's father had not put much energy into enhancing the New Palace beyond remodeling the private quarters he himself had occupied. Selim had spent much of his reign away from Istanbul, limiting his opportunity to attend to the needs of the imperial residence. This warrior-sultan, moreover, was not particularly interested in the Hall of the Maidens. Ambassador Antonio Guistinian commented in 1514, "He does not want to have more sons, so he no longer encumbers himself with women."[5] Forty-three when he seized the throne in 1512, Selim had finished with the reproductive phase of his life. During his reign, the Old Palace world of women was also subdued—his children were grown, and his mother had died in Trabzon during his governorship there. When Hafsa arrived in 1520 following Suleyman's enthronement, she undoubtedly had work to do.

As mistress of the Old Palace, Hafsa presumably contributed advice on the upgrading of the New Palace's female section. It is tempting to wonder if Roxelana voiced her own opinions or even lobbied for the reconstruction project. During the first years of her sexual relationship with Suleyman and the multiple conceptions it yielded, the sultan's favorite had logged considerable time in the Hall of the Maidens. She would know its routines and its limitations well.

ALTHOUGH CERTAINLY NOT a public figure before her marriage, Roxelana began now to practice an imperial seclusion parallel to that of the sultan. Bassano's voyeuristic perspective enabled his readers to envision her invisibility: "No one enters the palace of the Sultana except the Grand Turk, the eunuchs, and another person, highly trusted by the Grand Turk," he wrote. The sultana was not a prisoner of the New Palace, however. "She does not let herself be seen (so they say), and if she goes out, she goes at night in a closed carriage, as [do] all the wives of the great in Turkey."[6] (Bassano was not wholly correct as, at least in later years, Roxelana did make daytime excursions.)

Numerous individuals helped Roxelana maintain her seclusion. Foremost among them were eunuchs, castrated males uniquely able to cross thresholds separating male and female. Many royal regimes, including the Byzantine and Chinese courts, made use of eunuchs, although in evolving their own practices, the Ottomans looked primarily to earlier Muslim-ruled states.[7] The Venetian Giovanni Maria Angiolello, palace page from 1473 to 1481, described the eunuch corps of the Old Palace as it existed then. Guarding the women's quarters were some twenty eunuchs who "remain there day and night, serving and watching the women, in order that they may not be seen, except by these eunuchs and the sultan." Some were black, and some were white—a difference from the all-white eunuch guardians of the all-male interior courtyard of the New Palace. (Writing some sixty years after Angiolello, Bassano would put the number of the latter at thirty).[8]

The chief eunuch of the Old Palace wielded considerable stature and authority. "[He] has the right to correct and to chastise all persons in the palace, and [he] receives a salary of one hundred silver aspers, besides

"An eunuch, a sultana or noble woman, her wayting mayden." From *A Volume of Coloured Drawings of Costumes Worn in Turkey, Persia and Greece*. Late Sixteenth Century.

living expenses and a retinue of slaves," wrote Angiolello. This was "to say nothing of the many gifts from the Great Turk, a house outside the palace, and a large villa about six miles distant from Constantinople which has been presented to him." He enjoyed free time during the day but was required to remain in the palace at night.

When Roxelana took up residence in the New Palace, she would have at least one eunuch in her own service. As for the trusted individual who could also enter her quarters, "[he] is called the *procurator* of the Sultana," Bassano explained. Although the identity of this man is unknown, we can assume he served as Roxelana's steward, her *kethüda*, an office familiar in wealthy Ottoman households of the time. He would act as her link to the world outside the palace, the agent for transactions she might authorize and major purchases she might request. He may also have run interference for her within the palace, although the eunuchs could act as intermediaries with other palace functionaries. Suleyman apparently made sure that Roxelana's steward was recognized as a man of consequence: "[he] always comes and goes whenever he wishes, dressed most richly and accompanied by thirty slaves," noted the Venetian.[9]

Bassano provides us with both the earliest and the most intimate glimpse of Roxelana's new life in Suleyman's palace, and so we must ask how reliable his reporting was likely to be. Probably of Slavic origin, he hailed from Venetian-controlled Zara, a city on the Adriatic coast prey to Ottoman raids.[10] Bassano's languages presumably provided him with a range of interlocutors, and as a cultivated and informed man, he may have had contact, direct or indirect, with the envoys and dragoman translators of the Venetian embassy compound in Istanbul.[11] Bassano certainly had more information than many highly placed Ottomans did. However, the palace hearsay he was apparently privy to was bound be erroneous in some particulars: one hundred maidens in Roxelana's suite, for example, may be an exaggeration for this early moment in her occupation of her new quarters, as may the thirty slaves tracing the footsteps of her steward when there were only thirty eunuchs serving the inner quarters of the New Palace. On the other hand, Bassano's remark about the discreet conduct of women when they went out suggests some familiarity with the habits of Istanbul high society.

Social standards were changing in mid-sixteenth-century Istanbul, and pressure to conform was intensifying. "The great" set the tone for

those who aspired to improve their status in this increasingly cosmopolitan city. Under Ottoman rule, Istanbul was fast becoming one of the
largest urban settlements in the world. In addition to its polyglot native
population, the metropolis teemed with international traders, migrants,
refugees, and renegades. Seclusion behind walls in elegant residences
became the mark of the distinguished. Men of the elites avoided the
streets, receiving business associates and petitioners in stately reception
rooms in their homes. The imperial palace was the supreme model of
this practice, permitting only select ambassadors and top statesmen contact with the sultan in the palace's inner reaches. As for the New Palace
women's quarters, Jean-Baptiste Tavernier would comment in his 1675
book *A New Account of the Interior of the Grand Seigneur's Palace*, "I
include a chapter on the quarters of the women only to demonstrate to
the reader the impossibility of knowing it well. . . . Entrance is forbidden
to men with greater vigilance than in any Christian convent."[12]

Females seeking to gain social respectability emulated the wives of
"the great" who, as Bassano informed his readers, went guardedly into
public spaces. Women who hoped to elevate their social standing aspired
to recognition as *muhaddere*, an appellation that signified chaste virtue.
Apparently there was a certain social anxiety in Roxelana's day over
the boundaries of female respectability, for Ebu Suud, a respected jurist
and later the chief mufti of the capital, received a flurry of questions on
the matter. He confirmed that a woman of virtue was recognized by her
seclusion. But how aloof from the public must she remain to achieve this
standard of moral etiquette? The queries sought to determine just who
qualified for the attribution of female purity.

The mufti issued several fatwas in answer. He opined, for example,
that a village woman who fetched water at the well could not be *muhaddere*, but a woman escorted by a retinue to the baths, a wedding, or
another neighborhood could. Apparently impatient with the number of
queries he was receiving, Ebu Suud eventually pointed out that female
respectability was not a matter of Islamic piety. "It is not conformity to
the prescriptions of the noble Sharia that is the essential element in being
muhaddere," he stated. "That is why Jewish and Christian [literally, infi-
del] women can also be *muhaddere*. A woman is *muhaddere* if she does
not let herself be seen by males [outside the immediate family] and does

not set about taking care of her affairs in person."[13] Diplomatic missives sent later in the century from the Ottoman court to the Tudor queen Elizabeth I demonstrated this nonsectarian understanding of female moral honor—they hailed her as "the pride of the *muhaddere* of the Christian faith."[14]

Ebu Suud's dictum regarding *muhaddere* status made two points in addition to offering his judgment on the question of seclusion. First, moral virtue, as popularly understood and practiced in Istanbul, had less to do with precepts of Islamic conduct laid out in Sharia law than with wealth and social class. A woman of means with servants and attendants—regardless of her religious allegiance—could appear on the street and still maintain her distinguished status. An ordinary peasant could not.

Second, Ebu Suud recognized that a woman of high standing was likely to have "affairs" to take care of. Wealthy Ottoman women indeed had business interests. For the Muslims among them, a woman's right to independent control of her wealth meant that she might have real estate, investments, and money to manage. Seclusion, in other words, whether at home or within the portable harem provided by a retinue, was no bar to business—it just had to be handled through agents. Once again, the imperial palace was the model. Not long after her marriage and Suleyman's return from the east, Roxelana would launch her own "affairs" in the form of her first philanthropic foundation, on which she would presumably be spending some of her dower. No doubt her steward and his retinue would play a key role.

With her elevation to unprecedented prominence, Roxelana's comportment became an object of greater scrutiny. With the departure of Mahidevran and Mustafa to the provinces, the death of Hafsa, and Suleyman's campaign in the east, Roxelana would become a main target of royal watchers. In the absence of her husband and master, the new queen's conduct had to be conspicuously circumspect.

WHEN ROXELANA TOOK up residence in the New Palace, it had been a resolutely male establishment ever since Mehmed the Conqueror separated imperial business into two domains. The government of the empire would reside with the sultan in the New Palace, while the management and education of the dynastic family remained in the Old Palace.

The architecture of Mehmed's new palace broadcast the notion that the monarch was an exalted figure, access to whom must be carefully restricted. One moved inward toward power, the Ottomans believed, unlike contemporary metaphor in which movement is upward toward greater authority. The spatial organization of the palace was linear: three courtyards aligned in order of increasing difficulty of access. Large portals connected the courtyards, each with its own company of guards. A corps of white eunuchs enforced virtual impenetrability of the innermost courtyard, where the sultan resided.

Unlike the massive multistoried palaces of European monarchs, the New Palace was composed of separate, mostly single-storied structures situated around large open courtyards adorned with flower beds and cypress trees. As one architectural historian has put it, this conglomerate of individual structures is likely to appear to contemporary visitors as "a haphazard aggregate of modest buildings."[15] But in the Ottoman view, it was not massive residences but rather the control of massive manpower that conveyed the monarch's might.[16] Monumentality was better suited for structures dedicated to God—and the mosques built by members of the dynastic family were indeed monumental. Only in the mid-nineteenth century, partly under the political and aesthetic influence of European states, did the sultans abandon the New Palace for the Dolmabahçe Palace, an ornate colossus in comparison.

Suleyman's decision to install his queen in the New Palace, the very heart of politics, was a dramatic break with the past. It had the potential to disturb traditionalists even more than Roxelana's multiple sons or her transformation from slave concubine to royal wife. The blueprint of the sultan's palace was something of a saving grace in this regard, for new structures necessary to accommodate the new imperial harem could be situated alongside the second and third courtyards without impinging on their hierarchy of majesty.

The principal entrance to the New Palace compound was the Imperial Gate, the largest passageway in the high walls surrounding the entire palace complex. Royal guards stationed here permitted or refused access to the most public of the palace's three courtyards. Petitioners with routine requests and others with official business could enter the first courtyard but go no further. It is highly doubtful that Roxelana made use of the Imperial Gate when she exited or entered the palace. Its very nature as a public entrance, however restricted, was unsuited to her dignity as a female. She may have chosen to use the less monumental Iron Gate, which had the advantage of being closer to her quarters.[17]

The first courtyard was the least regimented of the three, at times noisy and hectic. The appeals and complaints of petitioners were received in the large kiosk of the supervisor of documents, who would, they hoped, deliver a positive response. Also located in this vast first courtyard was an array of service divisions that provided for the palace: the former church of St. Irene, turned into an armory; the royal mint; the workshops of court painters and jewelers; warehouses and waterworks; and an infirmary. Pages of the palace interior were said to feign illness and bribe servants escorting them to the infirmary to move slowly so that they could communicate with relatives and friends who had managed to gain entry.[18]

Animals as well as humans populated this initial courtyard. Suleyman followed ancient tradition by keeping in it a menagerie with elephants and the occasional giraffe. Horses, the favored mode of personal transport, were permitted to accompany their masters into the courtyard, while cavalry troops stationed there added color and motion. (Until recently, the first courtyard was host to modern forms of transport—it functioned as a parking lot for buses ferrying tourists to the Topkapı Palace Museum.)

Only the sultan could ride on horseback through the Middle Gate into the expansive second courtyard—all others could proceed only on foot. A new ruler was formally installed on the throne in this official "government" court of the empire. Here too, according to the protocols laid out by Mehmed II, the sultan appeared on the two principal Muslim religious holidays to greet and receive greetings from his ministers and his troops—all splendidly outfitted, carefully positioned, and strictly disciplined.

In its capacity as a ceremonial stage, the second courtyard also served as an open-air reception hall for foreign embassies. An account of the audience given the French ambassador François de Noailles in 1573

Second courtyard of the New Palace. The Imperial Council is in session on the left, the sultan observes from the Tower of Justice. The entrance to the palace precincts, at bottom, is guarded by Janissaries, and the wall separating the second and third courtyards, at top, by white eunuchs. Seyyid Lokman, *Hünernâme*.

provides a vivid sense of the ritual order imposed during such occasions: "We observed with great pleasure and the greatest admiration the frightening number of Janissaries and other soldiers lined up along the walls of this court, their hands joined in front of them in the manner of monks. . . . And they remained immobile in this way for more than seven hours, not a one of them uttering a sound or making the slightest movement." Once the audience was over, however, the French party was horrified by the troops' furious stampede out of the palace—"all those thousands . . . who had seemed like a palisade of statues in the court, now transformed, not into men but into starved animals or unchained dogs."[19]

The second courtyard was a working space as well as a ceremonial one. The heart of government was the great hall in which the Imperial Council—the Divan—assembled. Here the empire's viziers, the head treasurer, the chancellor, and the two military judges of Anatolia and

Rumelia met several times a week, with the grand vizier presiding. They deliberated, heard petitions from Ottoman subjects, and made policy decisions regarding domestic, military, and diplomatic affairs. Council members were attended by various scribes, money counters, couriers, and guards, making Divan days a bustling affair. The first courtyard too was congested during Divan meetings, as the dignitaries left their steeds and their servants there to await the end of the day's business.

Like those of other states during the sixteenth century, the government of the Ottoman empire was expanding, and with it the volume of revenue and paperwork. The Venetian Marco Minio, on his second embassy to Suleyman, this time to congratulate him on the brilliance of his 1526 victory in Hungary, noted that the sultan had had the old Divan Hall razed and a more beautiful one built in its place.[20] In addition to the council meeting room, the new structure provided space for the chancery and for a state archive to hold the increasing bulk of records and correspondence generated by the proliferation of imperial affairs.

The costs of the splendid new home for the Imperial Council were allegedly borne personally by the grand vizier Ibrahim Pasha. As Minio observed, it was there that "il magnifico Embraim" gave audience. The vizier also directed its construction, as he did much of the remodeling of the 1520s. Next to the Divan Hall, an imposing eight-domed public treasury was erected. The empire's reserves of gold and silver were then transported there from the Seven Towers, a massive fortress that Mehmed had built into the old Byzantine land walls soon after the Ottoman conquest.

At some point in the late fifteenth century, a small grilled chamber had been built into the tower rising above the Divan Hall. Here the sultan could station himself invisibly so as to monitor the integrity of his officials' work—"checking the truth of affairs," as Suleyman's private secretary put it.[21] A story about Mehmed the Conqueror attempted to explain the origins of this chamber: one day, a rude peasant from Anatolia approached Mehmed and his ministers in council with a petition and asked in the dialect of his region, "Which one of you is the sultan?"—an intolerable insult to the imperial dignity.[22] Ordinary subjects, it seems, had no idea what their sultan looked like. True or not, the legend underlines the increasing withdrawal of sultans from the quotidian business of government once they had become masters of Constantinople, ancient seat of august emperors who excelled in the arts of imperial theater.

The skyline of the second courtyard advertised the sovereign attributes of justice and munificence. The tower that crowned the Divan Hall loomed above the palace walls. Known as the Tower of Justice, this structure advertised that the core compact of government—the justice provided by the sultan in return for the loyalty of his subjects—was enacted in this very location. In later decades, Roxelana's female successors were said to have observed events in the second courtyard from the tower; perhaps Mahidevran and Hafsa stationed themselves there to watch Mustafa's investiture as governor.

Also visible from afar was the procession of chimneys rising from the imperial kitchens and running the entire length of the second courtyard's seaside outer wall. Food and its service were a metaphor for the giving of largesse, and the royal kitchens fed hundreds if not thousands each day. Together with the pencil-like minarets of the imperial mosques, these two palace features—tower and chimneys, justice and

"The kitchen of the Great Lord." Seventeenth-century European drawing of the New Palace kitchen featuring great cauldrons, kitchen chimneys, and domes and towers.

generosity—would be the first sights remarked by travelers as they sailed into the capital.

IF THE DIVAN Hall generated the energy of the second courtyard, the large portal that separated it from the third, innermost domain dominated architecturally. The very name of this structure, the Gate of Good Fortune, signaled that one was about to encounter the essence of empire. The rich Ottoman vocabulary of gates, doors, and thresholds reflected respect for the integrity of interior spaces, inherited in part from Byzantine precedent, in part from Near Eastern royal tradition.

Good fortune, *saadet*, was a resonant term among the Ottomans. Derived from Arabic, it approximated the old Turkish concept of *kut*, the divine grant of sovereignty that had legitimated the rule of eastern and central Asian khans before the arrival of Islam among the Turks. In the Ottoman view, the sultan's palace enshrined this blessing of sovereignty. The royal residence was often referred to as *Dar ul-Saadet*—House of Good Fortune—and so sometimes was Istanbul, whose aura of greatness came from the presence in it of the monarch and his residence. *Kut* and *saadet* both carried connotations of happiness, luck, fortune, and destiny. Westerners attempted to capture these meanings in phrases such as Sublime Porte or Gate of Felicity.

A major goal of Ibrahim and Suleyman's program of renovation was to make the interior palace as magnificent as its public and semipublic sections. The time had apparently come to bring the imperial residence in line with the empire's growing power in the world. The opulence of the redesign, however, also reflected the grandiose ambitions of Ibrahim and Suleyman. The monarch would become more august and less accessible, while the grand vizier would represent him in splendid array. To be sure, the selective seclusion of the sultan was not a new idea: in the imperial protocols he issued, Mehmed the Conqueror had passed official judgement, for example, on who was sufficiently distinguished to sup with him. Ibrahim and Suleyman's effort to further elevate the ruler's person was manifested in the upgrading of the Chamber of Petitions, a throne room that lay immediately beyond the Gate of Good Fortune. Here the sultan received only the highest dignitaries: important ambassadors, the chief mufti, and the grand vizier. The 1520s renovations added marble columns, wall mosaics of azure and gold, a silver fireplace, a throne studded with jewels, and more.

Beyond this last link with the world of politics lay the private universe of the Ottoman sultan. Situated in the inner courtyard's far left corner was the Privy Chamber. Selim's only significant contribution to the palace was the remodeling of these royal apartments. Suleyman's contribution was to reinforce and enhance the terrace that looked out over their hanging garden.[23] In situating his new palace on the acropolis, Mehmed the Conqueror had provided himself and his descendants with magnificent views. From the private garden the sultan could see all four districts of the capital, the Asian as well as the European (Istanbul and the "three boroughs" of Galata, Eyüp, and Üsküdar). Also visible was the conjunction of the Bosphorus and the Sea of Marmara, the two bodies of water that linked the Black Sea and Mediterranean sea. The intersection of these waters confirmed that Mehmed was indeed "lord of the two seas and master of the two lands," a title that he had arrogated to himself.

It is worth dwelling on Suleyman's refinements to the Privy Chamber terrace, for the architectural enhancements appear to carry a romantic subtext. The garden gate that linked Suleyman's quarters to Roxelana's suggests that he shared with her the delights of the terrace. At the same time that the "splendid" chambers were rising up on the female side of the gate, Suleyman was embellishing the terrace with new marble paving, a kiosk (the familiar haven of leisure and contemplation preferred by the sultans), and a room adjacent to a small bath.[24] Even if it was only the view that Roxelana would experience from this inner sanctum of power, it was an awesome vista for a former peasant from Ruthenia. But let us respect the taboo on breaking into the privacy of the inner courtyard and leave Roxelana and Suleyman to their pleasures.

In contrast to the second courtyard's dedication to the public good, the perimeter of the third, innermost, courtyard was occupied by structures that served the dynastic family. In the far-right corner was the imperial treasury (separate from the public treasury housed in the second courtyard). It was a great stronghold whose four chambers were stocked with the riches of the sultanate—among them thrones (including that of Ismail the Safavid, plundered by Selim) and the revenues of the rich province of Egypt. But the most remarkable feature of this secluded court was the conglomerate of buildings devoted to training the most promising of male slave recruits for high government office. Even in the sultan's most private domain, it seemed, the personal could not escape the political. The royal pages of the New Palace had been assessed and judged to possess more aptitude than the majority of male recruits, who were routed to other, secondary training institutions or directly into the corps of the military. The quarters of these slaves in training comprised five chambers occupying two sides of the courtyard.

Approximately five hundred such youths were said to be living and studying in the inner palace in 1534, the year of Roxelana's arrival next door.[25] The curriculum devised by Mehmed II perfected its students' bodies and minds, trained their hands in a vocational skill, and gave their tongues facility in Turkish, Arabic, and Persian.[26] Around 1577, by which time the French had gained knowledge of the Ottomans on a par with the Venetians', the French humanist Blaise de Vigenère commented, "It should be understood, first of all, that the whole establishment of the sultan's court, the foundation of his empire, and the strength of his army, depend upon a permanent seminary of young boys."[27]

The most accomplished of the pages were honored by selection for personal service to the sultan in the Privy Chamber. Selim had raised their number from thirty-two to forty when he had improvements made to these apartments. Wherever the sultan went, the four most favored of this elite group accompanied him. Prior to elevating Ibrahim in 1523 to the grand vizierate directly from the inner household, Suleyman had singled out his male favorite by making him head of the Privy Chamber during the Rhodes campaign of 1522—after having already awarded him the head pageship during the 1521 Belgrade campaign. Pages who did not make it as far as the sultan's personal suite had the consolation of knowing they were already among the chosen. Their continued loyalty and excellent performance, they were assured, would gain them other favors from their master. So foolproof was this system, it seemed, that Nicolò Machiavelli informed his Medici prince that one reason the Ottoman empire would be difficult to conquer was that the ministers, slaves, and dependents of the sultan could not be corrupted.

In 1534, Roxelana was joining a New Palace made splendid through the efforts of Ibrahim and Suleyman. Its two inner courts broadcast the majesty of her husband to targeted audiences of present and future power brokers. Roxelana was the first woman to inhabit this charismatic space. With the passage of time she would gain recognition as the founder of a female establishment within the New Palace that paralleled the male establishment created by the Conqueror. Each housed preeminent members of the dynastic family in elegant surroundings, and each trained chosen candidates to serve the empire. Over the next hundred years, the new wing of the palace would grow greatly, both in physical expanse and in political influence. Although Roxelana's grandson would establish rooms within it for his own use, it would remain a female-governed zone of the imperial residence. In the seventeenth century, it was from this wing of the palace that regent mothers would direct affairs of state in cooperation with their sons' viziers. Their collaboration would resemble that of Suleyman and Ibrahim, with the exception of the different inner quarters inhabited by the queen mothers.

Both the inner male and inner female spaces in the New Palace were referred to officially as *harem-i hümayun* (imperial harem). The comments of the early sixteenth-century historian Mehmed Neşri, as he described the construction of Mehmed the Conqueror's two palaces, suggest what contemporaries understood by the term "harem": "It is related that Sultan Mehmed first built in Istanbul a tower which he made into a treasury. And then he turned it into a palace, which he surrounded with a harem in the manner of a castle. He made that his residence. Later, displeased with it, he had another castle built, he made it a harem, and within it he built glorious palaces and made it the seat of his sovereignty."[28]

Neşri uses "harem" to refer to the space created by enclosure within an impregnable wall. The Old Palace starts as a tower to house the gold and silver of the recently conquered capital; then it becomes a palace, but only when Mehmed makes it a guarded, fortified "castle" does the entire structure become a harem. Likewise the New Palace, the "seat of sovereignty," is an interiorized space composed of a collection of residential and governmental "palaces." The spaces that were home to the sultan, and now to his wife, were harems within a harem, so to speak.

The Arabic roots of the word "harem" and its usage over time conveyed two general and clearly related meanings: a space that is forbidden or unlawful, and a space that has been declared sacred, inviolable, or taboo. A harem was a zone in which certain individuals or certain forms of conduct were forbidden—in other words, a kind of sanctuary. In the Ottoman world of the sixteenth century, the most revered spaces were known as harems—the interior of a mosque, the Muslim sacred compound in Jerusalem, and, above all, the two holy cities of Mecca and Medina.

That the Ottomans characterized the zone surrounding the sultan as a harem reminds us of how they understood and assessed power—that one moved inward toward it, not upward. The rich Ottoman vocabulary of gates, doors, and thresholds demonstrated the charisma of interior spaces. But Suleyman's majesty came from more than the royal privilege of remoteness. His Olympian remove was punctuated by public displays of splendor—the great Hippodrome festivals (Ibrahim's wedding in 1523, the circumcision festival of 1530), his processions to the city's mosques for Friday prayers, his departures for war, and his victorious reentries to the capital. The sultan was defined by his unique capacity to cross every significant threshold of the empire—from the inaccessible core of the palace through its successive walls to the public streets of Istanbul, through the ancient walls of the capital to the borders of his domains and beyond. His legitimacy was reinforced every time he plied the circuit from inner sanctuary to frontier and back.

Roxelana was now generating a circuit of her own as she moved between her apartments in the Old and New Palaces. Since her person was invisible, the very fact of her mobility between the two imperial spaces communicated the new queen's expanding orbit of authority. We do not know how often or how long Roxelana stayed in the Old Palace or whether her children moved between the two residences. But whatever the case, her familiarity with both royal households presented the opportunity to strengthen coordination between them.

Although the sole woman of stature in the palace of men, Roxelana would understand much of the dynamics of its male harem from the fourteen years she had spent in the Old Palace. With their training regimes, their hierarchies of slave recruits, and their well-guarded interiors, the

New and Old Palace harems deliberately resembled each other. Pages were as scrupulously monitored by their eunuch guards and their teachers as were the virgins of the Old Palace. Although New Palace males might be in their twenties when they "graduated out," their sexual adulthood was latent. Intimate physical contact with their fellow trainees was strictly forbidden. Only when awarded public office could they demonstrate full masculinity by growing a beard—or so Europeans reported.[29] Likewise, Old Palace trainees who had distinguished themselves gained sexual maturity when they graduated out—either to become the concubine of a sultan or prince or, more commonly, to be united with a New Palace graduate in marriage.

Such unions were frequent and often the product of deliberate design. Bassano noted that Roxelana married her "damsels" to pages of the palace, some of whom succeeded in becoming "great personages."[30] As loyal satellites of the two Istanbul palaces, these new households played a critical role in propagating dynastic authority among the population. The parallel stipend scales of the female and male training establishments suggests that such marriages were considered unions of equals. According to the wage register kept for Suleyman's princely household at Manisa, his pages received slightly less than the women in his harem.[31] This slim edge enjoyed by females persisted: in 1664, the average page received a stipend of 8.5 silver aspers a day, while his female counterpart received 8.7 aspers (stipends in Suleyman's day were less than half that).[32]

No sooner had Roxelana become Suleyman's wife than he left Istanbul for the confrontation with Iran, not to return for a year and seven months. This was not his first absence from her, but it was certainly the longest. During the five campaigns Suleyman had led so far, four in Europe and one in the Mediterranean, Roxelana had been surrounded by others in the Old Palace, sharing many of the daily routines that kept them all occupied. Now she faced the lot of a queen in an age of warring kings.

While Suleyman had reason to want Roxelana to serve as his eyes and ears in the New Palace during his long sojourn, he may also have trusted her to keep watch over the Old Palace. After fourteen years of Hafsa's government, it was without an obvious leader of royal stature. Admittedly, the institution could run on its own under the management of the Lady Steward, who administered the household of several hundred with the help of her female and eunuch staffs. But this imperial establishment did best when enhanced by a royal head. Roxelana may have cooperated in that role with one or more of Suleyman's sisters. They were likely to be widows who returned to their original home upon the death of their husbands, either to stay or to leave again if remarried.

It no doubt fell to Roxelana to organize at least some banquets and entertainments in the Old Palace, or at a minimum to attend them. Just a little over a week after Suleyman's departure, Istanbul celebrated the Festival (or Feast) of the Sacrifice, one of the two most important religious holidays in the Islamic calendar. Commemorating the willingness of the prophet Abraham to comply with God's command to sacrifice his son, the custom entailed the sacrifice of a sheep and the sharing of the meat with family, friends and neighbors, and the poor. To Muslims, Abraham is known as Ibrahim, and it is not Isaac but a different son, Ismail, whom the angel Gabriel instructs his father to spare. The religious festival would be an occasion when women of high rank—the wives of viziers and other notables—were invited to the Old Palace as honored guests. Etiquette called for those of lesser rank to attend those of greater rank. All these women presumably recognized and honored Roxelana's elevated status.

Gatherings that brought palace women together with women of elite households were more than social events. The wives of prominent Ottoman statesmen were very likely to be politically sophisticated and well informed. Some might themselves be products of an Old Palace education, perhaps already known to Roxelana, or alternatively of grandee households that prided themselves on the quality of their female and male slaves. (Recall that Roxelana herself may have come to Suleyman from such a household.) Others might be freeborn Muslims selected for Suleyman's men because of their pedigree and the loyalty of their families to the sultanate.

Like Roxelana, these women stayed abreast of the news by employing the networks available to them through servants and family clients.

Especially if their husbands had joined the "government on horseback" in the east, they would be eager to learn whatever information the queen was willing to share and in turn impart any news of their own. While we lack explicit information about Roxelana's other networks, she likely had several. With a range of suppliers and associates in the city, her steward might pry from them the latest street talk. Eunuchs in her service would transmit palace talk. No doubt they enjoyed their own networks stretching beyond the New Palace walls—the chief eunuch, for example, perhaps had a suburban villa as well as a residence near the sultan's palace.

From Hafsa, Roxelana had inherited a valuable asset in the network game: the female go-between who had assisted the queen mother in acquiring strategic information. Her name was Strongila, or Stranhilla, as the French ambassador Antonio Rincon called her. Her family belonged to the Karaite Jewish community of Istanbul.[33] This woman had presumably been in Hafsa's service since the start of Suleyman's reign, if not earlier, since some months after his accession she was rewarded with a grant of exemption from taxes as well as the right to own slaves (although not Muslim slaves). It was she whom Hafsa had dispatched in 1526 to seek information from the Venetian ambassador on Suleyman's movements during the Hungarian campaign. Strongila eventually converted to Islam, acquiring the name Fatma Hanım (Lady Fatma).[34] It is not clear if the practice of employing Jewish intermediaries originated with Hafsa, but it would continue at least until the end of the century.

Last but certainly not least of Roxelana's intermediaries was her eldest son. Mehmed had entrée, if circumscribed, into the world of men and politics. He may well have been present at meetings of the Imperial Council during his father's absence. When Hayreddin Barbarossa, the famed Mediterranean corsair whom Suleyman made admiral of his navy in 1533, repulsed an attack by the Spanish and their allies, both Mehmed and Roxelana separately wrote Suleyman with the news. Which of them heard it first? Mehmed's letter informed his father that the "infidel" fleet had attacked Hayreddin Pasha and that "with the aid of God, my sultan, he fought for the glory of your rule, defeated the enemy, captured one hundred eighty ships, and sank the rest."[35] Suleyman doubtless received the news independently, as soon as couriers could transmit it across Anatolia, but hearing it from his family may have had special value, both personal and political.

ONLY THROUGH ROXELANA and to a certain extent his older children could Suleyman maintain touch with the intimacies of family life during his long separation. The welfare of the dynastic family was always a major political concern, and this was his first campaign without his mother's trusted communications from the capital. But unless he specifically asked for news of his wife, it was taboo for others to mention her in their communications to him. The arrival of a letter from Roxelana, delivered to him in the sumptuous tent that was his home away from home, was surely an anticipated pleasure.

As a kind of postscript to the lengthy, stylized core of her letters, Roxelana typically added a paragraph or two of quotidian news. Whether the result of her imperfect (although increasingly fluent) Turkish or simply her personal style, Roxelana's letters are not always easy to follow. Mehmed's writing was more sophisticated, but then he had been schooled in the arts of language from the time he was little. Roxelana's writing tends to be cryptic, its ambiguities and ellipses arising in part because the letters are an ongoing epistolary conversation between wife and husband. The obvious gaps confirm that only some of Roxelana's letters to Suleyman have survived.

The health of their youngest son Cihangir, who suffered from a deformity of his shoulder, was apparently a serious preoccupation of his parents, since Roxelana wrote of it in the two surviving letters sent during the Iran expedition. In one, she describes a successful medical procedure that involved application of a plaster or salve to his shoulder, followed by what appears to be the surgical removal of a cyst. Cihangir is now improved, and Roxelana urges Suleyman not to lapse in his prayers for the boy. She has less good news about "the hodja [teacher]," possibly Suleyman's esteemed childhood preceptor, Hayreddin. He is "a virtual corpse," she writes, "neither dead nor alive," due to his great difficulty breathing. "No one but God knows his condition."

Roxelana's letters make clear that management of her new residential domain apparently presented some challenges. She may not yet have achieved finesse in handling her monies in general, or at least Suleyman had some concern about her ability to do so. Back in 1526, he had appealed to Gulfem, a trusted woman more experienced in the ways of the palace, to check on his favorite's expenditures. Now, during the Iran campaign, it seemed that Roxelana was again facing budgetary problems. The issue was bathing facilities, presumably those of the New Palace harem wing.

Renovated several years earlier, the hamam presumably served all residents of the expanded harem section. In one of her letters, Roxelana pours forth ecstatic thanks to Suleyman for his positive response to an earlier conversation about the hamam—in it she seems to have hinted that she would be pleased to have a private bath added to her suite of rooms. The letter also expresses gratitude for a directive Suleyman has sent from the field, presumably an order that the matter be sorted out.

As if to compensate for any presumption on her part, and perhaps also to cajole Suleyman into granting her request, Roxelana writes, "My sultan, may your blessed self never suppose that I, your slave, would request a hamam." Her excuse is that she is a perfectionist whose allowance doesn't go far enough. "You know, I am never content when the least little thing is not the way I want it," she continues. "It's just that fifty thousand of my silver pieces went on kitchen expenses." Apparently to assure Suleyman that she is not frivolous, she adds, "I have not put the remainder toward my own use." Whatever the problem, Suleyman paused in the midst of the most arduous military venture he had yet undertaken to make things right for his new queen.

The great bulk of Roxelana's letters, however, continued to be consumed with lament. Expressions of distress at Suleyman's absence and great longing to be reunited with him abounded. "If you ask after your wretched poor slave," she wrote, "day and night I burn in the fire of grief over separation from you." Although embroidered with copious poetic and scriptural ornament, the sentiments were apparently sincere. Mehmed wrote to his father that while at present his mother seemed well on the surface, underneath part of her was not. She was so caught up in missing him, Mehmed added somewhat dramatically, that her moaning and wailing echoed all the way to the world of the dead. "May Allah the Almighty quickly destroy that evil-doer [the shah of Iran] and make it possible for you to come soon," the prince concluded.

It is tempting to imagine that during the Iranian campaign Suleyman composed an undated but oft-quoted verse letter for his new wife.[36] In the fifth couplet, she is the empire that he knows intimately but also the eastern lands that he may never possess.

My solitude, my everything, my beloved,
my gleaming moon,
My companion, my intimate,
my all, lord of beauties, my sultan

My life's essence and span, my sip from
the river of Paradise, my Eden
My springtime, my bright joy, my secret,
my idol, my laughing rose

My happiness, my pleasure, lantern in my gathering,
my luminous star, my candle
My oranges bitter and sweet, my pomegranate,
the taper by my bed

My green plant, my sugar, my treasure in this world,
my freedom from woe
My Potiphar, my Joseph, my existence,
my Pharaoh in the Egypt of the heart[37]

My Istanbul, my Karaman, my lands of the Byzantines,
My Bedakhshan, my Kipchak Steppes,
my Baghdad, my Khorasan

Mine, you with the hair like vav [و], brows like ya [ى],
my languid and seditious eye,
If I die my blood is on your head, so come to
my aid, my non-Muslim[38]

As if I were a panegyrist at your door,
I sing your praises, I wish you well
My heart filled with grief, my eyes with tears,
I am your lover [Muhibbi],
you bring me joy [Hurrem]

Poets typically employed pen names, and Suleyman's was Muhibbi (the lover). In the poem above, the sultan addresses himself explicitly to Roxelana (that is, Hurrem, the name the Ottomans knew her by). In classic poetic fashion, Muhibbi is the besotted and the beseecher, she the elusive and powerful beloved. This inversion of power continues in the next-to-last couplet: she is the non-Muslim who must rescue him, the monarch of a great Muslim empire. By convention, the poet often included his pen name in the final line of a poem; Suleyman, however, also enshrines the memory of his queen by pairing her name with his own.

Love and desire permeated Ottoman poetry, and Suleyman's verse was no exception. The love and yearning of the sufi dervish for God, the pining and despair of the spurned or neglected lover, the celebration of the beloved—all filled the lyrics of poets. In the sixteenth century, the poet was everyman—and perhaps everywoman (although the little that scholars have recovered suggests that female poets may have kept some of their sentiments to themselves).[39] People ordered up poems the way lovers today buy valentines or roses. The popular poet Zati remarked, "I've struck it rich! Every two or three days somebody's servant comes along and brings me either a few silver coins or a few of gold accompanied by some delicious food or some halvah, and a letter that says 'write me such and such a kind of poem.'"[40] Reciting one's own or a well-known poem of another was a mark of cultivation. It is not surprising that among the sultans there were esteemed poets. Selim and Suleyman, father and son, were two of them.

9

THE TWO FAVORITES

MEHMED'S WISH FOR his father's victorious return from the east
came true, although not as quickly as he or his mother might
have desired. Not until January 8, 1536, did Suleyman make a triumphal
entry into Istanbul.[1] The two-year campaign against Iran captured Baghdad, ancient center of power, learning, and religious significance, while
the acquisition of the two large provinces of Erzurum and Van moved
the Ottoman frontier eastward into the Caucasus. It was no wonder that
victory celebrations were staged for five days and nights in principal
cities of the empire as well as the capital. When it came to Ottoman
grandeur, contemporary historians spared no hyperbole: there existed no
words to describe these festivities, they asserted, although they managed
to detail at great length the widespread "merriment and happiness."[2]

The people of Istanbul were doubtless ready to indulge the great
conqueror upon his return, and Suleyman may have found this an oppor-
tune moment to celebrate his marriage to Roxelana. The controversial
union had to be announced at some point, and the run-up to the Iran
campaign in spring 1534, when the contract of marriage was sealed, was
an inappropriate time for festivities, especially given the mourning for
Suleyman's mother Hafsa. Now that Suleyman was safely home, Roxelana may have pressed to have her stature as his legal wife made public.
Istanbulites had doubtless felt the sultan's long absence, and the jubilant
aftermath of victory provided an auspicious time to do so.

Suleyman's first five military campaigns had established the Ottoman empire as a major player in Europe and the Mediterranean, rivaled
only by the Hapsburgs. Now, under the command of the grand vizier
Ibrahim, the army had reduced the domains of the Safavid rulers of Iran
and stanched their territorial ambitions in Anatolia. Baghdad was a great
prize, even though the city in 1535 was not what it once had been. In

medieval times, it rivaled metropolises in China as the most populous in the world. Only with its seizure and sack in 1258 by Hulegu, brother of Khubilai Khan, the Mongol emperor of China, did Baghdad lose its stature. Privileging Iran over Iraq, Hulegu's successors went on to create a brilliant culture that fused Persian and Mongol traditions. Still, even if this once lustrous city had declined to the status of provincial capital, it was key to controlling Mesopotamia. In 1508, Shah Ismail, charismatic young founder of the Safavid dynastic house, had become Baghdad's sovereign, but Tahmasp, his son, had now given it up to the Ottomans.

The royal wedding apparently caught some in the foreign community by surprise. "This week there has occurred in this city a most extraordinary event, one absolutely unprecedented in the history of the Sultans," remarked the Istanbul representative of the Genoese Bank of Saint George. "The Grand Signior Suleiman has taken to himself as his Empress a slave woman from Russia. . . . There is great talk about the marriage and none can say what it means." If the palace anticipated negative reaction to the event, it offered palliative diversion. "At night the principal streets are gaily illuminated, and there is much music and feasting," noted the banker's dispatch. "The houses are festooned with garlands and there are everywhere swings in which people swing by the hour with great enjoyment."[3]

The public festivities highlighted entertainment just as the memorable circumcision celebration of six years before had. Although the 1530 event's duration and extravagance were greater, the venue was the same, as was, at least in part, the menu of amusements. This time, however, Roxelana was a center of attraction. "In the old Hippodrome a great tribune is set up, the place reserved for the Empress and her ladies screened with a gilt lattice," wrote the Genoese banker. "Here Roxelana and the Court attended a great tournament in which both Christian and Muslim Knights were engaged, and tumblers and jugglers and a procession of wild beasts." The giraffes had necks so long that to the unaccustomed spectator they appeared to "touch the sky."

The wedding prepared the way for Roxelana's public career. Soon she would begin the construction of a philanthropic foundation in Istanbul, the first royal mother to build in the Ottoman capital. Here, however,

Roxelana challenged yet another precedent. Architectural patronage was the traditional mark of maturity for a royal mother—one who had graduated to provincial service along with her son. Creating an endowed foundation in the city where her son served as prince-governor signaled her assumption of responsibility for the welfare of the empire's subjects. But Roxelana was still living with Suleyman, and all her sons were still living in the palace. By establishing a new, more prestigious profile for Roxelana, the marriage's publicity also opened the door to negative reaction.

IT WAS AROUND this time—the middle years of the 1530s—that unfavorable talk about Roxelana and Suleyman began to circulate on the streets of Istanbul. At issue was the sultan's unseemly devotion to his favorite, but the murmurs of discontent targeted Roxelana rather than Suleyman. She had, it was rumored, unnaturally seduced the sultan. Ever the pulse of popular opinion, Luigi Bassano commented, "Such love does he bear her that he has so astonished all his subjects that they say she has bewitched him, therefore they call her *Ziadi*, which means witch."[4] The talk of sorcery apparently did not dissipate over time. Nearly twenty years later, the Hapsburg ambassador Ogier Ghiselin de Busbecq wrote that Roxelana was "commonly reputed to retain [the sultan's] affection by love charms and magic arts."[5]

What did people imagine when they called Roxelana *Ziadi*?[6] The vast lands that made up the Ottoman empire encompassed different cultures of witchcraft and sorcery, with local traditions flourishing in the Balkans and the Caucasus, for example.[7] One shared vision of the witch was the old woman, poor and ugly, who might entrap her victim. Two couplets by the eighteenth-century Ottoman poet Shaykh Galip depict the menace of her abode and the fear of falling in thrall to her: "An old woman made a dwelling there / A frightful witch, demon-faced" and "Don't imprison me in the hands of a witch / Kill me, don't leave me mad like this."[8]

Perhaps not surprisingly, similar tropes of the rustic female witch existed in the Ruthenian lands of Roxelana's birth, at least in the eyes of the inhabitants' Polish overlords. In the words of a late sixteenth-century poet, "Poison and enchantment rule Ruthenia / The Ruthenian lands swarm with witches / Here I saw decrepit hags flying in the dark."[9]

Those who, in Bassano's report, called Roxelana *Ziadi* may, however, have been thinking of a different kind of female sorcerer—she who fettered men through love, the enchantress of the heart. Nedim, the seventeenth-century poet, spoke for the victim:[10] "Finally you have fettered my heart with your tresses. Hey, what sort of witch are you that you bound [me] with strands of your hair?" In the imaginative legacy of the Ottomans, the danger of the seductress was that it was men who suffered in love, not women.[11] On the other hand, it was overwhelmingly males who created the canons of love.

Just when popular antipathy to Roxelana emerged is difficult to say. Already in 1526 the Venetian Senate had learned that the sultan no longer paid attention to Mustafa's mother but instead "concentrated all his affection" on the mother of his three other sons.[12] Venetian diplomats, however, enjoyed privileged information, and this rift may not have been public knowledge. By 1540 or so, however, when Bassano's sojourn in Istanbul is thought to have ended, Roxelana's unpopularity in the capital was discernible.

More consequential than street gossip were the sentiments of the palace and the army. They too, apparently, were distressed by Suleyman's unorthodox devotion to Roxelana. "For this reason the Janissaries and the entire court hate her and her children likewise," observed Bassano, "but because the sultan loves her, no one dares to speak." The Janissaries were potentially the unruliest element in the military, and the military, at least at this point in Suleyman's reign, was the dominant element in government. Janissary revolts, threatened and real, punctuated the reigns of the strongest of Suleyman's ancestors. He himself had already experienced the wages of their discontent in 1525, when the soldiers rampaged in Istanbul over the simultaneous absence from the capital of both the sultan and the grand vizier.

One powerful impetus for the Janissaries' enmity toward Roxelana was the sultan's other family. Stationed in Manisa, Mustafa and his mother Mahidevran were out of Istanbul's sight but hardly out of mind. Even as a child of twelve, Mustafa had won popularity with his father's soldiers. Throughout his career, Venetian ambassadors continued to describe him in laudatory terms. Bassano wrote that he had "always heard everyone speak ill of the Sultana and her children and well of the first-born and his mother, who is repudiated."[13]

Already, apparently, the story of Mahidevran's rejection by the sultan had taken hold. It is not clear, though, whether in these years it included the accusation that later ages would make: that Roxelana was responsible for her rival's "exile" from Istanbul to Manisa. Although untrue in fact—Mustafa and Mahidevran merely followed the ancestral pattern of graduation to the provincial careers they had been trained for—this rumor probably contained the germ of truth that Roxelana was not unhappy to have her rival gone.

An experienced prince typically participated in his father's military engagements or else was assigned, as Suleyman had twice been, as "deputy sultan" in Adrianople or Istanbul. Mustafa had neither joined the recent operations in the east nor acted as a placeholder on his father's throne (Roxelana's eldest son Mehmed was by then old enough to act as dynastic figurehead in the capital). Instead, as Mustafa and his troops were a valuable asset, he remained stationed in Manisa during the Iranian war, deputized by his father to act as commander of all Anatolia.[14]

According to Bassano, the prince finally experienced the Ottoman-Safavid frontier himself with transfer of his post to the east, temporarily at least. "He stays in Asia, in a city called Charahechmith, thirty days from Constantinople . . . on the borders with the Sofiani."[15] (Europeans often called the Safavid shah "the Sophy," or Sufi, because the family originally had risen to prominence, at the dawn of the fourteenth century, as a mystical, or sufi, order.)

The Italian garbled the name of Mustafa's new post, Kara Amid (black Amid), the old name for Diyarbakır, the capital of the large eastern province also called Diyarbakır. The city was "black" because of the mammoth walls of black basalt that surrounded it. The province was both a bulwark against Iranian forces and, with its capital on the Tigris River, a gateway to Iraq and Baghdad. This was an important assignment strategically, a post that was likely to see action against renewed Safavid border sorties. But the rumor mill also could construe Mustafa's transfer eastward as Suleyman's deliberate distancing of the prince and his mother from the capital.

As Bassano represented him, Mustafa was a worthy successor to his illustrious ancestors. The Italian informed his readers that "the first-born has with him a most beautiful and magnificent court, no less than that of his father." Moreover, Mustafa was a man of the utmost justice and had won a name for great generosity. Bassano was not explicitly holding up Mustafa as the next sultan in the making, but his readers would recognize and approve the sovereign attributes of munificence, moral rectitude, and majesty. Mahidevran too came in for praise from Bassano as the model female parent to a prince: "his mother, who is with him, instructs him in how to make himself loved by the people."[16] The encomiums were exaggerated in at least one respect, for even if Mustafa had the audacity to rival his father's court, he would not have been permitted the resources to do so. The sultan must always and everywhere in his kingdom have no rival.

Had Bassano become a partisan of the prince and thus a natural critic of Roxelana and the advantage her sons might be assumed to enjoy? Had the force of the public opinion he reported perhaps swayed his thoughts? If Bassano was the chronicler of Roxelana's emergence as queen, he was also the purveyor of her portrait as witch. Self-interest was perhaps operating here: stories of harem intrigue could help sales of his book to an audience already curious about the Great Turk's women. On the other hand, Bassano's commentary may have offered a dispassionate reading of prevailing sentiment.

Whatever the case, Bassano's European readers would correctly presume that some antagonism was building toward Roxelana in the years following the revelation of her marriage. The seeds of the Ottoman queen's notoriety in Europe had been planted.

TWO MONTHS AFTER Suleyman and Ibrahim's victorious return to the capital, a shocking event occurred in Istanbul: the sudden execution of the grand vizier. Sometime during the night of March 14–15, 1536, Ibrahim was strangled by order of the sultan as he lay sleeping in his room in the inner palace. There had been some controversy over Ibrahim's leadership of the Iranian campaign, but there was no warning, no observable clue, that his monarch and the friend of his youth was displeased enough to do away with him—indeed, Ibrahim had that very evening gone to the palace to break the Ramadan fast with Suleyman. Returning to Istanbul after the eastern victory he masterminded, Ibrahim had resumed his role as director of the empire's affairs. Only a month before his death, he concluded negotiations with French diplomats that yielded a historic agreement on reciprocal trading privileges; the agreement marked the beginning of a long diplomatic and military alliance between the two kingdoms.

Was Ibrahim a martyr to political partisanship that allegedly drove Roxelana to lobby for his murder? In the last century or so, the grand vizier's fall has typically been viewed as one of her schemes to eliminate her rivals. As the standard story goes, Roxelana took control after Hafsa's death in 1534 and used her powers to turn Suleyman against anyone who might oppose her. Having banished Mahidevran to the provinces, she next convinced the impressionable sultan that Ibrahim was a danger to his reign.

The story has deep roots. Şemseddin Sami, an Albanian Ottoman writer and thinker and early proponent of women's rights, had this to say about Roxelana in the encyclopedia he published in 1891 (the first in Turkish): "A Russian slave who, because of her beauty and grace, and intelligence and shrewdness, acquired extraordinary influence and power. However she did not always use that influence and power toward good ends and was the cause of the execution of the grand vizier Ibrahim."[17] A prominent Turkish historian of the mid-twentieth century was more direct: in order to protect her sons, Roxelana's "first act was to do away with the grand vizier."[18] Recently, the "ruthless queen" motif acquired new life in a Turkish television series on the reign of Suleyman, which portrays both favorites as drunk with power: Ibrahim guilty of "mad arrogance," Roxelana of engineering his fall.[19]

The problem with this judgment is that there is no contemporary evidence of Roxelana's guilt. Venetians, the keenest and most vocal observers of the two favorites, had nothing to say on the matter of Roxelana's involvement. Their ambassadors, fascinated with Ibrahim, paid close attention to the ups and downs of the grand vizier's career. At the same time, like Bassano, they made a point of publicizing news of the sultan's new wife, so one might well expect to hear about any role she played in his downfall. Bassano had nothing to say on the subject beyond repeating the story that it was Ibrahim who originally presented Roxelana to Suleyman. Ottoman pundits and historians were likewise silent on the matter, although they analyzed at length the reasons for Ibrahim's fall from favor. Even the late sixteenth-century bureaucrat and historian Mustafa 'Ali, who did not hesitate to accuse the queen of malevolent scheming in her later career, made no mention of a connection between Roxelana and the grand vizier's execution.

We can safely conclude that the contemporary public did not hold Roxelana guilty for Ibrahim's death. But perhaps it was inevitable that these two individuals, who rose simultaneously, at the very outset of Suleyman's reign, as his favorites, were assumed, at least by later historians, to be rivals who would do anything to impede the other's influence on the sultan. The absence of a smoking gun, however, does not mean that Roxelana had no opinions regarding the man who occupied much of Suleyman's attention for the first thirteen years of her life with him or that she kept those opinions to herself. No one could be silent on the subject of Ibrahim, it seemed. He became controversial well before she did.

Ibrahim's execution did not entail the usual public beheading of a disgraced pasha. In the inner sanctum of the palace's third court, he was garroted with a bowstring, the mode of death usually reserved for Ottoman royalty. Mehmed II's favorite Mahmud Pasha, another lauded grand vizier struck down by his master, had also been strangled, but his murder took place in the Seven Towers prison fortress, a grim quasi-public affair. Was it symbolic that Ibrahim's illustrious career ended in the very place where it had begun when Suleyman appointed his best friend head page in his personal service? We will probably never know if it was a last honor bestowed on this servant of the sultanate or an expedient way to eliminate him without the encumbrance of protocol. Ibrahim's corpse was removed from the palace in secret.

We find a partial answer to these questions in the lack of a grave commensurate with the grand vizier's service to the empire. Devoid of the usual memorial tomb, his burial place was deliberately obscure—clear evidence of dishonor. Ibrahim's corpse was allegedly interred in the garden of a dervish hostel behind the imperial dockyard. It was later said that a single tree marked the site of his grave.[20] In other words, the man who was arguably the most powerful grand vizier the Ottomans had known was symbolically obliterated. Ibrahim's fall was as sudden and unexpected as his astoundingly rapid rise to the pinnacle of power. The alteration of a single letter in his nickname marked the overnight change of his status: once Makbul (the favorite), he would now also be known as Maktul (the slain). Only Ibrahim's wife Muhsine paid tribute to him by building a mosque in his memory in the Kumkapı district of Istanbul.[21]

Both the unprecedented ascent and precipitous descent of this illustrious statesman and commander affirmed the singular power of the sultan to make and unmake the careers of his highest officials. Four years after Ibrahim's fall, Henry VIII would similarly eliminate his powerful henchman Thomas Cromwell, as he had cut down his earlier political favorite (and Cromwell's mentor) Cardinal Thomas Wolsey in 1530. Both men, however, had at least been tried for their crimes. While an Ottoman sultan could not in principle execute a subject of the empire without a judicial trial, he held the power of summary punishment over the slave servants to whom he had delegated power.

Suleyman may have deliberately chosen March 15 for Ibrahim's murder. The anniversary of Julius Caesar's assassination was a telling choice for the elimination of a brilliant politician whose power had apparently grown excessive in the eyes of his executioner. By the Ottoman calendar Ibrahim perished on the twenty-second day of Ramadan in 942, but Suleyman could easily have ascertained when the Ides of March fell that year. Ibrahim had shared his love of ancient history with Suleyman, and the two may well have ruminated on Caesar's career. According to Pietro Bragadin, reporting in 1526, Ibrahim derived pleasure from having books about war and history read to him, especially the lives of Hannibal and Alexander the Great.[22]

Suleyman and Ibrahim shared more than an interest in the past. Each was the tutor of the other, perhaps a natural outcome of the fact that they grew together into sovereignty. One had the sultan as his father, the other a fisherman from Parga, a town on the Ionian Sea, but their lives came together when both were young men. Stories of Ibrahim's origins were various: He was captured in a raid by the Ottoman governor of Bosnia, Iskender Pasha, and presented to Suleyman during his princely service at Caffa; alternatively, he was abducted by pirates who sold him to a widow living near Manisa, the prince's second post.[23] Pietro Zen reported a more plausible account in 1523: captured by corsairs, the boy, called Pietro, was sold to the widowed daughter of Iskender Pasha. When Suleyman visited her home in Adrianople, she presented him with her slave Ibrahim, "who played [the violin], sang, and was of the same age."[24] Ibrahim's ties with the family were later solidified when he married Muhsine, the granddaughter of Iskender Pasha.[25]

IBRAHIM MOVED WITH the new sultan to Istanbul in 1520, having served as a page in Suleyman's princely household in Manisa. Their closeness was formalized with Suleyman's award to his male favorite of the top post in the New Palace's inner courtyard: head page of the Privy Chamber. More shocking was Ibrahim's elevation in June 1523 from personal service in the inner court directly to the grand vizierate, the highest office in public service. Suleyman's other viziers had worked their way up the ranks, gaining years of experience in government. They had earned their status; Ibrahim was given his. Suleyman's decision so alienated Ahmed Pasha, who believed himself next in line for the office, that he used the consolation prize of the Cairo governorship to stage a rebellion, thereby entering historical memory as "Traitor Ahmed."

Just as Ibrahim's elevation to grand vizier was unprecedented, so was the autonomy he enjoyed in the office. Already in June 1524, at the completion of Zen's first mission to Istanbul, the envoy informed the Venetian Senate that the new grand vizier "does everything, and whatever he wants is done."[26] Zen emphasized that Suleyman loved Ibrahim greatly and that they were always together. The sumptuous palace Suleyman built for his favorite on the Hippodrome not only impressed observers with Ibrahim's extraordinary status but had the additional advantage of inspiring wonder at how much more splendid the sultan's own palace must be.

The first full account of Ibrahim came two years later from Bragadin. Perhaps not coincidentally, this same report to the Venetian Senate also introduced Suleyman's other favorite, "the Russian" woman. Followers of the ambassadorial reports learned that both were small:

Roxelana was not beautiful but graceful and petite; Ibrahim was a thin man, with a small face, pale, not very tall, and graceful.[27] (Suleyman, on the other hand, was tall.) The sultan's affection for both was intense, wrote Bragadin: Suleyman focused all his love on Roxelana, ignoring Mustafa's mother, and people said that he would have perished from sorrow had Ibrahim stayed any longer on his mission in 1525 to restore order in Egypt. As usual, the Venetians knew a good story when they saw one, especially when it came to Ibrahim, to whom they enjoyed more than the usual access.

Bragadin was doubtless not the first to recognize the parallels in the precedent-shattering rise of the two favorites. Ibrahim's career, however, peaked first. News of Roxelana was just emerging in 1526, and she would attract open criticism only after she became a public figure in the mid-1530s. Ibrahim, on the other hand, was already controversial by 1526. In words strikingly similar to Bassano's later comment about popular dislike of Roxelana, Bragadin reported that "at first everyone hated the pasha, but now that they have seen how much the sultan loves him, they try to become friendly with him."[28] This included the mother and "the wife" of the sultan.

Some at least sought to get close to Ibrahim for good reason: he had considerable political patronage to dispense. As head of the Imperial Council, he made policy as well as routine appointments to office. Every day, noted Bragadin, the sultan wrote him about political matters, dispatching notes via one of the mutes who served in the inner palace. Ibrahim in turn wrote to Suleyman of everything he was doing. For high-level petitioners, particularly foreign ambassadors, Ibrahim was an indispensable channel to the sultan, especially since the process of royal removal from the quotidian business of administration that had begun with Mehmed the Conqueror was picking up. Reporting on his audience with Suleyman in 1527, Marco Minio commented on what seems to have been a recent convention: "They have imposed this rule, that the envoy neither speaks nor does the Signor answer, but [the envoy] only kisses his hand, and then the pashas dismiss him."[29]

Ibrahim had a great deal of personal patronage to dispense as well. According to Bragadin's report, the vizier's yearly income was an extraordinary 150,000 gold ducats: 100,000 for the grand vizierate and 50,000 for the governorship of Rumelia, the enormous Ottoman province in southeastern Europe.[30] The sultan would increase these sums over the years. Ibrahim's architectural largesse, which provided services to local communities and jobs for builders and workers, included mosques large and small, schools, dervish lodges, and hamams in places ranging from Mecca to cities in the Ottoman Balkans. Ibrahim was also a devoted patron of poets and writers. A work dedicated to him on the distinctions between apparent synonyms in Persian illustrates the extent of his erudition.

A good deal of the vizier's wealth went to maintaining his large palace and substantial household. He outfitted the 1,500 slaves he already possessed by 1526 in red silk embroidered with gold thread. For the time, this was a large pasha household, although it was not unique—that of the famously wealthy royal treasurer Iskender was allegedly grander. Ibrahim's patronage included his own family. He placed two of his brothers in palace service, his mother lived in a house adjoining his own palace, and for his father the vizier obtained a modest governorship in Parga, with an income of 2,000 ducats annually. All four converted to Islam, the father taking the name Yunus (the biblical Jonah, a prophet in Islam).

THE COMPANION OF Suleyman's youth was also the architect of the sultan's magnificence. Ibrahim was apparently gifted with an eye for visual sensation, be it architectural, ceremonial, or sartorial. For his part, Suleyman gave his favorite both the means and the opportunities to realize his talents. The 1520s renovations to the New Palace directed by the grand vizier greatly enriched the settings in which select observers viewed the Ottoman government at work. Venetian ambassadors referred to Suleyman as *il signor*, the king, but Ibrahim was *il magnifico*. They remarked that his dress was fancier than the sultan's and that his fingers were lavishly bejeweled. Ibrahim's wedding in June 1524 was the first gala event of Suleyman's reign, establishing the blueprint and the tone for future celebrations.

The wedding is worth dwelling on for an erroneous supposition that accompanies it. The panoply of the event has been attributed to the assumption that Ibrahim was betrothed to Suleyman's sister Hadice. A century later, the historian Ibrahim Peçevi wrote, "Spread before the eyes was such abundance and merriment as had never been observed at the wedding of a princess."[31] However, this assumption has been challenged more than once, and Muhsine, granddaughter of an illustrious statesman, is now largely accepted as Ibrahim's wife.[32] The older belief made sense because the custom of marrying Ottoman princesses to top statesmen had taken firm hold once Suleyman's grandfather Bayezid II made it policy, and all of Suleyman's other sisters married high-ranking officials.[33] In any event, the fanfare of Ibrahim's wedding was all the more remarkable if it was not for a princess.

An interesting question then arises: Why was Ibrahim, holder of high office, not honored with the hand of a princess? Perhaps it was considered improper, scandalous even, to ask a sister to tolerate her husband's continued intimacy with her brother. Perhaps Hafsa, the dynastic elder, questioned the propriety of an alliance between her son's sister and his intimate friend. According to Bragadin, a bed head to head with Suleyman's was kept for Ibrahim in the inner palace. It seems more likely that Ibrahim retained his old room in the Privy Chamber suite, but even that violated the custom that the only fully adult male present in the inner palace was the sultan. At the very least, the ambassador's comment reflected their uncustomary closeness.[34]

During Ibrahim's tenure as grand vizier, the cultivation of Ottoman magnificence was pursued with a competitive eye to Europe and the increasingly glamorous courts and persons of Renaissance kings and queens. Until he departed in 1535 on the eastern campaign, fifteen years into his reign, Suleyman's military attention was focused westward. So was the propaganda war, with its heavy dose of lavish display. European powers had been relieved at his accession in 1520, having spent the previous two years in great fear of an attack by the warrior-sultan Selim I.[35] Alvise Mocenigo, dispatched by Venice to congratulate Selim on his defeat of the Mamluk sultanate in 1517, remarked that the conqueror "hopes to become the ruler of the world, with Africa, Europe, and Asia under him."[36] The common presumption in Europe was that Suleyman was the gentle lamb to his father's angry lion.

Ibrahim was the right man for the task of convincing European powers that his master fully intended to realize his father's ambition.

"He delights in knowing the condition of the monarchs of the world, the location of their lands, and all other matters," noted Bragadin of the vizier. Ibrahim's linguistic abilities and network of contacts and informers, especially among the Venetians, bolstered this avid interest in world affairs. He was particularly close to Pietro Zen, the elderly envoy (born in the year of the Ottoman conquest of Constantinople) who represented his government three times during Ibrahim's vizierate. More important was Alvise (Luigi) Gritti, intimate collaborator with both Ibrahim and Suleyman.

Gritti was one of four sons born in Istanbul to Andrea Gritti, doge of the Venetian Republic from 1523 to 1538. The father had previously been a merchant cum diplomat in Istanbul for several years; his 1503 report to the Senate following his mission to negotiate peace was a model of the genre.[37] The four sons were the offspring of one or more concubines, presumably acquired locally by their father (he also had a legitimate son, whose mother was the niece of a doge). Receiving an education worthy of his father's station, Alvise studied in Venice and Padua, whose university was one of the great centers for the Renaissance revival of classical studies. Apparently his father's favorite, Alvise nevertheless settled in Istanbul, where he cut a resplendent figure and eventually lent his nickname—Beyoğlu (son of the lord)—to the large district in Istanbul where his palace once stood. A prime example of the culturally composite citizen of the sixteenth century, Gritti held court for merchants and humanists and provided entertainment for Christians and Muslims alike.[38]

Like his father, Gritti was a merchant who dealt in jewels, among other commodities, and Ibrahim introduced him to Suleyman in this capacity. Roxelana was conceivably also one of his clients, dealing through her Jewish agent, the woman Strongila. Gritti's real contribution, however, was in diplomatic and military service to the Ottoman empire. In his 1534 report to the Venetian Senate, Daniello de'Ludovici noted that Gritti had won Ibrahim's favor by educating him on "the world and the government of states," experience of which the grand vizier lacked at the time of his appointment.[39] Gritti participated in three campaigns and, more significantly, became the architect of the empire's policy in Hungary, an unending arena of contention with the Austrian Hapsburgs.[40]

This fascinating man was killed in 1534 by Transylvanian rebels while fighting for the sultan.

Gritti was a collaborator in the most explicitly competitive project in Ibrahim's program for displaying Suleyman's splendor. From Venetian artisans (including Pietro Zen's sons), the grand vizier commissioned and purchased an enormous four-tiered crown for the sultan, intended to visually challenge the claim of Suleyman's greatest rival, the Hapsburg monarch Charles V, to the mantle of the Roman empire. When in 1530 Pope Clement VII placed the crown of the Holy Roman Empire on Charles's head, he himself wore the iconic three-tiered papal crown. The new emperor entered Bologna, the city of his coronation, to cries of "Cesare, Cesare, Carlo, Carlo, Imperio, Imperio!"—Caesar, Charles, Empire![41]

Suleyman wearing the four-tiered jeweled crown. Woodcut, anonymous Venetian.

Mehmed II, however, had made his own claim to Roman successorship with his conquest of Constantinople, center of the Roman empire from 330 onward. Selim I's greatness as a conqueror rested on his reassembly of the eastern Roman empire through his annexation of former Mamluk territories in the Levant and Egypt. Now Suleyman would visibly challenge Charles on the basis of those claims as well as his further victories in former Roman domains in southeastern Europe and the Mediterranean.

In 1532, the Ottomans countered the elaborate processions in Bologna with a display of Suleyman's crown along the long route of his army's march to Austria, where he hoped (futilely, as it turned out) to engage the emperor in battle. In the southern Serbian city of Nish, Hapsburg envoys were compelled to watch the military parade from the minaret of a mosque, and in Belgrade the procession passed under Roman-style triumphal arches. Adding to the extreme opulence of the occasion was a whole ensemble of precious items acquired from Venice that accompanied the crown: a jewel-studded saddle, the rich head armor worn by Suleyman's horse, a scepter, and a bejeweled gold throne. So lavish was the parade that a prominent treasury official objected to the enormous cost on the grounds that the campaign itself was already a burdensome expense.[42]

IBRAHIM WAS THE public face of the sultanate: commander in chief of Suleyman's army as of 1529, master of diplomacy, and impresario of the sultan's image. Why was he so suddenly eliminated? In attempting to provide a single answer, commentators of the time pointed to the grand vizier's overweening pride. Ibrahim, they said, failed to remember that however much authority Suleyman delegated to him, the sultan was still the absolute master of the empire.

Drawing on one another, Ottoman historians listed a set of errors made by Ibrahim on the eastern front that justified his execution.[43] The vizier's tactical misjudgments overextended the war against the Safavids, causing harsh winter conditions to weaken and, perhaps worse, alienate the soldiers. Possibly more harmful in its consequences was Ibrahim's execution of the powerful royal treasurer Iskender, whose war counsel

Suleyman had instructed Ibrahim to seek. On the night of Iskender's hanging, Suleyman allegedly suffered a dreadful dream that revealed the error of his trust in his longtime grand vizier. Surrounded by a nimbus, Iskender accused Suleyman of forgetting his own many services to the sultanate and allowing his execution on the word of a troublemaker. Suleyman awoke in distress when Iskender began to unwind his turban to strangle the unjust sultan.[44]

In writing of Ibrahim's death, these same historians also gave equal space to the many virtues displayed by the vizier over the course of his career. They commended his scrupulous respect for the law (both Islamic Sharia and Ottoman dynastic law) and his veneration of the Qur'an. His downfall, they asserted, resulted from Ibrahim's gullibility—he was seduced on the frontier by the flattery of riff-raff (sometimes represented as Safavid sympathizers). These sycophants had corrupted his integrity, inciting him to refer to himself as "sultan" in his military commands and to blaspheme by treating the holy book of Islam with disrespect. (The sunni Ottomans were ever ready to accuse the shi'i Safavids of corruption and blasphemy.)

This "official" account of Ibrahim's rise and fall originated in large part with Celalzade Mustafa, son of a Muslim judge and Suleyman's private secretary, who rose to chief secretary of the Divan and then, during the eastern campaign, to royal chancellor. Celalzade's detailed history of Suleyman's reign was rarely critical of the sultan, its purpose largely to glorify his reign.[45] In like manner, he was generous in his judgment of Ibrahim, whom he had served as private secretary and principal collaborator in repairing the damage wrought in Egypt by "the traitor" Ahmed. Citing Celalzade in his own history, Solakzade Mehmed noted that the secretary had been the "confidant of Ibrahim's secrets."[46]

In their treatment of Ibrahim's fall, Celalzade and the early seventeenth-century historians such as Peçevi and Solakzade who drew on his history were displaying a common Ottoman habit: rather than directly criticizing powerful or popular individuals for their unpopular actions or breaches of conduct, they deflected blame onto their associates. If the sultan looked bad, it was because Ibrahim had committed errors, while in turn it was the riff-raff who lured Ibrahim from the right path. At worst, vizier and sultan were guilty of succumbing to self-seeking and treacherous intimates. The sultan, however, could only be chastised in a dream.

Providers of intelligence to the outside world, however, told a story that challenged this canonical view of a grand vizier who served well until the end. De'Ludovici, reporting to the Venetian Senate in 1534, was as critical of Ibrahim—and of Suleyman—as his predecessors had been admiring. The sultan lacked the virtues of a monarch, commented the envoy, leaving everything in the hands of Ibrahim, whose rise was the product of his wiles. Despite the empire's strength on land, its soldiers were wretched due to Ibrahim's neglect, and the navy was underdeveloped. The grand vizier sidelined capable men or ruined their careers; therefore talented men hid from him out of distaste or fear. De'Ludovici believed Ibrahim had known of the empire's weakening. He had simply loved himself more than he loved Suleyman.[47]

Like foreign observers, the Istanbul public did not hesitate to express its views of Ibrahim. Ever since the Janissaries targeted his palace in their 1525 uprising, the sultan's favorite had accrued unpopularity among some circles in the capital. Ibrahim's palace was again the object of discontent when he placed in front of it three bronze statues of Hercules, Diana, and Apollo he had seized in 1526 as spoils from the royal palace in Budapest. The poet Figani gave voice to popular reaction in a couplet: "Two Abrahams came into the world, one a destroyer of idols, one an idol-worshipper." The righteous Abraham was the biblical patriarch, for Muslims the prophet Ibrahim, whose holiness included the purification of sacred spaces; the idol worshipper was of course the grand vizier. For this offence, Figani was tortured and hanged in 1532.[48] According to the German Hans Dernschwam, the public believed the statues proved that Ibrahim was still a clandestine Christian.[49]

Doubt over the sincerity of Ibrahim's embrace of Islam was again provoked in 1533 when Suleyman and Ibrahim paid a three-hour visit to the palace of Alvise Gritti.[50] The context was difficult treaty negotiations with the Austrian Hapsburgs, whose Archduke Ferdinand, brother of Charles V, challenged Suleyman's claim to Hungary (Ferdinand's claim derived from his marriage to the sister of King Louis II, who was killed at Mohacs in 1526). Gritti's views were essential, as he probably understood Hungarian politics better than anyone in Ottoman government. But

Ibrahim's critics saw a pseudo-Muslim vizier in cahoots with a bastard infidel to induce the sultan to forget that his august station required all to come to him. Suleyman, no fool, no doubt had his reasons for making such a risqué move—perhaps he was sending a warning to Ferdinand.

In the end, Ibrahim's errors clearly accumulated to the point that Suleyman found it necessary or expedient to get rid of him. But he had obviously had sufficient trust in his grand vizier and respect for his military leadership to put him in sole command at the outset of the campaign against the Safavids. Suleyman had certainly tolerated, and presumably authorized, lavish expenditures such as the four-tiered crown and its retinue of precious objects. On the other hand, Ibrahim had made mistakes—the army under his command was turned back from Vienna in 1529, and the German campaign of 1532 fell short of its anticipated success. On the home front, Suleyman was undoubtedly sensitive to the opinion of his public and especially to the mood of his other pashas and governors.

The sultan did not lack for talented statesmen. In other words, Ibrahim was dispensable. Ultimately, it appears that Suleyman kept his grand vizier for as long as he needed him—that is, through his reign's first military venture across Anatolia (where Ibrahim had put down serious tribal disturbances in 1527) and the confrontation with Iran. But no matter how alienated by Ibrahim's misconduct, Suleyman could hardly have found easy the sacrifice of his friend of nearly twenty years and partner in government for thirteen. His resolve would have to be firm. Perhaps that resolve did not come quickly.

Hindsight enables us to see that in 1536 Suleyman was approaching a turning point in his reign, of which the grand vizier's removal was a signpost. Ibrahim was a visionary with talents supremely suited to the competition awakened by the extraordinary empire Charles V inherited and the Ottomans' extraordinary expansion. Both Suleyman and Charles could now lay claim to the old ideal of universal sovereignty, and Ibrahim could take a good deal of credit for placing his monarch on a par with Europe's most powerful ruler. The French political philosopher Jean Bodin, born in the year Charles was crowned Holy Roman Emperor, believed "the Turks" had the better claim to the mantle of Rome because they ruled over a far greater expanse of formerly Roman territories.[51] But the times were changing, and it was beginning to appear that the decisive clash of the two titans would not materialize.

The resounding victory over the Safavids, together with a truce granted to Ferdinand in 1533, freed Suleyman to devote more attention to matters of state building within the empire. His grandfather Bayezid II had labored to integrate the territories conquered by his own father, Mehmed II, but Bayezid's son Selim had devoted his short reign to yet more conquest. Suleyman and his government had work to do to solidify the empire. The modernization of imperial law and the consolidation of provincial administration marked the late 1530s and the 1540s. The sultan would be back in the saddle by 1537, but it was during this era in Suleyman's long reign that he would acquire the regnal nickname he would come to be known by—Kanuni, the lawgiver, the just administrator. Other minds than Ibrahim's were better suited to the challenges of this period.

The Safavids posed one of those challenges. The sixteenth century was one of sectarian antagonism. Just as Catholic and Protestant monarchs racked Europe with conflict, the most powerful Muslim rulers—the sunni Ottoman sultan and the shi`i Safavid shah—now attempted to divide the western Asian world. Each drove the other to a firmer embrace of doctrinal orthodoxy and a campaign to promote religious conformity among his Muslim subjects. Suleyman issued an imperial order in 1537 that every Muslim village must have a mosque.[52] The sultan, moreover, competed for another prophesied role: in addition to the long-awaited universal sovereign, the "renewer of religion" was expected at the start of each new Islamic century. The tenth sultan of the Ottoman ruling house, Suleyman had been born in 900 by the Islamic calendar, the beginning of the tenth century. But he had to earn that destiny.[53]

It was no coincidence that the year of Ibrahim's execution was the year Suleyman turned his attention to the old lands of Islam. In 1536, he ordered the rebuilding of the walls of Jerusalem, third holiest city for Muslims after Mecca and Medina and holy also to his Jewish and Christian subjects. In this same year Roxelana, having made her debut as Suleyman's lawful wife, began to plan the mosque that would become the centerpiece of her religious complex in Istanbul. Later in the queen's career, her magnificent hospice in Jerusalem would win her the accolade "the Zubaida of her times," after the venerated woman who, as the wife of the Abbasid caliph Harun al-Rashid, had sponsored numerous public works for the benefit of the Muslim community. In other words, Suleyman was now attending to the Islamic face of the empire, and it was Roxelana who would be his partner in this enterprise.

FRUSTRATINGLY LITTLE IS known of Roxelana's actual relations with Ibrahim apart from the scant evidence in her letters. One of the several stories of how she came to the sultan—as a gift from his male favorite—is dubious, since at that point Ibrahim was merely a member, if a distinguished one, of the Privy Chamber slave corps.[54] The story may preserve a germ of truth, however—a lack of tension between the two at the outset of Suleyman's reign. We find the only sign that Roxelana may have been less than happy with Ibrahim in a letter to Suleyman in 1526. "An explanation has been requested for why I am angry at the pasha," she, or more likely a scribe, wrote somewhat stiltedly. "God-willing, if it becomes possible to speak in person, it will be heard. At present, we still send greetings to the pasha, may he accept them." Twice during the Safavid campaign, Roxelana's postscripts included a simple "greetings to the pasha."[55] Perhaps she had acquired in the interim a renewed appreciation for the comfortable lodgings in the New Palace that she now occupied, which owed much to the grand vizier's efforts.

However, Roxelana did have one thing to fear from Ibrahim: a threat to her own status or that of her children. Mustafa was her sons' rival, and in the 1530s he was making a name for himself. Roxelana may have had reason to suspect a sympathy on Ibrahim's part with the oldest prince and his mother Mahidevran, especially as their mutual acquaintance went back to the years in Manisa. Contact between prince and vizier continued in Istanbul, or so Bragadin's stories of Ibrahim's kindly patience in soothing Mustafa's jealousies imply.

Letters exchanged between Mustafa and Mahidevran in Manisa and Ibrahim and his wife suggest a friendly relationship between the two families. In 1534, Mustafa wrote to Ibrahim, away fighting in the east, to inform him of affairs in the Aegean, and the grand vizier responded with news of Ottoman victories. Referring to himself in his letter as the prince's "sincere friend," Ibrahim expressed the wish to see Mustafa soon and to "take profit from and be gladdened by [his] noble and blessed grace." In a letter to the vizier's wife asking after her health, Mahidevran wrote effusively of the "sisterhood and brotherhood" that she and Ibrahim had shown and of their "truly sincere kind friendship and tender compassion."[56]

Are these letters evidence of Ibrahim's partisanship? Maybe, but maybe not. Had Roxelana's eldest son Mehmed been old enough for a princely post, Ibrahim would probably have written to him in a similar vein. The grand vizier would find it politic to maintain a cordial relationship with all Suleyman's potential heirs. Selim's last grand vizier continued as Suleyman's first until Ibrahim's appointment to the office unseated him; likewise, Ibrahim could expect to manage the transition from one reign to the next if Suleyman should meet with a fatal accident.

All this, however, does not mean that Roxelana would be unreasonable to worry about a cabal between the two families. Ibrahim's death probably allayed her concern over Mustafa's popularity, at least for the moment. For Mahidevran, however, Ibrahim's execution could well exacerbate the fear that Suleyman would privilege a son of his favorite over Mustafa. He had broken protocol for Roxelana before and might do so again in the matter of the succession.

A BIOGRAPHER OF Suleyman has asked whether the sultan displayed "a certain lack of character" in allowing others to influence him excessively. On the other hand, he observes, Suleyman was able to delegate authority, a skill his father lacked.[57] In a similar vein, ambassadors to Suleyman's court admired the sultan's judicious administration but repeatedly noted his susceptibility. Bernardo Navagero remarked twenty-three years into his reign that Suleyman tended to let himself be "the prey" of almost all his counselors.[58]

Perhaps the Venetians' republican bias made them less than sympathetic to rise of favorites so characteristic of the elaborate courts cultivated by Suleyman and his fellow monarchs of the early sixteenth century. Suleyman clearly displayed a bias throughout his reign toward governing in close association with individuals who enjoyed his personal trust and affection. In other words, he needed favorites, although nothing matched the intense collaboration he fostered with Ibrahim and Roxelana at the outset of his sultanate.

Suleyman was hardly alone among sixteenth-century monarchs in his devotion to his favorites. A biographer of Henry VIII has described as "flamboyant intimacy" the young king's association with the favorites who served in his Privy Chamber. New ordinances refashioning the chamber into a more private zone were issued in 1526, the same year that Ibrahim and Suleyman undertook a similar reworking of the New Palace.[59] In his work on friendship, the late sixteenth-century writer Luis de Zapata noted of Charles V that he had two *privados*, one his personal favorite, the other "the king's" favorite (Zapata followed European notions of the king's two bodies, the person and the office). Charles' relationship with the former, Don Luis de Avila, was like that of Alexander the Great and Hephaestion, wrote Zapata.[60] With their interest in past kings, perhaps Suleyman and Ibrahim also compared themselves to the celebrated pair. Hephaestion was Alexander's childhood friend, trusted commander, and possible lover.

A prince's early life experiences were bound to shape the idiom of his reign—in Suleyman's case, instilling a desire for intimate confidants. He had grown up with the debilitating competition among Selim and his siblings, only to witness a degree of intradynastic violence not seen since the devastating civil war of the early fifteenth century. Suleyman may have found with Ibrahim the fraternal relationship he never had. The slave from Parga safely filled a brotherly role, for he could presumably never rival his master. Suleyman's closeness to his mother Hafsa and to his tutor Hayreddin, who was still with him at the time of Ibrahim's execution, may also have been forged in these same bloody years.

There was a role and a title for the intimate confidant of the sultan: the *nedim*—the boon companion who provided relief from the cares of government, the courtier who could tell a good story. Ibrahim had certainly been that person to the prince, what with his music making and his love for history. But as sultan, Suleyman crossed the line when he made the talented slave his grand vizier in order to keep him close, or so it seemed to the public. Did Suleyman cross another line by persisting in openly demonstrating his devotion to the empire's highest statesman, to the point that a diplomat could inform a European audience that the sultan loved Ibrahim more than he was loved by his vizier, who only loved himself? Was Suleyman's great rival Charles, with his two favorites, wiser?

Ottoman society tolerated, and in some circles welcomed, intimate friendship among males. The sixteenth century has recently been dubbed an "age of beloveds," in which young men were objects of desire among powerful men, poets, and artists and "the inspiration for a rich literature of love."[61] Poetry was the principal medium for expressing love (of females as well as males), and several members of the royal family participated in this celebration of desire.

There were certain rules, however. The strong should not love the strong, thereby disrupting the convention of power disparity between lover and beloved and putting both at risk of a shameful loss of decorum. But if Suleyman's subjects perceived a problem in his intimacy with his powerful vizier, neither Ottomans nor Venetians cared to note it in writing. Bragadin, however, did transmit the angry words of Ferhad Pasha, husband of Suleyman's sister Beyhan. Stung by accusations of misgovernment, Ferhad retorted, "That whore Ibrahim is the cause of this."[62] It was the worst of insults: whatever Ferhad had uttered in Turkish Bragadin translated as *bardassa* (a promiscuous girl); the ambassador chose the feminine form of the word. The pasha's outburst occurred early in Ibrahim's ascendancy (he was executed in 1524 for his persistent misdeeds).

If Roxelana resented Suleyman's intimacy with his male favorite or shared Ferhad's opinion of him, the record is silent. Certainly she did not lack for evidence of Suleyman's continuing passion for her. He discarded one precedent after another to keep her at his side, culminating in her emergence as the first and only Ottoman queen. If 1536 was the year of Ibrahim's exit from the stage of history, it marked Roxelana's debut as a player. She was celebrated in Suleyman's poems and known as his beloved among Europeans, and also doubtless in Iran.

If the literary culture of the era honored male friendship, it also treasured the great romances of the Persian world, especially the tales of ancient kings and the women they loved and desired. Well known among the Ottomans was the story of Khosraw, who fell in love with the

Armenian princess Shirine, made her his queen, and killed her would-be lover Farhad. The romantic epic *The Seven Beauties*—named for the wives of the heroic king Bahram Gur, among them princesses of the Slavs, the Turks, and the Roman emperor—was a cautionary tale as well as a romance. So consumed was Bahram Gur in the seven pleasure pavilions he built for the beauties that his minister usurped power; after listening to seven victims of the empire's subsequent disarray, the king slew the minister and turned the pavilions into temples.

It was not that life imitated fiction but that the trials and temptations of sovereigns were timeless. Religion, law, and royal tradition guided kings and queens, but so did literature, which could teach ethics and history as it entertained.[63] In the poetic imagination inherited by the Ottomans, beloved queens were foreign, ministers could be tempted to fill the void opened by distracted kings, queens could be mere objects of desire or commanding figures like Shirine, and ultimately kings must rule.

10

BUILDING A REPUTATION

IN 1538, CONSTRUCTION began on a new mosque in an Istanbul neighborhood somewhat distant from the city's imperial core. It was the nucleus of a foundation that would soon expand to include two schools—a madrasa to provide advanced education to older youths and a primary school that taught letters and scripture to children of the neighborhood. The next structure to rise up was a large soup kitchen. Some years later, the complex gained a hospital, a rare amenity. A fountain on the soup kitchen's grounds brought fresh water to neighborhood residents, a further boon.

Roxelana's Istanbul foundation was the first of the philanthropic efforts that would punctuate the rest of her career. By the time of her death, major charitable institutions existed in her name in the holy cities of Mecca, Medina, and Jerusalem and in the Ottoman capitals of Istanbul and Adrianople, while smaller endowments were scattered across the empire in regional capitals and towns.[1] Works she built or supported financially included hostels for wayfarers, pilgrims, and religious devotees, as well as additional mosques and soup kitchens. Roxelana also attended to the second face of Ottoman piety, the mystical, by building sufi lodges and mosques for revered spiritual leaders.[2] But her first project was the most significant, for it was Roxelana's debut as a public servant.

Charitable giving was an obligation for all Muslims who had even a small amount of disposable income, and the Ottoman dynastic house was expected to lead. The great Istanbul foundations of Mehmed the Conqueror, his son Bayezid, and their leading statesmen had forged the recovery of Constantinople after its decline in the late decades of Byzantium. Roxelana recognized that undertaking a substantial philanthropic project was the single most effective means of legitimating her extraordinary elevation to queenhood. If anything would win the hearts and minds of Ottoman subjects in a lasting way, it was a graceful edifice that offered tangible benefits to ordinary people.

For Muslims, such donations to the public welfare were *hayrat*, good deeds or good works that won merit in God's eyes. Obituary notices of prominent figures regularly included their record of philanthropic projects. In other words, the users and admirers of Roxelana's mosque complex would recognize—and respect—an intentional act of piety. At the same time, both subjects and foreign observers of the sultanate understood that her foundation was a display of power. In a culture that disapproved of physical representation of the sovereign on statues and in portraits, even on coins, monumental architecture was the most obvious demonstration of wealth and influence. Like the foundations endowed by the sultans and many of their viziers, Roxelana's eventually gave its name to the area in which it was located—today the busy Istanbul district is officially known as Haseki (the royal favorite).[3]

For prominent women, who did not reveal their persons openly in public, building was an even more consequential gesture. Although her wedding had been celebrated, Roxelana enjoyed no public coronation like that in May 1533 of her contemporary Anne Boleyn, the favorite of Henry VIII. The lavish celebrations in London lasted four days (the ambassador from Milan estimated the total cost at 200,000 ducats). The first day featured a procession along the Thames of barges and smaller vessels numbering more than three hundred; on the last day the coronation itself took place.[4] Roxelana was queen by virtue of Suleyman's desire, as no traditional or legal category legitimated such a position. It was her act of charity toward Istanbul that was both proclamation and justification of her queenhood. It endured long after both Anne and she were dead.

The location and timing of her architectural debut announced Roxelana's maverick status. Her foundation was the first in Istanbul donated by and called after a woman. Tradition dictated that it was only after a royal mother graduated from the imperial center together with her son that she acquired the privilege of public patronage. Her projects tended to be located in or near the province where her son served as governor. And, like Hafsa, who began her Manisa project late in Suleyman's princely tenure, she typically initiated foundations only once her son was well established in his public career.

Philanthropic giving, in other words, was a privilege of mature political motherhood, a status Roxelana had yet to achieve by traditional measures. When the planning for the Haseki foundation began, Mehmed, age sixteen, had not yet departed from Istanbul for a provincial governorship; nor was it clear when he would. Roxelana's project was only the latest challenge to established dynastic practices already pushed aside to make way for the concubine's unprecedented ascent to freedom and marriage to the sultan. Moreover, the Haseki was the first foundation constructed in the builder's own name by a member of the current royal generation. At the outset of his reign, Suleyman had built a mosque complex in memory of his father Selim, but nothing since.

Hindsight allows us to see that the Haseki helped to redirect the momentum that drove Suleyman's reign. The execution of Ibrahim in March 1536 signaled a shift in priorities. Instead of lavishing resources on the splendor of the sultan's person, palace, and retinue, political work the grand vizier excelled at, spending would now be conspicuously focused on channeling resources into the public welfare. Roxelana's philanthropic donations were instrumental in Suleyman's efforts to consolidate a stronger sunni Muslim identity after the recent victory over the shi`i Safavids.

ROXELANA DOUBTLESS RECEIVED advice in the choice of a site for her foundation, but the final decision bore her imprint. The neighborhood selected for the mosque was associated with females—it held a weekly market commonly known as Avrat Pazar (women's market). John Sanderson, secretary to the English embassy at the end of the sixteenth century, described it as "the markett place of women, for thether they come to sell thier wourkes and wares."[5] It must have been unusual for the times, for the neighborhood had come to be popularly, if not officially, known as Avrat Pazar.

Writing a century later, the famous traveler Evliya Çelebi noted that people commonly called Roxelana's mosque "Haseki Avrat." Apparently the benefactor, her female beneficiaries, and the neighborhood had

The market at Avrat
Pazar, featuring Roxela-
na's mosque, the column
of Arcadius, and men
and women buying
and selling wares.

become intimately linked in the popular mind.[6] Women of the neighborhood could gain much from the queen's foundation. Males might be the
sole beneficiaries of its madrasa, but women could pray discreetly in the
mosque and line up for the fountain's water and the soup kitchen's dole.
Little girls sometimes attended primary schools, and Roxelana perhaps
encouraged coeducation in hers. She herself had had excellent teachers
and a cohort of fellow students as she struggled to learn, and she might
hope to offer something of the same opportunity to the less fortunate
girls in her adopted neighborhood. They lacked the privilege enjoyed by
daughters of better-off families, who might learn alongside the brothers
for whom private tutors were hired.

Though not what it had been in its Byzantine heyday, the Avrat Pazar
neighborhood boasted a distinguished history. Roxelana's mosque stood

on the long downward slope of Istanbul's seventh hill. It stretched from the fifth-century Byzantine city wall, still the city's defensive bulwark, to the Sea of Marmara. "New Rome," as Constantine I's capital was often called, mirrored the topography of Old Rome and its seven hills. Ottoman royalty chose the pinnacles or upper slopes of the hills for several of their most imposing foundations, both to provide greater visibility on the Istanbul horizon and to offer a panoramic outlook from the precincts of the complex. Later in her life, Roxelana and Suleyman's only daughter Mihrumah would endow a mosque at the peak of the sixth hill.

The Byzantine past echoed vividly in the Haseki complex, for its locale overlapped the old forum of the emperor Arcadius.[7] It was the last of the four great Byzantine city squares that punctuated the Mese (middle way), the principal thoroughfare of Constantinople under both the emperors and then the sultans. Constructed in 403, Arcadius's forum lay on the western branch of the Mese, which forked at the old Forum of the Bull. Suleyman's grandfather Bayezid II had situated his large mosque complex at this juncture. Both forums featured tall columns that signaled their location, each column adorned with a spiral sculptural band depicting the victorious exploits of the forum's founder. Arcadius's son, Theodosius II (builder of the city's outer wall) had placed an equestrian statue of his father atop the enormous column. The statue tumbled in an earthquake in 704, but the column still stood when Roxelana built her complex. In sixteenth-century panoramas drawn by European and Ottoman artists, Arcadius's truncated column marks the location of the Haseki.

When Roxelana adopted the site of the Byzantine forum for her project, she would know some, if not all, of its history. She probably knew something of the Forum of the Bull, as it was the closest of the four to the Old Palace. Originally designed by Constantine I, this forum was remodeled and embellished by Arcadius's father Theodosius I. Devotee of Byzantine imperial monuments, Mehmed the Conqueror commissioned an Italian artist to make drawings of this column's sculptural program.[8] Less reverent than his father toward the antiquities of the empire, Bayezid had the column dismantled and some of its stones placed in the walls of the new public bath he built for his foundation. Bayezid may have had good reason for remaking the old forum, for in late Byzantine times the area had become a refuge for robbers who hid among the wild trees that overran the once open space.[9]

That Roxelana had a strong hand in the early planning of the Haseki is suggested by her close oversight after the complex was completed—she appointed herself for the duration of her lifetime to the executive office of endowment supervisor. The careful detail with which the queen specified the qualifications and daily wages of the staff employed in the complex provides yet further proof of her intimate involvement in the implementation of her foundation.

The complex's Avrat Pazar location raises the question of whether Roxelana had as one of her goals the specific welfare of females. That one of the key administrative positions she specified for her foundation was a female scribe suggests that she did, but we can only surmise her motives.[10] This was an unusual stipulation, since female functionaries of the times were virtually unknown in public institutions. Perhaps the lady secretary's job was to facilitate women's access to the complex's services or to receive their petitions or complaints. It is not hard to imagine a neighborhood woman voicing concern about long lines at the fountain, or asking about her child's eligibility for the primary school, or perhaps seeking the dole from the soup kitchen.

But how was the female staff member of the foundation trained for the job? The one place in the capital that we know had a staff of skilled female scribes was the harem quarters of the imperial palaces. That a trained scribe put to paper Roxelana's own letters is evident from their refined penmanship. Even after the queen mastered enough Turkish to write her own communications, she continued to call on the services of a scribe and doubtless kept at least one on her personal staff. Entrusted with intimate or politically revelatory knowledge, a personal secretary was recognized as a confidential intimate, in Turkish a "scribe of secrets." Some palace staff would also be skilled in bookkeeping and budget balancing as they kept the accounts of high-ranking women's income and expenditures.

Roxelana may have chosen the lady scribe herself or made recommendations to the trustee of her foundation, manager of its operations. Perhaps the woman was a loyal member of her household, just as the trustee was of Suleyman's. Where the lady scribe actually worked is not obvious, whether in the sixteenth-century equivalent of an office at the foundation or out of the palace. If the former, Roxelana could meet directly with her on visits to the complex or summon her to the palace for a check on how things were going.

Whether Roxelana was a forward-looking equal opportunity employer or merely wanted a direct hand in the foundation's business is hard to say—perhaps it was both. But if anyone were to challenge the etiquette of women's employment, it would be Roxelana, who was busy fashioning an innovative career for herself. Her successors—both her own descendants and the queen mothers who built on the model of her career—would continue to show concern for other women, especially those unable to control their fates. Roxelana's great-granddaughter Aisha provided funds to ransom Muslim prisoners of war, with the proviso that female captives be liberated first.[11] At the end of the century, the queen mother Safiye intervened to suspend the sentence of drowning in the Bosphorus imposed on prostitutes by the chief eunuch. As John Sanderson, the English secretary, told the story, Safiye had sighted the execution in process as she strolled in the palace with members of her son's harem. "Shee, taking displeasure, sent word and advised the eunuch Bassa that her sonne [absent on campaign] had left him to govern the citie and not to devoure the women."[12]

BUILDING A MOSQUE complex required considerable advance work. Planning for Roxelana's project began well before the site was cleared for construction: potential locations had to be evaluated, funds had to be assembled to finance the building as well as the upkeep and staffing of the mosque, and architects had to draw up plans. Roxelana's dower might cover the expense of the mosque, but funding a whole complex would require a sizeable infusion from the imperial treasury. Moreover, endowing a major public foundation was an overtly political decision as well as a considerable budgetary expense, one that Suleyman's viziers might conceivably be called to weigh in on. A large endowment, especially in the capital, also touched on the empire's religious policy, since the rules for establishing charitable foundations were spelled out in Islamic law.

Roxelana's complex had two architects. The first, designer of the mosque, was in all probability Alauddin Agha, popularly known as "Persian Ali," chief royal architect until his death the year before construction of the mosque was completed.[13] The second was his successor, Sinan, who became chief royal architect in 1539 and built the charitable complex anchored by the mosque.[14] Consultation with the architects could be carried on through Roxelana's own staff—her steward or perhaps a specially chosen project liaison designated by Suleyman. While such agents would initially scout possible sites for the mosque and its affiliated structures, Roxelana probably visited the Avrat Pazar district herself, traveling in her covered carriage with a suitably impressive retinue. She would want to assure herself that the neighborhood truly needed of the services her endowment would provide. The column of Arcadius doubtless piqued her interest, but perhaps the women's market was the deciding factor.

The Haseki complex did more than provide a set of services to the people of the Avrat Pazar district. The construction of the five component buildings over the course of more than a decade furnished jobs and income to a whole array of laborers, artisans, engineers, and suppliers of materiel. Once the foundation was operational, marketers of different commodities would service its buildings, purveying wood for heating and cooking, oil for lamps, foodstuffs for the soup kitchen, and more. Some 130 staff positions would furnish income to a range of employees, at least some of them drawn from local districts. New shops were likely to open as the neighborhood picked up, and the buzz of activity around the complex surely helped business at the weekly market held at the foot of Arcadius's column.

It is no wonder that foundations famously functioned as nuclei of urban development. Roxelana's would inject vigor into an area of Istanbul that was still recovering from the severe population decline experienced during the last years of the Byzantine regime. Hafsa had demonstrated effective measures to stimulate population growth in Manisa, where she provided incentives to encourage settlement in the vicinity of her mosque—for example, she made lots available for rent or purchase and, with Suleyman's support, offered tax exemptions to those who built houses on them. Roxelana had less urban space at her disposal, but she

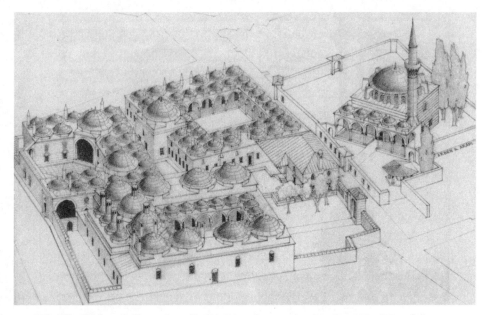

The Haseki foundation at Avrat Pazar. Directly opposite the mosque is the roofed primary school, followed (clockwise) by the soup kitchen, hospital, and madrasa.

did furnish rental units near the complex. The success of the Avrat Pazar initiative would be demonstrated in 1612, when the mosque was expanded to accommodate its enlarged congregation, acquiring a second dome in the process of reconstruction. Composing his history a few decades later, Ibrahim Peçevi remarked that the "exalted mosque" and the various other "good works" of the Haseki Sultan were "known to all humankind."[15]

With the exception of the hospital, all the components of the complex—mosque, madrasa, primary school, soup kitchen—were complete by late 1540. It was now time for Roxelana to draw up the customary charter that established the blueprint for the foundation's operations. Such deeds were long and, in the case of royalty, highly ornamented. Charters typically comprised three principal components: first, the requisite praise of Allah, the Prophet Muhammad, and the reigning sultan, followed by a tribute to the patron of the endowment for his or her beneficent qualities; next, the enumeration of all the sources of income that would fund the maintenance and daily activities of the foundation's institutions; and finally a lengthy description of the foundation's various staff positions, including their essential qualifications and daily wages.[16]

Charter deeds were heavily formulaic in their composition, but Roxelana's voice lent color and vitality to the prose of hers. The queen's influence is especially direct in her repeated insistence on kindness, compassion, and good character as essential qualities of the Haseki's principal personnel. For example, in addition to possessing firm knowledge of the Qur'an and the proper form of its recitation, the primary school's teacher must treat his young pupils as if they were his own children and must not favor one over the other. His apprentice should behave similarly as he took the children through the recitation of their lessons (they were to study the Qur'an, language, and grammar).

The list of requisite qualities for the head of the soup kitchen—its shaykh—was especially long, no doubt because he came into regular daily contact with the Haseki's largest number of patrons. The soup kitchen's mandate encompassed more than the feeding of the hungry, for the Qur'an stipulated several categories of deserving recipients of Muslim giving, including not only "the poor and the indigent" but also members of the religious establishment and those whose employment had to do with the delivery of charitable services.[17] The numerous beneficiaries of Roxelana's soup kitchen included the students of the madrasa, the employees of the foundation, and patients at the hospital (whose meals were tailored to their medical conditions and prepared by a separate staff).

In fact, only twenty-four indigent persons were eligible for regular meals. Each was awarded a patent of eligibility, and the shaykh was warned, when one of the twenty-four died, not to succumb to bribery or influence when reassigning the patent but to apply a kind of poverty standard. However, any leftover foods were to be distributed to the poor on the condition that they consume their portion on the premises.[18]

The shaykh's job requirements were tailored to meet the challenge of managing a large mixed clientele—teachers, doctors, and administrators; students selected for their spiritual and intellectual promise; the mosque's large staff; and the needy. Obviously he needed to be an effective marshal of his guests, but the charter emphasized his moral characteristics, listing them one by one and making clear that the reputation for piety and ethical conduct required of all the complex's employees was especially critical for the office of shaykh. Speaking through her deed, Roxelana urged the same compassion that the teacher must possess: the shaykh must greet his guests with humility, sweet words, and a friendly mien. He must never injure their self-esteem (literally, break their hearts), curse at them, or even act sternly. In other words, the shaykh had to be a man of great forbearance, for disputes over precedence, the amount and quality of the food, and its service undoubtedly broke out from time to time.

The Haseki's madrasa was an institution of a different order from the primary school and the soup kitchen. Madrasas were critical to the empire's ability to generate a homegrown class of experts in religious learning, specialists in Islamic jurisprudence, and qualified judges for cities and towns across Ottoman domains. To lessen reliance on foreign-educated learned men, Mehmed the Conqueror had accelerated the production of local expertise with his endowment of the Semaniye, the famous complex of eight madrasas attached to his mammoth mosque complex.

While Roxelana's madrasa provided a valuable educational service, it had an additional purpose—to bring prestige to the foundation and its founder. Ottoman madrasas were ranked, with those endowed by royalty at the top. The index to a madrasa's standing was the stature of its professor—specifically, the amount of his daily stipend. The Haseki professor would receive fifty silver aspers per day, a handsome sum equivalent to the stipend carried by the Semaniye. The pay was admittedly less than the sixty-asper stipends of subsequent royal madrasas, but it made the professorship of Roxelana's new madrasa a plum opportunity indeed.[19]

The principal qualification of the professor was, unsurprisingly, not his kindliness but his reputation. The charter stipulated that he must be esteemed by the luminaries of his time and superior to his peers, among whom his accomplishments—"his learning and his faith"—should be well known. In turn, presumably to bolster the standing of his profession, he should strive to cast positive light on his superiors by praising their merits. The professor's lofty salary was surpassed within the foundation only by the fifty-five-asper stipend of the royal architect Sinan. The soup kitchen's shaykh earned ten aspers; the schoolteacher, six; the mosque's preacher, ten; its prayer leader, eight; and each of the two callers to prayer, ten. When the hospital was established, the two doctors earned twenty-five and fifteen aspers, respectively.

Naturally, the Haseki professor should also be a good teacher, able to "instruct and enlighten" his charges—highly select scholarship students slated to become judges, jurisprudents, scholars who composed studies of religion and law, and perhaps professors like himself. Here, his ability to "explain challenging intellectual problems and to probe the most intricate of matters" was critical. If madrasa students should choose not to follow such career paths—there were well-known graduates who took government office and might compose histories or political treatises on the side—they would be at the very least well-educated members of the Ottoman intellectual elite.

As for the sixteen students at the madrasa, they had little to complain about, it seems. Each had the luxury of his own room, outfitted with a fireplace and opening onto the madrasa's spacious courtyard. In addition to two free daily meals, they received a daily stipend of two aspers (the same pay the soup kitchen's assistant pantry man received). Some Haseki students may have noted the elegance of the madrasa's architectural adornment. On the other hand, not all may have been happy with their monitor, a student chosen from among them who received a five-asper stipend.

DAILY LIFE AT the Haseki, as Roxelana envisioned it, comes to life in the charter's details. On Fridays and religious holidays, people may have attuned their ears to the summons to prayer, recited on these special days not by the regular callers but by one of three staff persons appointed for "the beauty of their voices." These gifted individuals were also on stand-by to perform the call to funeral prayers. A more material attraction was provided by the soup kitchen's refectory. Its relatively rich menu featured the luxury of meat twice weekly as a supplement to the daily wheat- and rice-based fare. Roxelana's charter also provided a detailed list of special ingredients for more festive dishes, including butter, saffron, chickpeas, honey, plums, apricots, figs, almonds, currants, and mint. It is easy to see why passes were required to distinguish the local deserving poor from petitioners who might flock to the Haseki from other neighborhoods.

Employees of the Haseki Foundation Soup Kitchen

Daily wage per person in aspers
(standard silver coin) follows office

Overseer (the shaykh)	10
Two assistants	2
Purchasing manager	6
Pantry head	4
Assistant	2
Scribe (in charge of paperwork)	4
Scribe (secretary of soup kitchen expenses)	2
Head cook	5
Cook	4
Two assistants	4
Two bakers	8
Two apprentice bakers	2
Dish washer	2
Three hullers and sorters of rice, wheat	2
Porter of meat from butcher	2
Four custodians of plate ware, cutlery, storage jars, etc.	2, 1
Two sweepers	2
Two custodians of wood supply, storeroom	1
Maintenance man	4
Six miscellaneous employees	10.5
Total employees: 36	Total daily wages: 106.5 aspers

Source: Taşkıran, *Hasekinin kitabı*, 48.

While the foundation's users doubtless took care to conduct them-selves with circumspection, the Haseki complex was rarely silent. In warm weather, the voices of children reciting their lessons might waft beyond the foundation's walls from the open porch that served as the schoolhouse's summer classroom. From the mosque echoed a variety of sounds—some, like the call to prayer, were meant to be heard from a distance; others were more subdued. In the intervals between the five daily prayer times, a buzz of voices echoed on a nearly around-the-clock schedule, except for the hours between the last prayer of the day and the dawn prayer of the next. Roxelana's charter provided support for a roster of forty-seven individuals to recite portions of the Qur'an or repeat the Shahada, the succinct Muslim declaration of faith. The most elaborate recitations occurred after the noon prayer, when thirty men in unison each recited a different *juz'*, a thirtieth part of the Qur'an.

All such mosque staff would naturally be trained in recitation techniques. Their small stipends suggest that perhaps they had other occupations or were retired. Roxelana was not unusual in her devotion to prayerfulness, for even Muslims of modest means habitually endowed such recitations, in part to secure the well-being of their souls after death. The Qur'an and Shahada reciters supported by Roxelana's largesse would dedicate their effort to her posthumous spiritual welfare. Those who lingered between prayers might recognize the purpose of the steady hum and offer their own prayer to the mosque's benefactress.

Who made sure that Roxelana's detailed vision for the Haseki was realized, so far at least as human and material resources allowed? The queen's appointees to the two top managerial posts were the principal enactors of her will: the executive supervisor of the foundation, responsible for its financial well-being, and the trustee, responsible for on-the-ground operations. Although Roxelana assigned the office of supervisor to herself for her lifetime, she also named as "honorary" supervisor the chief eunuch of the New Palace.

This honorary supervisor no doubt handled most of the work of overseeing the complex, including scrutiny of the trustee's performance. But Roxelana could communicate with the chief eunuch easily, even face to face. Later in the century, when black eunuchs rose to prominence along with the expansion of the New Palace's harem section, their chief would act as the overseer of all royal foundations. His office controlled a vast budget and by the eighteenth century ranked third in importance after those of the grand vizier and the chief mufti.

As her first trustee, Roxelana appointed one Mehmed son of Abdurrahman. Though not a eunuch, he had ties to the palace (his titles suggest he was a fairly high-ranking member of Suleyman's household).[20] The salary of fifty aspers per day, equal to that of the madrasa professor, was worthy of such a remarkable individual. In the graveyard of the Haseki mosque, one of the most beautiful tombstones belongs to a Mehmed Beg (Sir Mehmed), who died in 1562. He may well have been the foundation's first trustee.[21] Over the centuries, numerous other officials serving the complex would join him in the graveyard, as would both female and male members of their families.[22]

With her characteristic repetitive insistence, the queen required that her trustee be a man of "good and honest morals," forceful enough to carry out his duties as prescribed without breaking a single one of the numerous conditions of his hire. He must, moreover, be recognized as trustworthy.[23] The charter provided the trustee with three staff associates: a scribe, who apparently functioned as an executive secretary; an agent, who oversaw collection of rents on properties dedicated to the foundation; and the lady scribe. The component institutions also had supervisory staff: the soup kitchen and the hospital each had a scribe, the latter an accountant, and the mosque an overseer.

Roxelana's foundation was not without controversy. A story that circulated in Istanbul linked her mosque to the puzzle of her marriage to Suleyman. In his diary, Hans Dernschwam, member of an embassy sent in 1553 by the Hapsburg Archduke Ferdinand, suggested that the favorite may have used her desire for a monument to persuade Suleyman to marry her. "Before his Russian wife was freed by the sultan, she wanted to build and endow a small mosque for which she petitioned the clerics," wrote Dernschwam. "This was not approved by the mufti, who is the Turkish Pope, until she was freed by the sultan."[24] A more scathing account was penned several decades later by George Sandys, an English traveler and poet who journeyed in parts of the Ottoman empire in 1610. Crediting to Roxelana the knowledge that a sultan could not free a concubine without marrying her (otherwise any continued sexual relationship would constitute adultery), Sandys continued, "It being well knowne to the wicked witty Roxolana: who pretending devotion, and desirous for the health, forsooth, of her soule to erect a Temple, with an Hospitall, imparting her mind to the Mufti, was told by him that it would not be acceptable to God, if built by a Bond-woman. Whereupon she put on a habite of a counterfeit sorrow, which possessest the doting Solyman with such a compassion, that he forth-with gave her freedome, that she might pursue her intention."[25]

Sandys's account colored the story of Roxelana's hope for a mosque to conform with the scheming-wife motif present in storytelling traditions around the world. ("The wiles of women" tales were popular among the Ottomans,[26] while Londoners were pondering Lady Macbeth, who first appeared on the stage four years before Sandys's travels were published in 1615.) Still, his version probably contained germs of truth—that Roxelana received sanction from the empire's religiolegal authorities, possibly seeking it on her own initiative, and that her desire to create an endowment was not initially embraced by all. It was, frankly, an audacious idea to build a foundation in Istanbul, for no royal mother had done so before her.

Over the centuries, a complex politics of sex, gender, and power had come to underpin royal benevolence. The patronage of mosques, madrasas, and other charitable institutions was not a straightforward enterprise open to any member of the dynastic household with the wealth to endow them. A fundamental qualification of the builder was that his or her identity be dominated by an intimate connection to the Ottoman dynastic house. The Christian wives of the early sultans were not Ottoman builders since they retained their native dynastic loyalties and their Christian faith. The top convert slave recruits who served the dynasty as commanders, governors, and viziers, however, were eligible builders because their Christian identity was overtly erased and replaced with Islam and affiliation to the House of Osman. Ottoman largesse traveled to remote corners of the empire via the hundreds of foundations built by pashas, viziers, and occasionally prominent eunuchs who had risen to positions of wealth and power. With the reign of Suleyman's grandfather Bayezid II, royal mothers began to join this elite in notable numbers.

Adulthood was a second prerequisite for philanthropic building. But maturity was measured not in years but in terms of the significance of one's political function. When the Ottomans first appeared on the horizon, princes were builders. The madrasa in Nicea endowed by Suleyman, son of the second Ottoman ruler, Orhan, was one of the very first; his father completed it after the prince's premature death in 1357. But as royal sons were gradually subordinated to their father's charisma and authority, it was mothers who provided patronage on behalf of their prince-governor sons. As for princesses, once they ceased marrying foreign princes in the later fifteenth century and began to marry high-ranking Ottoman statesmen, their identity was wholly Ottoman, and they too became builders.

The options for patronage open to top-ranking female slave recruits were trickier to navigate than those open to statesmen. A politics of sexuality defined these women's full adulthood and thereby determined which could be builders. Only in the postsexual phase of a royal mother's life, when she had moved to the provinces with her son, was she considered fully mature, hence eligible to endow a prominent foundation. Roxelana, however, thirty-five or so when construction began on her mosque, could be presumed to still be sleeping with the sultan. The dynasty's formula for assigning political adulthood subordinated her motherhood to her sexual partnership with Suleyman. It took the invention of a new tradition—creating a favorite, then freeing and marrying her—to open the way for the Avrat Pazar mosque.

Roxelana's mosque has come in for a certain amount of debate among art historians. The discussion concerns the architectural judgment that the mosque was insubstantial, lacking in robust design, and unusually conservative, especially in comparison to the subsequent components of the foundation.[27] In other words, such a modest structure, one that looked backward architecturally rather than forward, has been considered unworthy of Roxelana's stature as queen. But this seemingly academic matter in fact casts light on aspects of Roxelana's mind-set when she undertook her building project—her piety, her ambition, and her awareness of the political snares she had constantly to avoid.

The personal and political considerations that occupied Roxelana during the planning of the Haseki can help account for the gap in elegance between the mosque and its neighboring structures. The story told by Dernschwam suggests that Roxelana earnestly dedicated herself to the goal of endowing a mosque, one that fitted her station and personal budget. Perhaps a modest yet pious endeavor is all she initially wished for—Dernschwam noted that, once freed, Roxelana funded the mosque she had built herself.

The simplicity of Roxelana's mosque can be linked to the timing of her building debut and the probability that the then head royal architect Persian Ali designed it. As chief architect, Persian Ali had been in charge of Hafsa's great initiative in Manisa.[28] Completed around 1522, two years after Suleyman's accession, the Manisa complex comprised a mosque, a madrasa, a primary school, a sufi lodge, and a soup kitchen. At the time, Hafsa's was the largest foundation endowed by a royal mother and also the most prestigious. Not one but two minarets flanked the mosque, a prerogative until then reserved to sultans.[29]

Hafsa's foundation was the first step in the ramping up of monumental architecture as a propaganda vehicle for Suleyman's reign. The Ottomans were still working to consolidate the empire's legitimacy as a world power in the eyes of the Muslim east as well as the Christian west. In 1538, while Roxelana was planning her mosque, Suleyman was adding a hospital and a public bath to the Manisa foundation in his mother's name. The timing of these two projects—the sultan's completion of his mother's memorial and his wife's initiation of her first act of public patronage—was unlikely to have been coincidental.

The joint timing helps to explain the unpretentious nature of Roxelana's mosque, since a muted start to her debut project would not draw attention from Suleyman's aggrandizement of the queen mother's monument. The architect would presumably be sensitive to the protocol involved in the two projects, as of course would the royal couple. Once Hafsa's foundation was complete, however, Roxelana was free to pursue her own philanthropic ambitions in a more grandiose fashion, with the support of the new royal architect Sinan and the financial backing of her husband. The Avrat Pazar initiative, with its unassuming mosque but magnanimous public services, could be construed (and justified, if need be) as the favorite's homage in the capital to the queen mother's benevolence in the province.

Roxelana's foundation was not an isolated undertaking. With Suleyman's reign, the clear separation of the philanthropic theater of the sultan from that of royal women came to an end. Suleyman was the architect of a policy that no longer reserved patronage in the capital to males—Ottoman monarchs and their principal statesmen. By the early 1540s, female patronage had emerged in Istanbul as a signature feature of his reign. In addition to his wife, Suleyman's sister Shah Sultan would prove a prolific patron, although of relatively modest projects (over the course of her long lifetime, she endowed three mosques, three dervish lodges, and other smaller structures in three different Istanbul neighborhoods).[30]

And in 1543, Roxelana and Suleyman's only daughter Mihrumah would initiate construction of the elaborate mosque complex that still graces the waterfront of Üsküdar, the Asian suburb that was the departure point for the annual pilgrimage to Mecca. Istanbul's changing skyline was an unambiguous sign of the rising stature of the dynasty's women.

The Istanbul endowments of Roxelana, Shah Sultan, and Mihrumah stretched from the shrine of Eyüp north of the city, to the suburb of Silivri to the west, down along the western city walls and across the city proper, over the Bosphorus straits to Üsküdar. Each of these structures helped to broadcast the dynastic house's piety and benevolence. While the sultan's own immense complex, the Suleymaniye, broke ground in 1548, it was not inaugurated until 1557. In the meanwhile, it was the women of his family who answered the dynasty's mandate to provide for the public welfare. The Haseki complex set the model for large-scale foundations endowed by females in the imperial capital—not only for Suleyman's reign but also for the powerful queen mothers of the future. They would build on the precedents established by this bold and munificent woman.

There was a loser in all this, however: Mahidevran, the mother of Suleyman's eldest son Mustafa. When ground was broken for the Haseki mosque, Mustafa was in his sixth year as governor of Manisa, somewhat early for Mahidevran to consider an endowment of her own. If Suleyman's marriage to Roxelana had widened the gap between the two royal mothers, the Haseki foundation opened a chasm between the provinces and Istanbul. Even if Roxelana had not intended to outshine Mahidevran—the trajectory of her career produced its own compelling need for a mosque—it was as if Suleyman's two families were living in different epochs of history, with different rules of conduct and status. Neither Mahidevran nor Mustafa nor their numerous partisans could have been pleased.

W HAT DID ROXELANA'S foundation mean to her, both politically and personally? Her status as Suleyman's queen now had a literal foundation. The discussion of such a project had perhaps been under way for some time, perhaps as early as the 1520s, when it was obvious that

Roxelana was no ordinary royal concubine. In fact, as a royal mother she had always known that she would be expected to engage in some form of architectural patronage. Responsibility for philanthropic gestures would certainly be an element in the instruction Hafsa imparted to the mothers of her son's children.

With marriage, Roxelana became a wealthy woman. The jewels that Suleyman had heaped on her and her large dower were known to envoys and elite circles and probably to the Istanbul street as well. Were people wondering what this new wife of the sultan, living next to him in the splendidly renovated New Palace, planned to do with her riches? Roxelana's newfound status and wealth were a virtual imperative that she perform a noteworthy act of generosity. It is impossible to exaggerate the profound obligation to give in Ottoman society of Roxelana's day. All over the empire, modest women were making their own charitable donations. In the southeastern Anatolian city of Aintab, for example, Aisha gave her share of a jointly owned house to her local mosque in 1541 (eventually the entire dwelling was donated by its four shareholders). The mosque could then raise funds by renting or selling it.[31]

The urban jewel that was the Haseki dispelled any doubts about the sultan's endorsement of his queen's influence. Even if Roxelana financed the building of the mosque herself, it took Suleyman's support to expand the complex. Rather than directly underwrite the "good works" of his household affiliates—Roxelana included—the sultan made them legal gifts of crown lands, now their private property to dispose of as they wished. Builders generally dedicated these properties to support their endowments. The income generated by the properties, for example tax revenues from villages or customs duties, then went to upkeep and operating costs. Among the most exquisitely rendered documents in the possession of the Topkapı Palace Museum Archive are the property deeds drawn up for Roxelana's use.

These deeds were formally witnessed by the signatures of the empire's top echelon of statesmen. The act of witnessing had the effect of forcing any pasha with reservations about the queen's building privilege to implicate himself in her project, if only on paper. One deed issued in 1539 was signed by the grand vizier, Lutfi Pasha; the other three viziers, Suleyman, Mehmed, and Rustem; the chief justices of

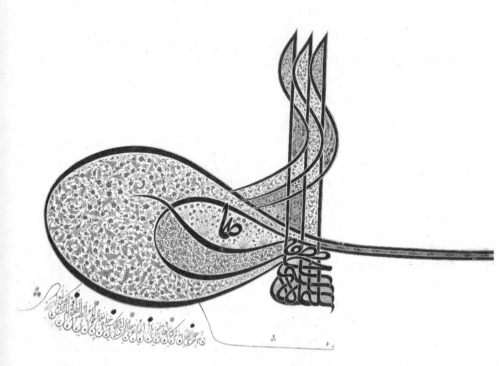

Tughra, or calligraphic emblem, of Suleyman, ca. 1555–1560. Highly decorated and containing the name of the reigning sultan and his father as well as the motto "ever victorious," the *tughra* was drawn at the head of imperial decrees, such as the property deeds for Roxelana's foundations.

Rumelia and Anatolia; the chief finance ministers; and "other states-men."[32] The Haseki foundation charter of 1540 bore an even longer list of distinguished signatures. With the signatories presumably summoned en masse, these signings were highly ceremonial occasions. The deeds themselves were probably kept in the Divan Hall's archive annex or the inner treasury of the New Palace, with access given to the honor-ary eunuch supervisor if he needed to check the details of the charter's provisions.

The magnitude of the queen's first public project would gradually impress itself on other elite cadres in Istanbul. Among them was the cor-poration of top madrasa graduates—the religious, legal, and academic backbone of the sultanate, collectively known as the *ulema*. Since the best jobs, the best students, and the most conducive environments for scholarly research and writing were found in the imperial foundations, endowment of any new royal madrasa was a notable event. Selim I, third sultan to rule from Istanbul, died before he could establish a foundation for his capital. Finally, a new madrasa appeared in the memorial complex Suleyman built for his father, completed in 1522. The *ulema* doubtless prized it and would not have been insensitive to its prime location on the fifth of Istanbul's hills. But no royal madrasa had emerged during the long heyday of Suleyman and Ibrahim's expensive competition with European powers.

If the identity of the newest madrasa founder surprised aspiring professors and hopeful students, the school's opening in 1539 could only have pleased them. The two chief justices recommended to Suleyman the first professor appointed to the Haseki, Molla Bostan. His poverty had impelled him to leave his post as a "twenty-five asper" professor in Bursa and accept the more lucrative but less prestigious job of provincial judge. Molla Bostan must have been grateful that Roxelana's patronage brought him back to the capital, for he went on to become a chief justice himself.[33] Subsequent holders of the Haseki professorship lent it even more stature: Kınalızade Ali, author of an influential Ottoman work on ethics, and Şemseddin Ahmed, son of the renowned jurist and chief mufti Ebu Suud.

Much further afoot, the queen's name and reputation for good works would gradually seep into the villages whose revenues belonged to her foundation by virtue of the property rights she now retained over them. Peasants on royal endowment lands might enjoy certain protections and privileges, such as lighter taxes. Inhabitants of the Bulgarian village of Bobosevo, once part of the holdings of Roxelana's granddaughter Ismihan, still remembered in the 1970s that their ancestors had been "under the veil of a sultana."[34] By the close of her philanthropic career, Roxelana's "veil" would cover much of the empire. Several of her endowments included waterworks, dervish lodges, and hostels for pilgrims, boons to the tired and thirsty traveler who might carry forth news of the benefactress.

But what personal meaning might her foundation have had for Roxelana? Was her first act of philanthropy more than just a performance of royal noblesse oblige? Muslim notables in all parts of the empire were endowing similar, if more modest, foundations in their towns and cities. Let us return to Aintab for our yardstick for provincial notables: in

1548, a prominent family from the wealthy village of Sam completed construction of Aintab's second madrasa and a primary school alongside it. To support the two institutions, they built a large commercial center that brought in 9,600 aspers annually.[35]

Giving was more than just duty, however. From the waters of the Haseki's fountain to the hospital's cures and the mosque's recitations, the benefits to the Avrat Pazar community also counted in God's eyes as Roxelana's good works. Even after her death, she would continue to earn grace, so long as her foundation's services and the prayers for her soul endured. Aisha of Aintab took similar care of her spiritual welfare: shortly after donating her house share to her mosque, she sold a gold bracelet to her stepson for two hundred aspers and used the money to finance the recitation of the Qur'an after her death ("for my soul," she told the judge who registered her bequest).[36] The Qur'an was most likely recited in the mosque to which Aisha contributed.

Roxelana was almost certainly a sincere Muslim believer when she undertook the construction of her mosque. Converted at a young age, she spent her formative years among the Ottomans in the company of other converts, not all of whom had yet learned to forget their Christian origins. Perhaps they never really had to in a world where every Ottoman prince and sultan had a Christian convert mother and a retinue of convert servants, consorts, and statesmen. Moreover, Muslims honored Jesus, recognized in Islam as the prophet Isa, and the nineteenth chapter of the Qur'an is devoted to his mother Maryam, the only woman mentioned by name in the holy book. Mehmed the Conqueror commissioned the Venetian artist Gentile Bellini to paint an image of the Virgin and Child to add to his collection of Christian relics, although his famously orthodox son Bayezid had the assemblage sold to the king of France.[37]

If there were syncretic tendencies in the palace, they were more than balanced by the doctrinal and ritual weight of Islam. The office of the chief mufti, arbiter of the religiolegal practices of the empire, was becoming more influential, and Suleyman was developing a lifelong friendship with the future mufti Ebu Suud. For Roxelana, raising her children within the daily occupation of being Muslim—the five prayers, the calendar of fasting and feasting, the occasional visiting of graves— imbued her life with the culture of Islam. Suleyman's wars might be determined primarily by strategic considerations, but they were hailed as victories for Islamic orthodoxy.

Pursing the career of a pious Muslim benefactor apparently did not require Roxelana to mask her origins: the violent uprooting from her childhood home, the enslavement and transport to Istanbul, the forced allegiance to a new family and a new religion. The plight of slaves apparently remained on her mind (she would later demonstrate compassion toward young slaves who labored on Suleyman's own complex), and her benevolence toward them seems to have inspired others to follow suit. Her trustee Mehmed created an endowment to provide footgear for needy male and female slaves and jugs for children and slaves who carried water from the Haseki fountain. Her own slave woman Nevbahar used materiel left over from the Haseki's construction to renovate a small nearby mosque originally built by Mehmed the Conqueror's head baker; it came to be called after her, noted Ayvansarayı, the eighteenth-century historian of Istanbul's mosques, because she caused it to flourish.[38]

The sensitivity to slaves and females revealed in Roxelana's charitable work probably grew in part from the long years she spent in the Old Palace among other foreign captives and in part from the newfound power she possessed to express public sympathy with those who had suffered in one way or another. Although life in the harem generated jealousies, it must also have aroused compassion, perhaps especially for those who did not advance. If Suleyman's support of his female relatives' charitable endeavors had the tactical goals of improving community services around his empire and undergirding his religious agenda, it greatly facilitated his wife's ability to reward those she deemed worthy of her support.

Suleyman was indeed proving a sixteenth-century feminist of sorts. He did not lack for inspiration—and probably encouragement (he had his mother, his favorite and wife, his daughter, and at least one sister). Although—or perhaps because—another sister, Beyhan, had broken with him over the execution of her husband Ferhad Pasha, Suleyman rallied to support Shah Sultan in her marital difficulties. Shah was wed to the Albanian Lutfi Pasha, grand vizier from 1539 until his dismissal and forced retirement in 1541. The rupture was precipitated by an argument between the couple over Lutfi's harsh punishment of a prostitute, possibly circumcision or the branding of her genitals. In the heat of dispute, the vizier committed an unpardonable act—he struck his princess wife, grounds for their divorce and his banishment. A notable patron of dervishes, Shah continued to observe her sufi piety through further endowments. (Still loyal, Lutfi went on to write a treatise on Ottoman government.)

Heirs to both Christian Byzantine emperors and Islamic Middle Eastern caliphs and sultans, Ottoman monarchs were necessarily great builders, especially in the century following the fall of Constantinople. Suleyman, however, stands out among his ancestors and descendants for elevating his favorite to partner in his philanthropic planning. Would Suleyman and Roxelana recall that the emperor Justinian I—original patron of Hagia Sophia, now the premier Ottoman mosque—had raised the popular entertainer Theodora to empress? He then made her collaborator in his massive building program to glorify Constantinople. Theodora, who died in 548, by the Christian calendar a millennium before the building of the Haseki hospital, was held to be particularly responsible for charities devoted to the relief of poverty.[39]

If they remembered this most famous couple in Byzantine history, Roxelana and Suleyman could not openly emulate them—they were Christian. Moreover, Theodora's reputation was marred by historians who were unfavorable to both her past and her power; the analogy could be tempting to Roxelana's detractors. Muslim history, however, provided a perfect couple to invoke: the legendary Abbasid caliph Harun al-Rashid, made famous in part by his appearance in the tales of *One Thousand and One Nights*, and his wife Zubaida, also legendary as a great philanthropist. To be hailed as "the Zubaida of the times" was the highest accolade a female patron could aspire to. But Roxelana could not yet claim the comparison, for the Haseki, however grand, was only her first charitable undertaking. It would take an elaborate philanthropic establishment in Jerusalem some years later to earn her the honor.

POLITICS

11

FAMILY MATTERS

FOLLOWING THE IRANIAN campaign of 1534–1535, Roxelana and Suleyman began to spend more time in the winter palace at Adrianople (today's Edirne). Late November 1540 marked the start of one such sojourn. Roxelana's transit to Adrianople was apparently an occasion for display—she traveled in "marvelous pomp," accompanied by a substantial volume of belongings. A few days later, Suleyman himself set out. This brief item of news about the movements of the "grand seigneur" and "la souldane," his wife, made its way to the French king Francis via the ambassadorial grapevine. The news was contained in a letter dispatched by the Venetian envoy in Istanbul, Alvise Badoer, to Guillaume Pellicier, bishop of Montpellier and Francis's trusted ambassador in Venice. Pellicier passed it on to his king.[1]

Adrianople was a bustling city some three days' journey northwest of Istanbul. The ancient city became the de facto capital of the Ottomans, displacing Bursa once they controlled enough territory in the Balkans to put a safe distance between the city and the frontier with Europe. When Istanbul became the imperial center after 1453, both former capitals retained a special status. Adrianople was filled with mosques and churches, bazaars, schools, and a palace expanded by Mehmed the Conqueror.[2] Framed by three rivers—the Maritza, the Tundzha, and the Arda—it enjoyed a pastoral setting and a milder climate than Istanbul. It was a favorite of sultans like Suleyman who were devoted to the hunt. The gateway to Ottoman Europe, Adrianople was the launching pad for military campaigns that followed major arteries traversing the Balkan domains of the sultans. Between 1535 and 1548, Suleyman would fight his wars exclusively with European powers, making the city an even more attractive second home for the royal couple.

Custom did not permit Ottoman writers to expose the sultan's wife to view. But Roxelana was newsworthy, and Europeans did not hold back. The Genoese bank official who recounted her wedding festivities and the ambassadors like Badoer who tracked her public movements tacitly acknowledged that she was becoming a vehicle for showing off the dynasty's wealth and power. The long baggage train that followed her to Adrianople was a key element in the desired effect, although spectators along the route would have to imagine the queen within her handsome carriage and the luxuries carried on the backs of the mules and camels. Suleyman's favorite Ibrahim, that walking treasury of riches who dazzled the eyes of the masses as well as the envoys of sovereigns, was gone. Married, dowered, living royally in the New Palace, and now with a mosque to affirm her status, Suleyman's favorite was increasingly recognizable as a bearer of the empire's glamour.

During her travels between the two capitals, Roxelana was conspicuously invisible, so to speak. Glimpses of her carriage and her retinue were likely to be all the more tantalizing now that she was recognized as a political force as well as the object of Suleyman's extraordinary attentions. Europeans were free to record what they observed, but one combs the writings of Ottomans in vain, at least during Suleyman's reign, to find mention of her journeys or even of a work as public as the Avrat Pazar foundation. This scant historical record can leave the impression that Roxelana's life had reached a plateau where her sole preoccupation was her family.

On the contrary, Roxelana's marriage in 1534 gradually opened the door to significant, if unpublicized, exercise of power: the move into the New Palace, physical locus of sovereign authority, and then her first philanthropic project. We find Roxelana in this period seizing obvious opportunities as well as unexpected moments that looked open to manipulation, either for her own advantage or that of her husband's reign. The decade following the marriage was in fact the phase of Roxelana's career during which she consolidated a political foundation that set the stage for future queen mothers of the dynasty. But Roxelana did not build her role as queen at the cost of her domestic responsibilities. The integrity of the family she shared with Suleyman continued to be her topmost charge, a political office on its own, even if it was at the same time the source of her stability and contentment.

IT HAD BEEN a long while since the Ottoman public had a queen to watch. Nearly two centuries earlier, a daunting precedent was set by Theodora, daughter of the Byzantine emperor John VI Kantakuzenos. This usurper-emperor sought the military support of Orhan, the second Ottoman ruler, and rewarded him with Theodora's hand. In 1346, the Byzantine court bid farewell to the princess with great ceremony in Selymbria (Silivri), on the northern coast of the Sea of Marmara, where a delegation of prominent Ottomans received her. A convoy of thirty ships transported the wedding party to the southern shore of the Marmara, whence a large cavalry division escorted the Greek princess overland to Bursa, then the capital.[3] It was a late marriage for Orhan, in his fifties at the time. Theodora became the mother of his youngest son, Halil.

The political benefits of such ritualized journeys were many, among them the pride and perhaps even sense of community experienced by participants and observers alike. Sitti Khatun, princess of the southeastern Anatolian Dulkadir dynasty, was perhaps the last Ottoman bride to arrive in pomp, to be wed in 1450 to Mehmed, the future "Conqueror." Women were regularly key figures in the recruitment of brides—in this case, the wife of an Ottoman governor inspected the five Dulkadir daughters and singled out Sitti, while the party sent to escort her to Adrianople included a cohort of distinguished women, including Mehmed's governess.[4] Sitti apparently entered Adrianople atop an elephant.

Five decades earlier, the new capital Adrianople had received the ill-fated Serbian princess Oliviera Despina. She was the daughter of Lazar Hrebeljanović, who would be famously martyred in 1389, fighting the Ottomans at Kosovo. A Serbian partisan made an equally legendary battlefield martyr of Murad I, Orhan's son. In her last journey as royal consort Oliviera followed her husband Bayezid I in 1402 into his disastrous Anatolian captivity at the hands of Timur. The Turko-Mongol conqueror allegedly humiliated Oliviera (and the sultan) by forcing her to perform menial tasks. In his *Tamburlaine the Great*, first presented in 1590, the English playwright Christopher Marlowe dramatized this unendurable shame, rendering it the cause of Bayezid's alleged suicide. Released in 1403 after Bayezid's death, Oliviera spent the rest of her life in the courts of her siblings.

Roxelana was not the first Christian-born consort to be charged with malign influence on the Ottoman dynasty. Foreign wives furnished a scapegoat to fit the Ottoman penchant for blaming the flaws of a powerful personage on corruption by associates. Historians of the early Ottomans held Oliviera responsible for Bayezid's love of the royal high life. "Drinking parties and banquets were held, the infidel girl came and wine cups were passed around," wrote the populist historian Aşıkpaşazade around 1500. Addressing the dynasty's first ruler (and perhaps reproaching him for enlisting Christians in his battles), he continued, "What do you expect, Osman? Many things happened because of the infidels."[5] Too much carousing, one could infer, had contributed to Bayezid's defeat by Timur.

Oliviera's fate was still talked about in Roxelana's time. Writing in 1555, the Hapsburg ambassador Ogier Ghiselin de Busbecq noted that Suleyman had broken the custom of his ancestors by taking a legal wife and explained why sultans after Bayezid I took only concubines as their consorts—Oliviera's shame was so great that it discouraged future sultans from contracting interdynastic marriages.[6] Busbecq's account wasn't wholly correct, for the sultans in fact kept making marriages into the 1460s. They did, however, cease producing children with their foreign wives. The practice of reproducing the Ottoman royal line exclusively with slave concubines in fact took root around the start of the fifteenth century. The primary rationale was not that foreign princesses could bring shame on the House of Osman but that children born of mixed royal matches might only be half loyal to the dynasty. Şükrullah, who completed his history of the Ottomans in 1465, claimed that all the sons of Bayezid I, who ruled from 1389 until 1402, had concubine mothers.[7] If so, the Serbian Oliviera was one of the first childless wives.

The Ruthenian Roxelana perhaps had a particular interest in tales of women from the edges of the Slavic-speaking world. Another Serbian queen, one Roxelana likely knew of, was Mara Branković, wife of Murad II and stepmother of Mehmed the Conqueror. The story told about her by statesman George Sphrantzes in his history of the fall of

Byzantium offers vivid testimony of another childless wife. When Murad died in 1451 and the Byzantines considered newly widowed Mara for marriage to the emperor Constantine XI Paleologos, they hesitated, thinking she was not a virgin. But Sphrantzes dismissed the objection on the grounds that "she, it is generally believed, did not sleep with [the sultan]." The marriage did not proceed, however. "The sultan's widow had made a vow to God and decided that if He freed her from the house of her late husband she would not remarry for the rest of her life, but would remain in His service," wrote Sphrantzes.[8] Mara chose wisely, as Constantinople fell two years later. The former queen went on to a distinguished career as a patron of monasteries and intermediary between foreign powers and the court of her stepson Mehmed, toward which she remained well disposed.

By the mid-fifteenth century, opportunities for queen watching had come to an end. As royal spouses disappeared, concubine mothers rose to prominence. They doubtless drew crowds of onlookers as they traveled in state to and from provincial capitals, but it was their sons, princes of the blood, who bore the thrilling (and to some enthralling) majesty of royalty. The newfound ceremonial prominence of Suleyman's queen clearly did not sit well with all, but the political as well as entertainment value of her public presence was a resource to exploit.

If Roxelana's carriage and its train had become a locally recognized attraction, outside Adrianople and Istanbul the favorite was scarcely more than a name. Roxelana was a much less traveled royal mother than her fellow consort Mahidevran. Mustafa's mother had made the Manisa-Istanbul circuit at least twice, and soon she would undertake the rare journey to the eastern frontier with her son. Luigi Bassano's assertion that Diyarbakır, where Mustafa was posted in 1541, was thirty days from Istanbul seems an underestimate. Still, even thirty stops across the highly varied geography of the empire offered an encyclopedic lesson in its many populations, resources, and needs to the maybe future sultan and queen mother.[9]

Roxelana's regal progresses to and from Adrianople were testament to her unique stature, but they must also have sparked conversations about why she was not moving in a different direction—into Anatolia, with her eldest son. In 1540, Mehmed was nineteen years old. His half brother, Mustafa, had been eighteen in 1533 when Suleyman dispatched him to his post in Manisa. Suleyman himself had been only fifteen when his father Selim secured an assignment to Crimean Caffa for his son's first princely governorate. But Mehmed still lived in the capital with his parents and siblings.

It was not that Mehmed was unready. He and his younger brother Selim had accompanied their father on the 1537 campaign that ultimately abandoned its goal of seizing Naples (the French failed to attack Milan, their role in the joint maneuver). The decision to withdraw and leave the initiative to Hayreddin Pasha—the famous corsair turned Ottoman admiral—was perhaps as instructive to a prince as victory would have been, as it taught conservation of resources. The following year, Mehmed most likely participated in the sultan's successful campaign to punish the vassal ruler of Moldavia and strengthen the empire's hold on this Danubian territory.

The Anatolian provinces, used to the presence of multiple princes, eagerly awaited the arrival of Suleyman's sons. The cities of Konya, Kütahya, and Amasya rivaled Manisa as traditional seats of princely governorates. But since the bloodbath of 1513 that eliminated Selim's rival brothers and their sons, all of them at posts in Anatolia, only Manisa had been graced by a royal presence—Suleyman for eight years (three of which he spent as deputy sovereign in Istanbul or Adrianople) and now Mustafa, for the past seven years. The public was well aware that the sultan had three more eligible sons—Mehmed, Selim, and Bayezid—the two elder of whom were now plausible candidates for governorships.

There is no overt evidence of popular frustration with Mehmed's confinement to the capital. Nor was there open criticism of either Suleyman or Roxelana for this apparent breach of dynastic tradition. But there surely was impatient speculation. The organization of a new household for a prince-governor and his mother provided jobs for many. Aspirants for these positions were aware that newly enthroned sultans frequently filled top posts with men and women who had caught their eye during their princely apprenticeship. Females as well as males would be drafted for Mehmed's household when the time came, although in lesser numbers and with a smaller range of specializations. There must have been many hopefuls among the Janissaries, cavalrymen, New Palace pages in training, scribes, cooks, groomsmen, and falconers (Ibrahim had got his start as Prince Suleyman's chief falconer). Which of his trusted statesmen would Suleyman choose for the honorable post of *lala*, the tutor-guardian who would ensure the prince's compliance with his father's orders? What promising young women would Roxelana select to fill out the new harem?

The great question on everyone's mind, however, was almost certainly Roxelana herself. In 1540, she was around thirty-seven years old, the age at which a woman's oldest children would typically have established their own families. Would the sultan's beloved, who had now been with him for twenty years, finally leave his bed to take up the traditional role of the royal mother? Could a queen become the mistress of a small harem establishment in the provinces? Conversely, could Roxelana bear to let Mehmed go without her? She had learned to be Ottoman together with her firstborn, with all the privileges and privations that entailed.

THE FAMILY HAD indeed been growing up. When Roxelana wrote to Suleyman during the 1537 campaign, it was apparently with mixed feelings of pride and apprehension that she included "thousands and thousands of prayers and praises" for Mehmed and Selim.[10] Selim turned thirteen during the march from Istanbul to the Adriatic coast, somewhat young to experience a complex war plan that anticipated the invasion of Italy. Perhaps he was included on the grounds that Mehmed would be there to encourage and counsel him. This was Mehmed's first combat experience too, but for Selim his elder brother stood somewhere between sibling and parent. Selim would address Mehmed not by name but respectfully as "older brother," as Mehmed and his younger siblings would address Mustafa. The brothers, however, shared the honor of joining their father in the most important of his duties as sultan, the defense of his realm. Both were now semipublic figures, but Mehmed enjoyed the status of Roxelana's senior son.

Mehmed's education in the military arts, religion, and history had begun at an early age. In an undated letter to his father, most likely during Suleyman's German offensive of 1532, the prince demonstrated

Suleyman in his private library conversing with Mehmed. The sultan sits at his writing table, with books stacked behind him. Palace officials and dwarves accompany father and son. Talikizade, *Şemâilnâme-i Âl-i Osmân.*

that his political education was also advancing.[11] Reporting on the state of the city, Mehmed noted that all was well despite the outbreak of fire twelve times since Suleyman's departure; alarms had been sounded and the fires put out rapidly. Much of the letter, however, was taken up with enthusiastic and effusive thanks to Suleyman for reinstating one Pilak Mustafa, a statesman of some standing whom others had apparently criticized. "You have obliged your servant [i.e., himself] by accepting the request I humbly made to you and making your slave Pilak Mustafa governor," wrote the prince. "I beseech my sultan not to listen to what people say and [then] cast your longtime men to the wayside." Suleyman had granted Pilak Mustafa high office: the admiralty in 1521, when the naval campaign for Rhodes was on the horizon, and the governorate of Damascus in 1531. But the pasha was dismissed from the latter post in the year of his appointment, perhaps as a consequence of the bad-mouthing. Pilak chose to go into retirement in Cairo.[12] His return to favor apparently owed something to the prince.

Mehmed's education also included the arts of language. In addition to the requisite Arabic, Persian, and literary Ottoman Turkish, his reading competency may have extended to Italian, probably with the assistance of a tutor. "My sultan, I am reading the second volume of Menavin," the prince noted in the same letter.[13] In 1504, corsairs had captured Giovanni Antonio Menavino, son of a Genoese merchant, while on a voyage with his father. The boy found himself in Istanbul, enslaved, serving as a page to Suleyman's grandfather and then father. Bayezid II, who spoke some Italian, had scrutinized the twelve-year-old personally on his entry into the New Palace. By his own account, Menavino learned to read and write Turkish alongside the sultan's grandchildren.[14] Escaping in 1514, he went on to write *The Five Books of the Laws, Religion, and Life of the Turks*, published in 1548 in Venice but perhaps completed earlier. How a copy of the manuscript made its way to the palace library is not clear. Perhaps the grand vizier Ibrahim requested it, although Menavino himself possibly sent a presentation copy to Suleyman. The two may have crossed paths when the prince served as deputy ruler in Istanbul in 1512 and 1513.

A pattern was emerging in the careers of Roxelana and Suleyman's sons, with Mehmed and Selim a senior pair to the junior pair of Bayezid and Cihangir. The two eldest brothers had shared the great circumcision festival of 1530 with each other and Mustafa. Now Bayezid and Cihangir's turn had come. The circumcision of the two youngest was celebrated in November 1539, when Bayezid was around twelve and Cihangir eight. It was a time of general good feeling and delight, noted Solakzade Mehmed in his history, due to the latest victories in the Mediterranean and Europe. Suleyman had taken a hunting holiday near Bursa earlier that fall. Roxelana, however, was presumably occupied with readying her children for their public debut.

The program of receptions and popular entertainments for this gala event was similar to that of 1530 and the venue—the Hippodrome—the same. The festivities, directed by the grand vizier Lutfi Pasha, were a week shorter, however (Ibrahim Peçevi thought Lutfi negligent; Solakzade deemed him efficient).[15] The imperial budget may have been temporarily tight; much money had gone into the navy in recent years, and in 1538 the Ottomans had seen simultaneous combat on three fronts (the Mediterranean, central Europe, and the Indian Ocean). Perhaps it was also a deliberate scaling back of the lavish expenditure that had been so characteristic of the Ibrahim years.

On the other hand, the empire was more powerful now, a reality seemingly underlined by the royal menagerie on display, with its lions, tigers, leopards, panthers, lynx, wolves, and awe-inducing giraffes. More nations sent their ambassadors this time—Venice of course, but also France, the Austrian Hapsburgs, and Hungary (or what remained of the kingdom after Ferdinand and Suleyman had staked claims to large parts of it). Once again, the Persian Safavids were not invited.

MORE SIGNIFICANT IN this family extravaganza than the circumcision was the marriage of Mihrumah, Roxelana and Suleyman's second child and only daughter. Despite the fact that a princess's marriage was the equivalent of a prince's departure for his provincial governorship—marking entry into the adult world—the event went unmentioned in the

Portrait of Mihrumah, second half of the sixteenth century. The Latin caption reads, "Cameria daughter of the emperor Suleyman, wife of Rustem Pasha."

eyewitness histories of the times composed by Celalzade Mustafa, Suleyman's private secretary, and Lutfi Pasha himself.[16] This silence reflected in part the usual Ottoman reticence in speaking of royal women
but also the fact that the signing of the marriage contract and the wedding celebrations were both private affairs, held within the walls of the
palace. Town criers would circulate, however, calling out invitations to
the celebrations. The crowds enjoying the clowns and fire artists were
surely aware that it was a princess's marriage in part that drew them to
the Hippodrome.

Mihrumah was seventeen, an appropriate age for a young woman to
wed. The groom was Rustem, a man of Croatian origin and a product of
the elite training system. Rustem was a successful statesman who had
worked his way up through the ranks. From service to Suleyman in the
Privy Chamber, he had progressed to the prestigious office of master of
the horse in the New Palace outer service. Then, in 1533, he graduated to
public office. After serving as governor of Diyarbakır, he earned a promotion in 1538 to the governorship of Anatolia (second only to European
Rumelia in the hierarchy of Ottoman provincial offices). In preparation
for the marriage, Suleyman appointed Rustem third vizier.

Becoming a vizier of the Divan required that Rustem reside in Istanbul, at least in peacetime. Mihrumah was thus relieved of starting
married life in a provincial capital, as several of Suleyman's sisters had
done. Here we might suspect the hand of Roxelana, for Mihrumah would
be the first of the children to leave her care. But Suleyman too, affectionate by nature, may have been loath to allow his only daughter to depart
from the family circle as his sons inevitably would. Mihrumah may also
have put her own foot down and insisted on a marriage that would keep
her in the capital. Very much her mother's daughter, she would prove
spirited and strong willed.

It was her parents' duty to ensure the best match possible for Mihrumah. The ideal union for a princess was not simply a compatible one that
would keep her happy, however. It would also be a political alliance, and
the royal parents would choose Rustem primarily because they judged
him to possess the talents for superior long-term service to the dynastic family. Princesses around the world—and their husbands too—had
always been destined for marriages that operated as strategic tools for

creating or strengthening political bonds. The Ottoman sultans ceased betrothing their daughters and sons to foreign royalty in part because the empire had subjugated the very powers it once needed as allies. But it was also partly because the slave service nobility had demonstrated itself to be the most effective and, more important, the most loyal force for consolidating the dynasty's control of its conquered lands.

The union of Mihrumah and Rustem was in all probability not a love match. Rustem was twice Mihrumah's age. Apparently he was not Roxelana's first choice for her daughter. The queen had her eye instead on the handsome governor of Cairo, or so reported the Venetian ambassador Bernardo Navagero (according to whom Rustem was not handsome—he was small and red faced). Rustem, however, allegedly foiled her plan by inducing the royal doctor Moshe Hamon to say that the governor was afflicted with syphilis.[17]

Mihrumah herself may have been reluctant to accept the older statesman. She had theoretical grounds on which to resist, for Islamic law gave a virgin the right to refuse the husband selected by her guardian (typically the father). While the sultans tended to ignore the law when political exigency trumped legal propriety, in this case religious duty and affection most likely conspired to gain her parents' respect for Mihrumah's sentiments. But in the end, it seems, the princess consented, possibly after a good deal of persuasion or pressure. Like all children of the dynastic family, Mihrumah was called upon to sacrifice personal desire to public duty.

The safety valve for an Ottoman princess who could not marry for love was the privilege of divorcing her husband should the union turn out badly. Two years after Mihrumah's wedding, Suleyman's sister Shah Sultan divorced her grand vizier husband Lutfi for his physical violence toward her. Fatma, another of Selim I's daughters, was already divorced from her first husband, governor of the Mediterranean province of Antalya, who showed more interest in males than in his new wife.[18] The young but eloquent Fatma complained by letter to her father, pleading to return home: "I have fallen into the hands of someone who treats me worse than a dog. Since coming here, I have not had a single hour of happiness, I have donned none of my robes. I have risen from the dead like a widow. . . . My sultan, dear father, let

me wear cloth of coarse wool instead of the cloth of rudeness, let me
eat barley bread, just let me live in your shadow."[19] Fatma's bad luck
would continue when her second husband was executed, but she is
said to have found happiness with a third, the eunuch Ibrahim Pasha.
Kindness and consideration apparently triumphed.

Mihrumah probably knew something of her aunt Fatma's first marriage, but she could not help knowing that her aunt Beyhan was deeply
angry over the execution of her husband Ferhad. But alongside these
cautionary tales, Mihrumah perhaps entertained romantic notions of
love. Hers was an unusual upbringing for the daughter of a sultan. She
was accustomed to a father who composed copious love poetry and a
mother who suffered during his absences. Her parents were a monogamous couple whose relationship was clearly cemented by mutual devotion. And because Suleyman broke with the dynasty's reproductive
protocols, Mihrumah had four full brothers, to three of whom she was
older sister. Indeed, if her father had conformed to protocol, Mihrumah
would never have been born at all, for Roxelana would have departed
from his bed once she gave birth to Mehmed.

BY THE ISLAMIC calendar, Suleyman turned forty in August 1533, the
age of full male maturity. Fittingly, this was also the year he dispatched
Mustafa, his eldest son, to take up the post of governor. With a prince
in the field and a wealth of pashas capable of leading the Ottoman army
(as Ibrahim had for most of the Safavid war), Suleyman could well have
delegated command to his grand viziers. He had already proven himself
a great warrior in the mode of his ancestors, and war was not the only
domain of rule that called for the sovereign's attention. But there was
also the unceasing summons to compete with the extraordinary cast of
powerful European monarchs who had been born within twelve years of
each other: Henry VIII in 1491, Francis I and Suleyman himself in 1494,
Charles V in 1500, and his brother Ferdinand in 1503.

Roxelana had presumably learned to manage during Suleyman's absences. After the death in 1534 of his mother Hafsa, a seasoned politician, she became his most trusted family correspondent. When Mehmed,
now also an epistolary confidant of his father, joined him on campaign,

Roxelana was his sole correspondent. The political acumen her letters began to exhibit tallied with the increasing authority she had accrued over the years. Among Roxelana's few surviving letters to Suleyman, one she composed in the summer of 1537 suggests that she no longer needed a harem scribe to translate her thoughts into tolerable Turkish, although she continued to employ one for drafting the final copy. Suleyman was doubtless pleased to receive his wife's own words of affection but less so her candid assessment of conditions in the capital.

The epidemic-ridden city was suffering once again. "There is still sickness, although it is not as bad as before," Roxelana reported. "Our saintly ones say that it will pass when the autumn leaves fall." She reassured Suleyman that all would be well by his return. Meanwhile, however, there was a different problem—Istanbul was not receiving enough bulletins from the front, although earlier news of a victory had, as Roxelana put it, "brought the whole world from darkness into the light of God's mercy."[20]

The city's inhabitants were inclined in wartime to believe that no news was bad news, and in 1537 they turned out to be partly right. Roxelana could warn the sultan of the dangerous consequences of poor communications more outspokenly than his pasha lieutenant in the capital was likely to. "I ask you, I beg you, to send news quickly, very quickly, because—and I swear I am not lying—no courier has come for the last week or two," she pleaded. "The whole world is clamoring, all kinds of rumors are circulating." This was not just a pretext for eliciting a letter from her absent beloved. "Don't think it is just for myself that I am asking."

Although this was a shorter, more succinct letter than Roxelana's earlier missives, she still devoted the first half to multiple expressions of yearning for Suleyman's return and prayer to God to hasten the moment she could bow to the ground before him. She is drowning in the sea of longing; she can no longer tell night from day; she is the nightingale whose song goes unheard. Her condition is direr than that of Majnun and Farhad (great heroes of legend who went mad from loving women who eluded them). Then, after an abrupt "Amin" (amen), Roxelana gets down to business. Suleyman has "lifted her up from the ground" by dispatching a gift of 5,000 gold florins. "Now my sultan, what great trouble you went to," she writes. "A single hair of your beard is worth more to me than one hundred thousand florins." If Roxelana's playful voice and fondness for colorful images had shown here and there before, now they dominated her personal missives.

Roxelana also had homelier reasons for wanting Suleyman to write more frequent letters—namely, the practicalities of supervising the family she shared with him. For one thing, sojourns in Adrianople were becoming routine and required significant advanced planning. Between fall 1537 and spring 1541, the winter palace was Suleyman's capital for all or part of three winters, and possibly all four. These were no mere seasonal holidays, for much of the court moved with the sultan, as did foreign ambassadors resident in Istanbul—the French ambassador Antonio Rincon, for instance, reported by dispatch from Adrianople in the winter of 1538–1539.[21] Roxelana would want to know if her husband planned for the whole family to join him there or wanted any of them, even her, to remain in Istanbul. The Adrianople palace needed to be informed about domestic arrangements, as did the two palaces in Istanbul. And Roxelana would want to keep up with news of the Haseki foundation's progress. The famous Ottoman *chiaus*, royal messengers and heralds, could handle rapid communications, but if the queen was to leave Istanbul for the winter, she had responsibilities that would require arrangements in her absence.

One of these was the Old Palace. Although her principal residence was now the New Palace, whose harem division she was actively developing, the Old Palace still maintained quarters for the queen. How frequently she spent time there, or for how long, is unknown, although Suleyman's absences at war and on hunting expeditions were likely opportunities for prolonged stays in her old home. It is unclear if any of her five children were still living there or if all had moved with their mother to the New Palace in or after 1534.

If the younger boys, Cihangir and Bayezid, remained in their original home to take advantage of the care and education that was its stock in trade, their mother's visits were probably quite frequent. Cihangir's back possibly required continued medical attention, either for treatment of discomfort or additional procedures like the one Roxelana had described by letter to Suleyman during the eastern war. If so, the Old Palace, with a hospital geared toward treating women and children, was the more appropriate home. But the child, still young, perhaps insisted on being with his mother rather than remaining with his governess.

With the death of the queen mother Hafsa, supervision of Old Palace affairs had passed into Roxelana's hands. While the day-to-day management of both residences was the business of experienced female administrators and eunuch officials, Roxelana was the authority for major decisions and serious problems. Irresolvable tensions, budgetary difficulties, important promotions or dismissals—such matters required executive input. Her principal collaborator in the Old Palace was the Lady Steward, the institution's majordomo. In the 1555 register of palace stipends, hers is a lofty 150 silver aspers, three times that of Ali Agha, the highest-paid palace eunuch official (45 aspers).[22]

One aspect of Old Palace management that surely engaged Roxelana was the training of the young slave recruits. The queen could hardly help but have an interest in them. Her own enslavement was the transforming event of her life, and she had progressed through the same processes of molding that they were now undergoing. Moreover, Roxelana's close access to Old Palace personnel put her in an excellent position to select talented females and eunuchs for transfer to her own service in the New Palace. And when the time came, both harems would be resources for the princely households of her sons.

As Bassano noted, Roxelana made a practice of marrying her "damsels" to graduates of the male palace training regime, and she may well have made alliances for other women in the Old Palace school. One wonders if Mehmed's championing of Pilak Mustafa Pasha had to do with such a harem connection. According to Peçevi, the pasha's marital alliance had boosted his career: "After he rose to the rank of governor general, he was married to a lady named Shahhuban, one of the slave women of the imperial harem, and because of this he was graced with the vizierate."[23] Peçevi was wrong about the vizierate (Pilak never rose that far), but the marriage did precede Pilak's promotion to Damascus governor, a prestigious post that controlled all of the Levant except the Aleppo region. Here, Hafsa rather than Roxelana may have taken the lead in matching Shahhuban to Pilak Mustafa, but Roxelana succeeded the queen mother as the ultimate matchmaker.

When Suleyman and Roxelana arranged compatible matches for imperial slaves, they could be said to act in loco parentis. Their motivations were not wholly unlike the ideals (if not always the realities) of typical Ottoman slave-owning families: to create capable servants, eventually free them, but remain associated with them after manumission. Ottoman practice, underpinned by Islamic law, set ground rules for a servitude that was ideally only temporary, since many Muslims considered freeing a slave a good deed in the eyes of God. Pilak Mustafa had been manumitted when he graduated from New Palace training to public office (his first post had been a junior governorship in Ioannina on the Adriatic coast); Shahhuban was manumitted when she left the palace to marry him.

Freedom was not absolute, however. For one thing, the master or mistress retained certain inheritance claims over the estate of a former slave at his or her death. This was a rule stretched by the sultans to justify government seizure of the rich estates of deceased pashas. On the positive side, Muslim masters and mistresses were enjoined to ease the passage of manumitted slaves into free adult society, most immediately by helping them establish a marital household. Mutual ties of patronage and clientage could continue to connect the two families, and freed persons frequently worked for their former owners, with the result that their households tended to move in tandem with the social status of their former owners.

The ruling regime exemplified this phenomenon. Former imperial slaves would raise their own slaves, inculcating in them the culture of loyalty and service that they themselves had absorbed during their training. The domestic establishment of the lady Shahhuban and the statesman Pilak Mustafa was only one of countless satellites propagated by the sultanate. Having gradually dispossessed the Turkish and Christian-convert lords who fought beside them in their early conquests, the sultans created a kind of proxy nobility to take their place. Roxelana's job was to ensure the availability of Old Palace graduates as talented as she herself.

On January 27, 1541, the Old Palace was struck by a disaster about which we know surprisingly little: a devastating fire nearly burned it to the ground. A week earlier, the same fire had consumed some houses in Pera, the Istanbul district where most Europeans lived. It also destroyed the Pera arsenal, presumably in an explosion, taking with it forty men working there.[24] Pellicier, the French ambassador in Venice, informed King Francis that restoring the women's palace would require no less than 400,000 scudos. (According to current exchange rates that Bassano claimed Jewish bankers and Christians employed, this sum equaled 20 million aspers.)[25] Apparently, the Old Palace had its own treasury, for Pellicier added that the riches guarded in its stronghold were gone: 1 million gold pieces and half that value in jewels and other items. Roxelana lost "the best and most beautiful of what she possessed," noted the ambassador. Strongila, the Jewish agent who served Hafsa and then Roxelana, lost a large cache of gold coins.[26]

Pellicier commented that the fire was so fierce that the women of the palace had survived only by "throwing themselves into the public square," where they had to remain for some time. For most of them, their flight would be their first exposure to the public without the protection of a carriage or a phalanx of eunuchs since entering palace service. They must have suffered enormously, doubly wounded by the loss of both their home and the seclusion that defined them. Perhaps they were rescued, or at least sheltered, by local Janissary troops, the primary firefighting corps of the capital, whose barracks were luckily not far from the Old Palace.

At the time of the fire Roxelana was safely in Adrianople with Suleyman. If any of their children were home in the Old Palace, the first response of their caregivers was undoubtedly to shepherd them to safety. In any event, Roxelana most likely returned to Istanbul immediately, perhaps for the sake of the children but certainly to assist with the daunting task of housing the hundreds of displaced palace residents. For his part, Suleyman declared the hunting season shortened and came back to Istanbul, although he made this decision in part to organize the dispatch of his navy into the Mediterranean.[27] The Old Palace was eventually restored, though at what actual cost is unknown. In an ironic twist of fate, it was as if the fire symbolically finalized Roxelana's departure for a larger stage in her queenhood.

12

HOME AND ABROAD

I N NOVEMBER 1542, the judge of Manisa instructed one of his scribes to make an entry in the city's official register, an "annal" that marked a significant date in the provincial capital's history: "Sultan Mehmed son of Sultan Suleyman arrived in Manisa and acceded to the throne. Recorded on 3 Sha`ban 949 [12 November 1542]. In the same year Sultan Selim acceded to the throne in Karaman [at Konya]." A year and a half before Mehmed and Selim arrived in Anatolia, the Manisa register had noted the transfer of Suleyman's eldest son to his new post in Amasya: "Sultan Mustafa set out from Manisa for Amasya. Recorded on 17 C.E. 21 Safer 948 [June 16, 1541]."[1]

There were now three princes in the field, two of them Roxelana's sons. All three were stationed in Anatolian cities with distinguished historical pedigrees. Each was a post worthy of a prince, since each had formerly been the capital of a royal domain conquered by one of Suleyman's ancestors. Indeed, many cities of Anatolia reached far back into time, for the peninsula had been a veritable cradle of civilization and a stage upon which empires had displaced one another. The imperial lineage of the region included the Hittites, the Greeks, the Persians, the Armenians, the Romans (who called the three cities Magnesia, Amaseia, and Iconium), and finally the Byzantines. Then the Turkish invasion from the east that began in the later eleventh century opened the way to waves of migration from Central Asia and Iran that gradually rendered Anatolia predominantly Muslim and Turkish. Once Mehmed and Selim were settled, Roxelana would set out to visit her sons, traveling for the first time across this antique land.

Located on the south-central Anatolian plain, Konya was arguably the most prestigious of the three cities, at least in terms of its recent history. It had been the capital of the Anatolian Seljuks, who dominated the twelfth and much of the thirteenth centuries as sultans of the first major Turkish-ruled state in the region. The Seljuk polity was sophisticated and wealthy, more interested in trade and connoisseurship than conquest. "What a miracle is this Seljuk architecture!" wrote the art historian Bernard Berenson in 1958. "It has an elegance, a distinction of design and a subtle delicacy of ornament surpassing any other known to me since French Gothic at its best."[2]

After an interlude of domination by the Mongol khans of Iran, Konya passed under the rule of the Karaman dynasty, one of the most formidable of the dozen or so Turkish princely houses that competed in post-Seljuk Anatolia (the House of Osman was originally one of the smallest). The chronic and vicious Karaman-Ottoman wars finally came to an end when Mehmed II, "the Conqueror," took Konya in 1467 and his son Bayezid annexed the entire principality twenty years later. Among the several prominent Islamic monuments of the city was the tomb of the great thirteenth-century sufi master Jalal al-Din Rumi. Over time the venerated shrine expanded, reaching its present configuration with endowments by Bayezid II and Suleyman, but it was under Karamanid patronage that it gained its iconic green-tiled dome. In both its political and religious legacy, Konya was a distinguished post for Selim.

Amasya, Mustafa's new post in north-central Anatolia, sat in the valley cut by the River Iris (Green River in Turkish). Its rock hills still contain tombs of the Pontic kings who ruled over the southern shores of the Black Sea; Strabo, geographer of the ancient world, was born in the city in 64 B.C.E. under one of the last of these kings. Like Konya, Amasya had been governed by the Seljuks and then the Mongols (the city's museum features eight mummified Mongols, testimony to the far-flung presence of Chinggis Khan's successors). When Amasya fell to Mehmed the Conqueror in 1461, he appointed Bayezid, at fifteen his eldest son, its governor. During his twenty-year tenure there, the prince upheld the city's long-standing reputation for learning; poets and sufi dervishes were particular beneficiaries of his largesse. Partly with Bayezid's generous patronage, the Amasya poet Mihri Hatun became the first Ottoman female whose work is known to have been compiled in a *divan*, or collection.[3]

Manisa, Mehmed's post, had an equally venerable and colorful history, passing through the hands of the Greeks, the Persians, and the

Romans. Alexander the Great settled a Macedonian colony in this western Anatolian city, and the Roman emperor Tiberius rebuilt it when a massive earthquake in 17 C.E. ravaged much of Anatolia. Làtin Christian Crusaders from the west encountered resistance in Manisa, first from the Orthodox Christian Byzantines and then from the Muslim Seljuks. During the era of Turkish principalities, the House of Saruhan, another rival of the House of Osman, governed Manisa for almost a century. Saruhan too ultimately gave way to the Ottomans, in 1410.

Everywhere that Ottoman princes went in Anatolia, remnants of past eras were a tangible reminder that their empire was only the most recent in a long succession of illustrious but vanished kingdoms. Mehmed the Conqueror allegedly gave voice to this inevitability as he surveyed the ruins of Constantinople following his army's sacking of the city. According to legend the young sultan recited a Persian couplet that mused on the transience of victory by imagining the deserted palaces of an ancient Iranian king and his principal adversary: "The spider is curtain-bearer in the palace of Chosroes, the owl sounds the relief in the castle of Afrasiyab."[4]

THE ARRIVAL OF Roxelana and Suleyman's sons must have delighted the citizens of Manisa and Konya. The presence of princes and their households not only conferred distinction but also stimulated local economies. Their mothers might add philanthropic foundations, to the benefit of both the city's infrastructure and its skyline. The downside, potentially ruinous but less frequent, was the risk of collateral damage if combat were to break out among royal sons. In 1513, for example, Suleyman's father Selim had besieged his brother Korkud in Manisa. Once he had concluded his bloody march to the throne, neither Konya nor Amasya saw a resident prince for three decades. Manisa's palace, on the other hand, had recently housed two—Suleyman for eight years and then, after a gap of thirteen years, Mustafa also for eight years.

When Mustafa moved to Amasya in 1541, he was twenty-six. The Amasya palace would find itself accommodating a princely household that had grown larger since Mustafa left Istanbul for Manisa in 1533. Mahidevran, who traveled with her son as head of his domestic court, would acquire more attendants, and Mustafa's harem had doubtless expanded, adding more concubines and staff. This prince was not a prolific reproducer, however, at least in comparison to his half brother Selim, who would have three concubines pregnant not long after his arrival in Konya.

Mehmed was twenty-one when he became governor of Manisa, older than the age at which Ottoman princes had typically embarked on their public careers. Selim was probably nineteen by the time he arrived in Konya. Neither had his mother with him. Unlike Mustafa, the brothers lacked one of the two most important counselors who traditionally accompanied prince-governors into the field (the other was the *lala*, the tutor-guardian appointed by their father). Of these two, only the loyalty of a prince's mother was undivided, for *lalas* had been known to desert charges whose fortunes looked bleak.

But Roxelana's loyalty could never be undivided. This novel dilemma emerged the moment the sultan's favorite gave birth to a second son, breaking the rule that a concubine could have only one male child, the better to devote herself to his career. Repeated debate between Suleyman and Roxelana must have ensued over the years before they came to the decision that the queen would remain in Istanbul with her husband while her sons took up their provincial duties. It is impossible to know the content of their deliberations—possibly that the role designed for her could not survive isolation in the provinces or that her large family made it infeasible. Cihangir was only twelve or so when Mehmed and Selim left Istanbul, still growing and coping with his handicapped body; Mihrumah might become a new mother at any minute; and Bayezid, fifteen, still needed polish. This was to say nothing of the royal couple's need and desire for each other.

The second-level consideration—which son should have his mother with him—had perhaps also been broached: Should Roxelana go with her eldest, the option closest to Ottoman tradition, or was it wiser to accompany Selim, less mature, farther away from the capital, and in a palace that would need to be started up again? In the end, she went with neither. The decision to abandon the traditional career of the concubine mother was the last of several ruptures in the politics of dynastic reproduction that Roxelana and Suleyman had brought about.

Mehmed's relatively late graduation to provincial service may have stemmed in part from the wait for Selim to mature. The princes had been paired in their preparation for public service, apparently so that they might depart simultaneously for the provinces. It is not inconceivable that this plan was intended to deflect attention from their mother's failure to go with one or the other. Parental affection cannot be ruled out, however—a desire to prolong the time when the whole family could be together. Roxelana and Suleyman had created that rare thing: a nuclear family. Both knew that its innocence would be irretrievably lost once the two princes entered the contest for the succession, to be pitted against Mustafa and each other. If this period in Roxelana's life appears relatively serene on the surface, the politicization of her children's lives could only undermine the illusion of security.

THE DYNASTIC FAMILY'S personal arrangements were never free from the shifting constellations of military competition and international diplomacy that dominated the era. In the late 1530s and early 1540s, these complexities were no doubt also a factor in Mehmed's postponed graduation to his public career. Given the increasing intricacies of great power rivalries, Suleyman may have intentionally prolonged his sons' training. This was not time wasted, however, for Mehmed and Selim were gaining an education in keeping peace as well as making war. The two princes would graduate to governorships at a point in their father's reign when conquest was not as feasible as it had been in the past. For her part, their mother was getting used to the princes' transition from her tutelage to their father's profession.

Suleyman and his commanders had been scoring victories ever since the failed siege of Vienna in 1529. In 1532, the Ottomans rallied with the so-called German campaign, which succeeded tactically in inducing Ferdinand, archduke of Austria, to sue for a truce and accept payment of a hefty annual tribute to the sultanate. The campaign's larger political agenda, however, was to demonstrate to Ferdinand's older brother, the Holy Roman Emperor Charles V, that Suleyman was as great a world conqueror as he, if not greater (the sultan liked to deny Charles his empire by referring to him merely as "the king of Spain"). It was during this campaign that Suleyman asserted his claim to the mantle of ancient Rome by famously parading under Roman-style ceremonial arches with the elaborate four-tiered crown. The diadem conveyed the message that only the combined forces represented by the three tiers of the pope's crown and the single one of Charles's could match Suleyman's prestige and power.

In the east, the long campaign of 1534–1535 against the Safavids in Iran had ended in victory, with immense gains both territorially and ideologically. The Ottomans were now free, temporarily at least, to concentrate once again on their European front. Mehmed and probably Selim had participated in the inconclusive Italian offensive of 1537, but 1538 was a banner year. The princes again accompanied their father, this time on a successful foray into Moldavia that subdued a restless vassal and led to the annexation of the northwestern Black Sea coast. The brothers would be instructed in the long-range value of this accomplishment: the Ottoman military system north of the Black Sea was now rounded out and linked more closely to another vassal, the powerful khan of the Crimean Tatars.

In September of the same year, the Ottoman navy scored a resounding victory over a "Holy League" comprising the pope (who issued the call to arms), Venice, Genoa, and the forces of Charles V. The battle was a clash of two great soldiers of fortune: the Genoese *condottiero* Andrea Doria, Charles's commander, versus the Mediterranean corsair-turned-admiral of the Ottomans, Hayreddin Barbarossa. The latter's momentous triumph secured Ottoman dominance of the Mediterranean for almost thirty years. The trifecta of 1538 was completed when the governor-general of Egypt, Hadım (the eunuch) Suleyman, sailed into the Indian Ocean with a fleet of seventy-two ships, seizing Aden on the way, besieging a Portuguese fortress on the Indian coast (unsuccessfully), and organizing Yemen as an Ottoman province on the way home.[5]

Then, while apparently at the top of his game, Suleyman took a break from fighting for two and a half years. The hiatus was due in part to military exhaustion and the financial drain of combat on three fronts. As for Roxelana, she probably uttered aloud her usual "thousands and thousands of prayers" for Suleyman to stay home and rest. And to an extent, he did—the palaces of Adrianople and Bursa bustled with extended hunting seasons. Perhaps Roxelana also pointed out that she had been holding down the fort for too many years. It was a time for attention to family—Mihrumah's marriage and the circumcision festival for Bayezid and Cihangir. Mehmed and Selim, on the other hand, might reasonably be showing impatience to move on to their public careers. Not until June 1541 would the older princes set out to war again when their father left Istanbul to deal with trouble in Hungary. They would return victorious.

The Austrian historian Joseph von Hammer thought that the years from 1540 to 1547 were the apogee of Suleyman's power.[6] His evaluation was based primarily on the military successes that the Ottomans enjoyed in Europe and on the seas. Other historians looking at other geographies and using other measures—Anatolia, the restless mood of Ottoman subjects—have spoken of a spreading malaise and discontent in the first years of the decade.[7] The Safavid challenge figured prominently in the disposition of the times.

Although Suleyman's reign saw the occasional trial and execution of a schismatic or messianic figure who challenged his legitimacy, the persecution of Safavid partisans and suspected sympathizers was systematic, taking a particular toll on communities, especially in central and eastern Anatolia. There was little overt violence, as Safavid sympathizers were typically prosecuted through the courts and often punished or exiled on trumped-up charges.[8] It was something of a witch hunt.

It was no coincidence that stricter moral regulations were imposed by Suleyman's new law code, issued around 1540. New mandates required stepped-up surveillance, with local people sometimes coerced to report on one another.[9] Partisans of the shah were known as "red-heads" for the color of their headgear, and the whole episode is reminiscent of the "red scare" of the McCarthy era in American history, down to accusations of sexual misconduct leveled against suspected sympathizers.[10]

These two views of the times—stress and success—are not necessarily incompatible. Political and social strains were to a degree inevitable in an empire as large as Suleyman and his father had made it. Learning how to manage was one reason princes apprenticed in the provinces. Suleyman's own training took place in the highly disturbed aftermath of his grandfather Bayezid II's death. But Roxelana may have been reluctant to send her sons into Anatolia despite appreciation that her fundamental duty, shared with her husband, was to prepare them for rulership. We do not know if she disagreed with Suleyman over the issue. If she did, perhaps a combination of factors convinced her that the optimal time had arrived: the decisive Ottoman victory in Hungary in 1541, the fact that both princes had participated in it, and the danger to their reputations of any further delay.

EUROPE HAD NOT been quiescent after the losses of 1538. Suleyman and his viziers were occupied with a series of truces that were the intricate aftermath of the recent conflicts. The greatest diplomatic tensions in Europe were the rivalries between the Spanish Hapsburgs and France in the west and the Austrian Hapsburgs and the Ottomans in central Europe; the one constant for the Ottomans in these years was their alliance with the French king Francis. Along with Suleyman's viziers and his older sons, Roxelana was an important sounding board for the sultan, what with her own by now substantial knowledge of foreign affairs.

Diplomacy could be a more drawn-out affair than a military campaign, in large part because the sultan's empire had become a major player in the discordant concert of Europe. On the Ottoman side, much of the negotiation process was handled by the viziers, who enjoyed the collaboration of the empire's multilingual dragoman translators. An audience with the sultan himself was a coveted if potentially tense event. When the French alliance threatened to collapse in one of those brief moments of French-Spanish rapprochement—Charles V was welcomed in Paris in 1540—Suleyman reacted in anger to this apparent deception, allegedly threatening to kill the French ambassador Antonio Rincon. But the skilled envoy was so conciliatory that instead he achieved his full agenda. Rincon even received a robe of honor from the sultan, who declared that once again he trusted France.[11] Alas, the poor man was murdered by bandits on his return to Istanbul from a sojourn in Venice.[12]

Meanwhile, trouble was brewing at the other end of the empire. In September 1540 Pellicier, the French ambassador in Venice, informed Francis that several of the sultan's "lords and captains" in the eastern frontier region had risen up for lack of pay. Nothing remained of the grand seigneur's conquests, he added, except Baghdad. The rebels had defected to the Sophy ("the Sufi," as Europeans tended to refer to the shah of Iran—the Safavids had got their start in the fourteenth century as a sufi brotherhood). Pellicier followed up in October with the comment that "the Sophy business" troubled Suleyman more than ever, in part because Hungary was flaring up once again.[13] War on two fronts— or rather two conflicts that called for the sultan's personal leadership— was a threat that the Ottomans assiduously tried to avoid.

Predictably, both Roxelana's and Mahidevran's sons were enlisted in their father's military strategies. Suleyman moved to Adrianople in November 1540, taking 3,000 Janissaries and Mehmed and Selim with him (Roxelana had already gone ahead). The Thracian capital was an advantageous location should the sultan need to leave in haste to protect Ottoman interests in Hungary. Finally, in June 1541, Suleyman set out for the western frontier. Making war in Hungary was no easy matter, as the army could literally bog down in terrain vulnerable to flooding. Moreover, this was a critical showdown with the Hapsburgs.[14] Mehmed and Selim accompanied their father, their reputation for standing by him in combat already established; Ferdinand countered by bringing his two sons to the confrontation.[15] Once again Roxelana represented the royal family in the capital, now with Bayezid at her side.

It was in this same month Suleyman ordered Mustafa's transfer from Manisa to Amasya. Although historians often interpret the reassignment as banishment disguised, it was clearly a key element in Suleyman's war plans to protect his eastern front as he himself went west. The prince's transfer was a promotion in fiscal terms—Suleyman granted him a generous boost in stipend.[16] Pellicier reported that another 3,000 Janissaries marched east with Mustafa.[17] From Amasya, he was temporarily dispatched to southeastern Diyarbakır to counter any opportunistic Safavid moves. As the young commander moved from one end of Anatolia to the other, spectators in cities, towns, and villages could angle to catch a glimpse of the prince, his mother, and their retinues.

The dispatch of Mustafa to the eastern front was a pointed announcement to the shah that the next Ottoman generation was formidable. It also let European powers know not to count on an Iranian thrust that would distract Ottoman attention from their western front. In the end, the Safavids did not pursue an offensive, having informed themselves of Suleyman's treaties and his firm liaison with France.[18] The princes proved to be a huge asset to the security and welfare of the whole empire. If Suleyman was its living embodiment, "God's shadow on earth," his adult sons radiated the charisma and might of the dynasty that Allah had blessed with good fortune. Displaying the royal sons to the public was an effective strategy for impressing both domestic and international publics. No one knew which one would succeed his father; therefore all would receive careful scrutiny.

EVEN THE PRINCESS Mihrumah was being drawn into international affairs, if only indirectly. Her husband Rustem, who became second vizier in 1541, was Suleyman's top officer during the Hungarian campaign of that year. (The eunuch Suleyman, the victor at Aden and now grand vizier, was stationed in Anatolia.) As chief campaign vizier, Rustem was responsible for aiding the sultan in sorting out the tricky situation that had developed in Hungary. In July 1540 John Zapolya, king of Hungary, governor of Transylvania, and vassal to Suleyman, had died unexpectedly, leaving his two-week-old son and heir and the infant's mother Isabella vulnerable to the pretensions of Ferdinand. The archduke, who controlled western Hungary, lost no time in occupying Buda and seizing the crown. Suleyman responded by expelling him and putting central Hungary under direct Ottoman rule. Vassal rule in this critical frontier zone had proven too risky.

It was Rustem who parlayed with the young queen during negotiations that eventually secured the surrender of her son's claim to the Hungarian crown in exchange for the regency of Transylvania. Isabella was no minor princess, for she was the eldest child of Sigismund I, "the Old," king of Poland and grand duke of Lithuania and a monarch the Ottomans strove in this period to maintain as an ally. It was again Rustem who took Isabella's side when Suleyman considered removing her and Zapolya's little heir to Istanbul, where they would be political hostages, however distinguished. Isabella's rich gifts to Mihrumah had allegedly helped win over the avaricious vizier.[19]

In February 1542, Isabella sent an envoy to Suleyman, technically her overlord, to petition for the freedom of two Hungarian noblemen taken prisoner during the 1541 campaign and now held in the fortress of the Seven Towers in Istanbul.[20] The sultan answered with a firm refusal, and the two men eventually died in captivity. However, Isabella received another response to the affair—a letter from Roxelana, carried by a royal courier. In it, the queen announced that she was taking Isabella and her son under her protection. Isabella should trust Roxelana's authority, as the Ottoman queen did hers: "I am the person most close to the emperor [Suleyman] and you are the true queen of the kingdom of Hungary."[21]

Roxelana's letter, put into Latin, opened with a specifically female salutation: *Filia charissima* (dearest daughter). "We are both born from one mother, Eve," it continued, "and we are both created from the same matter." Pointing to Isabella's allegiance to Suleyman and tacitly underlining the young queen's indebtedness to the sultanate, Roxelana wrote, "And we both serve the same man." Unspoken but doubtless understood by both women was their shared responsibility as mothers of young heirs in uncertain political environments.[22]

Isabella's response to this invitation to a female diplomatic alliance is unknown, but Roxelana pursued the connection through Isabella to the Polish monarchy. In a further act of female solidarity (and Ottoman partisanship), she let it be known that she supported the wishes of Isabella's mother Bona Sforza in the matter of the marriage of her son, Isabella's younger brother Sigismund Augustus. In an age that teemed with remarkable kings and queens, Bona was an unusually fascinating woman. Princess of the powerful House of Sforza, which had ruled Milan for almost three-quarters of a century, Bona became Sigismund the Old's second wife in 1518.[23] She brought with her to Cracow an entourage that introduced Renaissance learning and artistry, and she soon established herself as a political force. Roxelana had come to the Ottomans with no such cultural or political credentials, but she could recognize another queen with ambitions to make her mark on her adopted country.

The marriage of Sigismund Augustus was of critical interest to the Ottomans, for the Polish prince had long been betrothed to Elizabeth, daughter of Archduke Ferdinand, Suleyman's prime rival in central Europe. Bona's strong opposition to this Hapsburg alliance opened another door to Roxelana's diplomatic ambitions. Now she sent an envoy, one Said Beg, to Cracow, who arrived on January 28, 1543. (The envoy, Polish by origin, had been captured as a child in 1498 during the siege of his family's castle in Ruthenia; converted to Islam, he was noticed by Ibrahim Pasha and assigned to Polish embassies.)[24]

The pretext for Said Beg's journey was a personal matter that had put him on the outs with the grand vizier Suleyman, but he was apparently traveling at Roxelana's behest: she wished to assure Bona that she would back her in the matter of the marriage. Roxelana doubtless spoke for both herself and Suleyman, who appears to have appreciated, if tacitly, the utility of this emerging network of queens. He was planning a new campaign for the spring to confront Ferdinand yet again over Hungary.

Bona reacted to Roxelana's message immediately. She called for a secret council on January 29. Discussion of the optimal policy toward the Ottomans and the status of Isabella in Transylvania ensued. Opinions were divided, but a consensus emerged that hopes should not be placed on the outcome of the anticipated confrontation between the feuding monarchs (Ferdinand was favored by some attending the council) and that pacts with "the Turks" should not be overly trusted. Sigismund the Old, partisan of his son's engagement, opined that the Turkish emperor was "faithful neither to us nor anybody else." To this cautious stance, Bona apparently responded that she would rather Isabella and her boy die or fall into Turkish captivity than for Ferdinand to acquire Hungary in a peaceful manner (through the marital alliance of Austria and Poland).[25]

Bona remained a partisan of the Ottomans. Two years later, for instance, the peace with Istanbul came under threat when Lithuanian Cossacks attacked Ochakov, the Ottoman-controlled Black Sea fortress city, and Polish collusion was suspected. Bona was instrumental in heading off a potential rupture by arranging a settlement between Polish and Ottoman commanders stationed in the region. Queen Bona eventually returned to Milan, having broken with her son over his second marriage. (The unfortunate Elizabeth died just two years after the 1543 wedding, and the prince married his very unpopular mistress.) Roxelana and Suleyman, however, kept up the habitual Ottoman cultivation of peace with Poland. When Sigismund Augustus inherited the throne in 1548, a hearty round of correspondence would ensue that included the princess Mihrumah, who persisted in the distaff approach to diplomacy that her mother had put into action.

ROXELANA NEVER FORGOT her domestic concerns. Once Mehmed and Selim settled into their respective governorships, she lost no time in visiting them. In the summer of 1543, she traveled to both Konya and Manisa. Another annal was entered in the Manisa registry: "While the fortune-favored sovereign was on his way to the fortress of Pécs, the Haseki Sultan together with their majesties the sultans came to Konya, and from there to Bozdağ, and from there to Manisa. In the year 950."[26] The "sultans" were presumably Cihangir and Mihrumah; Bayezid had succeeded his elder brothers as his father's confederate at war.[27] The attraction of Bozdağ (ash-brown mountain) was that it offered one of those retreats to summer pastureland so beloved of the Ottomans. Probable site of the luxurious palace belonging to the ruler of Aydin, one of the Turkish principalities absorbed by the Ottomans, Bozdağ was celebrated in poetry.[28]

Desire on both sides for a family reunion doubtless motivated the journey. Whether deliberate or not, however, the visits to Konya and Manisa were also a political maneuver. Finally, Suleyman's queen could compensate for her permanent residence in the capital by showing herself in the great Anatolian heartland. Like her journeys to Adrianople, her progresses to and from her sons' posts were a perfect opportunity to display her majesty. Roxelana could also display interest in and a concern for the empire's subjects during the frequent stops in cities and towns along the route. On a more personal level, Roxelana had found a solution to the loneliness so often described in her letters when her menfolk were absent (Suleyman was now back on the Austrian frontier bolstering Ottoman control of Hungary).

Roxelana had last seen Mehmed and Selim at their gubernatorial inauguration as provincial governors. Like Mustafa in 1533, Mehmed and then Selim had been formally invested by their father and members of the Imperial Council in a traditional ceremony where Suleyman bestowed on each a banner and a drum, old symbols of Ottoman sovereignty.[29] Their mother may have observed their investiture from the Tower of Justice, perhaps accompanied by Mihrumah and the boys' childhood governesses. The loyal service of the latter was intended to be lifelong, and in some ways each knew her prince better than his mother did. In fact, these women may well have left Istanbul as members of Mehmed's and Selim's households. Prudent counselors and loyal to the queen (who would otherwise replace them), the governesses were logical stand-ins for Roxelana.

The only records documenting Roxelana's journeys into Anatolia are the bare-bones Manisa annals, leaving us with a frustrating silence on the whole new world that the queen was about to absorb. With her trips back and forth to the Adrianople palace, Roxelana had become familiar with a rural panorama of small towns and villages. But Anatolia presented a larger and more variegated canvas as well as a radically new historical geography.

Roxelana's first business in Konya was to reunite with Selim and to rest from the long journey. Then would follow formal receptions—it was only proper that the prince introduce his mother and siblings to his household. Selim would later be known for his proclivity to drink, but these festivities were more restrained, taking place as they did in the Konya palace's domestic quarters. While only Cihangir would be introduced to the military and administrative wings of the palace compound, Roxelana would doubtless confer with the prince's *lala*. Although Selim carried on direct correspondence with his father via couriers, Suleyman no doubt sent instructions with his wife, possibly including an inspection of the palace and orders for any necessary alterations and additions.

Like any son with visiting relatives, Selim would show off the venerable city of which he was now in charge. Konya was a museum of delights for a maturing maven of architecture like Roxelana. Seljuk and Karaman princes and Mongol governors had strewn the city with mosques and madrasas. The queen's first foray into the city proper was doubtless to the shrine of Jalal al-Din Rumi, the great mystic who was said to have welcomed Christians and Jews as well as Muslims to his teaching circles.

From a strict religious perspective, praying at the graves of the dead was tantamount to breaking the cardinal precept of Muslim faith—that there is no god but Allah. But deeply embedded in the spiritual practice of many Ottoman subjects was the habit of visiting the shrines and tombs of revered persons to offer prayers for the deceased and often to seek their intercession. Such was the power of the dead that people of one faith might venerate the saint of another and shrines might acquire new spiritual identities through the sheer volume of pilgrims.[30] Before exiting the capital to go to war, sultans themselves routinely stopped at the tombs of their ancestors and at the shrine of the martyr-saint Eyüb north of the city walls. Eyüb, a companion of the Prophet Muhammad, allegedly fell in 670 during the first attempt of Arab Muslims to capture Constantinople. According to Ottoman legend, the tomb of Eyüb was miraculously discovered during Mehmed II's siege of the city; the Byzantines had allegedly prayed at the grave for rain in times of drought.

With the rise of the Safavid "Sophys," their adoption of shi`i Islam, and especially the fervent religiosity fostered by the shah himself, it behooved the Ottomans to sanction veneration of sufi saints that might offset their suppression of Safavid sympathies. On the other hand, Suleyman and his advisers were also now pursuing a policy of stricter sunni Islamic conformity. The proliferation of mosques in Istanbul and elsewhere in the late 1530s and 1540s was one manifestation. But while royal women built mosques, they also shouldered responsibility for propagating acceptable modes of sufi spirituality. Konya was an excellent environment for Roxelana to apprentice herself in the diverse expressions of Islamic faith.

So great was the saintly charisma of Rumi that Suleyman could hardly have failed to visit his tomb during the army's halt in Konya on

"Dance of the Mevlevi dervishes." Seventeenth-century European drawing.

its 1534 march eastward.[31] Sixteen years later Selim would do his part by
supervising the construction of a mosque that his father endowed adjacent to the shrine.[32] When she paid her own respects in 1543, the queen
and her children were perhaps honored with a performance of the ritual
distinguishing the sufi order that Rumi's followers established after his
death. Known as the Mevleviye, the order took its name from the title
of respect accorded to the revered mystic—*Mevlana* (our lord). The familiar moniker "whirling dervishes" tends to mask the deeply spiritual
liturgy that informed the circular movement of Mevlevi celebrants and
its mournful instrumental accompaniment.

The spiritual biography of Rumi emphasized his many female patrons, among them donors and builders.[33] So when Roxelana visited the
sanctuary, its custodians were perhaps eager to inform their sultan's beloved queen that a foreign princess, Tamar of Georgia, had built Rumi's
original mausoleum.[34] Daughter and granddaughter of queens, better
known to history as Gurji Khatun (the Georgian lady), Tamar was the
wife of the Anatolian Seljuk sultan Kaykhusraw II. His love for her was
so great, it was said, that he insisted she be represented on Seljuk coins
as the sun shining above the lion that stood for himself. Allowed to retain her Christian faith as well as her priests and her icons, Gurji nevertheless became one of Rumi's most fervent followers and, partly through
his influence, a convert to Islam.[35]

Gurji's Christian predisposition persisted however, at least in a legend according to which she commissioned a portrait of the mystic, a
very un-Islamic act. But the artist could not capture a likeness of Rumi,
who had said of himself, "How devoid of color and sign I am!" Gurji
allegedly carried the twenty images that resulted wherever she went.[36]
Whether this story was still told in Roxelana's day is not certain, but it
is tempting to imagine the affinity the Ottoman queen might have felt,
despite her lack of noble pedigree, with this Christian-born consort and
beloved of a Muslim monarch who became a convert to, and patron of,
Islam.

Perhaps Roxelana also discussed with the shrine keepers her own
plans to channel more of her philanthropic work toward the support of
sufi piety. Across the years, she would provide support to several sufi
shaykhs by endowing mosques and/or dervish lodges in Istanbul and

Anatolia where they could preach and train disciples.[37] Shah Sultan, Suleyman's sister and a patron of sufis, doubtless provided inspiration to Roxelana. Shah's career as a sufi devotee began early, in Ioannina in western Greece, where she accompanied her husband Lutfi to his post as governor. There the princess became a lifelong follower of the popular sufi order of the Halvetis. Returning to Istanbul when Lutfi was promoted to vizier, Shah built the first of three mosques with an attached dervish lodge, this one for her Ioannina shaykh.[38] The next lodge-mosque was dedicated in 1537 to the Halveti shaykh Merkez Efendi, who had recently become Shah's new spiritual guide; the last was a memorial foundation erected after his death in 1552.

Merkez Efendi was already known to Roxelana, at least by reputation. His affiliation with the royal family had begun when his own sufi master sent him to Manisa in response to Hafsa's request for a shaykh to serve the dervish lodge she endowed as part of her foundation.[39] There the prince Suleyman first met Merkez Efendi. Later the sultan would appoint him "army shaykh" to the 1537 campaign, during which Mehmed and Selim would become acquainted with him. Shah Sultan was also present on this campaign, traveling in her husband's suite, and it was during the couple's return to Istanbul that she allegedly attached herself to the shaykh— his miraculous appearance on the road rescued wife and husband from bandits.[40] As for Roxelana, she would later do her part to honor the mystic by endowing a lodge-mosque in the Anatolian village of his birth.

DEPARTING FROM KONYA with Mihrumah and Cihangir, Roxelana made her way northwest toward Bozdağ, where Mehmed presumably met her and her traveling court. She was already familiar with the Ottoman passion for summer upland retreats, having accompanied Suleyman and the children on hunting trips to Bursa. First capital of the nascent empire, Bursa lay on the slope of the famous Uludağ (great mountain), to the ancient Greeks one of the several peaks called Olympus. As for the ash-brown mountain, its highlands offered a restful setting for recovery from the second leg of the family's overland travels. The first stage of their journey from Konya permitted lakeshore halts, but the last segment was an arduous trek across foothills and mountains.

Whether Selim escorted his mother and siblings to Bozdağ is not known; he may have needed to get back to the business of governing in Konya. Perhaps, however, he relished the opportunity to meet up as fellow governor with the brother to whom he had been junior partner for so long. If the princes did in fact reunite, they doubtless conferred with each other and their mother. Suleyman and Roxelana may in fact have organized her trip with a family conclave in mind.

Once in Manisa, Roxelana would feel the weight of recent Ottoman history far more than she had in Konya. She now found herself in the city where her beloved Suleyman had grown from a prince into the man who became sultan, just months before she first encountered him. The Manisa palace now belonged to their firstborn, but it was also where her rival Mahidevran had become her husband's lover. Mustafa, Suleyman's senior son, may well have been born in the harem quarters that housed the queen during her visit.

Manisa offered much to distract Roxelana from uneasy thoughts about the past. It was another city laden with sights to see, these erected closer to her times than Konya's. The two newest and largest monuments were the work of her female predecessors—Christian captives turned Muslim royal mothers. Husnushah, mother to one of Suleyman's uncles, had built the first of these, "the Hatuniye" (the honorable lady's [foundation]), in 1490. Her seal, "Mother of Sultan Shehinshah," signed the letter she would send in 1511 to the prince's father Bayezid II informing him of his son's death.[41]

Husnushah's endowment was geographically innovative: it moved the zone of royal patronage northward into the rich Manisa plain, away from the slope of Mount Spil, where the old Byzantine fortress and the Great Mosque, built in 1366 by a Saruhan prince, looked down on the ancient city.[42] Given the location of the complex on the outskirts of Manisa, near intercity roads, Husnushah's decision in 1497 to add a caravanserai to bring in revenue to support her foundation (rather than, say, a public bath) made sense. Income was generated from renting space in the expansive two-storied structure (thirty-six rooms downstairs, thirty-eight upstairs) to traveling merchants and local businessmen. The caravanserai's amenities included a large stable and a courtyard graced with a pool.

One of the earliest Ottoman mosques in Manisa (1427) had been the work of one Ali Beg, a notable man of property. His estate included a large park that featured gardens, streams, and an arboretum with fruit-bearing trees. A section of the park, purchased by Suleyman's mother, became the site for her own foundation. The Sultaniye (the imperial), as Hafsa's complex was known, certainly warranted a family outing arranged by Mehmed for his visiting relatives. No doubt each family member felt a sincere obligation to honor the late queen mother, who had died nine years earlier. Hafsa had been mentor to Roxelana in her progress as favorite concubine, and she was the only grandparent that Mehmed, Mihrumah, and Cihangir had ever known.

Among the Sultaniye's services to the community was the dervish lodge where Merkez Efendi had served at Hafsa's invitation. So affecting were his spiritual assemblies and his preaching that they allegedly brought Prince Suleyman to tears.[43] Also trained in the medical sciences, the mystic was said to have developed a homeopathic paste made up of some forty herbs and spices; the medicament allegedly relieved an illness Hafsa suffered. The annual spring equinox festival, whose main event is still today the casting of bits of this tasty remedy from the Sultaniye's two minarets to crowds below, had already begun to take shape by Mehmed's tenure in Manisa.

Perhaps inspired by Merkez Efendi, Suleyman had recently given Manisa a medical center by adding a hospital to his mother's complex. Roxelana no doubt made a point of inspecting it if she was already planning a hospital for her Avrat Pazar foundation—the layout of the Manisa hospital and the procedures it followed could offer ideas. Mihrumah too could store up thoughts for the future; her first philanthropic venture was just breaking ground in Istanbul.

The most captivating of all Roxelana's preoccupations in Manisa, however, had nothing to do with the city's delights. It was Mehmed's impending fatherhood. A granddaughter named Huma Shah would be born to Roxelana and Suleyman sometime before the late fall. The little girl's exact birth date is not known, so it is possible she became a babe in arms during her grandmother's visit.

Making their way home from Manisa, Roxelana and her party may have traveled directly to Istanbul. Or they may have chosen to return by way of Adrianople in order to meet up with Suleyman and Rustem on their march back from several new conquests in Europe. But what should have been a joyful and triumphant reunion turned into a ghastly tragedy. As the Ottoman army neared Adrianople, the sultan received the devastating news of Mehmed's death.[44] Couriers may have reached Roxelana first. In any event, the couple apparently learned separately of the shocking loss of their firstborn, unable to console each other for a matter of days.

The longest of the Manisa annals records the story of Mehmed's fatal illness:

> At the start of the month of Sha`ban in the year 950, on the day when the agha who came bringing glad tidings of the conquest of Usturgun-Belgrade and many other fortresses arrived [in Manisa] and a fireworks celebration ensued, the fortune-blessed prince Sultan Mehmed fell ill. He took to his bed for six days. During the night before the seventh he died. Following a brief mourning period, the Lala Pasha, Ibrahim Chelebi the treasurer, and many aghas departed for Istanbul with [the dead prince and] his suite, on the aforesaid month's ninth day, a Wednesday. By this reckoning, the prince lived one year and two days in Manisa.[45]

The record went on to note, "Now it was during the spring of this year that the plague appeared, and many families were consumed by the earth." The prince, it seems, succumbed to one of the periodic eruptions of the disease that engulfed Ottoman communities.[46]

According to contemporary historians, Suleyman ordered the transport of the prince's corpse to the capital. The Manisa annals, however, suggest that the lala understood the urgency of ushering the royal cortege to Istanbul and acted on his own. On the eighteenth of the month, the procession arrived on the Asian side of the Bosphorus at Üsküdar, where Mehmed's body was transferred to a casket. Accompanied by sufis proclaiming the unity of God, the prince was carried in state to the mosque of his great-grandfather Bayezid II. Mehmed would be buried in the center of the city, near the Old Barracks belonging to the Janissaries. With shops closed for the three-day mourning period that followed, the city's soup kitchens furnished sustenance to the crowds offering prayers.[47]

Nearly a century later, the historian Peçevi would reflect on the confluence of military triumph and personal tragedy: "In this never-ending world it is certain that every [act of] power carries with it an unrealized goal and that every pleasure is followed by pain."[48] Mehmed's death was an eerie echo of the ruined victory of Suleyman's first campaign in 1521, when he learned of the demise of three of his children as he returned to Istanbul in the midst of great jubilation. It was around that time that the young sultan's new concubine gave birth to the son whose promising life was now so cruelly cut short.

13

RECOVERY

SULEYMAN'S GRIEF OVER the loss of Mehmed was legendary. Utterly distraught during the prince's burial, the sultan wept for more than two hours, refusing to let the body be interred; he then attended prayers for the dead for forty days instead of the customary three. "They say that the Grand Turk has exhibited his sorrow and appeared in public dressed in black, to signal his pain," noted Luigi Bassano.[1] So perforce did leading Ottoman officials, who were required to remain in black garb for the forty days. To mark the prince's death, Suleyman composed the chronogram "My Sultan Mehmed, distinguished among princes."[2]

No one could or did chronicle Roxelana's sorrow. She and Suleyman had already lived through the death of a son, the toddler Abdullah, but this was a loss of a different order. Mehmed was their firstborn, said by some to be their favorite. He was the child who created a new family for his mother after the horrific loss of her own. We cannot know if Roxelana went wild with grief or if she composed herself so she could console those close to her. But if ever there was a moment when she regretted the decision not to accompany the prince to his provincial post, this would be it. Roxelana may now have clung even more tightly to Bayezid, the last of her sons destined to take the field. He would not depart for Anatolia until 1546, when he was twenty.

Neither Roxelana nor Mihrumah, the sibling closest in age to Mehmed, was present at the funeral prayers. Women did not participate in public funerals, although separate services were doubtless observed in the Old Palace, the prince's original home. No protocols could keep Mehmed's mother from visiting his grave, however. Perhaps Roxelana was luckier than Suleyman, for she was soon plunged into the distractions of family responsibilities. Most importantly, she had the arrival of

Suleyman mourning the death of Mehmed. Seyyid Lokman, *Hünernâme.*

Mehmed's infant daughter Huma Shah and her mother to prepare for. Roxelana may have been too distracted with mourning to pay heed to all her son's female attendants, some of whom she had gotten to know only months earlier, but she would certainly look after any woman who might be pregnant. The coming months made clear, however, that Huma Shah would be Mehmed's only progeny.

The unpleasant duty of interrogating the newly arrived Manisa contingent on the circumstances of Mehmed's death fell to both Suleyman and Roxelana and their staffs. Two concerns would be uppermost: determining that the prince had not been poisoned and ascertaining whether the plague had spread to others in the palace. Like most monarchs of the time, the Ottomans were always on guard against political sabotage from whatever discontented corner of the empire—or beyond. Roxelana would address her questions to Mehmed's former governess and whoever else had headed his female staff. Suleyman would turn to his son's *lala* and to the officers of the prince's domestic and military services, not only to assure himself of the cause of death but also to ensure that measures had been taken to guard the health of those who remained behind in Manisa.

THE SUDDEN BLOW of Mehmed's death appears to have dampened Suleyman's ardor for war. For four and a half years, from late 1543 on, Roxelana would have the comfort of her husband's steady presence and companionship. While combat continued on the empire's frontiers, the sultan remained at home, allowing his generals to take command. In May 1543, he turned fifty by the Islamic calendar. With ten victorious campaigns to his credit, he could delegate military authority with no threat to his reputation as a formidable commander. There was, however, a political rationale behind Suleyman's holiday from fighting: yet another set of negotiations over a peace treaty with Austria, this time a drawn-out process. The treaty was finally signed in 1547 when Ferdinand agreed to an annual payment to Suleyman of 30,000 gold ducats (the Ottomans called it tribute; the Hapsburgs did not). Until the western frontier stabilized, Suleyman would not take on the Safavids in Iran again.

The royal family were not wholly creatures of the capital in these years. Winter sojourns in Adrianople and seasonal hunts in Anatolia punctuated their life in the Istanbul palaces. In the summer of 1544, Bursa was the site of a gathering that brought the prince Selim together with Suleyman, Roxelana, Mihrumah, and her husband Rustem, now second vizier in the Imperial Council. (Bayezid and Cihangir presumably stayed behind to represent their father in Istanbul.) An annal entered into the Manisa city register noted, "The fortune-favored prince Selim was invited to Bursa for the purpose of a family reunion. After an audience was held, they remained there for forty days."[3] Selim had been appointed in March to succeed Mehmed in Manisa, but his move from the governorship of Konya was postponed due to the lingering plague.[4] Bursa was famous for the fresh and healthful air of Mount Olympus.

Suleyman undoubtedly took advantage of the season to hunt with his son and the "very many" soldiers who accompanied him. (Bassano claimed that the sultan never hunted with fewer than 300 soldiers and that a massive hunt in Thrace had numbered 50,000, including Christians and Jews.)[5] The Bursa reunion was not merely a convivial occasion, although it was surely that as well—a welcome distraction from the trials of the previous fall. Both Roxelana and Suleyman may have longed to see Selim, now alone among their children in Anatolia, but the formal language of the annal—the audience, the "performance" of a reunion—suggests that there was business to discuss. Selim may have been debriefed on affairs in Konya and in turn briefed on what his father expected him to accomplish in Manisa. The annal went on to note that Selim arrived in his new post on August 7.

Roxelana continued her habit of making journeys in Anatolia. When Bayezid finally graduated to provincial service in 1546, the fourth and last of Suleyman's sons to take up his public career in Anatolia, Roxelana had fresh reason to travel south from Istanbul. In the early spring, she journeyed to Konya, Bayezid's assigned governorate. It is entirely possible that she traveled with him to his post. It was perhaps her last chance to behave like the classic mother of a prince, if only briefly.

Having lost Selim to Manisa, the city must have been pleased to welcome a new prince and now his mother. As during her 1543 journey to Anatolia, Roxelana was accompanied by Cihangir. This youngest son, it was beginning to seem, would not graduate to provincial service. Suleyman now had three sons stationed in the field, evenly spaced across Anatolia. Two were Roxelana's and one Mahidevran's. Only one of the three could follow their father to the sultanate.

Having blessed Bayezid's political adulthood, seen to his welfare, and settled his female household, Roxelana then went on to spend the month of April with Selim in Manisa.[6] Both she and Cihangir were doubtless delighted to meet the three daughters who had been born to the prince in his first year as governor in Anatolia.[7] The mother of one, Nurbanu, would go on to become Selim's favorite consort and mother of his first son, Murad. Roxelana did not linger for the birth of this grandson, who arrived in July, but she surely established a relationship with Nurbanu, as she would with other mothers of her grandchildren.

During the mid-1540s, both Suleyman and Roxelana found solace in planning a memorial mosque for Mehmed. In 1544 builders broke ground next to the exquisitely adorned tomb constructed to house Mehmed's grave.[8] Completion of the mosque and its attendant structures—madrasa, soup kitchen, caravanserai cum hostel, and primary school—would take five years.

The Mosque of the Prince, as it became known, is remembered today as Suleyman's tribute to his son. Contemporary observers, however, also credited Roxelana as an active force behind the project. According to the Venetian ambassador Bernardo Navagero, "The Grand Signor and [the prince's] mother wanted to honor him with a most beautiful and most sumptuous mosque." Domenico Trevisano echoed his predecessor, commenting also that all who knew him loved the prince for his graciousness, comeliness, and habits, "being by nature humane and generous."[9] Even the late sixteenth-century historian Mustafa 'Ali, bitterly critical of Roxelana's political influence, wrote that the mosque's unusual plan, fit more for a sultan than a prince, stemmed from the exceptional love that Mehmed's "fortune-favored mother and illustrious father felt for him in their hearts."[10] While these comments credit Roxelana's involvement to parental devotion, the queen could also bring a practical voice to the planning from her experience with her own foundation.

In authorizing Mehmed's complex, unprecedented for a prince in its magnificence and the long period of its construction, Suleyman was taking the risk that he might never build a monument of his own in the Ottoman capital. It was certainly time for the sultan to contemplate construction of his own foundation. His great-grandfather Mehmed II had begun his mosque in the twenty-second year of his reign, and his grandfather Bayezid II in the twentieth year. His father Selim I had not lived to undertake this endeavor, the crowning material donation of an Ottoman sovereign to his subjects. In 1544, Suleyman entered the twenty-fifth year of his sultanate; he could hardly have predicted the extraordinary longevity of both himself personally and his reign. Fortunately, or perhaps by design, Suleyman had the women in his family to rely on in the meanwhile.

Mehmed's burial in Istanbul was exceptional, noted Trevisano, for it was "usual for all the sons of the emperors to be buried in Bursa."[11] The royal Bursa tombs were elegant, but a modesty of scale was maintained in the pastoral precincts of Murad II's mosque, where graves clustered from the mid-fifteenth century onward. Not only was Mehmed's eternal presence in the capital a highly visible break with tradition, but the choice of the Janissary barracks as the site of the foundation was also laden with meaning.

It was Mustafa, Suleyman's oldest son, who was famously admired and hailed by the Janissaries. Everything about Mehmed's memorial seemed carefully designed to demonstrate that the sultan's firstborn with Roxelana was likewise a defender of the empire's welfare, having given his life in dutiful service. We can only speculate whether Mustafa felt threatened by the uncanonical aggrandizement of Mehmed's memory, or whether he too mourned the passing of the prince to whom he had been elder brother for the twelve years they lived together in the Old Palace.

The importance of the Janissaries, seemingly the only force in the empire that could effectively challenge the sovereign, was not lost on Roxelana. During the construction of Mehmed's mosque, she culti-vated an association with them, or so it seems from a flattering story recorded in *Customs of the Janissaries of the Imperial Household*. This anonymous text of 1606, addressed to Roxelana and Suleyman's great-great-grandson Ahmed I, complained of eroding military standards and looked back to the "good old days." According to the account, "Her Highness the Haseki Sultan" paid a visit to the construction site, during which she noticed young Janissary novices, bareheaded and barefoot, hauling sacks filled with earth and stones. Presumably overcome with concern, she urged Suleyman to provide them with a five-asper monthly raise to furnish them with shoes. When he did, she allegedly sold her gold, pearls, and jewels and transferred the funds to the treasury to cover the raise, which Suleyman later wrote into law.[12]

The story ends by wishing the Haseki heavenly reward for her good deed. However embroidered it might be, the tale is emphatic with re-gard to Roxelana's compassion and generosity. One of its morals is that sultans sometimes need to be encouraged to do the right thing, and it is good to have hasekis who can tutor them. The tale also suggests Rox-elana's recognition that quotidian good works might be as effective in cultivating a reputation for benevolence as endowing large complexes, especially among the Janissaries. On the other hand, the gesture may simply have been spontaneous. This was not the only time Roxelana would make provision for slaves. The memory of her own early days as a captive of the Ottomans perhaps stimulated her concern for the novices, all of them young slaves of the dynasty drafted into heavy manual labor.

Stories such as this one did not make their way into the reports of European ambassadors. For them, news of the queen's political sway was both more available and more saleable than testimony about her human touch. Laborers and master craftsmen working at the construction site, however, might notice and comment favorably. And who knew which novice might rise to high rank in the Janissary corps, perhaps even becoming its commanding *agha*, and recall Roxelana's thoughtfulness?

WHEN BAYEZID TOOK up his provincial post in Konya in 1546, his mother was in her early forties. She had been Suleyman's partner for twenty-five years, virtually the whole of his reign. Little more than a decade had passed since she had become his wife and taken up residence in the quarters carved out for her in the New Palace. Only a gate and a stroll through Suleyman's private gardens separated their rooms. But like most kings and queens of the time, the couple spent a good deal of time apart, moving and working in separate realms.

If Suleyman was responsible for the defense and administration of the empire, Roxelana was accountable for the smooth running of the domestic households of both the New and Old Palaces. As the mourning period for Mehmed came to an end, she perhaps spent more time than usual in the latter, overseeing the allocation of rooms and attendants to Mehmed's daughter Huma Shah and her mother. The last women from the Manisa harem would be integrated into service in Istanbul or married to men in the sultan's service (a skeleton harem staff had no doubt remained in Manisa to await Selim's arrival). Roxelana would play a directing role in choosing and preparing other women for Bayezid's harem.

Roxelana was not the only high-ranking royal figure to spend time in the Old Palace during this period; so did Suleyman's sisters, some of whom, widowed or divorced, returned to the capital. Even if they chose to reside in domiciles of their own, the Old Palace was a center of sociability as well as a resource for female medical care. An odd hierarchy of status appears in imperial expense registers that differentiated the princesses, women of royal blood, from the Haseki, a former slave: the princesses had the title "sultan" plus honorifics; Roxelana had neither of these, but what she did have was a superior stipend that bespoke her influence and, consequently, her numerous financial responsibilities.

The daily stipend furnished to all members of the dynastic household served not only as material support for the expenses of office but also as an index of status. Roxelana's far exceeded that of other women—a queenly 2,000 silver aspers a day (roughly thirty gold ducats). Her income is documented in the first extant Old Palace account register of Suleyman's reign, dated 1555 to 1556. Bureaucratic practice combined both Istanbul harem residences into a single bookkeeping whole, under the rubric of the Old Palace, which still counted as the principal residence of women.[13] Perhaps Roxelana's residence in the New Palace was considered an aberration of Suleyman's reign.

Because Roxelana did not rely wholly on her stipend—most royal women had other sources of income—it was impressive more in scale than amount. The 2,000-asper per diem was ten times greater than the 200 received by the next-highest-ranking women, two sisters of Suleyman now resident in the palace—the widowed Shehzade and Shah, divorced and then widowed. Two junior princesses—offspring not of a sultan but of a prince or princess—received one hundred aspers. Their "thinner" blood was mirrored in their identification not by name but by their royal parent: "the daughter of Shehzade Sultan" and "the daughter of the deceased Sultan Mehmed, may he rest in peace" (Huma Shah).

Ranking lowest in the 1555–1556 register were ordinary concubine mothers. The stipend of Shah's mother, a former consort of the mighty Selim I, was only seventy-five aspers daily, and Huma Shah's mother received a mere thirty. Mehmed's governess, however, received forty-one aspers, her fiscal status greater than the dead prince's concubine. Stipends, it seems, indexed active power and present status in the imperial household where converted slaves might outrank princesses of the blood. The 150-asper stipend of the Lady Steward, administrative manager of the Old Palace and, like Roxelana and the governess, a product of palace training, gave further evidence of this principle.

Woven into this fiscal hierarchy was a different ranking, however, one that distinguished royal blood from royal service irrespective of stipend. The title "sultan" and the formula "long may they live" accompanied the names of Suleyman's sisters Shah and Shehzade, an acknowledgment that these daughters of Selim I carried the blood of the Ottoman dynasty. They, of course, had been born free. Roxelana, nameless, is listed merely as "mother of the royal children." In the formal logic of the finance department, her elevation to freed woman and queen to the sultan was irrelevant to her essential status as his concubine. Suleyman's regard for his favorite was apparently a nonfact in the canon of scribal practice.

Stipends were not the only source of support. To varying degrees princesses enjoyed wealth in the form of inheritance from relatives, gifts of valuables, ownership of slaves and real property, and so on. Mihrumah, for instance, would become the richest female in the empire after her mother's death, although she was arguably exceptional as the only surviving princess born during Suleyman's long reign and, moreover, the offspring of an exceptional mother and father. Especially during the years when her husband Rustem Pasha occupied the post of grand vizier, their combined wealth was as outsized as their combined influence.

Despite the large household over much of which she presided, Mihrumah spent a good deal of time in her parents' home. Navagero noted that she "goes very frequently to the palace of the Grand Signor to meet with her mother."[14] One virtue of Roxelana and Suleyman's multiple parenthood was that at least two of their children remained in the capital. Cihangir, the last of the siblings, was fifteen or so when Bayezid departed for Konya. As if in compensation for his ineligibility for governorship, the youth became his father's close companion. Alvise Renier, resident Venetian ambassador in the late 1540s, noted that father and son were devoted to each other—Suleyman greatly enjoyed the company of the clever and talkative Cihangir, whom he took with him wherever he went. Perhaps because of his frequent public presence, some mistakenly thought the prince would graduate to governor, Renier among them: "Soon [Suleyman] will send him from the palace and give him a title as he has done with his other sons."[15] But it was not to be.

Roxelana presumably discouraged any talk of a provincial post for Cihangir, and not only in light of his condition. She was doubtless as devoted as Suleyman to her youngest child. His birth several years after her first five arrived in rapid succession gave her more time to savor his early years. His affliction, moreover, necessitated a different bond than she had with the others. And now Cihangir could be his mother's travel companion as well as his father's, chaperoning her on her solo Anatolian journeys. In addition to the 1543 and 1546 visits to Konya and Manisa recorded in the latter city's public register, they probably made additional journeys to the two princely courts. One ongoing attraction was the rapidly growing number of grandchildren for Roxelana and nephews and nieces for Cihangir to dote on. Bayezid is said to have produced eleven children and Selim seven.[16]

Apparently an outgoing personality, the teenage Cihangir may have been the perfect uncle to his two little nieces Huma Shah and Aisha, the daughter of Mihrumah and Rustem.[17] Huma Shah and Aisha were close in age and may have been educated together as they grew up. Their grooming and training was serious business, for the two princesses could expect marriages to top statesmen in which their partnership and political acumen would be critical assets. Just as Suleyman would supervise the choice of their husbands when the time came, Roxelana would in the meanwhile choose their governesses and tutors—or at least Huma Shah's, as Mihrumah, like her mother, had opinions of her own.

ALTHOUGH THE OLD Palace and Mihrumah's residence were always homes away from home for Roxelana, the New Palace held a particular attraction for her in these years: the presence of her husband between his return from Hungary in November 1543 and his departure in late March 1548 on a new Iranian campaign. This was the longest period the couple had spent in proximity to each other. It was uninterrupted except for Roxelana's trips to see her sons and Suleyman's hunting expeditions and sojourns in Adrianople during which she, for whatever reason, might not accompany him. New forms of intimacy and companionship may have developed between them, while older forms intensified or became less important. The changes that middle age wrought in the sultan—in his demeanor, habits, and health—are well chronicled, but once again we are left guessing with regard to his queen.

The sexual passion that was a driving force in Roxelana and Suleyman's early years together may have grown into a comfortable intimacy.

Portraits of Suleyman and Roxelana, late sixteenth century. From Jean Jacques Boissard, *Vitae et icones sultanorum Turcicorum, principum Persarum...*, Franckf. ad Moem, 1596.

Or so the royal couple would want it to seem, for there was a customary reticence among the Ottomans regarding sexual desire at middle age. Not that sex between the middle-aged should or was assumed to cease, but one's demeanor should suggest that it was no longer a preoccupation. This was the stage in life when one's own children became the sexually active generation, giving life to their own families.

It is hard to know if Suleyman's subjects regarded his reputation for faithfulness and devotion to Roxelana as a virtue. They would not necessarily see constancy as a meritorious quality in a sultan, the size of whose harem signified his power to take other nations' females captive and use them. As de'Ludovici reported in 1534, the year of the royal marriage, the consensus was that "the sultan has loved his wife very much from the moment he met her" and that "according to the rumors that circulate, he has never been together with any woman except her." In the mid-1550s, Ogier Ghiselin de Busbecq, Archduke Ferdinand's envoy to Istanbul, confirmed this view, at least partially: "It is generally agreed that, ever since he promoted her to the rank of his lawful wife, he has possessed no concubines, although there is no law to prevent his doing so."[18]

Alongside Roxelana and Suleyman's long-standing affection and shared interest in the progress of their children, a new concern emerged during these domestic years—the vagaries of health that came with middle age. In describing the sultan as he observed him in the first years of the 1550s, Navagero reported that he suffered from gout and edema.[19] When these maladies first affected Suleyman is not clear, but his lengthy respite from military campaigning in the mid-1540s may have been intended in part to address his physical well-being. During a winter layover in Aleppo during the new Iranian campaign of 1548, Suleyman would write to Roxelana that the pain from his gout kept him from walking. She dispatched a reply full of condolences and wishes for his recovery so that he might enjoy the hunting he so loved.[20] Shortly after leaving Aleppo in June, Suleyman suffered an attack of illness that puzzled his doctors and would cause him to spend part of the second fighting season recuperating.

None of Suleyman's conditions was fatal, and at first they were episodic. However, any sign of his ill health was, for Roxelana, cause for anxiety. He would always be sultan, with or without her. Were he to lose her, he would doubtless always mourn her, but he would of necessity carry on. But to lose Suleyman was for Roxelana to lose the fulcrum of her life. And while she was politically consequential as mother of three princes and a princess, without Suleyman she lacked the principal source of her protection—unless and until one of her sons became the next sultan. Roxelana must have felt trepidation every time Suleyman set off for war. His health, however, she could do something about.

Suleyman clearly followed a medical regime prescribed by his doctors. Luckily for posterity, the ambassador Navagero reported at length on his physical appearance and his health, the latter being a subject of obvious concern to the Venetian government. Suleyman was thin and rather tall. In his dark-complexioned face Navagero saw "an admirable greatness together with a gentleness that makes him agreeable to all who see him." The sultan was meticulous about his diet, rarely consuming meat and then only a small amount. Unlike in his days with Ibrahim, when feasting was more frequent, he now drank pure water beneficial to digestion, choosing among various springs according to the discomfort of the moment. Suleyman also took care not to remain sedentary for very long.[21]

Supporting Suleyman in maintaining these good habits would be a whole bevy of palace servants, from the cooks in the imperial kitchens to the select pages of the Privy Chamber, who were entrusted with the sultan's personal care both at home and on the road. His biggest booster, however, was surely his wife. We can imagine Roxelana consulting with the doctors, conferring with the kitchen, hectoring the pages, and most of all fussing over Suleyman. If her prayer-full letters are any indication, she constantly entreated God to keep the sultan healthy. Perhaps she too was experiencing the physical wages of growing older and appreciated the greater attention to dietary regime and exercise.

Cihangir rallied in support. Navagero noted that almost every day that Suleyman spent in Istanbul, he boarded one of the imperial boats, setting out for a variety of places but most particularly for the Asian shores of the Bosphorus, where he debarked for the exercise of hunting. It was on just such excursions that Cihangir accompanied his father. "He is Suleyman's principal amusement," reported the ambassador, "and this is a certainty, because [the sultan] always takes him along on the hunt and wherever he sails in his brigantine."[22]

Navagero also commented that one reason Suleyman enjoyed Adrianople was that he could step outside the door and find ready spaces for hunting and entertainment.[23] Since the government was wherever the sultan was, many top Ottoman officials as well as foreign ambassadors would make the trek to the empire's second capital in Suleyman's wake. Roxelana perhaps made a particular effort in these years to accompany him, clearing her calendar by delegating tasks to members of her staff. Adrianople was close enough to the capital that couriers could move back and forth fairly rapidly.

Sometimes Roxelana stayed behind. A short note she wrote to Suleyman, sent from Istanbul to Adrianople, apparently accompanied "papers" she was forwarding to him via some pilgrims returning from Mecca (presumably trusted individuals). In it she asks after Suleyman's health and inquires if anything is amiss. Bayezid must have accompanied his father, for his mother sends him greetings and "kisses his eyes" (an expression of affection for a younger person). As usual, Roxelana devotes most of her words to missing Suleyman—she burns in the flames of longing, but God's help and the protection of his mystic devotees bring her salvation. If "her fortune-favored one, her sultan" were to send news from time to time, the fire in her heart might subside.[24] Alas, few notes like this brief communication survive to reveal the myriad ways in which Roxelana participated in the daily routines of governing.

IN ALL THE years of Roxelana's association with Suleyman, there were surely moments of tension, if only passing disagreement or misunderstanding. She did not hesitate to express her emotions, or so it would seem from the story relayed in 1526 to the Venetian Senate of the jealous tantrum she pitched when the sultan received a gift of two Russian slave women. But however compatible she and Suleyman might be, their private relationship could not be shielded from the politics that were the daily agenda for him and increasingly for her as well. The issue ripest for tension was doubtless the future of their sons.

In 1546, when Bayezid joined Selim and Mustafa in Anatolia, all eligible successors to Suleyman were engaged in their public careers. Speculation about the succession was inevitable. The political stakes were heating up, if slowly, for no one could predict when the sultan would die. Three of the previous four Ottoman rulers had passed away before the age of fifty-five, all from natural causes. Suleyman was now fifty-three by the Islamic calendar, two years older than his father had been at his death.

Roxelana's sons were less experienced than Mustafa, who had the advantage of being the eldest prince and of having graduated to governor in 1533 at a younger age than either Selim or Bayezid. This gave him a considerable head start in building up a popular reputation. There were other imbalances. Roxelana's sons had a more powerful mother, but Mustafa had at his side a mother whose sole mission in life was ensuring the success of her only son. Rival foreign powers carefully tracked the three princes and the two mothers, for both Christian Europe and the Islamic east had a major stake in the Ottoman succession.

Tradition required that Suleyman maintain parity of opportunity for all his sons. A core principle of sovereignty among the Ottomans, from their very beginnings, held that all healthy males of the dynastic family were eligible to rule. At the same time, tradition required Roxelana to promote and protect her sons as assiduously as Mahidevran promoted and protected Mustafa. Herein lay Roxelana's unique dilemma. The role thrust upon every concubine mother of a prince—pushing for her own son to become the next sultan—was in inevitable tension with his father's prescribed role as neutral enabler of all eligible princes. Not that Roxelana was alone in running up against this tension. Mahidevran too was tasked with walking the delicate line between loyalty to the sultan and loyalty to her son. The additional risk for Roxelana—wife, queen, and palace coresident to the sultan—was that any overt exercise of her influence against Mustafa could disturb the special bond she enjoyed with Suleyman. The situation was even more anomalous: As queen, a role for which there was no precedent, was Roxelana expected to be neutral like Suleyman, remaining aloof from the contest for the succession? When her son-in-law, Rustem, was raised to the office of grand vizier in 1544, some perhaps began to wonder if the sultan himself was remaining impartial or if he was privileging the family he had created with Roxelana. In future years, some would come to regard the ties among Roxelana, Mihrumah, and Rustem as an unholy alliance.

Rustem Pasha was arguably becoming as powerful a grand vizier as Ibrahim had been. The signal difference was that Suleyman denied Rustem the intimacy that his male favorite Ibrahim had enjoyed. According to Navagero, Roxelana and Mihrumah failed in their attempts to persuade Suleyman to make him a court familiar: "I have learned through a reliable channel that they have tried many times to bring it about that Rustan might enter the palace of the sultan on such a familial basis as Ibrahim used to; the sultan has responded that committing folly once is enough."[25]

On the other hand, Rustem certainly cultivated the same intimacy Ibrahim had with foreign ambassadors, to whom he apparently liked to tell stories of his life. This son of a Croatian pig farmer had long been a prized servant to the sultan. He originally caught Suleyman's eye when he leapt from a window to retrieve an object that the sultan had dropped. Suleyman advanced him from inner-palace duties to master of the imperial stables, from which respected position the pasha went on to a series of governorships in Anatolia. Rustem was finally promoted to the rank of vizier in 1539 when he was chosen by Suleyman and Roxelana as husband for Mihrumah and acquired the title *Damad* (royal son-in-law). Five years later, when during an Imperial Council meeting the then grand vizier Suleyman and the fourth vizier quarreled in the sultan's presence, the former was dismissed and Rustem appointed in his place. (The second party to the quarrel, who had drawn his sword during the fight, was said to have starved himself to death from remorse.)[26]

In his later years as grand vizier, Ibrahim had obviously recognized Rustem as a potential rival, or so the story went that he removed him from circulation by posting him to the governorship of Diyarbakır, far to the east on the border with Iran.[27] The ruse failed, and at that point Rustem became a candidate for Mihrumah's hand. He also acquired the nickname "Lucky Louse." Rumors spread by his enemies that he suffered from leprosy (hence dared not marry the princess) were proven false when the doctor sent to Diyarbakır to examine him discovered a louse in his clothing, despite the fact that the fastidious pasha changed his garments daily.[28] (Lice were apparently known to avoid lepers.)

It was as much the promise of Rustem's future service to the state as his hoped-for compatibility with Mihrumah that had propelled his political ascent. Mihrumah was now emerging as her mother's protégée in public affairs, and it did not take long for mother and daughter to view Rustem as their ally. Suleyman presumably took the likelihood of this triple alliance into account when he promoted Rustem to grand vizier late in 1544. He could always dismiss his *damad* vizier if he were to take a serious misstep. Like all servants of the sultan, royal sons-in-law were not immune to destruction. Suleyman's execution of his sister Beyhan's husband Ferhad early in his reign stood as a warning to all future husbands of princesses.

To Suleyman, Rustem was valuable as a classically trained vizier who possessed familiarity with a wide range of government and military offices. Gone were the heady days when an inexperienced favorite could be rocketed to the most powerful office in the empire. Rustem was also shrewd—Busbecq considered him "a man of keen and far-seeing mind."[29] His consistent display of loyalty to the sultan was a habit that Ibrahim had failed to sufficiently cultivate, at least in his later years as grand vizier. Fidelity was critical, for Suleyman's style as sovereign was to delegate the execution if not the design of power to his grand viziers.

Renier, reporting to the Venetian government four years after Rustem's assumption of office, commented that he had seen the sultan only twice, for "it is Rustem Pasha who relays everything to us."[30]

The grand vizier would soon be recognized for his thrifty management of the imperial budget, another talent not cultivated by Ibrahim. Rustem reputedly ignored no plausible source of income, including sale of the flowers and vegetables grown on the palace grounds. The other side of the coin, unfortunately, was his reputation for stinginess as well as a greed that his opponents called graft. He was quite good at eliciting gifts from ambassadors, who sometimes had to apologize to their home governments for the expenses incurred in keeping communication channels open. Venetian ambassador Alvise Renier thought it a good idea to provide Rustem with one hundred gold ducats every year and not to wait until he asked, because then the amount might be larger.[31]

WHEN KING SIGISMUND the Old died in 1548, Roxelana resumed diplomatic correspondence with the Polish monarchy, writing personally to congratulate Sigismund Augustus, Bona Sforza's son and his father's heir to the double throne of Poland and Lithuania. This epistolary link with Poland would help establish a concrete foundation for the more expansive diplomatic role that would be adopted by her female successors. Roxelana's cultivation of contacts abroad was not reserved for Europe, for a few years later she would develop a cordial correspondence with Safavid royal women.

The Ottomans had made use of female diplomats before, but those emissaries had been the mothers or aunts of the sultans. As the seclusion of elite women became more fashionable over the decades, the practice of sending senior women to carry important messages or negotiate peace treaties died out. What Roxelana did was to establish a new mode of female diplomacy—the letter—to help Suleyman build alliances and keep peace among potential adversaries. By the end of the century, the mother of her grandson would be corresponding with the Venetian government as well as with Catherine de Medici, regent mother of the French king. The next queen mother would exchange both correspondence and gifts with Queen Elizabeth I of England. Gift giving was essential to consolidating the relationship—Elizabeth sent a carriage and received in return an Ottoman outfit such as her correspondent would wear.[32]

Roxelana's aim in her correspondence with Sigismund Augustus was to cement good relations by employing a more affective tone than Suleyman or Rustem, the grand vizier, could. In her first letter, she writes that she has learned that Sigismund Augustus has become king upon his father's death, for which honor she feels joy and pleasure. Then, offering consolation, she notes that one can do nothing (about death) but accept God's will. The short missive ends by stating that its deliverer, Roxelana's *agha* Hasan, can be trusted and can also convey to her anything the king would like to propose or relate.[33]

Roxelana wrote again to the new king in response to his reply. This letter carried more substance and more of her signature extravagance of expression. It is impossible, she says, to describe her delight in the king's letter, in which he spoke of his keen desire for friendship with her and his loving affection for the sultan. When she transmitted this news to the sultan, she writes, he too was delighted, to a degree that words cannot express. He was even moved to say, "The old king and I were like two brothers, and if it pleases God the Merciful, this king and I will be like father and son." Roxelana wants his majesty to know that she would be happy to pass along to Suleyman any matters that might occur to him.

Finally, so that her letter won't arrive empty-handed, she says she is sending gifts: two pairs of drawers, a shirt, and a waistband, six handkerchiefs, and a hand-and-face towel. In a show of modesty, Roxelana begs the king's forgiveness for these items and the wrapping in which they are enclosed, for the things being sent are unworthy of him. She made this demurral no doubt on behalf of her own handiwork, since she most likely embroidered and perhaps even sewed all the gifts, wrapping included, herself. The intimacy of the items perhaps underscored the familial relationship that was being asserted between the two monarchies.

Roxelana's familiar epistolary tone owed much to the bond she was assumed to possess with the "old king." Her very name announced her origins in the southeastern region of the Polish-ruled domains: Roxelana (the Ruthenian maiden). Sigismund had come to the throne in 1506 when Roxelana was a small child not yet carried off to Istanbul. That she remembered anything of the monarch of her childhood is doubtful, but the connection was useful for both sides to exploit. The Polish kings were traditionally among the Ottomans' staunchest allies. The Venetian Trevisano noted that the monarchy was one of four powers with whom Suleyman was on good terms (the others were the French king, the duke of Moscow, and "our most excellent Republic").[34] Sigismund I had made peace treaties with Bayezid II and Selim, and he went on to sign more with Suleyman.

Claims that Roxelana played a key role in facilitating this continuing goodwill between her natal and her adopted homes have rested, inaccurately, on the notion that Suleyman planned to attack Poland in the first years of his sultanate—the presumption being that the sultan's new favorite persuaded him to keep the peace.[35] More plausibly he or she or both began to appreciate the utility of promoting the captive from Polish domains as a symbolic link between the two powers. Frequent embassies from Cracow—more, allegedly, than any other state sent in the sixteenth century—no doubt consolidated Roxelana's reputed tie to Poland.

Diplomacy with the new king was a veritable family love affair. The courier Hasan also carried official correspondence from Suleyman and Rustem as well as letters from Mihrumah. Like her mother, the princess first sent a condolence-cum-congratulatory message and then a longer response to the king's own reply. Her style is formal in the first, effusive in the second. She writes that her father and her husband Rustem are indescribably overwhelmed by the king's expressions of love and friendship in his missives as well as in the verbal conveyance of his sentiments by the Polish envoy and by Hasan Agha. Sigismund should favor Mihrumah and her husband by letting them represent his wishes to the sultan. In short, everyone, according to the princess's letter, is simply thrilled about the liaison.

Mihrumah's second letter echoes Navagero's comment about the princess's close ties to her parents. Indeed, the households appear to be blended, as if her life with Rustem was a continuum that stretched from the New Palace to the couple's domicile. Hasan Agha appears at first as her husband the pasha's gentleman-in-waiting but then as "my mother the Haseki Sultan's servant." Mihrumah notes that she has dispatched a set of gifts, hers apparently intended for Sigismund's wife. Like the letters, the gifts sent by Mihrumah and Roxelana seem to have been a collaborative effort.

The apparent ease with which Mihrumah took part in the creation of a diplomatic entente makes one wonder if she was not already familiar to the Polish-Lithuanian royal family. It seems possible that she corresponded in 1541 with Isabella, Sigismund the Old's daughter, to send thanks for the gifts the Polish princess had sent her via Rustem. As regent queen of Transylvania, Isabella spent much of her adult life shielding the fragile sovereignty of her son by maintaining a delicate balance between the Hapsburg and Ottoman behemoths. Cultivating the sultan's beloved daughter, and perhaps his powerful wife, would be good policy. Conversely, the cultivation of the Polish siblings Sigismund Augustus and Isabella was necessary Ottoman policy, one of its aims to counteract overtures from Archduke Ferdinand.

ROXELANA'S GIFTS TO the Polish court were nothing compared to her lavish donations to the Persian prince Alqas Mirza, younger brother of Shah Tahmasp of Iran. When Tahmasp dispatched troops to punish Alqas for his alleged insubordination, the prince fled his post as governor of Shirvan, a province on the western Caspian shores, and took refuge at Suleyman's court. An inordinate degree of pomp and largesse was bestowed on this Safavid renegade upon his arrival in Istanbul in 1547. Alqas was a rare prize for the Ottomans. Just as European powers had used Cem Sultan, renegade son of Mehmed the Conqueror, to torment his elder brother Bayezid II with threats of a crusade, so Suleyman and Alqas might collaborate in an offensive against Tahmasp.

When Alqas Mirza arrived in the Ottoman capital, Suleyman was in Adrianople. Instead of summoning the Safavid prince, he left for Istanbul immediately, preferring to impress this scion of his only rival Muslim power with its splendors. He charged others with Alqas's care and entertainment in the meanwhile. If Roxelana was in Istanbul, she was no doubt called upon to receive the women in the prince's retinue, for he had fled with a substantial household. Suleyman's eventual entry into Istanbul apparently had more than the desired effect, for as he viewed the parade, Alqas kept asking, "Is that the sultan?" and rising to his feet as various top officials marched by. He was reportedly so overwhelmed by the grand vizier Rustem's appearance that he failed to register the sultan's arrival and remained seated.[36]

Following a formal welcome in the Imperial Council hall, the prince enjoyed the first of many banquets and receptions given in his honor. A veritable orgy of gift giving ensued. It included purses filled with gold and silver, robes of honor, sable and lynx furs, white and black slaves, swords and six-edged battle axes, carriages, horses, tents, pack animals, and more.[37] In other words, Suleyman's court was furnishing Alqas with an honorary princely household. The historian Ibrahim Peçevi commented, "All the leading figures showed extraordinary effort in giving gifts and favors."[38] He did not point out that the extravaganza doubtless took place at the sultan's behest.

Roxelana and her entourage did more than satisfy the imperial harem's duty in welcoming the defectors. Gifts reportedly worth the astonishing sum of 10,000 gold pieces issued forth. They included silk shirts for the prince sewn by the queen herself. The high value of the presents came in part from the lavish use of *sırma*, gilded silver thread, in the embroidery on other items of clothing as well as on quilt covers and pillows. For the women in the prince's suite, Roxelana and her court provided gifts of handiwork adorned with the same gilt thread and bedding items including quilts and sheets, these with gilt-thread tassels.[39] Countless hands were surely dedicated to the production of this armory of domestic comforts. The point was as much to generate talk of the queen's fabulous generosity as it was to equip and delight the prince and his female retinue.

The public was less impressed. Having been schooled in recent decades on the Safavid menace, people complained that Alqas was dangerous: he was a shi'i Muslim who "carr[ied] the virus of heresy and apostasy." Both Selim I and Suleyman had waged long wars to push back the double threat—sectarian and political—posed by the Safavids. Suleyman apparently answered the protests with the comment, "We have done what was required to uphold the honor of the sultanate; we have entrusted his punishment to God the Almighty should he betray us."[40] The remark about betrayal turned out to be prescient, for in the end Alqas Mirza proved a severe disappointment to Ottoman hopes.

The correspondence and exchange of gifts among queens, princesses, and kings was hardly trivial. The timing of Sigismund Augustus's accession and the confirmation of peace it brought turned out to be serendipitous, for the arrival of Alqas Mirza spurred Suleyman to go to war with Iran for the second time in his thirty-seven-year reign. He and his grand vizier would be comforted by the affirmation of stability on the Polish front to the north. So no doubt were Roxelana and Mihrumah, who would find themselves alone among their family to stay behind in Istanbul. Selim, Bayezid, and now even Cihangir were drafted to participate in the new war.

14

SHOWDOWN

ROXELANA WAS ACCUSED by her detractors of spurring Suleyman on to the Iranian campaign of 1548, one of his few flawed military endeavors. Ever eager for her sons to advance themselves, they alleged, she saw it as an opportunity for them to cultivate military favor. But it is more than likely that Roxelana opposed the war against the Persians, for it meant that Suleyman would be gone for almost two years. A compendium of sixteenth-century French diplomatic correspondence compiled in the mid-nineteenth exemplifies the evolution over time of Roxelana's reputation as a manipulative schemer.

In his forward to the documents he published, Ernest Charrière asserted that the campaign was the result of intrigues by "the sultana, absolute mistress of Suleyman," who wanted him away from the capital in order to enhance the reputation of Selim, who would be his father's deputy in Adrianople.[1] But the actual correspondence among diplomats and the new king, Henry II, suggests the opposite. Jean de Morvilliers, French envoy in Venice, reported in February 1548 that the sultana, fearing "the many accidents" that could occur during such a long absence, strove with all her means to keep Suleyman from going. He added that the sultan loved her so ardently he was loath to part from her.[2]

Suleyman's return ushered in a three-year interlude during which husband and wife renewed their building efforts. But then the sultan would again depart for the east, to be absent from August 1553 until July 1555. These two years would prove especially difficult, bringing down upon Roxelana's head the bitterest enmity she had yet experienced from the empire's subjects. She would also suffer great personal sorrow.

ADDED IN 1548 to Roxelana's usual reasons to dislike Suleyman's absences was concern about his health. In addition, the queen may well have shared the political objections voiced by Suleyman's viziers. Although opposed to the eastern venture, reported the Venetian ambassador Alvise Renier, they were unable to dissuade the sultan. "This is one of his principal traits," noted Renier of Suleyman's determination to hold to his decisions.[3] The grand vizier Rustem would afterward win esteem in the sultan's eyes for having predicted the dubious results of the expensive expedition.[4]

The two-season and nearly two-year campaign waged by Suleyman and his soldiers between spring 1548 and December 1549 met with limited success, making little overall headway against Safavid power. Worse, the assault would provoke Shah Tahmasp to strike back with punitive raids into Ottoman territory. If the Ottomans did come away with some gains—conquests in Georgia spearheaded by the vizier Kara Ahmed Pasha and the sultan's own victorious siege of the fortress of Van—they did so despite Alqas. During the first summer fighting season he had to be dissuaded from massacring the population of Tabriz, and during the second he evaded Suleyman's summons to rendezvous for fear of the sultan's wrath. The hapless prince returned to Iran and begged his brother's pardon, but Tahmasp ordered him imprisoned for life.

Renier recorded an incident that Ottoman chroniclers were less apt to note: Janissary novices and junior clerics in Istanbul took advantage of Suleyman's absence to commit acts of arson, their aim to plunder during the ensuing mayhem. A minor casualty of the arson was a workshop owned by Rustem Pasha.[5] The destructive outburst recalled the events of 1525, when a Janissary uprising in Istanbul demolished several elite residences in protest against the prolonged absence of both the sultan and the grand vizier from Istanbul. The present disturbance would be of particular concern to Roxelana, who would not have forgotten that Suleyman, away hunting in Adrianople in 1525, had feared to reenter his capital. Now serving as his father's deputy in Adrianople, Selim might be summoned by the Istanbul governor to add his heft and that of the troops under his command to a solution. As it turned out, the governor managed to quell the plot on his own, putting out the fires and publicly executing some of the guilty in the Hippodrome.

The Istanbul incident did not make its way into a letter Roxelana dispatched to Suleyman during his long absence in the east. Curiously so, for in the past she had informed him of urban discontents. This time she may have wished not to worry him, or perhaps she discussed the events in another letter that is not among the few that survive. In any event, Roxelana had other unhappy matters on her mind when she composed her message.[6]

Suleyman had obviously written to Roxelana of his physical troubles, and her letter was essentially a response to his. She returns again and again, in rather disordered prose, to his suffering. "In your noble letter, you said that your foot[7] had been aching for a day or two. God knows, my sultan, I was so upset I cried." Referring to Suleyman's subsequent comment that he was feeling better, Roxelana inquires what caused the pain. She hopes that now he will be able to hunt. At the same time, she urges him to waste no time and make every effort to come home! This hopeful note is followed by her lament over the fact that Suleyman's discomfort left him unable to walk. "Let me be the sacrifice [for your pain]!" she exclaims. Then, "please make an effort to send someone who can tell me of your *good* health and well-being."

This last train of thought—her great anxiety over the pain that kept Suleyman immobile and her plea for positive news—is reiterated, along with many invocations to God. Roxelana's concern was not misplaced. Morvilliers would report in September 1549 that Suleyman experienced a persistent inflammation of his legs while the army was stationed in the eastern capital of Diyarbakır. The pain caused him to cry out so loudly that he could be heard throughout the camp, compelling his pashas to mask the sultan's laments by summoning young men to sing and musical instruments to be played.[8]

As usual in her letters, Roxelana moves on from the emotional and sentimental to more pragmatic matters. "You asked me to forward the document you sent me to my Selim Khan," she writes; "I had already sent a porter to our Hajji Ali ... but I will send this as you order." Suleyman may have wished her to see the contents of the communiqué, or perhaps he entrusted more delicate information to courier links that went through the palace to Adrianople. What Roxelana had already sent with the porter and what role the apparently trusted Hajji Ali played are unclear, but this rare aside points to the usefulness of the queen's presence in the capital for private cross-empire communication. After Roxelana's death, Mihrumah would assume this function.

Finally, Roxelana provides, or rather the scribe formulates, rather stiffly, news of herself. "If you were to ask after your slave who is roasting in the fire of separation, it is due to the mercy of the Almighty and the prosperity of my sultan His Majesty's reign that my health can be said to be agreeable."[9] In closing, Roxelana sends greetings to Bayezid and Cihangir and passes along the respects of her granddaughter Huma Shah, Mihrumah, and Gulfem, her good friend in the Old Palace.

It is this greeting to Bayezid that dates Roxelana's letter to Suleyman's 1548–1549 winter layover in Aleppo between the eastern war's two fighting seasons. Renier and other watchers noted that Suleyman had summoned the prince from his post in Konya to pass the season with his father.[10] They made little mention of the fact that Cihangir had been with Suleyman since the two had marched out of Istanbul. However much pleasure this youngest, handicapped son brought to his father, his presence on campaign was not politically useful news. In times of war, it was the movements of Suleyman's potential successors that concerned observers of Ottoman politics.

Suleyman was apparently in good health at this point, for a great hunt was organized for March in the environs of Aleppo.[11] Experts were recruited to drive quarry into the designated area from surrounding verdant spaces and the desert region that lay to the east and south of the city. Such massive hunts were no idle pastimes. As exercises in strategy and coordination, they kept the soldiers active and entertained. Invitation to participate was also a way both to honor local dignitaries and to introduce the princes to an important segment of the empire's provincial leadership. The extended winter break would also provide sufficient rest and recuperation to prepare the sultan and his army for a second consecutive fighting season. The presence of his sons clearly added to Suleyman's ability to build recreation into the routine of business that always followed him on campaign.

Bayezid stayed in Aleppo until the army set out for the Ottoman-Safavid frontier in early June, at which point he returned to his post. A month later Suleyman crossed the Euphrates River to again head east.

He intended to reunite with Alqas Mirza, but the Persian prince failed to appear. The Ottomans moved on without him.

THIS EASTERN CAMPAIGN, the second in Suleyman's career, was the first time that all the males in Roxelana's family were away from Istanbul. Although she reserved her heartfelt expressions of "the pain of separation" only for Suleyman, she doubtless missed her princes. Bernardo Navagero, Venetian ambassador in the early 1550s, thought it worth reporting that she wanted her sons close to Istanbul.[12] This wish doubtless contained a strategic element: proximity to the capital would be advantageous if a contest for the throne were to erupt. Meanwhile, she and Mihrumah were able to join Selim in Adrianople, returning to the capital in January 1549, when Suleyman's deputy governor organized festivities to celebrate the empire's prosperity.[13] His aim was presumably to rally support for an unpopular war.

Did Roxelana ever wish that the Ottoman sultans were more like their Persian counterparts, who took their women to war? Perhaps so, but then there was the cautionary tale of the wife of Shah Ismail, Tahmasp's father, captured in the midst of battle by Selim I in 1514. Adding insult to injury, the sultan handed her over to one of his men as if she were an ordinary slave. If Ottoman custom required that Roxelana remain isolated from war, at least she now had two sons and a husband to write her news of their exploits. One would surely tell her the sad story of the elephant that had been acquired by the French ambassador Gabriel D'Aramon, who was traveling with the campaign. The poor creature expired from melancholy in Aleppo eight days after the death of its attendant, whom it loved and whose voice it liked to listen to.[14]

The farthest that Roxelana had ventured into Ottoman territory was Konya, where Selim and then Bayezid were posted. She was surely inquisitive about Aleppo, the northernmost of the legendary cities in the empire's predominantly Arab lands. This would be no idle curiosity, for the queen was no doubt contemplating sites for future philanthropic ventures in the old lands of Islam. Roxelana had already begun to plan for the welfare of the pilgrims who plied the Ottoman-secured routes to Jerusalem and Mecca. She would be aware that more people were finding it possible to undertake pilgrimages than earlier in the century, when the safety of the roads had been uncertain.

The reference in Roxelana's letter to the prosperity of Suleyman's reign was no hollow compliment, for ever since his victory over Shah Tahmasp in 1535 and the capture of Mesopotamia, the whole of the Fertile Crescent had begun to experience rising standards of living. Aleppo was recovering its former status as an international trading nexus and on its way to becoming a major diplomatic nexus and third city of the empire after Istanbul and Cairo. The sultan and his sons would find more than the hunt to entertain them during their Aleppo sojourn, for the city's intellectual and aesthetic appeal was considerable. The handsome physiognomy bestowed on the city by the great Mamluk sultans of Egypt was taking on Ottoman features, for Suleyman's viziers were starting to build mosques and commercial complexes in the Ottoman style.

If Roxelana missed her sons, she could take satisfaction in the knowledge that they were becoming familiar figures among the people of Anatolia and perhaps closing the gap with their long-admired half brother Mustafa. Suleyman had made a spectacle of his march to the east in 1548 by "inviting" each prince to stage a reception for his father along the route.[15] Selim had the longest trek, traveling from his post at Manisa to the town of Seyit Gazi (near today's Eskişehir). The itinerary was not unreasonable, for he would continue on from the reunion to wartime lieutenancy in Adrianople. Bayezid remained in Konya to greet the sultan, while Mustafa traveled from Amasya to the eastern Anatolian city of Sivas (Sebasteia to the Romans).

These ceremonial events were calculated to radiate Ottoman strength, especially to Tahmasp, who was dealing with a rebel brother while Suleyman was showing off the three sons he had at his beck and call. (Tahmasp had other, loyal brothers and also sons, but that was not the point at the moment.) The villages, towns, cities, and fortresses that lined the princes' routes to their rendezvous destinations composed another equally significant audience. Roxelana could participate vicariously in the receptions, or at least Selim's, for the prince surely gave his mother an account of the Seyit Gazi celebration when he stopped in Istanbul en route to Adrianople.

As for Bayezid, once in Aleppo he would participate in formal occasions and state banquets. While some divisions of the army were stationed in other winter quarters, Suleyman's top officials had accompanied him to the Syrian city. Bayezid would attend meetings of the Imperial Council, possibly offering information about Konya and neighboring regions. The visit was an opportunity for Suleyman to appraise and augment the prince's political skills.

One highlight of the Aleppo interlude was the arrival of many gifts to Suleyman from Alqas. A veritable catalogue of the fabled riches of the east, Alqas's offerings were the fruits of plunder gained from raids against his own relatives in central Iran: aloe, amber, and musk; muslins from India, shawls from Kashmir, carpets from Khorasan; weapons encrusted with diamonds and other costly stones; sacks filled with turquoise from Nishapur and rubies from Badakhshan.[16]

Suleyman would likely present some of these riches to his queen. He might work some of the gemstones into jewelry for her (she had lost much finery in the Old Palace fire of 1541). Alqas had also sent precious books—exemplary copies of the Qur'an, collections of the *Hadith* (the oft-quoted sayings and deeds of the Prophet Muhammad), and fine specimens of the *Shahnameh*, the great Iranian epic poem penned in the eleventh century by the poet Firdausi. Many or perhaps all of these works would enter the New Palace library. Bayezid, a budding bibliophile, was no doubt delighted; so probably was Rustem, whose estate was said to include 8,000 volumes.[17] Illustrated manuscripts in the imperial library might circulate among a fairly wide range of palace readers, including women of the court.[18] Perhaps Roxelana and her circle relished the *Shahnameh*'s cautionary tales of lovers and traitors. Other precious manuscripts might be carefully shown to little Huma Shah and Aisha, Mihrumah's daughter, both now six or so, to instruct them in the history of great queens and kings.

SULEYMAN AND ROXELANA were reunited at last in late December 1549. Soon after his return, both turned their attention to new building projects. The sultan finally ordered construction to begin on his own foundation in 1550. Rising on the third hill of Istanbul, the Suleymaniye, as it was called, would constitute the largest collection yet of royally endowed religious and welfare institutions. It would take seven years to build and cost a true fortune. But Suleyman had more than satisfied the

Ottoman tradition that such colossal expenditures must come from revenues gained in new conquests.

It was also in 1550 that Roxelana initiated work on the hospital that
would round out her foundation in the Avrat Pazar district of the capital. The timing was not coincidental, for its construction drew on the
resources already assembled for the Suleymaniye. The chief royal architect, Sinan, who had designed and built Roxelana's foundation with the
exception of its mosque, was in charge of both sites.

Roxelana had not been an idle philanthropist since the opening in
1539 of the Haseki, as her Avrat Pazar complex was becoming known.
One way she put her wealth to work was to underwrite foundations
built by others. For example, the queen's largesse provided financial
support for the memorial mosque built for Prince Mehmed by his *daye*,
the nurse-governess who may well have been at his side when he died
suddenly in Manisa. The Lady Daye chose to situate her memorial in
Kağıthane, today a busy district of Istanbul but then a village located
on a stream running into the Golden Horn. Mehmed's *daye* also built a
primary school and endowed durable stone water troughs in the vicinity.
When she died, she was buried in the graveyard of the mosque.[19]

It is not hard to imagine Roxelana making exploratory trips with the
daye to Kağıthane or consulting with her on the endowment, finished in
1545. She would visit the completed mosque, perhaps more than once.
The then-pastoral setting of Kağıthane and its stream, one of the so-
called sweet waters of European Istanbul, was an inviting, albeit bitter-
sweet, location for a family excursion. The *daye* apparently anticipated
the visits of Mehmed's relatives, for her mosque featured a screened gallery for members of the royal household. This small mosque was an intimate alternative to the lofty shrine to Mehmed's memory in the center
of the city.

While Suleyman was still away in the east, Roxelana occupied herself with the first of the charities she would sponsor in places sacred to
Islam. Turning her attention to Mecca and Medina, the two great Muslim
shrine cities, she endowed each with a hostel for pilgrims. Work began in
1549 when the chief eunuch of the Old Palace was dispatched to supervise construction. With these lodgings in Islam's two holiest cities, Suleyman's queen was achieving maturity as a patron of religious well-being.

Tile depicting the Ka`aba in
Mecca, ca. 1720–1730. The
Ka`aba is situated within
Islam's holiest mosque and
establishes the direction
to which all Muslims pray.
Labels for other structures
in the mosque's vicinity
may aid viewers unable
to make the pilgrimage.

The completion of these two structures overlapped with the renovation of the Ka`aba in Mecca, a project Suleyman undertook in 1551.[20]
Once again, the royal couple appeared to be coordinating their philanthropic efforts. Roxelana was the initiator and funder of the hostels, her
interest in assisting travelers and pilgrims by now a signature feature of
her patronage. Suleyman helped to pave the way for these far-away institutions by instructing local governors to facilitate the work of Roxelana's
agents. He presumably issued his orders somewhere along the eastern
campaign route.

Once Suleyman returned from his long absence, Roxelana finally
focused her attention on the Haseki hospital. She may have entertained
the idea of sponsoring a hospital ever since Suleyman added one in 1538
to his mother Hafsa's large complex in Manisa; she had had opportunities to explore it during her visits to the city. It seems Roxelana and
Suleyman discussed the need for more medical services in Istanbul, as
his own complex included a medical school in addition to a hospital.
There was definitely demand in the rapidly growing capital. Mehmed

the Conqueror had built a hospital as part of the city's first imperial foundation, but nothing had followed. His son Bayezid II included one in his large complex in Adrianople but not in his Istanbul foundation. The near-simultaneous arrival of hospitals in Roxelana's and Suleyman's names constituted a milestone in the history of Ottoman medical practice.

Aware that she was breaking new ground for Ottoman female builders in the capital, Roxelana perhaps imagined herself now joining a longer imperial tradition—that of queens of the city who enacted their charity in partnership with their husbands. Roxelana could hardly fail to recognize the parallel with Eirene, one of her Byzantine predecessors as benefactress of the city, if she knew anything of the twelfth-century queen. Eirene and her husband, the emperor John II Komnenos, endowed a monastery-church on the slope of the city's fourth hill, still one of the most visible monuments on Istanbul's skyline. Dedicated to St. Savior Pantocrator (Christ the Almighty), the large complex included two churches, the monastery, a hospice that cared for twenty-four old men, and a fifty-bed hospital with separate wards for men and women.[21] Soon after the conquest of Constantinople, Mehmed II converted the Pantocrator monastery-church into the first Ottoman madrasa in the city, thereby preserving it.[22]

John and Eirene can be seen today among the mosaics in Hagia Sophia, the great Byzantine cathedral that Mehmed turned into a mosque upon the fall of the city. Flanking the Virgin Mary, the empress offers a scroll and the emperor a purse of gold, symbolizing their religious donations. Eirene's story bears a striking resemblance to Roxelana's, except that she was a princess given in marriage to John while Roxelana was a country girl who came to Suleyman as a slave.

Born Piroska, daughter of the Catholic king of Hungary, Eirene converted to the Orthodox Church and gained her new name when she married. After giving the emperor eight children, she was impelled by her piety, according to hagiographic legend, to urge her husband to help her make this pious endowment an exceptional one.[23] Likewise, as mother of several children and then married queen, Roxelana had begun the work on her Haseki foundation, some of it with Suleyman's financial support.

When compared to other couples in history for the surpassing nature of their patronage, Suleyman and Roxelana were likened to Muslim rulers and their wives, not to Byzantine Christians. But the very stones of Constantinople might suggest models that were more immediately inspiring.

THE COMPLETION OF Roxelana's hospital in 1551 required the drawing up of a new charter. It would incorporate both the hospital and the other religious and charitable institutions she had founded since the charter of 1540. In this deed, as in the earlier document, Roxelana's concern for the qualities and qualifications of her foundation's staff stood out.

The hospital's two doctors had to observe an elaborate moral and social etiquette in addition to possessing a thorough medical education. In fact, the two charges, expertise in the practice of medicine and an exemplary bedside manner, were inseparable in Roxelana's deed. As they ministered to in- as well as outpatients, the doctors were to treat psyche as well as soma. Their character was critical. They must be "stouthearted, of noble and generous disposition, good-natured, and untroubled. They must demonstrate with every patient the kindness that they would toward an intimate friend." The doctors should not utter even the smallest of brutal or hateful words, for, as the charter noted, "one harsh word can weigh more heavily on a sick person than the worst of maladies." Comforting speech was not difficult to come by, for there were many words that were "purer than the river of paradise and sweeter than its springs" to the sick.[24] Roxelana's sensitivity to the patient's morale may have stemmed, in part at least, from the many painful hours Cihangir had spent in the hands of doctors.

This emphasis in the queen's charter on the health of the spirit as well as the body contrasts with the goals of the hospital constructed for Suleyman's foundation. In laying out the numerous qualifications of the hospital's three doctors, the charter for the Suleymaniye focused on knowledge of the various sciences and practices of healing (among them "expertise in the nature of the [four] humors"). Only in concluding did it prescribe that the doctors undertake their duties with care and consideration for their patients: "They shall approach medical matters and accomplish [their work] by attending with kindness and gentleness to the objectives and the needs of people of want and persons with urgent conditions."[25]

Might Roxelana have urged Suleyman to include this final note? Given that the Haseki hospital went up in tandem with the Suleymaniye, the couple may have consciously tailored their "houses of healing" (as hospitals were called in Turkish) to answer to different needs. Suleyman's could function as a teaching hospital alongside the medical school (a "madrasa for medicine"). We might think of the Suleymaniye as offering the latest in medical technology, while the Haseki provided a holistic approach to healing.[26] As its charter declared, Roxelana aimed for her hospital to be "the antidote to every affliction."

The Haseki hospital managed to provide a variety of medical services in a relatively compact space. It was structured around a courtyard that opened into two large circular halls, presumably the doctors' receiving rooms. These in turn gave onto nine rooms of varying sizes (or twenty-two domed spaces, as the Ottomans counted). In addition to the two doctors, the medical staff included two eye specialists, two surgeons, and two pharmacists. The latter had two assistants who prepared (literally, pounded) raw materials for medical use. Four nurses rotated day and night rounds, and two individuals monitored urine samples.[27]

Adding to the daily routine was a kind of outpatient service on Mondays and Thursdays, when the doctors were permitted to perform examinations and dispense medicines, mainly syrups and pastes, to petitioners. The charter firmly forbade the doctors from selling medicines or their own services outside the confines of the hospital. The deed does not make clear whether females were accepted as inpatients, but perhaps they could avail themselves of the outpatient resources.

By the time the hospital was added to the Haseki foundation, the green spaces that faced the hospice and surrounded the mosque had matured (they were now tended by a staff gardener). Fruits and flowers grown in these fertile areas were sold at the Avrat Pazar market and the profit returned to the foundation. The Haseki was far from poor, but it was clearly frugal—the garden products yielded only five hundred aspers. Frugality was perhaps the influence of Mihrumah's husband Rustem Pasha, an asper-pinching vizier who ordered the sale of flowers and vegetables grown on the extensive grounds of the New Palace. Some thought Rustem corrupt; others (including Suleyman) were grateful that he kept the imperial budget balanced.

WHILE SULEYMAN WAS occupied with his foundation and Roxelana with her hospital, the Safavid shah Tahmasp and his forces had been making devastating inroads into Ottoman territories. According to a Venetian report, the area lost to the Persians measured a thirty-day march north to south and eight days east to west.[28] The sultan was compelled to respond. Though not his last campaign, it was the most fateful.

Suleyman had not originally intended to lead this offensive. He had lately been delegating military leadership to his top viziers and governors, a policy that proved successful when two of his generals, the second vizier Kara Ahmed and the rising star Sokollu Mehmed, foiled yet another attempt by the Hapsburg Ferdinand I to dominate Transylvania.[29] The sultan assigned the grand vizier Rustem Pasha to act as commander in chief of the army that headed east in 1552. But alarming news from Rustem's camp at Aksaray in central Anatolia made clear that Suleyman could not afford to sit out this war.

According to Rustem, the Janissaries were exhibiting a dangerous tilt toward Mustafa, still governor of Amasya. Ottoman historians would later note that some soldiers could even be heard muttering that the sultan was too old and unwell to go against the enemy himself.[30] What needed to be done, they said, was to kill the grand vizier, who opposed Mustafa, and send the sultan into retirement in the palace at Dimetoka near Adrianople. They emphasized that that Mustafa was now forty years old, an age that balanced full maturity with the bravery and gallantry of youth he had long been admired for. Some partisans were even attempting to persuade the prince to take action to dethrone his father, but the honorable Mustafa refused, wrote the historians, despite accepting their reading of the political situation. "A strange spectacle," commented the seventeenth-century historian Solakzade Mehmed.[31]

The officer who delivered Rustem's dispatch provided an eyewitness account of Suleyman's reactions. The first was to vehemently discount the grand vizier's virtual charge of treason against Mustafa. Instead, the

Suleyman receiving Mustafa during the 1548 campaign against Iran. The prince's striking resemblance to his father, bearded and clothed in identical colors, may suggest his rumored intention to usurp the throne or perhaps his qualifications to succeed his father. Arifi, *Süleymanname.*

sultan placed the blame on partisan agitation—in the words attributed to him by the historian Ibrahim Peçevi, "God forbid that my Mustafa Khan should dare such insolence and should commit such an unwise move during my lifetime! It is troublemakers trying to obtain the rule for the prince they support who are responsible for such slander."[32] Suleyman's second reaction was to join the campaign. Setting out in late August 1553, he would lead the largest Ottoman army yet to confront the Safavids.

What happened next made a martyr of the prince and unleashed an outbreak of intense emotion across the empire. If the stated objective of the campaign was to contain the Safavid menace, Suleyman's own target had in the meanwhile become his eldest son. Mustafa was summoned to rendezvous with his father in the Eğreli valley, southeast of Konya. There was nothing unusual in this; Suleyman had already greeted Bayezid and Selim en route. Nevertheless, all Mustafa's advisers pled with him not to comply. Foremost among them was his mother Mahidevran.

Bernardo Navagero, Venetian ambassador from 1550 through 1552, had previously reported that the prince's mother "exercises great diligence to guard him from poisoning and reminds him every day that he has nothing else but this to avoid."[33] (Renier had reported several years earlier that Mahidevran prepared Mustafa's meals herself as a precaution.) Now the threat was palpable. But though his counselors anticipated the worst, the prince allegedly refused to believe his father would do him harm and pointed out that failure to go was construable as an act of defiance. Mustafa sent gifts ahead to the sultan and arrived in the imperial camp on October 5.

While the story of the prince's execution the following day has been told varyingly, nuanced by time or the narrator's view of the matter, most accounts concur on the following sequence of events. Despite a final warning of his probable fate, contained in a note delivered to his camp by an arrow, Mustafa made his way on horseback, accompanied by a train of officials, to the tent where his father awaited him. He entered alone, leaving his bodyguards outside—once again ignoring cautions that had been pressed upon him. The execution was a gruesome affair, with more than one botched attempt to strangle the prince. The executioners allegedly succeeded only when he tripped on his long robe trying to flee.

The prince's corpse was thrown outside Suleyman's tent as proof of the deed. Other commands of the sultan were carried out in rapid succession—all of them acts that symbolized the erasure of the dead prince's household. Two of Mustafa's men, stationed at the threshold of his tent, were executed; the horse he had ridden was transferred to the sultan's stables; the goods in his tent were confiscated for the imperial treasury; and, according to some, his effacement was symbolized by the ritual collapsing of his tent. Local religious dignitaries were summoned to participate in funeral prayers, and by the end of the day, the prince's body, now ready for burial, had departed. The cortege would make its way to Bursa, for Mustafa was denied the interment in Istanbul granted to his younger half brother Mehmed. At least he had the honor of resting among other Ottoman royalty in the imperial funerary complex that had grown up around the mosque of Murad II.

Grief and rage broke out in the camp the moment Mustafa's death was made public. There were clamorous cries for Rustem's head—he was blamed for persuading Suleyman of his son's perfidy. But the sultan disappointed his soldiers, for rather than execute Rustem, he dismissed him from the grand vizierate and sent him into a semiexile in a palace belonging to his wife Mihrumah on the outskirts of Istanbul. The vacated office was given to Kara Ahmed, who had recently triumphed in Europe. If it was a natural promotion for the second vizier, it was also a recognition that only someone who had been amicable toward Mustafa could calm the troops, many of whom had been devoted to the prince since his childhood. Some believed that Kara Ahmed himself had shot the warning arrow.

Suleyman sought to rekindle loyalty through reward: Janissaries received raises in their salaries, and he provided Mustafa's soldiers with grants of office in the imperial cavalry.[34] Hearts were not easily won, however. A further blow to Mustafa's partisans, as well as to sympathetic subjects around the empire, occurred several months later. Mustafa's only son Mehmed was hunted down and strangled. The little prince had taken protective flight with his mother. He was killed for fear that disaffected soldiers and possibly civilians would rally around him to form a threatening new faction. It is impossible to imagine the grief and perhaps the rage of Mustafa's mother Mahidevran, whose whole life's purpose had been obliterated.

WHAT WAS IT that convinced Suleyman to execute Mustafa after first protesting his innocence? However challenging to pin down, the answer is critical because the prince's killing became the fount of Roxelana's notoriety and the principal reason history has vilified her. Even unfounded accusations leveled earlier against the queen—the exile of Mahidevran from the harem, Mustafa's distant post in Anatolia—acquired an ex post facto plausibility for her critics, given that she had dared to eliminate what in their eyes was the Ottomans' best hope for the future.

Over the centuries, more scholars have found Roxelana guilty of deadly intrigue than innocent, with her reputation for scheming only increasing. So tenacious has the story of her domination of Suleyman become that distinguished historians of the twentieth century could censure her in uncompromising and unreflective terms: "After the success of [Roxelana], to whom Suleyman was extremely bound, in having her rival, the mother of Prince Mustafa, banished from the palace, she resorted to every kind of trick in her inordinate ambition to secure the Ottoman throne for her son."[35]

But only the rare Ottoman historian of the century following Mustafa's execution directly accused Suleyman's favorite of instigating the prince's death.[36] Some were silent; others found sufficient cause for Mustafa's demise in the competition for power among men. The explanation most frequently proffered was that the scheming grand vizier had duped the sultan. However, one could read this view, if so inclined, as an implicit accusation against Roxelana, for some believed both Rustem and his wife Mihrumah to be partisans of her full brothers Selim and Bayezid and thus allies of Roxelana.[37]

But the historical assignment of guilt to Roxelana contains a serious flaw: the assumption that the sultan could so easily be duped. At work here is the Ottoman habit of blaming subordinates so as to avoid holding the powerful accountable for unsavory acts. Suleyman was no fool, however. He routinely sought opinions and views other than Rustem's—indeed, he was said to keep his grand vizier at arm's length, allowing him into the palace for formal consultation only. By contrast, the eunuch vizier Ibrahim had free access to the palace and to Suleyman, who played chess with this experienced eighty-year-old statesman and constantly praised his actions.[38]

It is difficult not to conclude that the decision to sacrifice Mustafa was ultimately Suleyman's. It was a question of preserving the empire. Sometime between Rustem's accusatory report and his own arrival in central Anatolia, Suleyman came to believe that Mustafa represented a threat that was too great to tolerate, regardless of whether he was guilty of plotting for the throne or not. He had ample reason for concern over Mustafa's popularity. Soldiers' restlessness with eastern campaigns, long and relatively unrewarding, had erupted in 1515 and again in 1535. A Janissary defection to the prince's side would be especially threatening now that the empire was on the eve of a new war with Iran. The security of Anatolia was paramount, and it was there that Mustafa's greatest support was located.

It was not that Suleyman necessarily distrusted Mustafa. Twice when he himself was fighting in Europe, he put his eldest son in charge of Anatolian defense. Moreover, in fall 1549, when his second eastern campaign was going badly, Suleyman had even summoned Mustafa to Diyarbakır to rally the troops.[39] But now a coup in the prince's name, even if Mustafa opposed it, would be a godsend to the Safavids. The eastern half of the great peninsula, as yet tenuously integrated into Ottoman systems of control, harbored populations who might well defect to Tahmasp. "The Sufi," as Europeans referred to him, commanded not only an army but also a charismatic religious appeal that penetrated the frontier into Anatolia, where his adherents could conceivably turn into active partisans.

Historians who have judged Roxelana guilty have largely failed to consider Mustafa's part in the affair.[40] People had already been hailing the prince as "sultan." Venetian ambassadors reported in 1550 and again in 1552 that Mustafa was universally desired to follow his father to the throne.[41] He had become so popular, it seems, that Suleyman could not be certain that his troops would remain loyal to him in the event of a showdown. Later, in 1555, the Hapsburg envoy Ogier Ghiselin de Busbecq would write, "There was nothing that the Sultan so much dreaded, as that there might be some secret disaffection among the Janissaries, which might break out when it was impossible to apply any remedy."[42]

It was probably no secret that Mustafa was building support for himself. He had requested and received formal assurance from the governor of Erzurum, Ottoman bastion in northeastern Anatolia, that he would side with the prince at the moment of Suleyman's death, when the brothers would openly vie for the succession.[43] Mustafa had also exchanged correspondence with the Venetian government (and perhaps other powers), probably to the same effect.[44] On the other hand, a prince worthy of the throne might be expected to line up backers, and both Mahidevran and Roxelana were justifiably making it their business to rally support for their sons. Mustafa was clearly taking action, but there was no evidence of a planned insurrection.

If not guilty of direct action, neither prince nor queen was necessarily innocent of intent. Roxelana need not actively plot harm against Mustafa in order to influence Suleyman against him. She had had some thirty years of proximity to the sultan to plead on behalf of her own sons, to whom Mahidevran's Mustafa was by definition the greatest political danger. Both mothers, innocent young slave concubines with no security until they gave birth to a male child, came to understand the contract that would define their career: absolute fidelity to the son. Roxelana's devotion to that charge did not waver when her career took the exceptional turn toward queenhood and motherhood of multiple sons. She must have been a perpetual lobby for her princes and, implicitly if not explicitly, an ardent opponent of Suleyman's eldest son. Mahidevran operated by the same political calculation, but it was obvious to everyone that she enjoyed far fewer opportunities to draw Suleyman to Mustafa's side. Like Mustafa, Roxelana was guilty of the capacity to wield disproportionate power.

For Roxelana's part, we can only imagine the concern she felt as Mustafa became ever more popular while her sons seemed to enjoy little enthusiasm from the public. Upon his return to Venice in late 1554, Venetian ambassador Domenico Trevisano described the sons of Suleyman: "Sultan Selim is of portly build and is devoted to wine and women. Sultan Bayezid is of a more delicate build and is devoted to the literary arts. But neither the one nor the other has fame as a captain or has acquired the love and favor of the people and the Janissaries that Sultan Mustafa acquired."[45] Of Roxelana's sons, only Mehmed, the eldest, appeared to manifest qualities that made him readily popular, but he had died tragically a year after assuming his governorship.

Roxelana's anxiety must have grown exponentially when Suleyman made the decision to go to war himself in 1553. As in 1548, this time too he drafted all three of her sons into the war effort. Bayezid would take his turn as lieutenant in Adrianople, but Selim and Cihangir accompanied their father into Anatolia. The worst nightmare of Roxelana's life was becoming plausible: that her husband and sons could perish if internal dissent erupted into violence and Mustafa's partisans prevailed. The specter of Suleyman's natural death and the ensuing combat for succession was always present, of course, but the immediate possibility was catastrophic—that only she and Mihrumah would remain alive, widowed and doubtless facing some form of punitive exile. The pragmatist in Roxelana appears to have taken precautionary measures—Trevisano noted that Selim's sons had come from Manisa to stay with their grand-mother.[46] Bayezid's sons were presumably with him in Adrianople.

But how far would Roxelana go to influence Suleyman against his oldest son? She was too astute to jeopardize her own sons' future by overplaying her hand and alienating Suleyman. There is also the important question of the degree to which Suleyman tolerated Roxelana's importuning. The sultan was well named, for he had a Solomonic obligation to balance his two families—the traditional one he had created as prince with Mahidevran and the revolutionary one he built as sultan with Roxelana. There were very possibly moments when husband and wife clashed over the vexing issue of the succession.

There is little compelling evidence that Suleyman exhibited a sustained desire for a particular one of his sons to succeed him. According to Navagero, he even acknowledged the probability of Mustafa's success, for when Cihangir suggested that his physical deformity would allow him to escape the fate of execution, Suleyman allegedly replied, "My son, Mustafa will become the sultan and will deprive you all of your lives."[47] Accurate or not, the ambassador's sources apparently found the sultan's comment plausible. On the other hand, Suleyman cannot have entirely suppressed the awful prospect of the demise of the family he had created with Roxelana.

In the end, the most probable explanation for Mustafa's execution was his very success. Any reservations Suleyman held about his son's intentions were increasingly compounded by the sheer danger of a prince, however innocent, whose extreme popularity constituted a threat to his own sovereignty and thus the stability of the whole empire. On Suleyman's mind were certainly the events of his own youth, which now threatened to repeat themselves. His father Selim had overthrown his own father, Bayezid II, allegedly to retire him to Dimetoka—precisely what the discontented soldiers supposedly suggested to Mustafa. Bayezid had died on the way, allegedly poisoned by his son. His death unleashed a civil war among princes second only to that of the early fifteenth century, when the nascent state nearly dissolved in fragmentation.

Not to counter the challenge to Suleyman's sovereignty that Mustafa represented, even if unintentionally, was to risk invasion from the west as well as east while the empire went to war with itself. By mid-century, the Ottomans faced formidable powers on both fronts. Archduke Ferdinand had already exploited Ottoman distraction in the east by occupying Transylvania, while the threat from Iran was ideological as well as military. In this light, Suleyman knowingly made the painful and costly but politically prudent decision.

Venetian comments on the affair provide perspective. Navagero spoke extensively on the matter of the succession in his report of February 1553, eight months before Mustafa's execution.[48] Astute and well informed, he predicted that Mustafa would become sultan when Suleyman died. At present, he was in such great favor that there was no suspicion he might attempt a coup against his father. There was, however, universal dread among the populace that the prince's path to the throne would be a bloody affair. (Reporting after Mustafa's death, Trevisano noted, "Every Turk and every Christian was left in great sorrow.")[49]

Navagero did not need to spell out for the Senate that Suleyman's death (or dethronement) was expected to precipitate a civil war among the brothers. It did not matter that Bayezid was rumored to prefer Mustafa to Selim, his full brother, or that some believed the younger siblings would not challenge their half brother.[50] Even if Mustafa, the presumed victor in a showdown, were to spare the empire yet another deadly war among princes—by imposing strictly enforced exile or imprisonment on his half brothers or even by introducing a whole new system whereby junior siblings maintained their governorships (the practice of the Safavids)—his advisers would stress the necessity of their deaths. The factions backing Selim and Bayezid would take action.

As for Suleyman's own preference, Navagero reported, it was hard to tell, for all the princes were his sons. "But he always has near him his wife, who seeks to place her own [sons] in favor and Mustafa in disfavor."[51] Still, Navagero commented, she recognized that she could do little about Mustafa's eminence. Nor, in his opinion, could Suleyman, and this was one reason that he preferred to avoid war and pursue peace (as war would mobilize the troops and stoke their appetite for rallying around Mustafa).

Navagero's report vividly depicted an atmosphere of troubled speculation and widespread dread of the consequences of a war for the throne. Suleyman's longevity was apparently a constant topic of debate. But a

very different story, that of an empire secure and strong, would be told
by Navagero's successor Trevisano when he presented his report to the
Senate on the last day of 1554, fourteen months after Mustafa's execution. He went on to describe Suleyman as a tall man with a melancholy
mien that made him appear grave. The sultan had once been thought to
possess a humane and kindly nature, remarked Trevisano, but now many
believed the contrary because of the deaths he meted out to his own son
and grandson.[52]

> *You allowed the words of a Russian witch into your ears*
> *Deluded by tricks and deceit, you did the bidding*
> *of that spiteful hag*
> *You slaughtered that swaying cypress, fruit of life's orchard*
> *What has the merciless Monarch of the World*
> *done to Sultan Mustafa?*[53]

So the poet Nisayi accused Suleyman and Roxelana in the second verse
of an elegy she composed for Mustafa. Most likely a member of the circle of literati at the prince's court in Amasya, Nisayi apparently knew
Suleyman when he was young and later joined Mahidevran's retinue.
The poem's first verse denounced the sultan for tyranny and abandon-
ment of the compassion integral to Islam.[54]

The most famous of all elegies for Mustafa was that of the Albanian-
born soldier Taşlıcalı Yahya. He blamed the tragedy on the "deceit of
Rustem" (the phrase, a chronogram for the year of the execution, was
memorable).[55] The poem spread quickly among Mustafa's followers and
sympathizers. Unsurprisingly, it cost Yahya the favor of Rustem, who
had earlier been his patron. But the harshest words were reserved for
the sultan. I wonder who has ever seen or heard of such a thing, asked
the soldier-poet—that a great prince of just temperament should slay his
son?[56] The emphasis on injustice in both elegies targeted the epithet that
Suleyman was beginning to enjoy: Kanuni (the just), or *giustissimo*, as
the Venetian Renier recorded it a few years earlier.[57]

Suleyman appears to have borne in stoic acceptance the burden of
sacrificing his son for the integrity of the empire. The elegies pronounced
the sultan guilty, and Trevisano confirmed the raw anger directed at him.

Yet Suleyman is widely remembered as an exemplar of the good sovereign and his reign as the high point of Ottoman achievement. That he ruled creditably for another thirteen years after Mustafa's demise clearly helped to cement his abiding reputation, but more significant is the fact that Roxelana came to serve as the lightning rod for responsibility in the affair of Mustafa.

Later generations and centuries represented the prince's execution as the culmination of a career that, in the view of Roxelana's critics, was inexorably geared toward realizing her selfish ends—namely, the triumph of her sons over Mustafa. But this characterization overlooks the fact that Roxelana's sons were also Suleyman's. Roxelana was justifiably a strong advocate for them, and Mustafa may have done nothing more calculating than strive to be a great prince and worthy heir to his father. The tragic irony of Suleyman's generous regard for those closest to him is that their goals and their influence were at counterpurposes. It was the awful conundrum at the heart of the empire.

15

LAST YEARS

ULEYMAN REMAINED ON campaign following Mustafa's demise, for
no retreat was possible. A month later, he arrived in the northern
Syrian city of Aleppo together with Cihangir. There the sultan would
pass a long winter season before confronting the Safavids in the spring.
Selim was stationed with his troops a few days' march to the north in
the provincial capital of Maraş. Part of the army was camped in northern Anatolia, but Suleyman's viziers, other officials, and the bulk of the
armed forces remained with him.

An anonymous Venetian living in Aleppo, most likely a member
of the resident merchant community, penned a detailed description of
the Ottoman entry into the city on November 8, 1553.[1] No expense was
spared to dazzle the eye. Each of the various companies of soldiers was
splendidly outfitted in its own colorful uniform, as were the different
divisions of palace officials and attendants who served the sultan wherever he went. By the Venetian's count, more than 10,000 men marched
or rode into the city in utter silence, while the onlookers greeted them
noisily. The people of Aleppo were perhaps less torn by Mustafa's death
than the inhabitants of Anatolia, where the prince had been one of
them for twenty years. Aleppans were already familiar with Cihangir
and Bayezid, the sons of Roxelana; they did not know the dead prince
personally.

Once the column of soldiers reached the spacious square at the foot
of Aleppo's ancient citadel, they divided into two wings. The moment
the sultan came into view, riding his horse between them, fifty cannons
were fired. Suleyman's private secretary, Celalzade Mustafa, observed
that scholars, dervishes, and the notables of the city hailed their ruler;
the Venetian noted that all bowed low.[2] Cihangir entered before Suleyman, receiving the same obeisance that would shortly be accorded his

father. Riding behind the commander of the Janissaries, the prince "affectionately saluted all who demonstrated reverence toward him."[3]

The lavish parade sent a message to Shah Tahmasp that the Levant was strongly protected (Suleyman's governor in Erzurum had sent warning that the region could soon be under Safavid threat).[4] But the staging of the imperial entry presumably aimed equally to displace pernicious gossip about the recent tragedy. Smaller versions of the spectacle had likely been enacted in other cities along the army's route. The exposure of Cihangir and Selim made the point that Suleyman had other adult heirs; knowledgeable parties would recognize that a third son, Bayezid, currently represented the dynastic house in Europe.

How devastated then must all have been when Cihangir died three weeks after the arrival in Aleppo. Felled by a sudden sickness, he perished within four days, despite various remedies applied by the puzzled physicians. A formal procession of the highest-ranking Ottoman dignitaries accompanied the prince's casket to the funeral prayers, where leading dignitaries of the city doubtless thronged. For numerous villages and cities across Anatolia, Cihangir's would be the second royal cortege within a matter of weeks to pass by on its way west.

Word may have reached Roxelana before the arrival in Istanbul of the coffin and its retinue of soldiers and attendants. Bayezid most likely came from Adrianople to share his mother and sister's grief. Cihangir was interred in the sumptuous tomb built for his older brother Mehmed. The two princes rest side by side, the oldest and youngest of Roxelana and Suleyman's five sons. A memorial mosque for Cihangir would be constructed by the royal architect Sinan, set on a pastoral hill overlooking the Bosphorus. It was said that the prince had enjoyed excursions there and that his mother reminded his father of his wish to build a mosque in the area, whereupon Suleyman took action.[5] The neighborhood, today a lively bohemian quarter, retains the prince's name.

Roxelana's last years were perhaps the most challenging of her life, paralleled only by the traumatic loss of her childhood home and family. The new family she had built with Suleyman had lost its innocence and its one innocent member, and now her two remaining sons would perforce become rivals and perhaps enemies. Consequently she found herself mediating tensions that emerged among the men in her family.

As it turned out, her own health would decline more rapidly than Suleyman's. Meanwhile, the resilient queen carried on with the occupations
that fulfilled her, forging ahead with more philanthropic foundations and
corresponding on behalf of peace.

DURING HER HUSBAND'S prolonged absence, Roxelana had resumed her
role as key correspondent from the capital. Suleyman could count on
astute intelligence as well as loving words. A letter sent to the Aleppo
camp in late 1553, before she had news of Cihangir's death but after
news of Mustafa's, opens with her usual "thousands and thousands of
prayers and praises," accompanied by "one hundred and one thousand
kinds of longing and yearning" to be with him. She asks after his health,
especially his gout, and prays to God to protect him from all harm—
indeed, may he live to be as old as Noah! If he should ask after her, she is
capable of nothing but suffering in his absence. After repeated iterations
of her pain, she tells him (in plainer language) that she really misses seeing him. Roxelana closes the letter by kissing Cihangir's eyes, sending
the respects of Suleyman's two granddaughters Huma Shah and Aisha,
and informing him, should he wonder about his capital, that the city is
"safe and secure" and that all are praying for and missing him.

Three postscripts contained more candid news for Suleyman and
betrayed Roxelana's worries. These were inscribed in the usual Ottoman
epistolary style, running counterclockwise up the right-hand margin of
the letter, across the top, and onto the reverse side. As she had done before, Roxelana reminded Suleyman firmly of the critical importance of
positive news from the front. Given the general turmoil over Mustafa's
death and the concern that Suleyman was too old to fight, she would be
right to think it was even more crucial now. What prompted the first
postscript was the fact that the capital was unrealistically keyed up over
a report that a messenger was on his way (in Turkish, the word refers to a
bearer of good tidings). The long side note read,

> The city is clamoring that a messenger is coming, and everyone is get-
> ting ready to deck the city out. They are saying the messenger will arrive
> in two or three days and so they are standing ready to decorate the city. I

don't know if this is rumor or if it is true. Now, my sultan, it is very odd that a good-news messenger should come when you yourself are wintering in Aleppo. Furthermore, my sultan, neither the son of the heretic [the shah] nor his wife has been captured, nothing has been happening. Now if a messenger arrives saying "No progress here, nothing there," no one is going to be happy, my sultan.[6]

Roxelana had apparently been planning a visit to Bayezid in Adrianople. Now she tells Suleyman not to send letters there, since she has changed her mind and won't go until she has heard from him. Again taking up the matter of the messenger, she wonders whose idea it was to dispatch him, for people have been questioning why the sultan would send tidings merely to announce that he was settled in his winter camp. She could not know that the eagerly awaited messenger was in all likelihood the courier who would instead bring her the calamitous news

Letter from Roxelana to Suleyman, 1553. Her valedictory signature appears in the lower left corner: "And that's that. Your lowly slave."

about her youngest son. How painful it would be for Suleyman to receive these anxious but still innocent words from his beloved.

In the postscript at the top of the letter, Roxelana turns her thoughts to the impending war. She invokes divine support for the Ottoman venture, without which, it was believed, victory was impossible. "It is to be hoped, my sultan, that the Lord God brings that accursed one [Tahmasp] misfortune and failure," she writes.[7] "May the Lord God remove him to the place of Qarun [Croesus] and destroy him" (in the Qur'an, wealth and pride cause the earth to swallow up Qarun and his family).[8] Roxelana then turns to her concern about the conflict. "If he [the Shah] has set out [on campaign], then whatever is possible will be done. If he hasn't, please don't send your noble self there."

Receptive as usual to the words of sages, Roxelana was apparently influenced here by the counsel of a seer regarding the advisability of the confrontation with Tahmasp. "Just now, my emperor, a great holy man has sent word that it would be better if His Majesty the Sultan didn't go [to war] this year," she writes, "[but] if he has already gone, it was God's command, it was not forbidden." Apparently the holy man was reassured by the size of the army and its ample supply trains. In Roxelana's paraphrase, "By going with the soldiers and with the horses and the sheep, [the sultan] has headed off all kinds of misfortune and mishap. . . . With the help and grace of God, victory will henceforth be His Majesty's." She concludes, "This is what he said, my sultan, you know best."

The postscript on the reverse side of the letter was a plea on behalf of Rustem Pasha, still in semiexile on the outskirts of the capital, having lost the grand vizierate due to the furor of Mustafa's partisans. "My fortune-favored, my happiness . . . Rustem Pasha is your slave," pleads Roxelana. "Do not withhold your noble favor from him, my fortune-favored." She is concerned that Suleyman will pay heed to angry sentiments lingering among the military and perhaps even his close advisers. "Do not listen to what anyone says," she urges, "Let it be for the sake of your slave Mihrumah, my fortune-favored, my emperor, for your noble sake, and for my, your slave's, sake too, my prosperous sultan." This was a personal entreaty, but the politician in Roxelana would doubtless recognize that it was too soon to reinstate her son-in-law as the grand vizier. Perhaps she feared that Suleyman would find it necessary to sacrifice him to achieve stability while at war.

Of Roxelana's surviving letters to Suleyman, this one is richest in content. Some of its features are not new: she had been a barometer of the capital's mood before, and she had conveyed the well wishes of spiritual figures before. Nor had she held back her opinions of Suleyman's grand viziers (recall her postscript in 1526 telling Suleyman she would explain when he returned from Hungary why she was angry with Ibrahim Pasha). But this is the first time we see Roxelana openly pushing for a political favor from her husband. It is also the first time we see her palpably nervous, even agitated.

Roxelana worried about Suleyman's health—not only its fragility on an extended campaign but also its liability in the eyes of some factions in the army. This was not an overwrought concern, as an incident in Aleppo would demonstrate: when news of a death (Cihangir's) began to emerge from the Aleppo palace, it was assumed that it was the sultan who had died. Suleyman was compelled to make a hasty appearance, leaning on a cane, to stop the Janissaries from ransacking the bazaars (they claimed plunder as their traditional right during an interregnum). "There was a moment when we feared for our goods and our lives," wrote the anonymous Venetian who authored a long report on the eastern campaign. The loss was small, and the Janissaries were forced to return what they had taken, but they had effectively demonstrated their power to disrupt.[9]

THE CONFRONTATION WITH Iran began in earnest in spring 1554, and the mood of the troops would now be tested. Even in death, Mustafa posed a threat, for his young son was still alive when the war began. The anonymous Venetian in Aleppo reported a widespread and openly voiced desire to see to the dead prince's son on the throne. Roxelana and Bayezid, stationed in Adrianople, would be aware of this reality.[10] It was as if many had come to regard Mustafa as the rightful ruler and his son the natural heir to the throne. Partisans and sympathizers within the army could cause overt trouble or might withhold the loyalty and discipline the Ottoman military was famous for.

Suleyman himself very clearly understood the danger, for he rallied support in uncharacteristic sultanic fashion with "a very rare speech," first in Diyarbakır and again in Erzurum, the two Ottoman military bastions in the east.[11] At the open *divan* in Diyarbakır, he addressed not only his top officials but also numerous echelons of company commanders. He greeted his men, listened to their reports, and then explained at length why it was necessary to go deep into Safavid territory and how he had made every provision for their safety, expecting in return their devotion to the sultanate. Responding with fervor, the assembly enthusiastically pledged to follow their sultan beyond India and China, all the way to the mountain of Qaf (the legendary end of the earth).

It helped that pledges were solidified with bonuses of 1,000 silver aspers to every soldier (possibly in lieu of the accession bonus they would have received had Mustafa become sultan). The process—rally and reward—was repeated in Erzurum when the forces arriving from Ottoman Europe met up with the main body of the army. Not coincidentally, it was at this time that the eunuch Ibrahim, now second vizier, carried out the order to kill Mustafa's son Mehmed. Suleyman had waited until the troops were far away on the Iranian frontier. It would be too late for them to react as news trickled through, for a broken oath of loyalty could mean death. The campaign ended without major incident, although unwanted numbers perished in the east from disease and lack of rations.

The military results were inconclusive. Suleyman and his commanders had failed to draw Tahmasp into battle. The Ottoman army instead invaded the Safavid frontier zones of Nakhchivan and Karabakh, only to find that Tahmasp had purposefully despoiled much of the region. The final straw was the destruction by the shah's son Ismail of an Ottoman supply train coming from central Anatolia. The two empires had reached a draw, proving themselves equally capable of deadly raids into each other's territory but equally incapable of lasting conquests. Suleyman withdrew to Amasya to await negotiations for peace with the shah's emissaries. He would turn Mustafa's longtime capital into an arena of international diplomacy and thereby impress sultanic authority upon any lingering dissident sentiment.

Finally concluded in April 1555, the Treaty of Amasya established a frontier between the two powers: the Ottomans had retained Iraq and most of Kurdistan, while the Safavids recovered the southern Caucasus and Tabriz, their capital city until the Ottomans had seized it in 1548.[12] It was during the long negotiations with Iran that Archduke Ferdinand's ambassador, the Flemish diplomat Ogier Ghiselin de Busbecq, made his way to Amasya to sue for cessation of Ottoman raids into Austrian-controlled regions of Hungary. The negotiations with Ferdinand, however, would be drawn out until 1562. Busbecq passed some of that time as a hostage under house arrest, allowing him ample time to write four long letters that he would publish in 1581; widely read, they became a source of information (and misinformation) about Roxelana for future generations across Europe.

Roxelana was doubtless overjoyed at her husband's return to Istanbul in late July 1555. He had been gone one month short of two difficult years. That they could now mourn Cihangir's death together was among the comforts of his return for Roxelana. The peace treaty in hand and the extended parleys with Ferdinand were another gift for Roxelana, since Suleyman would not be taking his forces to war again anytime soon. The truce with Iran would hold until 1578 and that with the Hapsburgs until Ferdinand's death in 1564 and the accession of his ambitious son Maximilian II.

Despite the several trials of the war, the Ottomans appeared as powerful and threatening as ever to their Venetian observers. The ambassador Domenico Trevisano explained to the Senate in late 1554 why no European state could defeat them: their full treasury could support a war at any time, and the sultan enjoyed a particular obedience and loyalty afforded him by each member of his army and navy. (The ambassador attributed the latter more to fear than to love and to the fact that the soldiers were slaves.) In the opinion of a Turkish acquaintance, noted Trevisano, the army was strong because it tolerated no wine, whoring, or gambling.[13] Likewise, the anonymous Venetian in Aleppo wondered who could prevail against Suleyman and answered his own question: "All Christianity lives in division." European princes thought of nothing but quarreling, preferring to take land from one another instead of defending themselves against the Ottoman sultan, he lamented.[14]

The empire may have looked united to its rivals, but achieving a modicum of internal harmony would take some time. As Busbecq's second letter, composed in July 1556, demonstrated, all attention was focused on Bayezid. Suleyman's return from Amasya to Istanbul was marred by news of a pretender active around Salonika. Known to history as "Pseudo Mustafa," he claimed to be Suleyman's eldest son, another having been executed in his place. Considerable numbers of demobilized cavalrymen and assorted malcontents hastened to join his uprising, which was soon strong enough to threaten Adrianople. Bayezid, still his father's deputy for the European domains of the empire, sent troops to quell the rebellion, appointed a local governor to take charge of the operation, and notified his father. The pretender was executed on August 18, 1555, not quite three weeks after Suleyman finally arrived home.[15] But the affair did not bode well for Bayezid, for Suleyman came to consider the prince's response suspiciously slow. Roxelana would find herself acting as peacemaker between father and son.

Even though the pretender had no connection to Mustafa, certain of his supporters did, especially among the Ottoman cavalry. Some carried the soldier-poet Yahya's elegy by heart as they returned from the Safavid war to their stations in Thrace and the Balkans. Unlike the Janissaries, urban creatures in peacetime, cavalrymen were denizens of the countryside, where they lived and served when not at war. Those who had fought in the recent conflict received their campaign bonuses only to learn that the most lucrative allotments had gone to Janissaries of the capital—as if the sultan had purchased loyalty at the center at their expense. Anatolian cavalrymen had been similarly disillusioned a few years earlier when Rustem had denied Mustafa's appeals to repel menacing raiders from Georgia.[16] This discontent among sectors of the cavalry would bear on both Bayezid's and Selim's futures, as the brothers now became each other's sole rival for their father's throne.

SULEYMAN'S LONG ABSENCE in the east had not deterred Roxelana from pursuing her career as a patron. Apart from her family and her duties in the Old and New Palaces, fostering endowments continued to be the queen's principal diversion from politics, and now she would claim another new frontier for Ottoman women. Palestine was her next destination. While the Haseki hospital was being completed in Istanbul, construction on a large and well-funded complex in the holy city of Jerusalem was beginning. It would not formally open until 1557, but its first structure, a kitchen, was distributing food to the poor by late

1551.[17] The Jerusalem project would be the last major monument Roxelana completed.

An assembly of structures and courtyards housed the several services provided by the foundation. Roxelana's contribution to religious life consisted of a mosque and a fifty-five-room lodging for pious Muslims who followed a long tradition of taking up residence in Jerusalem to lead a life of contemplation. The foundation's charter deed described this section of the endowment: "The illustrious donor has gratuitously built and embellished [a building] with fifty-five doors to high-domed rooms [that are] pleasant dwelling-places of firm structure and solid construction, and she has set them aside for those devotees who dwell in the holy precincts."[18]

Those holy precincts were visible from Roxelana's complex. Located high on the slope of a hill, in the center of the old walled city, it had a clear view of the Noble Sanctuary, as Muslims called the Temple Mount. Holiest site to Jews, it was the third-most-sacred space to Muslims (Mecca and Medina were jointly known as the Two Noble Sanctuaries). On the Mount's elevated platform stood three structures built by caliphs of the first Islamic century: the mosque of Al-Aqsa, a small prayer house called the Dome of the Chain, and the Dome of the Rock, a shrine that enclosed a great rock. Thought by Jews to mark the site of the First and Second Temples, the rock is believed by many Muslims to be the place from which Muhammad ascended in his night journey to heaven, where God instructed him on the correct manner of prayer. The striking visibility of the shrine's golden dome makes it perhaps the most iconic feature of the Jerusalem skyline. The building's brilliant tile facade was the work of Suleyman's master craftsmen.

As the charter described it, Roxelana's foundation served the local community with "a spacious courtyard—a source of abundant favors— and beside it an exquisite specimen of a kitchen, a bakery, a cellar, a woodshed, privies, a refectory, and a store room."[19] Similar in makeup to the soup kitchen in Roxelana's Istanbul complex, this one apparently fed more "poor and needy"—some four hundred twice a day.[20] The final elements of the foundation were "a clean and fine caravanserai . . . and a spacious and tidy stable . . . for all those who travel and journey." The travelers, like the poor and the devotees, presumably also qualified for the soup kitchen's meals. Christians too may have been eligible—at least the charter deed did not exclude them, and the neighborhood was partially Christian.[21] Since the 1920s and the collapse of the Ottoman empire, the Muslim Vocational Orphanage has occupied the premises, and the kitchen still provides nourishment to the poor.[22]

The Jerusalem endowment could be called Roxelana's crowning accomplishment. It combined and aggrandized two features of her earlier endeavors—the substantial soup kitchen in Istanbul and the hostels for pilgrims she had founded in Mecca and Medina. Her work helped to bring an Ottoman style of charity to the old lands of Islam by adding these two features to the classic formula of mosque and madrasa.[23] Nearing her fifties, Roxelana was now building as a dynastic elder, no longer burdened by the potential for public disapproval that accompanied her Haseki foundation in the late 1530s. And once again, Roxelana's projects dovetailed with her husband's—in this instance the royal couple focused simultaneously on the most important cities of the Levant.

Suleyman was at the time directing his own efforts to Damascus, having already delegated responsibility for Aleppo to his viziers. He first endowed a soup kitchen, completed in 1552, to accompany the shrine-mosque and hostel his father Selim I had constructed in 1518 in memory of the great sufi master Ibn al-Arabi (the mystic was believed to have predicted Selim's conquest of the Arab lands). Then, in 1554, Suleyman undertook his own large foundation in Damascus. Situated on the route that passed through the Syrian capital and wound south to Mecca, it honored the critical role the city and its governors played as custodians of the annual pilgrimage.

In Jerusalem, Roxelana exploited a specifically female identity that enhanced the reputation of her project. She was the third notable woman to adopt the site she selected. The first was a great lady of the eastern Mediterranean world: Helena, mother of Constantine, the Roman emperor who founded Constantinople. Allegedly an innkeeper when she became the concubine of Constantine's father, Helena, like her son, converted to Christianity. In 326, the elderly empress famously journeyed to Jerusalem, where she is said to have uncovered sacred Christian sites and relics, most importantly the True Cross.[24] These discoveries, for which Helena was later sainted, were a critical element in the revival of

Jerusalem as an important locus of Christian pilgrimage.[25] Constantine had the Church of the Holy Sepulcher constructed near Golgotha, its location also an alleged discovery by Helena. Near her son's church was the site where she herself built a hostel for pilgrims.

The next prominent female to grace the hilltop location, halfway between the core Christian and Muslim holy places, was Lady Tunshuq al-Muzaffariya. Sometime in the late fourteenth century, she built herself a palatial residence with an enormous second-floor reception hall and ground-floor stables with adjacent paddocks. A slave of disputed origins who converted to Islam, this mysterious but wealthy woman lived in Jerusalem as a religious pilgrim.[26] By this time Helena's hostel was long gone, as Byzantine Jerusalem had given way to various Muslim dynasties that ruled the city from 638 onward, except for a Crusader interlude from 1099 to 1187. The roadway facing Tunshuq's mansion became known as Street of the Lady, a name that endures today alongside Street of St. Helena and Street of the Soup Kitchen.[27]

Roxelana's selection of the site was perhaps partly a matter of convenience, as Lady Tunshuq's palace needed restoration. But the association with Helena was fundamental. Roxelana had likely learned of this first female patron among the Byzantines either in Ruthenia, as a child getting acquainted with the saints of the Orthodox Church, or in Istanbul, where she might be informed by royal agents scouting possible sites for her project. Learning more about Helena and the model she provided to future empresses through her *philanthropia* (love of mankind) would not be difficult in the old Byzantine capital.[28]

Association with this site, whose status and pious nature had been preserved over the centuries, advanced Roxelana's personal and political goals. Like Helena, Roxelana was a convert to the religion she honored with her foundation in Jerusalem. Likewise, she was the first female of the Ottoman dynasty to establish a presence in the holy city, as Helena had been for the Byzantines. Roxelana could feel a personal affinity with this long-ago queen at the same time that she appreciated the site's political utility in the larger philanthropic agenda she shared with Suleyman.

At work here was that old imperial practice of preserving continuity with the past while introducing new laws, styles, and customs. Especially in the Near East, where so many faiths and sects had flourished for millennia, monarchs were virtually compelled to tolerate—or at least not to obliterate—religions that differed from their own. Suleyman could never emulate his European counterpart the emperor Charles V, who agreed in 1555 to a new religious policy summed up in the formula *cuius regio, eius religio* (whose realm, his religion). By ruling that a king's own religion would be that of his subjects, the agreement was aimed at ending armed conflict within the Holy Roman Empire between Catholic and Protestant leaders generated by the Reformation.

Suleyman, on the other hand, inherited the dogma that a Muslim monarch must acknowledge Judaism and Christianity as legitimate faiths, although his own religion claimed the superior distinction of being the final and most perfect of the three monotheistic dispensations. A special tax, as well as a range of social restrictions, could be imposed on non-Muslims, but their freedom of worship should not be curtailed. Especially in Jerusalem, a pilgrimage destination for all three religions, Ottoman authorities were charged with enforcing an etiquette of mutual toleration, lest sectarian violence break out (though some officials were less than assiduous[29]).

The subtext of Roxelana's foundation was that it acknowledged the work of a pious Christian queen of the past but signaled that the privilege of religious patronage now belonged to a Muslim queen. Patronage, in other words, was a form of colonization, first by one empire, then by the next. The spirit of the hilltop was preserved, but now it purveyed a specifically Ottoman charity.

By 1555 or so, Suleyman's family had contributed a remarkable number of good works to the Islamic world through donations to the Muslim holy cities and the major capitals. The collaboration of sultan and queen now enabled them to claim one of the highest accolades that the old world afforded to royal patrons—the mantle of the Abbasid caliph Harun al-Rashid and his wife Zubaida. Harun "the Just," who died in 809, is remembered for the epoch of cultural and intellectual efflorescence that marked the height of an empire stretching from North Africa eastward beyond Iran. Zubaida, who like Harun made several pilgrimages to Mecca, is best known for the extensive system of waterworks she sponsored to serve pilgrims along the arid Arabian roads and to bring water to Mecca.

The charter deed to Roxelana's Jerusalem complex hailed her as "the quintessence of the queens among women, the Zubaida of her time and age . . . who is unique and to whom there is no second queen in prosperity and good fortune."[30] Both Zubaida and Harun's mother Khayzuran, a former slave, acquired renown as notable patrons, their philanthropy focused on Mecca and the pilgrimage. Khayzuran purchased the house where Islam's prophet was allegedly born and restored it as a mosque. Despite engineers' objections to Zubaida's Mecca project, she allegedly persevered to complete the construction of a difficult subterranean aqueduct. Mihrumah would keep up her family's link with the Abbasid golden age by undertaking repairs to the waterworks and extending the Mecca water supply.[31]

There were other honorifics Roxelana could now call upon. The highest epithets for a Muslim female were association with the Prophet's first wife Khadija, his daughter Fatima, and/or his third and favorite wife Aisha. If Suleyman's Turkishness prevented him from claiming affinity with the first Muslim generation (Muhammad and the caliphs belonged to Meccan Arab lineages), the female members of his family could more easily do so. Describing the funeral of Suleyman's mother Hafsa, Celalzade Mustafa's history of Suleyman's reign praised her extravagantly as "a woman of great asceticism and a lady of righteous thought, queen of the realm of chastity and the Khadija of the capital of purity, builder of charitable foundations and doer of pious deeds, the Fatima of the era and the Aisha of the age."[32]

The charter deed lauded Roxelana's maturity as a pious patron in the familiar formula: "the Aisha of the time, the Fatima of the age."[33] A decorous restraint, however, ascribed these accolades sparingly, to both Hafsa and Roxelana, in death or late in life. But some forty years after Roxelana's death, Talikizade Mehmed, author of celebratory histories of Suleyman's reign, extravagantly compared her countless good works with the philanthropy of Zubaida. About the Abbasid queen he wrote, "Books of history are filled with that great lady's glory and generosity."

Talikizade emphasized the humanitarian aspect of Roxelana's benevolence with verve. "Wherever there was a pious shaykh deserving veneration . . . wherever there was a dilapidated mosque," she made it right. For pilgrims, there were "medicines, saddled beasts, horses, and resting places." There were funds for Janissaries who lost baggage during campaigns. Talented scribes wrote "books of excellence to be distributed to students throughout the empire." From Egypt Roxelana brought "a thousand pairs of Yusufi turtledoves" to be used as mail pigeons by the Imperial Council. "The Lady of Time has not seen such an abundantly benevolent dame!"[34]

POLITICS, BOTH DOMESTIC and international, continued to absorb Roxelana's attention during the years before her death in 1558. Suleyman granted her plea when in late September 1555, one month after his return from campaign, he reinstated Rustem as grand vizier. The sultan, however, had his own good reasons for wanting his longtime vizier back at the helm. Rustem had proven himself dependable, effective, and loyal, if not universally popular. That he was Mihrumah's husband was no small consideration, as the princess continued to enjoy her parents' special favor. She was, moreover, becoming a valuable political asset, in several ways her mother's alter ego, but her stature came in part as half of a husband-wife team. Rustem's exile was to a degree her exile.

Although it was Suleyman's decision, Rustem's reappointment to the grand vizierate came about through yet another political rupture for which some would blame Roxelana. The way was cleared for Rustem when Kara Ahmed, made grand vizier in the wake of Mustafa's execution, was himself executed. An array of charges were mounted against him, from mismanagement of the Iranian campaign to corruption in administration.[35] A core plank in Ottoman statecraft was the protection of taxpaying subjects from mistreatment by the state's officials. Failure to observe this principle scrupulously—or accusations thereof—had been the downfall of many a governor and vizier.

There was something of a trumped-up feel to the docket of Kara Ahmed's wrongdoing, however, with the result that his execution has been attributed by some to Roxelana's influence—unsurprisingly, since those so inclined could lay almost anything Suleyman did that directly benefitted the family he made with his favorite at her feet. Two seventeenth-century historians disagreed on the matter: Ibrahim Peçevi surmised that Suleyman was disappointed with Kara Ahmed's management of the Iran campaign but noted that the rationale for the execution was unclear. Solakzade Mehmed, however, spared no words in castigating "the evil meddling of the virtuous monarch's wife."[36] In the end, Roxelana's lobbying may well have contributed to Rustem's rehabilitation, and thus Ahmed's fall, but Suleyman had apparently intended to reinstate Rustem, although not until he himself had returned from the war in the east. Kara Ahmed was disposable, having served his purpose by pacifying pro-Mustafa sentiment among the troops during the campaign.

Roxelana seemed to be paired with Rustem in many eyes, and not always for the worse. Upon the completion in 1558 of the Suleymaniye, the sultan's great foundation, Shah Tahmasp made a gift of Persian carpets to cover the floor of the mosque.[37] His sister Sultanim sent a congratulatory letter to Roxelana on the occasion, informing her that the carpets were coming and that the people of Iran all prayed for the sultan and the continuation of his reign. The happy message reflected the afterglow of the treaty ratified in Amasya in 1555.

Suleyman and the Suleymaniye mosque. Engraving by Melchior Lorck, ca. 1574. Altered in 1688 to represent Ibrahim (r. 1640–1648), an inferior sultan known to posterity as "the Mad."

Sultanim made a point of commending the achievement of peace between the two empires. There was no doubt, she asserted, that Roxelana and the grand vizier Rustem were "the authors and the cause of this good deed" and "partners and associates" in bringing it about.[38] The praise was a smart move on the Safavid princess's part, for it must have seemed likely to the observant world that Roxelana would outlive the ailing Suleyman and become queen mother to whichever of her sons inherited the throne. In that event, Rustem might well retain his position as grand vizier.

Much of the rhetoric in Sultanim's letter and Roxelana's reply expressed intentions to keep the peace. After giving thanks for the gifts to the mosque, Roxelana assured Sultanim that the sultan was devoted to the agreement between the two monarchs. She emphasized that Suleyman had not undertaken his earlier campaigns in Safavid territory for the purpose of "destroying the lands of the Muslims" but rather with the aim of "repairing the houses of religion and adorning the lands of God's law." This was a patently disingenuous reference to the Ottoman conquest of Iraq in 1535, when Suleyman captured Baghdad, former seat of the sunni caliphate of the Abbasids, from the shi'i Safavids. There the sultan "discovered" the tomb of Abu Hanifa, founder of the school of sunni law followed by the Ottomans. The tomb had allegedly fallen into disrepair under the Safavids. Roxelana affirmed the friendship with her Iranian counterpart but did not miss the opportunity to reassert the legitimacy of her side's claim to Iraq.[39]

Just as in 1548 when she wrote Sigismund Augustus to celebrate peaceful relations with Poland, here too Roxelana was serving as a goodwill ambassador for the empire. Her successors would follow the epistolary model of female diplomacy she established and taught to Mihrumah. When two Turkish women were captured at sea by the brother-in-law of Henry III of France and made members of the court of the regent queen Catherine de Medici, Mihrumah and her niece employed this model to intercede on their behalf.[40]

Two of Roxelana's successors in particular—Nurbanu, favorite of her son Selim and queen mother to Murad III, and Safiye, Murad's favorite and then queen mother—would correspond with a range of European leaders, including Catherine de Medici, Elizabeth I of England, and the Venetian Senate. Elizabeth apparently solicited Safiye's support for an alliance between England and the sultanate, for Safiye wrote, "Be of good heart in this respect. I constantly admonish my son, the Padishah, to act according to the treaty. . . . God-willing may you not suffer grief in this regard."[41] This communication among female royalty was testimony to the remarkable number of politically powerful women who flourished in the sixteenth century. They maintained an important diplomatic channel for making and keeping peace.

MUSTAFA'S DEATH RELIEVED Roxelana of immediate fear for her children's lives. Now, however, a new specter confronted her: only one of her two sons, Selim or Bayezid, could succeed. The fate of the other, and his sons, was almost certainly death. To become queen mother under such circumstances would constitute a Pyrrhic victory. Her response was the only one possible, to attempt to maintain parity between the brothers. For the most part, however, this meant protecting Bayezid, whose relations with his father were becoming strained. As it turned out, mercifully perhaps, Roxelana would not live to witness Selim's triumph and Bayezid's tragic death in 1562.

Much ink has been spilled over the centuries on the subject of which prince Suleyman and Roxelana preferred as heir to the Ottoman throne and whether they differed. Some believed Mehmed, their firstborn, had been their shared favorite. Some thought even the handicapped Cihangir had been in the running. But most disagreement has surrounded the question of Selim and Bayezid, Roxelana's only plausible heirs following Mehmed's death in 1543. In theory, neither sultan nor queen would or should express a preference. The decision had to be in God's hands or, depending on how one conceived destiny, in the configuration of the celestial universe. Otherwise, the Ottoman way was pernicious.

But these were not ordinary times. Suleyman's own advancing age and the rupture over Mustafa's death rendered him deeply wary of permitting any challenge to his sovereignty to fester. Roxelana's position was less clear-cut. Her lifelong charge to protect her sons might clash with the equally powerful charge of loyalty to whatever political decision Suleyman made. And so the devoted couple could find themselves with disparate goals—he determined to suppress any threat to stability, she desperate not to see her own son die.

Following the eastern campaign, Selim returned to his station in Manisa, where he had lived since 1541. Bayezid was set to return from his lieutenancy in Adrianople to Konya, his post since 1546, but events intervened. The affair of the rebel Pseudo Mustafa dogged the prince. According to the Austrian ambassador Busbecq, writing in July 1556, a year after the affair, Bayezid had not only failed to act with dispatch in quelling the uprising but had in fact considered joining it and marching on Istanbul (his father had not yet returned from the east).[42] If Busbecq's report carried any truth, Bayezid may have acted out of fear for his own future in the aftermath of Mustafa's sudden and shocking execution. His father had set a deadly precedent.

Busbecq had recently returned to Istanbul with new treaty terms Suleyman had demanded from Ferdinand, and his correspondent was eager for news of Bayezid. The ambassador opened his letter by announcing that great changes had taken place. The first item of news was that the prince "had freed himself from serious danger and was reconciled to his father." Roxelana, he wrote, had rescued her son by placating Suleyman. Taking considerable license in ascribing to Roxelana words presumably spoken in private, Busbecq wrote, "His wife, with her usual cleverness, easily read his thoughts. Letting a few days elapse in order that his wrath might die down, she touched upon the subject in the Sultan's presence."

Having "quoted similar incidents from the past history of Turkey," Roxelana pointed out that protecting oneself and one's family was a natural instinct in all men, that every man wanted to avoid death, and that evil counselors could easily lead young men astray. (This was doubtless an allusion to the terrible exigencies of the succession system.) "It was only fair, she said, to pardon a first offence; and if his son amended his ways, his father would have gained much by sparing his son's life; if, on the other hand, he returned to his evil ways, there would be ample opportunity to punish him for both his offences. She entreated Suleyman, if he would not have mercy on his son, to take pity on a mother's prayers on behalf of her own child."[43]

Busbecq imagined Roxelana adding "tears and caresses" and Suleyman "softening," but he perhaps wrote more realistically regarding

Suleyman's long lecture to Bayezid on his errors before pardoning him. Peace made, Bayezid's governorship was transferred from Konya to Kütahya in northwest Anatolia, undoubtedly a victory for Roxelana. Now both princes were roughly equidistant from Istanbul. This parity of location was not trivial, for it was commonly believed that whichever prince first reached Istanbul following the death of his father was likely to hold the throne.

In his letter to his old school friend, Busbecq was adamant that Suleyman favored Selim while Roxelana favored Bayezid. Her support, opined Busbecq, came from her pity for the fate that awaited the younger prince, or from his dutiful conduct toward her, "or else because he has won her heart for some other reason." Other foreign observers agreed that Bayezid was his mother and Rustem's choice. Regarding Selim, popular opinion was divided, noted the Venetian envoys, with some believing he would prevail as the eldest, others that his poor character weighed against him. The German Hans Dernschwam implied that Roxelana preferred Bayezid because of Selim's dissolute habits. These reports did not mention Suleyman's preference.[44]

Even if the envoys' surmise was overstated, Roxelana undoubtedly felt a great deal of concern for Bayezid and his future. She may also have felt remorse that Bayezid had been disadvantaged in his preparation for political life. He was not that much younger than Selim—approximately three years—but he had been paired with Cihangir, while Selim had been paired with Mehmed, the oldest of Roxelana's sons. Their public debut in the great circumcision festival of 1530 took place nine years before Bayezid's, and they had the benefit of early military training with a father who campaigned frequently and, with one exception, victoriously. Bayezid was tutored by an older Suleyman who was winning fewer clear victories. It was hardly Roxelana's fault if this imbalance affected Bayezid's actions, but she might well second-guess her conduct as his mother. No one could advise her on how to manage the preparation of multiple sons for the throne.

ROXELANA'S HEALTH HAD been declining, although just when it became a serious matter is not clear. Her death in the spring of 1558 apparently stemmed from a combination of chronic illness and more immediate factors. The Venetian ambassador Antonio Barbarigo, who had arrived in Istanbul in September 1556, informed the Senate in 1558 that she had become very reluctant to be parted from Suleyman. Because he suffered greatly from gout, his doctors counseled him to spend every winter in Adrianople for the change of air. "But as long as the Russian Sultana lived, she rarely let him leave Constantinople," Barbarigo noted. She was "the mistress of the life of this gentleman, by whom she was extremely loved. And because she wants him always near her and is doubtful for her own life on account of illness, she rarely or never lets him part from her."[45]

Roxelana's reluctance to be parted from Suleyman was doubtless influenced by his long and difficult absence in the recent war with Iran, during which time her health may have begun to deteriorate. Istanbul offered superior medical resources, hence perhaps her reluctance to leave it. The Old Palace probably provided the best female medical care in the empire, and now it could call on the support of the Avrat Pazar hospital and perhaps the medical team being assembled for the Suleymaniye medical madrasa and hospital. Istanbul also provided the queen with a circle of intimates—Mihrumah, her granddaughters Aisha and Huma Shah, her old friend Gulfem, and other palace stalwarts. The health of the empire's sovereign was paramount, however, and so he must go to Adrianople.

Roxelana had accompanied Suleyman there in earlier years, during some winters at least. Perhaps she made one last effort in the winter of 1557–1558, both to be near her husband and to work on the foundation she was sponsoring just outside the city.[46] If not, perhaps she was strong enough to benefit from the salubrious air of the forest that lay northwest of the city, where Suleyman kept "country-houses, places of pleasure and delight," as Busbecq described them.[47] In the end, however, Roxelana died within the walls of the Old Palace.

On April 15, 1558, the new French ambassador to Istanbul, Jean de la Vigne, sent a letter to a colleague announcing the departure of a great Ottoman fleet headed to the Mediterranean (it would ultimately win the Battle of Jerba). He went on to report that "La Assaqui" (the Haseki) had died early that morning. So great was the sultan's grief that he aged greatly. "They say that the day before she died," wrote de la Vigne, "he promised her and swore by the soul of his father Selim that he would never approach another woman." The ambassador also noted that sorrow was felt by all those who owed their high stations to the queen. He predicted that change, whatever form it might take, could be expected, given that the majority of those who governed the empire were of her making.[48]

Another ambassador, also present in the capital, left a near-daily record of his doings from his arrival on March 30 until his departure at the beginning of June. This was Kutbeddin el-Mekki (the Meccan), an envoy sent by the sharif of Mecca, steward of the two holy cities. He came to register a petition of complaint with the sultan regarding the lawless behavior of Mecca's Janissary commander. Kutbeddin's suit for the Janissary's removal, ultimately unsuccessful, met with delay for a variety of reasons, one being an attack of malaria. Due to his stature as a learned Muslim and representative of the sharif, Kutbeddin was treated by the chief physician, who at their first meeting inquired if he had brought gifts for the Haseki Sultan. Indeed, he had, but he had nothing for the Lady Sultan (Mihrumah). The two agreed that the gifts for Roxelana could be shared with her daughter. Apparently, the queen was too ill to notice the slip in protocol.

Kutbeddin met with just about everyone in Istanbul who counted. This included more top statesmen than European envoys typically sought out, as well as leading Muslim scholars of religion and law. Kutbeddin must have come with a great train of pack animals, for he gave multiple gifts to every one of these individuals and sometimes to members of their staff (six officers of Rustem Pasha's household were recipients). The sultan's protection of the two Noble Sanctuaries did not come cheaply, although reciprocal tribute would of course be made to the sharif and other notables of the holy cities. The ritual delivery of the gifts detailed in Kutbeddin's memoir provides us with an intimate account of the mood of the city and its power brokers.

On April 4, Kutbeddin experienced "an attack of loneliness" from his medical confinement and went to call on Rustem. He found the grand vizier very upset and quite distracted, the cause being the Haseki's illness. On April 7, Kutbeddin went to the Old Palace, "where the Haseki Sultan was," and presented gifts for her to the eunuch Ali Agha. There was no possibility of even sending a greeting to her, it seemed. Next the envoy took Mihrumah's share of the gifts to her palace and was delighted when the princess responded by having her *agha* wrap the distinguished visitor with a brocaded robe of honor. "Up to this point I had seen nothing like this, she was the first," Kutbeddin commented.[49]

Finally, Kutbeddin achieved an audience with Suleyman in the New Palace, where he presented the sharif's many gifts in a formal reception. He was fortunate to get this far, for the sultan's distraction over Roxelana's condition had created a hiatus in imperial business. During the brief audience on April 11, Suleyman wore a green robe and sat at one side of a balustraded throne. He remained silent throughout the ceremony. He had become a saintly old man, thought the Meccan, with his thin body and his shining face. In the following days, Kutbeddin made frequent calls on Rustem and other viziers in hopes of learning Suleyman's decision regarding the accused Janissary, but they believed nothing would be forthcoming as the queen's illness had taken a decided turn for the worse.

On April 15, Roxelana died, "unable to recover from the illness she had been suffering for quite a while," Kutbeddin wrote, "and she was also stricken with malaria and colic." Funeral prayers were held at the mosque of Bayezid II, where prayers for Mehmed had been performed fifteen years earlier. It was the imperial mosque closest to the Old Palace, and it could accommodate a large number of mourners. Roxelana's coffin was carried to the mosque on the shoulders of the viziers, the procession doubtless observed by throngs of onlookers. Residents of the Avrat Pazar neighborhood perhaps made the half-hour trek to pay their final respects to the patron who had brought them comfort. The chief mufti, Ebu Suud, a close friend of Suleyman's old age, led the funeral prayers. The queen was interred in the cemetery enclosed by the walls of the Suleymaniye, where Ebu Suud buried her with his own hands. Soon an elegant tomb would rise to house her in death. Eight years later Suleyman would join his beloved for eternity in a nearby tomb of his own.

In his travel memoir, Kutbeddin composed a kind of epitaph for Roxelana:

There are many charitable foundations and good works of hers in the Noble Sanctuaries and Jerusalem and other cities. It is said that she was Russian by origin. . . . Because she pleased the sultan, he married her and in this way the deceased finally achieved the status she held. She influenced the sultan to the degree that the state of many affairs lay in her hands. She had many children, they are Selim, Bayezid, Mehmed, Cihangir, and the Lady Sultan. As long as their mother lived, these siblings got along well but after her death, discord arose among them. It is said that her name was Hurrem Sultan. The sultan loved her to distraction and his heart has broken with her death.[50]

Epilogue

A LTHOUGH THE DEATH of Roxelana left her family unsettled in the short run, the accomplishments of her career strengthened the Ottoman dynasty in the long run. The rivalry between Selim and Bayezid ended in bitter strife and the execution of Roxelana's younger son four years after her death. But when the throne passed to Selim in September 1566, he proceeded to take the model of his parents' exceptional relationship and make further adaptations to what we can only call the refashioning of Ottoman sovereignty. It had all begun when Suleyman cast Roxelana as his favorite and she responded by embracing the possibilities of her role with vigor.

Abducted and thrust into a fate she was helpless to resist, Roxelana made the best of it, generating bonds of loyal devotion and real affection with Suleyman and their children. She fulfilled with dedication and imagination the obligations to the empire that came with the new vocation of queen that Suleyman and she brought into being. Hindsight lets us recognize that the disparity between the sultan's two families—the traditional one with Mahidevran and Mustafa and what we might call the experimental one with Roxelana—was a symptom of the changing times. Traditional politics had produced stellar sultans, but now the rise of strong empires to the west and the east (and soon to the north) made internal conflict too costly. Moreover, the sixteenth century was an age of great kings but also of great queens, who played their own roles in the international game of thrones, and Roxelana was one of them. The Ruthenian slave gave the Ottoman empire an exemplar of new possibility.

IT WAS THE consensus of foreign observers that Roxelana supported Bayezid in her last years. That did not necessarily mean partisan favoritism directed against Selim. Rather, Roxelana's efforts to boost the younger prince appear to owe more to her old mandate to protect her sons—that is, to keep them viable as contenders for the succession. Bayezid had lost ground in the Pseudo Mustafa affair, and Suleyman had grown closer to Selim during the long and trying eastern campaign of 1553 to 1555. With Roxelana's intervention, Bayezid returned to his father's good graces. Once his mother was gone, however, he began to abandon caution as he confronted the prospect of Selim's victory.

Their mother's death released the princes to gear up for the contest. Four months later, Suleyman ordered both transferred to posts more distant from Istanbul—Selim to Konya, Bayezid to Amasya—to prevent either from attempting a coup. Bayezid at first refused to move and only grudgingly complied. It may have been at this point that father and son communicated through an exchange of poetry, as the Ottomans were wont to do. The prince pled his case—"Forgive Bayezid's offense, spare the life of this slave / I am innocent, God knows, my fortune-favored sultan, my father." Suleyman replied, "My Bayezid, I'll forgive you your offense if you mend your ways / But for once do not say 'I am innocent,' show repentance, my dear son."[1]

Bayezid began to rally an army; Suleyman responded by giving Selim permission to do the same and dispatching the vizier Sokollu Mehmed to aid him. The sultan had finally made a choice. Bayezid would lose the Battle of Konya in May 1559 and flee to Iran.

In offering asylum to Bayezid and his sons, Shah Tahmasp violated the recent treaty with the Ottomans. He was wise enough, however, to hold Bayezid hostage rather than reverse the scenario of 1548, when Suleyman had used Alqas Mirza, Tahmasp's renegade brother, to mount an invasion of Iran. The sultan was forced to pay the shah a steep price to recover his wayward prince: the fortress of Kars on the Ottoman-Armenian border and 1.2 million gold florins. For his part, Selim wrote to Tahmasp pledging to keep peace with Iran when he became sultan. Suleyman obtained religious sanction for Bayezid's execution with fatwas declaring him a rebel and his punishment execution.

In July 1562, the prince and the four sons who had fled with him were handed over in the Safavid capital Qazvin to Selim's head sergeant at arms and immediately strangled. Denied honorable burial in Bursa, Bayezid and his sons were interred outside the walls of Sivas, an eastern Anatolian provincial capital. The site was presumably chosen to avoid a train of coffins traveling across Anatolia that could rekindle partisan agitation. Bayezid's fifth boy, an infant, was hunted down in Bursa and killed, an eerie replay of the murder of Mustafa's only son.

Roxelana had apparently foreseen that Bayezid would have fewer resources in the inevitable confrontation. It later came out that she had deputized her daughter Mihrumah to provide him with financial assistance. Marcantonio Donini, secretary to the Venetian ambassador, reported in 1562 that Mihrumah "dared to send to the late Sultan Bagiasit her brother many sums of dinars at different times and on different occasions, and especially just before he resolved to take up arms against his brother." The last of the specially dispatched monies were presumably to boost Bayezid's chances at the coming battle, for which Suleyman had amply supported Selim. Later, when the sultan learned of the situation, Mihrumah "freely confessed [she] had done this to execute the will of the mother, who had arranged this in her testament."[2] There is no record of Suleyman's response to his daughter.

Mihrumah apparently did not learn immediately of Bayezid's execution. News reached her in the midst of a triple wedding that Suleyman quickly arranged in Istanbul for Selim's three eldest daughters. The princess's "enormous expressions of grief" impelled her to forbid any signs of happiness during her nieces' marriage festivities. Suleyman was deeply hurt by this, reported Donini, but he never showed it. Selim, on the other hand, demonstrated no such forbearance. In the heat of the moment, he allegedly declared that he had never loved his sister, his mother, or his brother-in-law (Rustem). The secretary speculated that his indignation was aroused less by what they had done for Bayezid than by Mihrumah's great wealth.[3] (This story is only as trustworthy as Donini's sources.)

Mihrumah, like her mother, was devoted to the one who seemed destined to lose. The news of Bayezid's execution, coming soon after the deaths of her mother and then Rustem in 1561, no doubt intensified her grief. But these were keen losses for Suleyman as well. Perhaps he felt a certain admiration for Bayezid despite the anguish they had caused each other. Busbecq had already given the prince's resistance a positive spin in his 1556 letter: "He deems it more honorable to fall fighting for the throne and trying his luck than to be butchered ingloriously, like a victim for sacrifice, by the hand of his brother."[4] The same might have been said of Bayezid's grandfather, except that he won the fraternal contest.

Selim had been an increasingly "inglorious" contender. Donini would describe him in the year of Bayezid's execution as a glutton become so fat that he could not sit atop a horse. Lascivious by nature, he forced men and women to submit to him, reported the Venetian, including, allegedly, the wife of the governor-general of Anatolia.[5] But Selim had one cardinal virtue: he avoided conduct that could arouse his father's suspicions.

The stakes in Bayezid's demise, as in Mustafa's, were more consequential than any preference of Suleyman or Roxelana or Mihrumah. Factions of the army that had been loyal to Mustafa, some of whom had rallied behind Pseudo Mustafa, could easily rally behind Bayezid, especially in Anatolia.[6] The younger prince seemed like the answer to the widespread desire for a return to the dynamic world of Suleyman's young sultanate. But in Suleyman's eyes, it was Selim who promised a continuation of the hard-won modus vivendi he had painstakingly achieved with the Hapsburg and Safavid empires. The times had changed. Hence Suleyman's severity toward a son he had tried more than once to rehabilitate.

In the month of Bayezid's execution, Andrea Dandolo told the Venetian Senate that Suleyman was "held by all to be very wise and very just but extraordinarily cruel to those who attempt, or who in his judgment might attempt, anything against either his sovereignty or his person."[7] Suleyman's dedication to guarding the Ottoman sultanate cost him his sister Beyhan's affection, his male favorite Ibrahim, two sons, and six grandsons. For this, he bore both the responsibility and the personal anguish alone.

HAD A BREACH opened up between Roxelana and Suleyman in their last years together? To her critics, Roxelana's partisanship of Bayezid was yet one more instance of imposing her will on the political life of the empire. Working together with Mihrumah and Rustem, the story goes,

Roxelana plotted Bayezid's victory as she had Mustafa's fall. The reality
could never be that simple.

The late sixteenth-century bureaucrat and author Mustafa ʿAli instead placed the blame for Bayezid's downfall on the nefarious work of
one Lala Mustafa Pasha. Once known for his closeness to the prince,
having been his political tutor, Mustafa switched sides, as *lalas* were
sometimes wont to do. Moving to Selim's service, he secretly assured
Bayezid that he was actually better placed to support his candidacy;
instead, he double-crossed the prince by revealing his plans to Suleyman. The seventeenth-century historians Ibrahim Peçevi and Solakzade
Mehmed both considered Mustafa ʿAli's account believable.[8] ʿAli would
blame the conniving of Roxelana and Rustem in the Mustafa affair for
what he saw as the decline of the empire; his silence in this affair suggests that the two princes were the protagonists of their own fates.

Still, if accurate, Donini's story about Roxelana's testament suggests
a semblance of pro-Bayezid conspiracy, at least between mother and
daughter. Roxelana's and Suleyman's different responsibilities could,
and apparently did, put them at legitimate odds with each other. That
there appears to be no record of tension between them suggests they understood, and perhaps accommodated, their divergent duties. The concubine Roxelana had been trained in the obligation of promoting and
protecting her son, and that mandate held even when she and Suleyman
produced an unprecedented five boys. As sultan, Suleyman's mandate
was to promote and protect the integrity of the empire, which, as more
than one ambassador observed, required the monarch's defense of his
own person. Ultimately, for the astute queen, family still must trump
political mandate, while for the sultan, affectionate by nature, family
might have to be sacrificed to the greater good of the dynasty's future.

Suleyman made it his business to secure Selim's future. The hastily
arranged weddings of three princesses accorded with two time-honored
Ottoman techniques of rule: mounting a celebration to distract from bad
news and binding the loyalty of leading statesmen to the dynasty by
marrying them to Ottoman princesses. Selim's daughter Ismihan was
wedded to Sokollu Mehmed, Gevherhan to the admiral Piyale, and Shah
to the head falconer Hasan Agha; all three men were or would become
viziers. Suleyman engineered the occasion to consolidate a circle of

trustworthy talent around Selim as well as to introduce Istanbulites to their next sultan and his family.

In the same fashion, the sultan prepared for his own last years. When Rustem's death in 1561 ended Mihrumah's own political marriage, passage to the next grand vizier, Semiz Ali, was smooth because he had already become the husband of their only daughter Aisha. When Ali died in 1565, Suleyman appointed Sokollu Mehmed, now Selim's son-in-law, to take his place. Sokollu continued as the sole grand vizier of Selim's eight-year reign and the first five years of Murad's. Roxelana would probably have approved his tenure, for although Sokollu had been pitted against Bayezid, she would have recognized a superior vizier, who could ease the transition from the titanic reign of Suleyman toward a more modest form of rulership appropriate for the changing times.

If Suleyman suffered from Roxelana's absence, his lifelong companionship with his only daughter Mihrumah helped to fill the void. After Rustem's death, the princess moved into the Old Palace and became her father's close companion. Following in her mother's footsteps, Mihrumah acted as Suleyman's intimate counselor and sent him news and forwarded letters when he was away from the capital. She was instrumental in the decision to undertake the siege of the Mediterranean island of Malta in 1565, for which she offered to outfit four hundred galleys. It was in these years that Mihrumah worked with the royal architect Sinan on two of Istanbul's most exquisite mosques, one in Rustem's memory in a busy market neighborhood near the Golden Horn and the other in her own name at the Adrianople gate in the old Byzantine city wall.

Suleyman's life ended on the western frontier of his empire. On September 7, 1566, he died in southern Hungary near the walls of the Szigetvar fortress. It fell to the Ottomans two days later, giving the sultan his last victory. Sokollu Mehmed masterminded the delicate task of returning the army to Istanbul while keeping Suleyman's death hidden. The soldiers were loyal to the reigning sultan, not the state, rendering interregnums potentially fraught with disorder.[9] The historian Mustafa Selaniki, participant in the campaign, described Sokollu's illusionist stratagems, which involved a page made up to impersonate the sultan and wave from the imperial carriage.[10] Selim hastily made his way from Kütahya to Belgrade, where the army awaited his arrival. By this point, everyone understood that the sultan was dead. The transfer of sovereignty was formalized, and Selim distributed sufficient accession bonuses to keep the soldiers marching home.

Selim's journey through Istanbul on the way to Belgrade, however, had hit an obstacle when local Janissaries and palace personnel refused to recognize him as the new sultan. Mihrumah resolved the standoff by rushing to her brother's side and providing him with 50,000 gold coins, whose distribution as a kind of pre-accession bonus finally garnered Selim entry to the palace. Even when Selim returned with his father's cortege, the Janissaries twice balked as the procession crossed the city, until more gold coins were distributed to them.[11] Selim II was robbed of a dignified accession, no doubt in part because he was the least favored of Suleyman's sons among the army.

If the royal siblings had not already reconciled during their father's lifetime, they did now. Mihrumah lived into the reign of her nephew Murad, at whose court this last surviving of Roxelana and Suleyman's children was a respected elder. When she died in 1578, she was buried beside her father, her mother not far away in her own tomb. There Roxelana was joined by Mehmed, a grandson who died during his father Selim's reign.[12]

It was Selim's duty to order the construction of his father's tomb, but he also built another monument that Suleyman had apparently refused to sanction: one in Bursa, for his half brother Mustafa. Following the prince's execution, his mother Mahidevran had fallen on hard times, unable to pay her rent, her servants cheated in the market. In other words, her lot was banishment. Finally, in the 1560s, Mahidevran's circumstances improved, almost certainly at Selim's behest, once he was the obvious heir to the throne.

Decrees ordered payment of Mahidevran's debts and punishment of those who had mistreated her. Finally a large house with a garden was purchased for her.[13] Mahidevran now had the financial wherewithal to endow the upkeep of the prince's tomb, which Selim had sponsored after becoming sultan. A bereaved mother for twenty-seven years, Mahidevran would come to rest near her son in 1580. The street where the house stood, in the citadel district of Bursa, is named for this steadfast concubine.

HOWEVER SHORT SELIM fell of the formidable standards set by his ancestors, he advanced the process of dynastic transformation begun by his parents. The Ottomans were not abrupt reformers but rather cautious modifiers of their political practices. They preferred, when they could, to accustom both governing cadres and public opinion to change, with the goal of preserving loyalty and continuity. Roxelana and Suleyman's alliance had been an exception in that regard. What Selim did was to develop certain features of his parents' relationship while discarding others.

Selim left behind the onetime experience of a politically active queen working alongside a monogamous king and its perhaps unintended corollary, a mother dividing her loyalty among several princes. Selim did, however, establish a favorite: Nurbanu, mother of his first son, Murad. He was far from monogamous; nor was she celebrated as his queen, although he allegedly married and dowered her. Nurbanu's prestige would

A view of the queen mother's apartments as they appeared in the eighteenth century. The photo shows the "Tower of Justice" in the background and to the right the dormitories of harem servants and women in training.

come as queen mother to Murad, a new twist to an old formula. It is fair to say that Nurbanu's career brought Roxelana's accomplishments into closer compatibility with the ingrained political habits of the Ottomans.

Key to Nurbanu's success was Roxelana's establishment of a queenly domain in the New Palace. When, after an eight-year reign, Selim died in 1574 following a fall in the bath, Nurbanu became queen mother to their son Murad. Her presence at the political center made her own passage to her new role a natural succession and Murad's passage to the throne far easier than his father's had been. Nurbanu's first act was to have her dead husband's body preserved in ice until her son was safely in the capital, while Sokollu Mehmed, now grand vizier, once again concealed the demise of a sultan. This was the first of similar stratagems employed by queen mothers to head off trouble during interregnums, when Janissaries might loot or even attempt to put a different prince on the throne. Over time, this role as avatar of sultanic authority enabled queen mothers to assume the regency of minor or disabled sons, a frequent occurrence in the seventeenth century.

Possibly tutored by Roxelana, Nurbanu admirably executed the responsibilities that Suleyman's queen had taught the Ottoman public to expect. As queen mother, she took the epistolary practice of diplomacy developed by Roxelana to a new level. She not only intervened to protect Ottoman subjects, rescuing captives and protecting Jewish merchants, but also undertook her own relations with Venice and France. As the dynastic elder of Murad's reign, she enjoyed a freedom of diplomatic authority that Roxelana could not assert as consort to the powerful sultan—or at least not publicly.

"She has done me many favors," noted a Venetian ambassador of Nurbanu, but his French counterpart complained of her "lack of goodwill." (One story of Nurbanu's origins held that she was born Cecelia Baffo-Venier, illegitimate daughter of two Venetian noble families captured at age twelve by the Ottoman admiral Hayreddin Barbarossa.) The Frenchman was perhaps unaware that Nurbanu corresponded directly with the regent mother of his king, Catherine de Medici. At one point, she invited Catherine to send an embassy to Istanbul to strengthen mutual relations. Catherine addressed a letter requesting Nurbanu's help in renewing French trading privileges with the empire "from the

Queen Mother of the King to the Sultana Queen Mother of the Grand Seigneur."[14]

Roxelana's philanthropic accomplishments were another inspiration for Nurbanu. The queen mother's charitable foundation, located in Asian Üsküdar, was more expansive than Roxelana's. It added to the formula of the Haseki complex a school for the study of prophetic tradition, a school to teach the illiterate to read, a sufi lodge, a public bath, and a large multistructure complex for travelers and the homeless. The choice of site, the New District, followed the pattern of Suleyman's reign when females made endowments in less developed areas of Istanbul. However, Nurbanu's had the distinction of being the only royal foundation endowed in the capital during Selim and Murad's reigns. They built in lesser cities graced by the dynasty—Selim in Adrianople, Murad in Manisa—allegedly because they had not earned the privilege through leading their armies to victory in battle as their ancestors had.

It was the now famous "Blue Mosque," commissioned by Ahmed I and completed in 1616, that revived the sultanic prerogative of building in the capital, regardless of the fact that sultans now rarely went to war. Selim and Nurbanu's great-grandson, Ahmed chose the old Byzantine Hippodrome for his foundation, his mosque rivaling Hagia Sophia in grandeur. The two stately structures were linked visually by a double bath built by Roxelana and located between them. The bath opened shortly before her death and, unusually, provided facilities for women as well as men. Royal mothers continued to endow major foundations in Istanbul (three in the seventeenth century and two in the nineteenth), seemingly alternating with sultans (two in the eighteenth century, plus another who built in his mother's name).[15]

This aggrandizement of the queen mother appeared to be conceived in tandem with Selim's second significant dynastic innovation: he dispatched only Murad to a provincial governorship, in Manisa, a move designed to solve the perennial problem of princely rivalry for the throne by designating the eldest prince as heir apparent. Selim's own battle with Bayezid would be the last of the fratricidal contests that characterized the heyday of Ottoman expansion. The reform—for this move to primogeniture should be recognized as such—had the added utility of fitting the evolving mode of sultanic administration. Like sovereigns elsewhere, the Ottoman sultans were becoming palace rulers. Neither Selim nor Murad led the Ottoman army to war; nor did their successors for the most part. Murad's eldest son Mehmed was the last prince dispatched to the provinces to learn his craft.

Although Suleyman commanded thirteen military campaigns over the course of his reign, he also demonstrated that honor was not lost in appointing viziers and pashas as commanders. Suleyman's grandfather Bayezid II provided a durable model of the sultan who governed effectively without establishing legitimacy primarily through martial valor. Suleyman himself fashioned an imposing palace persona, employing a ritual silence and immobile posture on his throne in the sumptuously refitted throne room, leaving communication with petitioning dignitaries to his viziers.

The palace sultanate called for additional adjustments. Interregnums acquired a new threat now that they unfolded in the capital. The populace could tolerate neither licensed looting by soldiers nor an emerging mode of fratricide that would dampen popular enthusiasm at the accessions of Murad and his son Mehmed. The enthronement of each was followed by the execution of all his younger brothers. A report prepared for the English ambassador in 1595 noted that the crowd of mourners for Murad's funeral was half the size of the following day's, when the long line of the slain princes' coffins wended its way from the palace "amidst the tears of all the people."[16] Not surprisingly, a new pattern emerged—automatic succession of the oldest living male dynast regardless of his relationship to the deceased sultan. Henceforth a prince would live out his life in the New Palace precincts.

This new mode, evolved by the early seventeenth century, preserved the fundamental Ottoman tenet that eligibility for the sultanate was a right belonging to all royal males—a principle that Selim II's solution had bypassed by excluding his other sons from the opportunity to rule. Not all who came to the throne in this new manner were stellar sultans or even fit to rule, but a rocky start—a regicide in 1622—gave way to an evolving formula for deposing incompetent or dangerously unpopular rulers. One might plausibly call it an Ottoman version of quasi-constitutional sovereignty.

THE CHANGES THAT had been set in motion by Roxelana and Suleyman kept the dynasty intact through its second three hundred years, until the dissolution of the sultanate by the Turkish Grand National Assembly in 1922. Suleyman's long reign was the hinge between the two halves of Ottoman history. While Roxelana's career aroused anxiety as well as admiration, the model she constructed of royal female authority provided the empire with new leverage in the creative modification of Ottoman political structures.

It was not a simple process. Nurbanu's career did not lack controversy, for, like Roxelana's, her choices did not sit well with all. Upon her death in 1583, the Venetian ambassador Giovanni Francesco Morosini commented, "Some are saddened by this lady's death and others consoled, each according to his or her own interests, for just as she provided enormous benefits to many as a result of the great authority she enjoyed with her son, so conversely did she deprive others of the hopes of obtaining what they desired. But all universally admit that she was a woman of the utmost goodness, courage, and wisdom."[17]

In 1599, the empire's chief mufti Sunullah Efendi lamented a number of harmful developments, among them the meddling of women in "matters of government of sovereignty."[18] He also castigated eunuchs, quintessential denizens of palaces, a sign that some people were still reconciling themselves to the transition from warrior to sedentary sultan. Sunullah's effort was in vain, however. In that regard, it recalls *The First Blast of the Trumpet Against the Monstrous Regiment of Women* issued by the Scottish clergyman John Knox in the year that both Roxelana and the Tudor queen Mary I died. Knox contended not only that women were unfit to rule but also that a realm so ruled was itself monstrous, a body lacking a head.[19]

One measure of the persistent power of female monarchs in Knox's world was the political rivalry between two queens, Mary Stuart of Scotland and Elizabeth Tudor. The Ottomans would experience their own version of two women competing for political dominance in the mid-seventeenth century when the young queen mother Turhan challenged the powerful dowager queen mother Kosem, who refused to retire from the office when the second of her sultan sons was deposed. Kosem planned to govern as regent to her six-year-old grandson, ignoring his

A contemporary image of Turhan Sultan's mosque. The French caption reads, "The Valide, built by the Sultana, mother of the Grand Seigneur." From G. J. Grelot, *Relation nouvelle d'un voyage de Constantinople*, Paris 1689.

mother Turhan. It was an act of usurpation of what was now legitimate female royal authority. Queens were no strangers to political violence: Turhan ordered Kosem's execution as Elizabeth did Mary's.

Kosem's partisans mourned, but Turhan used her authority more judiciously by returning government to the grand vizier. While Turhan was the last key figure in the "sultanate of women," as the transformations initiated with Roxelana have been called, the office of queen mother remained influential through to the end of the empire's life. This does not mean that Roxelana reformed the institution of slave concubinage or that those who followed her escaped the trauma of captivity. But the fact that this feature of imperial practice persisted after male slave recruitment was abandoned underlines its utility.

The rationale was the same in the nineteenth century as it had been in the early fifteenth, when the practice originated: if every dynastic male was eligible for the throne, each required and deserved a politically savvy mother whose life was devoted to his cause. Roxelana shouldered the burden of parceling her loyalties among her sons, arguably the most difficult challenge encountered by any Ottoman consort. On the other hand, her princes, like her only daughter, were the bounty of an extraordinary partnership—that of an extraordinary woman with an extraordinary monarch.

Acknowledgments

I WAS THINKING about Roxelana long before I began writing her life story. This book came about through a happy confluence of individuals who were also thinking about her. Caroline and Andy Finkel and Günhan Börekçi put me in touch with literary agent Howard Morheim, who skillfully helped me turn Roxelana's story into a book proposal. I was fortunate that Lara Heimert of Basic Books acquired the book and became my editor; her insights as well as her editorial suggestions not only enriched my writing but also stimulated my thinking. Leah Stecher's sensitive editing sharpened both prose and ideas, and Melissa Veronesi made the final production process a pleasure. I am also indebted to Jen Kelland, Amy Quinn, and Alia Massoud.

Others made critical contributions to the writing of the book. Joanne Omang read the first draft of every chapter, making valuable suggestions, and also answered endless questions. Eric Bogosian generously read parts of the manuscript and gave me tips on how to make the narrative more compelling. Kerim Peirce gently reminded me not to get overly academic. NYU students asked challenging questions about the Ottomans that gave me fresh perspectives on why they are interesting and what needs to be explained about them.

For repeated conversations over the years that yielded insights and encouragement, I owe special thanks to Refia Akgök, Günhan Börekçi, Lale Can, Karen Kupperman, Alan Mikhail, Aslı Niyazioğlu, Lynda Ozgur, Amy Singer, Joshua White, and Sara Wolper. My colleagues at NYU have been unstinting in their support. Larry Wolff shared his knowledge on many occasions and has also been Roxelana's keenest fan, while Karl Appuhn patiently helped with translations from Italian. I am also grateful to Sibel Erol, Linda Gordon, Molly Nolan, and Everett Rowson. A special thanks goes to Guy Burak for his enthusiastic support and bibliographic expertise.

318

Evdoxios Doxiadis and Joshua White provided welcome forums for discussing the challenges of writing about an individual whose life is not well documented. Robert Dankoff's expertise was invaluable in unlocking the meaning of passages in Roxelana's letters to Suleyman. Others kindly answered queries, debated issues with me, or suggested sources I was not aware of, among them Rıfat Bali, Deniz Beyazit, Erdem Çıpa, Natalie Zemon Davis, Lerna Ekmekçioğlu, Caroline Finkel, John Freely, Didem Havlioğlu, Christine Isom-Verhaaren, Sait Özervarlı, Ünver Rüstem, Baki Tezcan, Hülya Tezcan, Başak Tuğ, Jane Tylus, and Fariba Zarinebaf. Dariusz Kołodziejczyk, Almut Bues, and Mateusz Falkowski acquainted me with an aspect of Roxelana's career and reputation I was hitherto unaware of. Many others have helped me along the way, and I am sorry not to have named them all.

I am grateful to the numerous individuals who facilitated my research in Istanbul. Fuat Recep, Director of the Reading Room of the Prime Ministry Ottoman Archives, pointed me to valuable registers of Suleyman's princely household. At the Topkapı Palace Museum Archive, Sevgi Ağca Diker suggested relevant documents and miniature paintings, and generously shared her knowledge of the palace and its history. I also thank Zeynep Atbaş and Merve Çakır for their assistance. Muhittin Eren has kindly advised me over the years on sources, old and new publications, and scholarly trends. Mahir Polat, specialist at the General Directorate of Foundations, generously gave his time to guiding me around Roxelana's foundation in the Avrat Pazar district, then undergoing renovation; without this tour, I fear Chapter 10 of the book would be rather lifeless.

The writing of the book overlapped with the worldwide popularity of the Turkish television series *Muhteşem Yüzyıl* (Magnificent Century), which dramatized Suleyman's reign and featured Hurrem (Roxelana) as one of its key figures. Time and again I have been asked what I thought of the show; my answer is that I learned from it, although its goals and my goals were quite different. The royal children, for example, were key players in the television drama, inspiring me to give them a greater presence in the book than I might otherwise have. In addition, the show and my book shared a concern with the fortunes of captives drafted into the service of the Ottoman dynasty. Thanks to Arzu Öztürkmen and Nermin Eroğlu, I was able to visit the set during a filming session and to converse with directors and some of the actors about their characters.

To Joanne Omang, Lynda Ozgur, Nancy Öztürk, Linda Robinson, and the late Jude Ülgen, old friends who share a love of Turkey and its history, I am enormously grateful for their encouragement, willingness to traipse around old monuments, and toleration of my frequent complaints about the rigors of writing. Finally, there is a reason that acknowledgments such as these often end with family—for one thing, they keep pulling you away from the computer. The writing of Roxelana's story has developed along with Samson, almost three, who has learned to love books instead of chewing on them. His mother Amy, also a book lover, has been an attentive and intelligent supporter of this project, while my son Kerim has been not only my most reliable sounding-board for sorting out knotty problems of interpretation but also this book's biggest booster. Thank you!

Who's Who and What's What

BRIEF IDENTIFICATIONS AND GUIDE TO PRONUNCIATION

The Ottoman Dynastic Family

Abdullah: Fourth child of Roxelana and Suleyman, born c. 1525, died as a small child

Bayezid: Fifth child of Roxelana and Suleyman, born c. 1526–1527

Cihangir: Sixth child of Roxelana and Suleyman, born c. 1530; suffered a physical disability

Daye Hatun: Title for the governess of a prince or princess, as well as for the female head of the harem administration

Gulfem: Harem woman of high standing, exact role undetermined: possibly former concubine of Suleyman, possibly Daye Hatun

Hafsa: Concubine of Selim I, mother of Suleyman

Hurrem: Ottoman name of Roxelana

Mahidevran: Concubine of Suleyman, mother of Mustafa

Mehmed: First child of Roxelana and Suleyman, born 1521

Mihrumah: Second child and only daughter of Roxelana and Suleyman, born 1522; married to Rustem (see "Government")

Mustafa: Only child of Mahidevran and Suleyman, born 1515

Roxelana: Concubine then wife and queen of Suleyman, mother of six children

Selim I: Ninth sultan, father of Suleyman, born 1470; remembered as a great conqueror

Selim: Third child of Roxelana and Suleyman, born 1524

Shah: Sister of Suleyman, wife of Lutfi (see "Government"); also called Shah Sultan

Suleyman: Tenth sultan of the Ottoman empire, born 1494; became sultan in 1520

Government

Divan: Imperial Council. The sultan's council of advisers (viziers, treasurer, chancellor, military judges, and others); met in the Divan Hall in the New Palace's second courtyard

Ferhad: Governor, executed in 1524 for unlawful conduct; married to Suleyman's sister Beyhan

grand vizier: Highest-ranking vizier

Gritti: Alvise Gritti. Adviser to Ibrahim and Suleyman; son of Andrea Gritti (doge of Venice 1523–1538)

Hayreddin: Hayreddin Barbarossa. Corsair turned Ottoman admiral, founder of the Ottoman imperial navy

Ibrahim: Suleyman's male favorite, grand vizier 1523–1536; from Parga (Epirus) on the Adriatic Sea

lala: Title for statesman appointed as tutor to an Ottoman prince in government service

Lutfi: Governor, grand vizier 1539–1541; married to Suleyman's sister Shah, then divorced; of Albanian origin

Ottoman: European name for the dynasty, derived from Osman, name of the first ruler

Pasha: Title for most prominent statesmen and military leaders; placed after name (e.g., Grand Vizier Ahmed Pasha)

Rustem: Governor, grand vizier 1544–1553, 1553–1561; married to Mihrumah; probably of Croatian origin

Sinan: Mimar (architect) Sinan. Chief royal architect, builder of the Avrat Pazar foundation and the Suleymaniye; of central Anatolian origin

Sokollu: Sokollu Mehmed. Governor, grand vizier 1565–1579; married to a granddaughter of Roxelana and Suleyman; of Serbian origin

sultan: Title connoting possessor of sovereign authority; used also for Ottoman princes and high-ranking dynastic women (e.g., Sultan Mehmed, Hafsa Sultan)

vizier: Title for ministers of the sultan; they numbered three or four under Suleyman

Religion

chief mufti: From the sixteenth century, highest-ranking member of the body of Muslim clerics (muftis, judges, jurisprudents, notable religious scholars, and madrasa professors)

dervish: Synonym of "sufi" in Ottoman lands of the period; also connoted poor, humble, itinerant, and/or ascetic

Ebu Suud: Celebrated jurist and scholar, chief mufti 1545–1574

hostel: Accommodation for travelers and pilgrims, sometimes a resident community

Merkez: Merkez Efendi. Sufi preacher; patrons included Hafsa, Suleyman, Shah Sultan, and Roxelana

mufti: Religiously learned Muslim who provides answers to queries on points of Islamic law

Rumi: Jalal al-Din Rumi, d. 1237. Great Persian mystic who settled in central Anatolia; his tomb in Konya remains a popular pilgrimage destination

sufi lodge: Common term for a hostel for itinerant sufis or one where a sufi community might meet or reside; sometimes accompanied by a mosque where the resident sufi master preached

sufi: Muslim mystic, seeker of closeness to God; often a follower of a holy man or spiritual leader

the two Noble Sanctuaries: Term for Mecca and Medina, today in Saudi Arabia; Mecca is the principal destination of the annual pilgrimage (hajj) taking place in the twelfth month of the Muslim calendar

Sultans Before Selim I and Suleyman

Bayezid I: R. 1389–1402. Known as "thunderbolt" for rapid expansion of borders; taken prisoner by Timur (Tamerlane) and died in captivity, initiating civil war among his sons

Bayezid II: R. 1481–1512. More a state builder and consolidator than conqueror; fostered greater prominence of royal concubine mothers; overthrown and possibly poisoned by his son Selim I

Ertuğrul: Father of Osman, subject of legends of migration into Anatolia

Mehmed I: R. 1413–1421. Victor in civil war, 1402–1412; reunified the Ottoman state

Mehmed II: R. 1444–1446, 1451–1482. "The conqueror" of Constantinople; began its Ottomanization; expanded empire into Black Sea, western Balkans, Serbia, and central Anatolia; expanded roles of slave-convert servants of the state

Murad I: R. 1362–1389. Led expansion into southeastern Europe and Anatolia; martyred at Battle of Kosovo

Murad II: R. 1421–1444, 1446–1451. Fought constantly against Christian lords in the Balkans and Muslim rulers in Anatolia; abdicated, then was recalled to face European crusade; made Adrianople second capital

Orhan: R. 1324–1362. Made Bursa the capital; expanded Ottoman principality into Byzantine lands

Osman: R. 1299(?)–1324. Local Turkish warlord; counted as first Ottoman ruler

Foreign Political Actors

Safavid Iran

Alqas Migrza: Renegade brother of Tahmasp, received in Istanbul in 1547

Ismail: First Safavid shah, r. 1501–1524; converted Iran to shi'ism; lost major battles to Selim I in 1514

Tahmasp: Son of Ismail, r. 1524–1576; lost war to Suleyman in 1535; subsequent wars ended in a draw in 1548 and 1555

Western Europe

Charles V: Heir to multiple royal legacies (Spain, Holy Roman Empire, House of Hapsburg), d. 1556; enemy of Suleyman

Ferdinand I: Brother of Charles, Archduke of Austria, Holy Roman Emperor following Charles, d. 1564; enemy of Suleyman

Francis I: King of France from 1515 until his death in 1547; ally of Suleyman

Republic of Venice: Relatively good relations with Suleyman; represented in Istanbul by numerous ambassadors and special envoys

Central and Eastern Europe

Bona Sforza: Wife of Sigismund I of Poland-Lithuania; Ottoman partisan, contacted by Roxelana

Giray Tatars: Rulers over Crimea and northern Black Sea region; allies of the Ottomans

Isabella: Daughter of Sigismund I and Bona; regent mother of Transylvania, supported by Roxelana and Suleyman

Sigismund Augustus: Son and successor of Sigismund I; corresponded with Roxelana

Sigismund I the Old: King of Poland, Grand Duke of Lithuania, d. 1548; kept peace with Suleyman

Pronunciation Guide

Every letter in Turkish words and names is pronounced. For example, Sultaniye (the imperial), the name of Hafsa's foundation, is pronounced "sul-tan-i-ye" (with vowels enunciated according to the guide below). Syllables tend to have equal stress; for example, the three syllables of Istanbul have equal stress in Turkish pronunciation, as opposed to "Is-TAN-bul" or "IS-tan-bul." Longer words, such as the four-syllable name of Mustafa's mother, Mahidevran, may have a slight stress on the final syllable.

a   a as in star

c   g as in George

ç   ch as in church

e   e as in bet

ğ   unvocalized, lengthens preceding vowel (exception to "every letter pronounced" rule)

i   ee as in see

ı   io as in motion

o   o as in okay

ö   French eu, as in *deux*

ş   sh as in ship

ü   French u, as in *tu*

u   oo as in boo

List of Illustrations and Credits

viii **Map of the Ottoman empire:** Reprinted by permission of Oxford University Press (p. xix, map, "The Ottoman Empire and Its Vassals" from *Imperial Harem: Women and Sovereignty in the Ottoman Empire* by Leslie Peirce, 1993).

5 **The young Roxelana:** Courtesy of the Amram Family Collection, Istanbul.

28 **Vavassore's map of Istanbul:** Courtesy of Harvard University, Houghton Library, 51-2570.

49 **First courtyard of the New Palace:** By permission of the Topkapı Palace Museum Library, Istanbul, H. 1523, fol. 15b.

56 **Headband and handkerchief belonging to Roxelana:** By permission of the Topkapı Palace Museum, Istanbul, 31/1473, 1477.

70 **Venetian ambassadorial residence:** From Franz Taeschner, *Alt Stambuler Hof- und Volksleben: Ein Türkisches Miniaturen Album aus dem 17. Jahrhundert*, Hanover: Orient-Buchhandlung H. Lafaire, 1925. Taeschner Album, No. 48.

75 **Talismanic shirt:** By permission of the Topkapı Palace Museum, Istanbul, 31/1477.

105 **Circumcision festival, 1530:** By permission of the Topkapı Palace Museum Library, Istanbul, H. 1524, 103b–104a.

124 **Sultana, eunuch, and lady-in-waiting:** Ms. possibly in the collection of Henry, Prince of Wales, son of James I/ VI (d. 1612), All Souls College, Codrington Library, Ms. 314, nos. 29-30-31. Courtesy of The Warden and Fellows of All Souls College, Oxford.

130 **Second courtyard of the New Palace:** By permission of the Topkapı Palace Museum Library, Istanbul, H. 1523, 18b–19a.

132 **New Palace kitchen:** From Franz Taeschner, *Alt Stambuler Hof- und Volksleben: Ein Türkisches Miniaturen Album aus dem 17. Jahrhundert*, Hanover: Orient-Buchhandlung H. Lafaire, 1925. Taeschner Album, No. 12.

159 **Suleyman wearing the four-tiered crown:** Courtesy of the Metropolitan Museum of Art, New York, 42.41.1.

173 **The women's market:** Museo Civico Correr, MS Cicogna 1971, "Le Memorie turkische." Photo credit: bpk Bildagentur / Art Resource, NY.

178 **The Haseki foundation at Avrat Pazar:** From Gülru Necipoğlu, *The Age of Sinan: Architectural Culture in the Ottoman Empire*, Princeton, NJ: Princeton University Press, 2005. By permission of Gülru Necipoğlu.

190 *Tughra* **of Suleyman:** Courtesy of the Metropolitan Museum of Art, New York, 38.149.1.

203 **Suleyman and Mehmed conversing:** By permission of the Topkapı Palace Museum Library, Istanbul, A. 3592, f. 79a.

205 **Portrait of Mihrumah:** Photo credit: HIP / Art Resource, NY.

228 **"Dance of the Mevlevi dervishes":** From Franz Taeschner, *Alt Stambuler Hof- und Volksleben: Ein Türkisches Miniaturen Album aus dem 17. Jahrhundert*, Hanover: Orient-Buchhandlung H. Lafaire, 1925. Taeschner Album, No. 29.

236 **Suleyman mourns the death of Mehmed:** By permission of the Topkapı Palace Museum Library, Istanbul, H. 1524, 171a.

245 **Portraits of Suleyman and Roxelana, late sixteenth century:** From Jean Jacques Boissard, *Vitae et icones sultanorum Turcicorum, principum Persarum...*,

Franckf. ad Moem, 1596. Courtesy of Rare Book Division, Department of Rare
Books and Special Collections, Princeton University Library.

265 **Tile depicting the Ka'aba in Mecca:** Courtesy of the Metropolitan Museum of
Art, New York, 2012.337.

270 **Suleyman receiving Mustafa:** By permission of the Topkapı Palace Museum
Library, Istanbul.

283 **Letter from Roxelana to Suleyman, 1553:** By permission of the Topkapı Palace
Museum Archive, Istanbul, E 5038/2.

295 **Engraving of Suleyman and the Suleymaniye:** Courtesy of the Metropolitan
Museum of Art, New York, 59.570.35.

311 **View of the queen mother's apartments:** Photo by B. Diane Mott.

316 **Turhan Sultan's mosque:** From G. J. Grelot, *Relation nouvelle d'un voyage de
Constantinople*, Paris 1689. Courtesy of Rare Book Division, Department of Rare
Books and Special Collections, Princeton University Library.

Notes

Abbreviations

BOA: Başbakanlık Osmanlı Arşivi (Prime Ministry Ottoman Archives). Istanbul, Turkey.

EI2: *Encyclopaedia of Islam, Second Edition.* Edited by P. Bearman, Th. Bianquis, C. E. Bosworth, E. van Donzel, and W. P. Heinrichs. Leiden: Brill, 2012.

EI3: *Encyclopaedia of Islam, THREE.* Edited by Kate Fleet, Gudrun Krämer, Denis Matringe, John Nawas, and Everett Rowson. Leiden: Brill, 2015.

G-SICIL: Gaziantep Şeriye Sicilleri (Gaziantep Sharia Court Registers). National Library, Ankara, Turkey.

İA: *İslam Ansiklopedisi* (Encyclopedia of Islam). Edited by M. Th. Houtsma. Istanbul: Maarif Matbaası, 1940–1986.

TDVİA: *Türkiye Diyanet Vakfı İslam Ansiklopedisi* (Turkish Religious Foundation Encyclopedia of Islam). Istanbul: TDVİA Genel Müdürlüğü, 1988–2012.

TSMA: Topkapı Sarayı Müzesi Arşivi (Topkapı Palace Museum Archive). Istanbul, Turkey.

Chapter 1: The Russian Concubine

1. Quoted in Young, *Constantinople*, 135.
2. Ives, *Life*, 296.

Chapter 2: Abduction

1. Alberi, *Relazioni*, 3:102n1; Hammer, *Histoire*, 5:487.
2. Isom-Verhaaren, "Royal French Women," 174.
3. The term "Ruthenia" has shifted over time with regard to the regions it refers to.
4. Halenko, "How a Turkish Empress," 109–110; Yermolenko, "Roxolana in Europe," 53.
5. Alberi, *Relazioni*, 3:102.
6. Valensi, *Birth*, 12–17.
7. Busbecq, *Letters*, 28,
8. Neşri, *Cihân-Nümâ*, 1:32–33.
9. Ibn Battuta, *Travels*, 2:454.
10. Uluçay, *Padişahların kadınları*, 30–31.
11. Inalcık, *Economic*, 284.
12. Halenko, "How a Turkish Empress," 112.
13. Fisher, "Muscovy," 580–582.
14. Ibid., 580.
15. Abrahamowicz, "Roksolana," 543.
16. Evliya, *Seyahatname*, 5:213–214.
17. Quoted in Kizilov, "Slave Trade," 1.
18. Golden, "Codex," 40.
19. Fisher, "Muscovy," 583.
20. Evliya, *Seyahatname*, 7:527.
21. Hrushevsky, *History*, 160.

22. Bennigsen and Lemercier-Quelquejay, "Marchands," passim.
23. Fisher, "Muscovy," 585; Kizilov, "Slave Trade," 13–14.
24. Kizilov, "Slave Trade," 13–14.
25. Quoted in Fisher, "Muscovy," 585.
26. Yermolenko, "Roxolana: The Greatest Empresse," 234.
27. Kołodziejczyk, *Crimean Khanate*, 87.
28. Fisher, *Crimean Tatars*, 27–28.
29. Halenko, "How a Turkish Empress," 114.
30. Twardowski, *Legation*, 225.
31. Abrahamowicz, "Roksolana," 543.
32. Halenko, "How a Turkish Empress," 114.
33. Yermolenko, "Roxolana: The Greatest Empresse," 234.

Chapter 3: In the Old Palace

1. The map was published by Giovanni Andrea Vavassore from an older print. Necipoğlu, *Architecture*, 6.
2. TSMA, E 10292.
3. Alberi, *Relazioni*, 3:78.
4. Seng, "Fugitives," 138–139.
5. Ibid., 160–162.
6. Spandouginos, *Origins*, 224.
7. Inalcık, *Economic*, 284.
8. Dernschwam, *Diary*, 186.
9. Bassano, *Costumi*, chap. 15.
10. Alberi, *Relazioni*, 3:101.
11. Ibid., 3:101.
12. BOA, D 8030, f. 1b.
13. Uluçay, *Padişahların kadınları*, 39.
14. Alberi, *Relazioni*, 3:108.
15. Ibid., 3:108.
16. Angiolello, *Historia*, 128.
17. Ko, *Every Step*, 85–88.
18. Withers, *Serraglio*, 300.
19. Postel, *République*, 33.
20. Bassano, *Costumi*, chaps. 15, 17.
21. Necipoğlu, *Architecture*, 159–162.
22. Campis, *Records*, 44.
23. Necipoğlu, *Architecture*, 160.
24. Postel, *République*, 32.
25. Kafesçioğlu, *Constantinopolis*, 214–216.
26. Sertoğlu, *Paşalar*, 5.
27. Sumner-Boyd and Freely, *Strolling*, 39.
28. Angiolello, *Historia*.

Chapter 4: The Politics of Motherhood

1. BOA, D 8030.
2. The first years of the 1520s were plague years in which the disease returned in naturally repeating waves (Nükhet Varlık, personal communication, May 26, 2016). See also Hammer, *Histoire*, 5:20.
3. Angiolello, *Historia*, 128.
4. Barkan, *Istanbul*, 7ff.
5. Alberi, *Relazioni*, 3:102.
6. Angiolello, *Historia*, 128.
7. For more on birth control, see Chapter 7.
8. Alberi, *Relazioni*, 3:78, 96.

9. Ibid., 3:102.
10. Bassano, *Costumi*, chap. 15.
11. Hammer, *Histoire*, 5:63.
12. Alberi, *Relazioni*, 3:78.
13. On the execution, see Danişmend, *İzahlı*, 2:5; Peirce, *Imperial Harem*, 85.
14. Peirce, *Imperial Harem*, 85.
15. Finkel, *Osman's Dream*, 98.
16. Ibid., 100–103.
17. Gökbilgin, "Süleyman," 100.
18. Hammer, *Histoire*, 5:10.
19. Alberi, *Relazioni*, 3:58.
20. Sanuto, *Diarii*, 25:352.

Chapter 5: Lovers and Parents

1. Sanuto, *Diarii*, 41:534–535.
2. Veinstein, "Süleyman."
3. Inalcık, "Istanbul." Inalcık emphasizes that estimates vary widely.
4. Other children may have died in infancy and not entered the historical record.
5. Alberi, *Relazioni*, 1:74–75.
6. Finkel, *Osman's Dream*, 117, 122.
7. TSMA, E 5662 (also in Uluçay, *Osmanlı sultanlarına*, 29–33).
8. Thanks to Robert Dankoff for his invaluable help with translation and interpretation.
9. TSMA, E 5426.
10. Tezcan, *Tılsımlı gömlekler*, passim.
11. Again, thanks to Robert Dankoff for sorting out this passage.
12. See Chapter Three, 35.
13. TSMA, E 5426.
14. Sanuto, *Diarii*, 42, quoted in Hammer, *Histoire*, 5:87n1.

Chapter 6: Roxelana's Rival

1. Alberi, *Relazioni*, 3:102.
2. Ibid., 102.
3. BOA, D 743, D 8030.
4. Uluçay, *Haremden mektuplar*, 36–40.
5. Angiolello, *Historia*, 69–70.
6. Reindl, *Bayezid*, 77.
7. Sakaoğlu, *Kadın sultanları*, 141, 148.
8. BOA, D 8030, f. 2a.
9. Seng, "Standing," 204.
10. Celalzade, *Selim-nâme*, 336.
11. Uluçay, "Notlar," 231.
12. Uluçay, *Manisa'daki Saray-ı Amire*.
13. Sanuto, *Diarii*, 29:549.
14. Alberi, *Relazioni*, 3:103.
15. Ibid., 103.
16. Ibid., 102.
17. Alberi, *Relazioni*, 1:74–75.

Chapter 7: Coming of Age

1. See Peirce, *Imperial Harem*, 36–37, for the probable concubine status of Orhan's consort Nilufer, mother of his successor, Murad I.
2. Menavino, *Libri*, 134.
3. Reindl, *Bayezid*, 77. Seven of the princes were Bayezid's sons; the other (Oğuz Han) was Cem Sultan's.

4. Yelçe, "Evaluating," 77–79.

5. In fact, the original plan was to include all Suleyman's sons, but Bayezid was withdrawn (ibid., 87); a possible explanation is that Roxelana was pregnant at the time and she might (as she did) give birth to another son to anchor another circumcision celebration with Bayezid.

6. This account of the festival relies on Hammer, *Histoire*, 5:139–145 (drawing on Ottoman historians Celalzade Mustafa, Ibrahim Peçevi, Solakzade Mehmed, and others). Other sources differ on the date of the festival opening (e.g., June 1, July 27).

7. Richardson, *Renaissance Monarchy*, 41ff.

8. Yelçe, "Evaluating," 93.

9. Peçevi, *Tarih*, 1:116.

10. Sanuto, *Diarii*, 57:632–633.

11. Alberi, *Relazioni*, 1:13.

12. Musallam, *Sex*, chap. 1 ("Why Islam permitted contraception").

13. Ibid., 61ff.

14. Alberi, *Relazioni*, 3:101.

15. Celalzade, *Geschichte*, 239b–240a.

16. Peçevi, *Tarih*, 1:127.

17. Sanuto, *Diarii*, 56:263–264.

18. Alberi, *Relazioni*, 1:29.

19. Peçevi, *Tarih*, 1:131; Solakzade, *Tarih*, 2:181.

20. Finkel, *Osman's Dream*, 106.

21. Busbecq, *Letters*, 118.

22. Alberi, *Relazioni*, 1:360.

Chapter 8: A Queen for the New Palace

1. Bassano, *Costumi*, chap. 13.

2. Alberi, *Relazioni*, 1:52–53.

3. Necipoğlu, *Architecture*, 162–163, 261.

4. BOA, Maliyeden Müdevver 5633.

5. Alberi, *Relazioni*, 3:48.

6. Bassano, *Costumi*, chap. 5.

7. Hathaway, "Eunuchs," passim; Ringrose, *Perfect Servant*, passim.

8. Angiolello, *Historia*, quoted in Miller, *Sublime Porte*, 91.

9. Bassano, *Costumi*, chap. 13.

10. Babinger, "Bassano."

11. Dursteler, *Venetians*, passim.

12. Tavernier, *Relation*.

13. Düzdağ, *Fetvalar*, 55.

14. Public Record Office (UK), S.P. 102/61/237.

15. Necipoğlu, *Architecture*, xi.

16. Necipoğlu, *Architecture*, xi and passim.

17. Ibid., 32, plate 10.

18. Bobovius, *Mémoire*, f. 278.

19. Canaye, *Voyage*, 64–72, 237–240.

20. Alberi, *Relazioni*, 3:116–117.

21. Necipoğlu, *Architecture*, 85.

22. Solakzade, *Tarih*, 268–269 [1879].

23. Necipoğlu, *Architecture*, 189.

24. Ibid., 184–190.

25. Ramberti, *Turchi*, 135.

26. Miller, *Sublime Porte*, 66.

27. Ibid., 70.

28. Neşri, *Cihân-Nümâ*, 2: 710–711.

29. Pakalın, *Deyimleri*, 3:331.

30. Bassano, *Costumi*, chap. 13.
31. BOA, D 8030, fs. 1b, 2a.
32. BOA, Cevdet Saray 1834; Maliyeden Müdevver 774.
33. Charrière, *Négotiations*, 1:470.
34. Rozen, *History*, 204–205.
35. Uluçay, *Osmanlı sultanlarına*, 33.
36. Andrews and Kalpaklı, *Age*, 243.
37. See chap. 5 for Joseph; Potiphar is the king whose wife lusted after Yusuf.
38. Andrews and Kalpaklı, *Age*, 243: The letters *vav* and *ya* together can connote "alas," a play on the usual cry for help, "Muslims, come to my aid!"
39. Havlıoğlu, "On the Margins," passim.
40. Andrews and Kalpaklı, *Age*, 35.

Chapter 9: The Two Favorites

1. Hammer, *Histoire*, 5:228.
2. Solakzade, *Tarih*, 189.
3. Report of Genoese Bank of St. George, in Miller, *Sublime Porte*, 93–94.
4. Bassano, *Costumi*, chap. 15.
5. Busbecq, *Letters*, 49.
6. In modern Turkish, *cadı*; in Ottoman orthography, *cadu*.
7. Sariyannis, "Ghosts," passim.
8. Pakalın, *Deyimleri*, 1:253.
9. Ostling, "Witchcraft," 497, passim.
10. Pakalın, *Deyimleri*, 1:253.
11. Kuru, "Representations," 495.
12. Alberi, *Relazioni*, 3:101–102.
13. Bassano, *Costumi*, chap. 15.
14. Hammer, *Histoire*, 5:211.
15. Bassano, *Costumi*, chap. 14.
16. Bassano, *Costumi*, chap. 15.
17. Quoted in Sakaoğlu, *Kadın sultanları*, 163.
18. Uzunçarşılı, *Osmanlı Tarihi*, 2:358; the Turkish word for "job" can also mean "trick."
19. Although the phrase "mad arrogance" is von Hammer's (*Histoire*, 5:229), it fits well with the depiction of Ibrahim in the television series.
20. Mustafa 'Ali, *Künh*, 122b; Ayvansarayı, *Garden*, 365.
21. Ayvansarayı, *Garden*, 31–32.
22. Alberi, *Relazioni*, 3:103.
23. Gökbilgin, "Ibrahim," 5/2:908.
24. Turan, "Marriage," 8.
25. Ibid., 11–12; Uzunçarşılı, "Kanuni," passim.
26. Alberi, *Relazioni*, 3:95.
27. Ibid., 3:102–103.
28. Ibid., 3:104.
29. Ibid., 3:116.
30. Ibid., 3:103.
31. Peçevi, *Tarih*, 1:63.
32. Turan, "Marriage," passim; Uzunçarşılı, "Kanuni," passim.
33. Uluçay, *Padişahların kadınları*, 31–34.
34. Alberi, *Relazioni*, 3:103.
35. Setton, *Papacy*, 3:152.
36. Alberi, *Relazioni*, 3:53–54.
37. Valensi, *Birth*, 18; Alberi, *Relazioni*, 3:xxiii, 6ff.
38. Valensi, *Birth*, 19–20; Necipoğlu, "Suleyman," 404–405.
39. Alberi, *Relazioni*, 1:30.

40. Hammer, *Histoire*, 5:90–225, passim.
41. Necipoğlu, "Suleyman," 410.
42. Ibid., 408–409.
43. Peçevi, *Tarih*, 1:139–140; Solakzade, *Tarih*, 2:189ff; Celalzade, *Geschichte*, 277b–287a.
44. Solakzade, *Tarih*, 2:187–188.
45. Şahin, *Empire*, 166ff. and passim.
46. Solakzade, *Tarih*, 1:189.
47. Alberi, *Relazioni*, 1:10–13.
48. Karaman, *Figani*, 13:57–58.
49. Dernschwam, *Diary*, 139–140.
50. Hammer, *Histoire*, 5:195.
51. Bodin, *Method*, 292–293.
52. "Ma`ruzat," 2:338.
53. Fleischer, "Shadows," 58ff.
54. Bassano, *Costumi*, chap. 15.
55. TSMA, E 5662, 6036, 6056.
56. Uluçay, "Notlar," 255–257.
57. Veinstein, "Süleyman."
58. Alberi, *Relazioni*, 1:89.
59. Starkey, *English Court*, 9.
60. Feros, "Twin Souls," 32–33.
61. Andrews and Kalpaklı, *Age*, back cover.
62. Alberi, *Relazioni*, 3:107.
63. Meisami, "Kings," passim.

Chapter 10: Building a Reputation

1. Necipoğlu, *Age*, 268–280.
2. Ibid., 271.
3. Ayvansarayı, *Garden*, 115.
4. Ives, *Life*, 215ff.
5. Sanderson, "Sundrie," 77.
6. Evliya, *Narratives*, 1:84.
7. See Kafesçioğlu, *Constantinopolis*, passim, on Byzantine forums.
8. Ibid., 216. The artist may have been Gentile Bellini, whose well-known portrait of Mehmed II hangs in the National Gallery in London.
9. Ibid., 124.
10. Taşkıran, *Hasekinin kitabı*, 47. The original document was unavailable to me.
11. Uluçay, *Padişahların kadınları*, 45.
12. Sanderson, "Sundrie," 436.
13. Goodwin, *History*, 187.
14. Necipoğlu, *Age*, 275, expresses reservation about the soup kitchen.
15. Peçevi, *Tarih*, 1:127.
16. The following section is drawn primarily from Taşkıran, *Hasekinin kitabı*, 47–49, 133–134.
17. Chapter 9, verse 60 of the Qur`an names deserving recipients of Muslim tithing.
18. Thanks to Mahir Polat for raising the question of who was fed at the soup kitchen.
19. Repp, "Some Observations," 21–22.
20. Necipoğlu, *Age*, 271.
21. Taşkıran, *Hasekinin kitabı*, 64.
22. Ibid., 67–68.
23. Ibid., 63.
24. Dernschwam, *Diary*, 187–188.

25. Sandys, "Relation," 158–159.
26. Sayers, *Tıfli*, passim.
27. Taşkıran, *Hasekinin kitabı*, 98–100; Necipoğlu, *Age*, 275.
28. Goodwin, *History*, 187, quoting L. A. Mayer, *Islamic Architecture* (1956), 50.
29. Uluçay, "Notlar," 230–231.
30. Necipoğlu, *Age*, 294–296; Uluçay, *Padişahların kadınları*, 33.
31. G-Sicil, 2:200b.
32. TSMA, E 9099, 9517.
33. Repp, "Some Observations," 27; Taşkıran, *Hasekinin kitabı*, 105–106.
34. Kiel, *Art*, 109–110.
35. Peirce, *Morality*, 44.
36. G-Sicil, 2:220b.
37. Raby, "Sultan," 4.
38. Ayvansarayı, *Garden*, 231.
39. Herrin, *Women*, 21–22.

Chapter 11: Family Matters

1. Charrière, *Négotiations*, 1:462.
2. Özer, *Ottoman*, passim.
3. Hammer, *Histoire*, 2:187; Bryer, "Greek," passim.
4. Singer, "Enter," 100–101.
5. Aşıkpaşazade, *Tevarih*, chap. 3.
6. Busbecq, *Letters*, 28–29.
7. Şükrullah, *Behçet*, 58, 62.
8. Sphrantzes, *Fall*, 61.
9. Bassano, *Costumi*, chap. 14; see Charrière, *Négotiations*, 1:473, for the date of Mustafa's eastern posting.
10. TSMA, E 5038.
11. Uluçay, *Osmanlı sultanlarına*, 33.
12. Süreyya, *Sicil-i Osmani*, 4:372.
13. Uluçay, *Osmanlı sultanlarına*, 33.
14. Menavino, *Libri*, 16.
15. Peçevi, *Tarih*, 1:158; Solakzade, *Tarih*, 2:201.
16. Lutfi, *Tevarih*, 371; Celalzade, *Geschichte*, 337a–340b.
17. Alberi, *Relazioni*, 1:99.
18. Uluçay, *Padişahların kadınları*, 31.
19. Sakaoğlu, *Kadın sultanları*, 156.
20. TSMA, E 5038.
21. Charrière, *Négotiations*, 1:passim.
22. Ibid., 5, 6.
23. Peçevi, *Tarih*, 1:24.
24. Charrière, *Négotiations*, 1:471.
25. Bassano, *Costumi*, chap. 2.
26. Charrière, *Négotiations*, 1:470.
27. Ibid., 1:473.

Chapter 12: Home and Abroad

1. Uluçay, "Notlar," 249.
2. Berenson, "Letter," 13.
3. Havlıoğlu, "On the Margins," 26.
4. Lewis, *Istanbul*, 7, 8.
5. Casale, *Age of Exploration*, chap. 3.
6. Hammer, *Histoire*, 5:319–320.
7. Turan, *Kanuni'nin oğlu*, 11ff; Ocak, "Idéologie," 189.
8. Imber, "Persecution," passim.

9. Peirce, *Morality*, 251ff.
10. Ibid.
11. Charrière, *Négotiations*, 1:421, 439, 462.
12. Hammer, *Histoire*, 5:332.
13. Charrière, *Négotiations*, 1:442, 473.
14. Finkel, *Osman's Dream*, 124.
15. Charrière, *Négotiations*, 1:498.
16. Ibid., 1:462.
17. Ibid., 1:473, 493.
18. Ibid., 1:467.
19. Hammer, *Histoire*, 5:335.
20. I am grateful to Dariusz Kolodziejczyk and Mateusz Falkowski for help with the Polish sources.
21. Dziubiński, *Polish*, 152.
22. Ibid., 152.
23. Bues, *Marriages*, 13–14, passim.
24. For Said Beg's mission, see Dziubiński, *Polish*, 151–153.
25. Pajewski, *Wegierska*, 57–60.
26. Uluçay, "Notlar," 250. The Islamic year 950 corresponds to April 6, 1543 to March 24, 1544.
27. Hammer, *Histoire*, 5:364.
28. Yıldız, "Aydınid," 225.
29. Ibid., 5:356.
30. Wolper, "Khidr," 142–144.
31. Hammer, *Histoire*, 5:496.
32. Necipoğlu, *Age*, 236.
33. Wolper, "Princess Safwat," 37.
34. Aflaki, *Feats*, 553.
35. Eastmond, "Art," 163.
36. Ibid., 164–165.
37. Necipoğlu, *Age*, 271.
38. Ibid., 293–295.
39. Öngören, "Merkez," 201.
40. Ayvansarayı, *Garden*, 280.
41. TSMA, E 3058.
42. Emecen, *Tarih*, 6–8.
43. Necipoğlu, *Age*, 293.
44. Hammer, *Histoire*, 5:377.
45. Uluçay, "Notlar," 250.
46. Varlık, "Conquest," 253.
47. Celalzade, *Geschichte*, 376v–377r.
48. Peçevi, *Tarih*, 1:189.

Chapter 13: Recovery

1. Bassano, *Costumi*, chap. 15.
2. Ayvansarayı, *Garden*, 18.
3. Uluçay, "Notlar," 250.
4. Hammer, *Histoire*, 5:385.
5. Bassano, *Costumi*, chap. 19.
6. Uluçay, "Notlar," 250.
7. Hammer, *Histoire*, 5:386; Uluçay, *Padişahların kadınları*, 40–42.
8. For a detailed description, see Sumner-Boyd and Freely, *Strolling*, 200ff.
9. Alberi, *Relazioni*, 1:76, 116.
10. Quoted in Necipoğlu, *Age*, 194.
11. Alberi, *Relazioni*, 1:116.

12. Akgündüz, *Osmanlı*, 9:167–168.
13. Barkan, *Istanbul*, 4–5.
14. Alberi, *Relazioni*, 1:90.
15. Pedani-Fabris, *Relazioni*, 47ff.
16. Alderson, *Structure*, tables 30 and 31.
17. Mihrumah's daughter is better known as Huma Shah Aisha; she is called Aisha in this book to avoid confusion with her cousin Huma Shah.
18. Busbecq, *Letters*, 65.
19. Alberi, *Relazioni*, 1:72.
20. TSMA, E 5859.
21. Alberi, *Relazioni*, 1:72–73.
22. Ibid., 1:77.
23. Ibid., 1:73.
24. TSMA, E 11480/1; Uluçay, *Osmanlı sultanlarına*, 40, 42.
25. Alberi, *Relazioni*, 1:90.
26. Hammer, *Histoire*, 6:6.
27. Alberi, *Relazioni*, 3:[96].
28. `Ali, *Künh*, 124a.
29. Busbecq, *Letters*, 29.
30. Pedani-Fabris, *Relazioni*, 74.
31. Ibid., 82.
32. Skilliter, "Three Letters," doc. 11.
33. Uçtum, "Hürrem," 712.
34. Alberi, *Relazioni*, 1:159.
35. Uçtum, "Hürrem," 709; Sokolniki, "La sultane," 236. Thanks to Dariusz Kolodziejczyk for confirming that the claim is unsubstantiated.
36. Hammer, *Histoire*, 6:8.
37. Peçevi, *Tarih*, 1:192; Solakzade, *Tarih*, 2:212–213.
38. Peçevi, *Tarih*, 1:191.
39. `Ali, *Künh*, 69a–b; Peçevi, *Tarih*, 1:192; Hammer, *Histoire*, 6:8.
40. Peçevi, *Tarih*, 1:191; Solakzade, *Tarih*, 2:212.

Chapter 14: Showdown

1. Charrière, *Négotiations*, 2:4.
2. Ibid., 2:44–45.
3. Pedani-Fabris, *Relazioni*, 73.
4. Alberi, *Relazioni*, 1:90.
5. Ibid., 1:70–71.
6. TSMA, E 5859.
7. The Turkish word for "foot," *ayak*, can also mean "leg."
8. Charrière, *Négotiations*, 2:103.
9. TSMA, E 5859.
10. Chesneau, *Voyage*, 163.
11. Hammer, *Histoire*, 6:14.
12. Alberi, *Relazioni*, 1:76.
13. Charrière, *Négotiations*, 2:89.
14. Chesneau, *Voyage*, 102–103.
15. Hammer, *Histoire*, 6:461–463 (note 1 lists all stops along the route).
16. Hammer, *Histoire*, 6:13–14.
17. Fetvacı, *Picturing*, 19.
18. Ibid., 35–36.
19. Ayvansarayı, *Garden*, 319.
20. Necipoğlu, *Age*, 276, 278.
21. Magdalino, "Foundation," 37.
22. Kafesçioğlu, *Constantinopolis*, 22, 99.

23. Magdalino, "Foundation," 38, 47, 53–54.
24. Taşkıran, *Hasekinin kitabı*, 133.
25. Kürkçüoğlu, *Süleymaniye vakfiyesi*, 40–41. The syntax of the original has been slightly altered to make it comport with English.
26. See also Necipoğlu, *Age*, 273.
27. Taşkıran, *Hasekinin kitabı*, 133–134.
28. Alberi, *Relazioni*, 1:77.
29. Hammer, *Histoire*, 6:26ff; Veinstein, "Sokollu."
30. Peçevi, *Tarih*, 1:213; Solakzade, *Tarih*, 2:229–230 (both following `Ali, *Künh*, quoted in Turan, *Kanuni'nin oğlu*, 27); Hammer, *Histoire*, 6:54.
31. Solakzade, *Tarih*, 2:229.
32. Peçevi, *Tarih*, 1:213. Peçevi relayed the account of Şemsi Agha (later Şemsi Ahmed Pasha), one of the messengers Rustem sent to the sultan.
33. Alberi, *Relazioni*, 1:77.
34. Hammer, *Histoire*, 6:57.
35. Altundağ and Turan, "Rüstem," 800–801. This view of Roxelana as a malevolent schemer stems primarily from the judgment, perhaps first put forth by Mustafa `Ali, that Mustafa's execution was a disaster for the Ottoman state, that she was responsible for it, and that Suleyman was helpless is the face of her intrigues. This view has persisted in the work of a remarkable number of well-respected twentieth-century scholars.
36. Most notable was Mustafa `Ali, who served Selim II, the son whom Roxelana apparently disfavored in her last years (Turan, *Kanuni'nin oğlu*, 2–3).
37. The authors of these views include Mustafa `Ali (d. 1600), *Künh*; Hammer (d. 1856), *Histoire*; and M. T. Gökbilgin (d. 1981), various writings.
38. Pedani-Fabris, *Relazioni*, 76; Alberi, *Relazioni*, 1:89.
39. Charrière, *Négotiations*, 2:104–105.
40. An exception is Turan, *Kanuni'nin oğlu*; this does not mean he exonerates Roxelana.
41. Pedani-Fabris, *Relazioni*, 74; Alberi, *Relazioni*, 1:77.
42. Busbecq, *Letters*, 158.
43. Turan, *Kanuni'nin oğlu*, 24.
44. Alberi, *Relazioni*, 1:240–242.
45. Alberi, *Relazioni*, 1:116.
46. Ibid., 1:116.
47. Ibid., 1:77.
48. Ibid., 1:77–79.
49. Ibid., 1:172.
50. Ibid., 1:76, 204–205.
51. Ibid., 1:79.
52. Ibid., 1:114–115.
53. Andrews and Kalpaklı, *Age*, 248.
54. Çavuşoğlu, "16. uü yüzyılda," 411–412; Havlıoğlu, "On the Margins," 46. Nisayi gave the same refrain to another memorial poem, this one addressed to the dead prince: "O Sultan Mustafa, what has the merciless monarch done to you?"
55. The sum of the numerical values of the letters equaled 960 in the Islamic calendar (1553).
56. Çavuşoğlu, "Şehzade," 656 ("Bunun gibi işi kim gördi kim işitdi `aceb Ki oğlına kıya bir server-i `Ömer-meşreb.").
57. Pedani-Fabris, *Relazioni*, 74.

Chapter 15: Last Years

1. Alberi, *Relazioni*, 1:230ff.
2. Ibid.; Celalzade, *Geschichte*, 440ff.
3. Alberi, *Relazioni*, 1:232.
4. Ibid., 1:202.

5. Necipoğlu, *Age*, 204.
6. TSMA, E 5038. Uluçay erroneously dates the letter to 1548 (*Osmanlı sultan-larına*, 42–43).
7. The shah was accursed because he was a religious deviant in the sunni eyes of the Ottomans—not only shi`i but a deviant shi`i.
8. Abdullah, *Meaning*, 981.
9. Alberi, *Relazioni*, 1:236.
10. Ibid., 204–205.
11. Ibid., 249–250; Hammer, *Histoire*, 6:62.
12. Veinstein, "Süleyman"; Finkel, *Osman's Dream*, 135.
13. Alberi, *Relazioni*, 1:154–156.
14. Ibid., 1:268–269.
15. Turan, *Kanuni'nin oğlu*.
16. Ibid., 21.
17. Necipoğlu, *Age*, 278.
18. Stephan, "Endowment," 182.
19. Ibid., 183.
20. Necipoğlu, *Age*, 278.
21. Singer, *Constructing*, 76.
22. Ibid., 3.
23. Stephan, "Endowment," 178.
24. Herrin, *Women*, 2, 245.
25. Holum and Vikan, "Jerusalem," 1033–1034.
26. Burgoyne, *Jerusalem*, 485–487.
27. Stephan, "Endowment," 173.
28. Holum, *Empresses*, 24, 26, 188.
29. Heyd, *Documents*, 162–184 and passim.
30. Stephan, "Endowment," 173.
31. Baysun, "Mihr-ü-Mah Sultan," 308.
32. Celalzade, *Geschichte*, 239a.
33. Singer, *Constructing*, 76.
34. Quoted in Necipoğlu, *Age*, 269–271.
35. Emecen, "Kara Ahmed," 358; Hammer, *Histoire*, 6:85–88.
36. Peçevi, *Tarih*, 243; Solakzade, *Tarih*, 1:246–247.
37. The remainder of this section is adapted from Peirce, *Imperial Harem*, 219–228.
38. *Shah Tahmasb*, 343–346. Thanks to Kathryn Babayan for alerting me to this letter and translating it.
39. Feridun, *Münşeat*, 2:65–66.
40. Skilliter, "Catherine," 47.
41. Skilliter, "Three Letters," 138–139 (slight changes have been made in the translation).
42. Busbecq, *Letters*, 81–82.
43. Ibid., 83.
44. Alberi, *Relazioni*, 3:134–135, 148–149; Dernschwam, *Diary*, 332.
45. Alberi, *Relazioni*, 3:148.
46. Necipoğlu, *Age*, 278–279.
47. Busbecq, *Letters*, 39–40.
48. Charièrre, *Négotiations*, 2: 464–465n1.
49. Kutbeddin, *Travelogue*, 73.
50. Ibid., 78.

Epilogue

1. Turan, *Kanuni'nin oğlu*, 208–210.
2. Alberi, *Relazioni*, 3:184.
3. Ibid., 185.

4. Busbecq, *Letters*, 80.
5. Alberi, *Relazioni*, 3:180.
6. Turan, *Kanuni'nin oğlu*, 6ff., passim.
7. Alberi, *Relazioni*, 3:164.
8. Peçevi, *Tarih*, 1:272ff.; Solakzade, *Tarih*, 1:264ff.
9. On the changing character of interregnums, see Vatan and Veinstein, *Sérail*.
10. Selaniki, *Tarih*.
11. Finkel, *Osman's Dream*, 151–153; Selaniki, *Tarih*, 40ff.
12. Ayvansarayı, *Garden*, 20.
13. Kepecioğlu, "Tarihi Bilgiler," 405ff.
14. Spagni, "Sultana," 320–321.
15. In order, the founders were Kosem, Turhan, Gülnüş, Bezmialem, and Pertevniyal (queen mothers); Mahmud I/Osman III, Mustafa III, and Ahmed III (sultans).
16. Rosedale, *Queen Elizabeth*, 27–28.
17. Spagni, "Sultana," 333.
18. Selaniki, *Tarih*, 826.
19. Weil, "Crown," 4.

Bibliography

Primary Sources

Abdullah, Meaning Abdullah YusufAli, trans. and com. *The Meaning of the Holy Qur'an.* Brentwood, MD: Amana Corporation, 1989.

Aflaki, Feats O'Kane, John, trans. *The Feats of the Knowers of God: Manāqeb al-'ārefin.* Leiden: Brill, 2002.

Alberi, Relazioni Alberi, Eugenio, ed. *Le relazioni degli ambasciatori Veneti al Senato.* Florence, 1840–1855, Serie III. Vols. I, III.

Angiolello, Historia Angiolello, Giovanni Maria. *Historia turchesca (1300–1514).* Edited by I. Ursu. Bucharest, 1909.

Aşıkpaşazade, Tevarih Aşıkpaşazade, Derviş Ahmed. *Tevarih-i Al-i Osman.* In *Osmanlı tarihleri,* edited and transliterated by N. Atsız. Istanbul, 1947.

Ayvansarayı, Garden Crane, Howard, trans. and annot. *The Garden of the Mosques: Hafız Hüseyin Al-Ayvansarayî's Guide to the Muslim Monuments of Ottoman Istanbul.* Leiden: Brill, 2000.

Barkan, Account Registers Barkan, Ömer Lütfü. *Istanbul saraylarına ait muhasebe deferleri. Belgeler* 9, no. 13 (1979).

Bassano, Costumi Bassano, Luigi da Zara. *Costumi et i modi particolari della vita de' Turchi.* Edited by Franz Babinger. Munich: Universität zu München, 1963.

Bobovius, Mémoire Bobovius, Albertus. *Mémoire sur les Turcs.* Harvard University, Houghton Library, MS. Fr 103.

Bodin, Method Bodin, Jean. *Method for the Easy Comprehension of History.* Translated by Beatrice Reynolds. New York: Octagon Books, 1945.

Busbecq, Turkish Letters Busbecq, Ogier Ghiselin de. *The Turkish Letters of Ogier Ghiselin de Busbecq.* Translated by E. S. Forster. Abr. ed. Baton Rouge: Louisiana State University, 2005.

Campis, Records Campis, Iacopo de Promontorio de. *De Aufzeichnungen des Genueses Iacopo de Promotorio de Campis über den Osmanenstaat um 1475.* Edited by Franz Babinger. *Sitzunberichte der Bayerische Akademie der Wissenschaften* 8 (1957).

Canaye, Voyage Canaye, Phillippe. *Le voyage du Levant.* Edited by M. H. Houser. Paris: E. Leroux, 1897.

Celalzade, Selim-nâme Celalzade Mustafa. *Selim-nâme.* Edited by M. Çuhadar and A. Uğur. Ankara, 1990.

Celalzade, Tabakat Celalzade Mustafa. *Geschichte Sultan Süleyman Kanunis von 1520 bis 1557, oder, Ṭabaḳāt ül-Memālik ve Derecāt ül-Mesālik.* Edited by Petra Kappert. Wiesbaden: Steiner, 1981.

Charrière, Négotiations Charrière, Ernest. *Négotiations de la France dans le Levant.* Vols. 1–2. Paris: Imprimerie Nationale, 1848–1860.

Chesneau, Voyage Chesneau, Jean. *Le voyage de Monsieur D'Aramon, ambassadeur pour le roy en Levant.* Geneva: Slatkine Reprints, 2010.

Dernschwam, Diary Önen, Yaşar, trans. *Hans Dernschwam—Istanbul ve Anadolu'ya Seyahat Günlüğü.* Ankara: Kültür ve Turizm Bakanlığı, 1992.

Düzdağ, Fetvalar Düzdağ, M. Ertuğrul. *Şeyhülislâm Ebussuud Efendi Fetvaları Işığında 16. Asır Türk Hayatı.* Istanbul: Enderun Kitabevi, 1983.

Evliya, *Narratives* Hammer-Purgstall, Joseph von, ed. *Narratives of Travel in Europe, Asia, and Africa, in the Seventeenth Century.* New York, 1968.

Evliya, *Seyahatname* Dağlı, Yücel, Seyit Ali Kahraman, and Robert Dankoff, eds. and trans. *Evliya Çelebi seyahatnamesi.* Istanbul: Yapı Kredi Yayınları, 2003. Vol. 5.

Feridun, *Münşeat* Feridun Ahmed Beg. *Mecmua-yı Münşeat üs-Selatin.* Vol. 2. Istanbul, 1831–1832.

Galip, *Beauty* Şeyh Galip. *Beauty and Love.* Translated and introduced by Victoria Roe Holbrook. New York: Modern Language Association of America, 2005.

Ibn Battuta, *Travels* Ibn Battuta. *The Travels of Ibn Battuta.* Edited and translated by H. A. R. Gibb. Hakluyt Series No. 117 (Second Series). Cambridge: Cambridge University Press, 1962.

Kutbeddin, *Travelogue* Kamil, Ekrem, ed. and trans. *Gazzi Mekki seyahatnamesi.* In *Tarih semineri dergisi* 1–2 (1937): 3–90.

Lutfi, *Tevarih* Lutfi Paşa, *Tevarih-i Âli Osman.* Istanbul: Enderun Kitabevi, 1990.

Matrakçı, *Menazil* Matrakçı Nasuh. *Beyan-ı menazil-i sefer-i Irakeyn-i Sultan Süleyman Han.* Edited by Hüsayin G. Yurdaydın. Ankara: Türk Tarih Kurumu, 1976.

Menavino, *Libri* Menavino, Giovanni Antonio. *I cinque libri delle legge, religione, et vita de' Turchi: et della corte, et d'alcune guerre del gran Turco.* Venice, 1548.

**Mustafa `Ali, *Künh*** `Ali, Mustafa. *Künh ül-Ahbar.* Vol. 1. Istanbul: Darüt-tıbaatil' Âmire, 1860–1861.

Neşri, *Cihân-Nümâ* Neşri, Mevlana Mehmed. *Cihân-Nümâ: Neşri Tarihi.* Edited by F. R. Unat and M. A. Köymen. Vol. 2. Ankara: Türk Tarih Kurumu, 1987.

Peçevi, *Tarih* Baykal, Bekir Sıtkı, ed. *Peçevi Ibrahim Efendi—Peçevi Tarihi.* Vol. 1. Ankara: Başbakanlığı Matbaası, 1981.

Pedani-Fabris, *Relazioni* Pedani-Fabris, Maria Pia, ed. *Relazioni di ambasciatori veneti al Senato.* Padua, n.d. Vol. XIV.

Postel, *République* Postel, Guillaume. *De la république des Turcs et là ou l'occasion s'offrera, des meurs et loys de tous Muhamedistes.* Poitiers, [1560].

Ramberti, *Turchi* Ramberti, Benedetto. *Libri tre delle cose de Turchi.* Venice, 1543. Excerpted and translated by Albert Howe Lybyer in *The Government of the Ottoman Empire in the Time of Suleiman the Magnificent.* Cambridge, MA: Harvard University Press, 1913, Appendix 1.

Sanderson, *Sundrie* Sanderson, John. "Sundrie the Personall Voyages." In S. Purchas, *His Pilgrims,* 9:422–486. Glasgow, 1905.

Sandys, *Relation* Sandys, George. "A Relation of a Journey Begun Anno Dom. 1610." In S. Purchas, *His Pilgrims,* 8:88–248. Glasgow, 1905.

Sanuto, *Diarii* Sanuto, Marino. *I diarii di Marino Sanuto, 1496–1533.* Venice, 1879–1902. Vols. 25, 29, 41, 42, 56, 57.

Selaniki, *Tarih* Ipşirli, Mehmet, ed. *Selaniki Mustafa Efendi—Tarih-i Selaniki.* Istanbul: Edebiyat Fakültesi Basımevi, 1989.

Shah Tahmasb Navaii, `Abd al-Husayn, ed. *Shah Tahmasb-e Safavî, Mujmu'a-yi Asnad ve Mukatibat-i Tarihî.* Tehran, 1931–1932.

Solakzade, *Tarih* Çabuk, Vahid, ed. *Solak-zâde Mehmed Hemdemi Çelebi—Solak-zâde Tarihi.* Vol. 2. Ankara: Sevinç Matbaası, 1989.

Spandouginos, *Origins* Spandouginos, Theodoros. *Delle historie, & origine de principi de Turchi, ordine della corte, loro vita, & costumi.* Lucca: Per V. Busdrago, 1550.

Sphrantzes, *Fall* Sphrantzes, George. *The Fall of the Byzantine Empire.* Trans. M. Philippides. Amherst: University of Massachusetts Press, 1980.

Şükrullah, *Behçet* Şükrullah. *Behçet ül-Tevarih.* In *Osmanlı tarihleri,* edited and transliterated by N. Atsız. Istanbul, 1947.

Süreyya, *Sicil-i Osmanî* Süreyya, Mehmed. *Sicil-i Osmanî.* Vol. 1. Istanbul: Matbaa-yı Amire, 1891–1897.

Tavernier, *Relation* Tavernier, J[ean] B[aptiste]. *Nouvelle relation de l'interieur du sarrail de grand seigneur.* Paris, 1681.

Twardowski, *Legation* Krzywy, Roman, ed. *Przeważna legacyja Krzysztofa Zbaraskiego od Zygmunta III do Sołtana Mustafy* [The sublime legation of Krzysztof Zbaraski from Sigismund III to Sultan Mustafa]. Warsaw: IBL: Pro Cultura Litteraria, 2000.

Withers, *Serraglio* Withers, Robert. "The Grand Signiors Serraglio." Translation of Ottaviano Bon, *Descrizione del serraglio del gran signore*. In S. Purchas, *His Pilgrims*, 9:322–406. Glasgow, 1905.

Secondary Sources

Abbreviations

EI2: *Encyclopaedia of Islam, Second Edition*. Edited by P. Bearman, Th. Bianquis, C. E. Bosworth, E. van Donzel, and W. P. Heinrichs. Leiden: Brill, 2012.

EI3: *Encyclopaedia of Islam, THREE*. Edited by Kate Fleet, Gudrun Krämer, Denis Matringe, John Nawas, and Everett Rowson. Leiden: Brill, 2015.

İA: *İslam Ansiklopedisi* (Encyclopedia of Islam). Edited by M. Th. Houtsma. Istanbul: Maarif Matbaası, 1940–1986.

TDVİA: *Türkiye Diyanet Vakfı İslam Ansiklopedisi* (Turkish Religious Foundation Encyclopedia of Islam). Istanbul: TDVİA Genel Müdürlüğü, 1988–2012.

Abrahamowicz, Zygmunt. "Roksolana." *Polski Słownik Biograficzny* 31 (1988–1989): 543–545.

Akgündüz, Ahmet. *Osmanlı kanunnâmeleri ve hukuki tahlilleri*. Vol. 9. Istanbul: FEY Vakfı, 1996.

Alderson, A. D. *The Structure of the Ottoman Dynasty*. Oxford: Clarendon Press, 1956.

Altundağ, Şinasi, and Şerafettin Turan. "Rüstem Paşa." In İA.

Andrews, Walter, and Mehmet Kalpaklı. *The Age of Beloveds: Love and the Beloved in Early-Modern Ottoman and European Culture and Society*. Durham, NC: Duke University Press, 2005.

Babinger, Franz. "Bassano, Luigi." In *Dizionario biografico degli Italiani*. Roma: Istituto della Enciclopedia Italiana, 1970, Vol. 7.

Baysun, M. Cavid. "Mihr-ü-Mah Sultan." In İA.

Bennigsen, Alexandre, and Chantal Lemercier-Quelquejay. "Les marchands de la cour ottoman et le commerce des fourrures moscovites." *Cahiers du monde russe et soviétique* 11, no. 3 (1970): 363–390.

Berenson, Bernard. "A Letter to Derek Hill." In *Islamic Architecture and Its Decoration, A.D. 800–1500: A Photographic Survey*, edited by Derek Hill and Oleg Grabar, 13–14. Chicago: University of Chicago Press, 1964.

Bryer, Anthony. "Greek Historians on the Turks: The Case of the First Byzantine-Ottoman Marriage." In *The Writing of History in the Middle Ages*, edited by R. H. C. Davis and J. M. Wallace-Hadrill, 471–494. Oxford, UK: Clarendon Press, 1981.

Bues, Almut, ed. *Royal Marriages of Princes and Princesses in Poland and Lithuania, c. 1500–1800*. Warsaw: German Historical Institute, 2016.

Burgoyne, Michael. *Mamluk Jerusalem*. London: Scorpion Pub., 1987.

Casale, Giancarlo. *The Ottoman Age of Exploration*. New York: Oxford University Press, 2010.

Çavuşoğlu, Mehmed. "16. yüzyılda yaşayan bir kadın şair Nisayi." *Tarih Enstitüsü Dergisi* 9 (1978): 405–416.

———. "Şehzade Mustafa Mersiyeleri." *Tarih Enstitüsü Dergisi* 12 (1982): 641–686.

Danişmend, Ismail Hami. *Izahlı Osmanlı Tarihi Kronolojisi*. Istanbul: Türkiye Yayınevi, 1947–1955. Vol. 2.

Dursteler, Eric. *Venetians in Constantinople: Nation, Identity, and Coexistence in the Early Modern Mediterranean*. Baltimore: Johns Hopkins University Press, 2006.

Dziubiński, Andrzej. *Stosunki dyplomatyczne polsko-tureckie w latach 1500–1572 w kontekście międzynarodowym* [Polish-Turkish diplomatic relationships

1500–1572 in an international context]. Warsaw: Wydanwictwo. Uniwersytetu Wrocławskiego, 2005.

Eastmond, Antony. "Art and Frontiers Between Byzantium and the Caucasus." In *Byzantium, Faith, and Power (1261–1557)*, edited by Sarah T. Brooks, 151–169. New York: Metropolitan Museum of Art; New Haven, CT: Yale University Press, 2006.

Emecen, Feridun. "Kara Ahmed Paşa." In TDVİA.

――――. "Selim II." In TDVİA.

――――. "Süleyman." In TDVİA.

――――. *Tarih içinde Manisa.* Manisa: Manisa Belediyesi Kültür Yayınları, 2005.

Feros, Antonio. "Twin Souls: Monarchs and Favorites in Early Seventeenth-Century Spain." In *Spain, Europe, and the Atlantic World: Essays in Honor of John. H. Elliott*, edited by Richard L. Kagan and Geoffrey Parker. Cambridge: Cambridge University Press, 1995.

Fetvacı, Emine. *Picturing History at the Ottoman Court.* Bloomington: Indiana University Press, 2013.

Finkel, Caroline. *Osman's Dream: The Story of the Ottoman Empire.* New York: Basic Books, 2007.

Fisher, Alan. *The Crimean Tatars.* Stanford, CA: Hoover Institution Press, 1978.

――――. "Muscovy and the Black Sea Slave Trade." *Canadian-American Slavic Studies* 6, no. 4 (Winter 1972): 575–594.

Fleischer, Cornell H. "Shadows of Shadows: Prophecy in Politics in 1530s Istanbul." *International Journal of Turkish Studies* 13, nos. 1–3 (2007): 51–62.

Gökbilgin, M. Tayyib. "Ibrahim." In İA.

――――. "Süleyman I." In İA.

Golden, Peter. "The Codex Cumanicus." In *Central Asian Monuments*, edited by Hasan B. Paksoy, 57–62. Istanbul: Isis Press, 1992.

Goodwin, Godfrey. *A History of Ottoman Architecture.* New York: Thames and Hudson, 1987.

Halenko, Oleksander. "How a Turkish Empress Became a Champion of Ukraine." In *Roxolana in European Literature, History, and Culture*, edited by Galina Yermolenko, 21–55. Burlington, VT: Ashgate, 2010.

Hammer, J. von. *Histoire de l'empire ottoman.* Vols. 5–6. Paris: Belizard, Barthès, Dufour et Lowell, 1836.

Hathaway, Jane. "Eunuchs." In EI3.

Havlıoğlu, Didem. "On the Margins and Between the Lines: Ottoman Women Poets from the Fifteenth to the Twentieth Century." *Turkish Historical Review* 1 (2010): 25–54.

Herrin, Judith. *Women in Purple: Rulers of Medieval Byzantium.* London: Weidenfeld & Nicolson, 2001.

Heyd. Uriel. *Ottoman Documents on Palestine, 1552–1651.* Oxford: Clarendon Press, 1960.

Holum, Kenneth G. *Theodosian Empresses: Women and Imperial Dominion in Late Antiquity.* Berkeley: University of California Press, 1982.

Holum, Kenneth G., and Gary Vikan. "Jerusalem." In *Oxford Dictionary of Byzantium*, edited by A. P. Kazhdan, Alice-Mary Maffry Talbot, Anthony Cutler, Timothy E. Gregory, and Nancy Patterson Ševčenko, 2:1033–1036. Oxford: Oxford University Press, 1991.

Hrushevsky, Michael. *A History of Ukraine.* New Haven, CT: Yale University Press, 1941.

Imber, Colin. "The Persecution of the Ottoman Shi`ites According to the Mühimme Defterleri, 1565–1585." *Der Islam* 56, no. 2 (1979): 245–273.

Inalcık, Halil. "Istanbul." In EI2.

Inalcık, Halil, and Donald Quataert, eds. *An Economic and Social History of the Ottoman Empire, 1300–1914.* Cambridge: Cambridge University Press, 1994.

Isom-Verhaaren, Christine. *Allies with the Infidel: The Ottoman and French Alliance in the Sixteenth Century.* London: I. B. Tauris, 2011.

————. "Royal French Women in the Ottoman Sultans' Harem," *Journal of World History* 17, no. 2 (2006): 159–196.

Ives, Eric. *The Life and Death of Anne Boleyn*. London: Blackwell, 2005.

Kafadar, Cemal. "How Dark Is the History of the Night, How Black the Story of Coffee, How Bitter the Tale of Love: The Changing Measure of Leisure and Pleasure in Early Modern Istanbul." In *Medieval and Early Modern Performance in the Eastern Mediterranean*, edited by Arzu Öztürkmen and Evelyn Birge Vitz, 243–269. Turnhout: Brepols, 2014.

Kafesçioğlu, Çiğdem. *Constantinopolis/Istanbul: Cultural Encounter, Imperial Vision, and the Construction of the Ottoman Capital*. University Park: Pennsylvania State University Press, 2009.

Karaman, Abdulkadir. *Figani*. In TDVİA.

Kepecioğlu, Kemal. "Tarihi Bilgiler ve Vesikalar." *Vakıflar Dergisi* 2 (1938): 405–406.

Kiel, Machiel. *Art and Society of Bulgaria in the Turkish Period*. Assen: Van Gorcum, 1985.

Kizilov, Mikhail. "Slave Trade in the Early Modern Crimean from the Perspective of Christian, Muslim, and Jewish Sources." *Journal of Early Modern History* 11, nos. 1–2 (2007): 1–31.

Ko, Dorothy. *Every Step a Lotus: Shoes for Bound Feet*. Berkeley: University of California Press, 2001.

Kołodziejczyk, Dariusz. *The Crimean Khanate and Poland-Lithuania: International Diplomacy on the European Periphery (15th–18th Century)*. Leiden: Brill, 2011.

Kuran, Aptullah. *Sinan: The Grand Old Master of Ottoman Architecture*. Washington, DC: Institute of Turkish Studies, 1987.

Kürkçüoğlu, Kemal. *Süleymaniye vakfiyesi*. Ankara: Vakıflar Umum Müdürlüğü, 1962.

Kuru, Selim. "Representations: Poetry and Prose, Premodern: Turkish." In *Encyclopedia of Women and Islamic Cultures*, edited by Suad Joseph. Leiden: Brill, 2003.

Lewis, Bernard. *Istanbul and the Civilization of the Ottoman Empire*. Norman: University of Oklahoma Press, 1963.

Magdalino, Paul. "The Foundation of the Pantokrator Monastery in Its Urban Setting." In *The Pantokrator Monastery in Istanbul*, edited by Sofia Kotzabassi, 33–55. Berlin: De Gruyter, 2013.

Mayer, L. A. *Islamic Architects and Their Works*. Geneva: A. Kundig, 1956.

"Ma`ruzat." *Millî Tetebbular Mecmuası* 2 (1916): 338. Istanbul: Âsâr-i İslâmiye ve Milliye Tedkik Encümeni.

Meisami, Julie. "Kings and Lovers: Ethical Dimensions of Medieval Persian Romance." *Edebiyat* (new series) 1 (1987).

Miller, Barnette. *Beyond the Sublime Porte: The Grand Seraglio of Stambul*. New Haven, CT: Yale University Press, 1931.

Musallam, Basim F. *Sex and Society in Islam: Birth Control Before the Nineteenth Century*. Cambridge: Cambridge University Press, 1983.

Necipoğlu, Gülru. *The Age of Sinan: Architectural Culture in the Ottoman Empire*. Princeton, NJ: Princeton University Press, 2005.

————. *Architecture, Ceremonial, and Power: The Topkapı Palace in the Fifteenth and Sixteenth Centuries*. New York: Architectural History Foundation, 1991.

————. "Suleyman the Magnificent and the Representation of Power." *Art Bulletin* 71, no. 3 (1989): 401–427.

Ocak, Ahmet Yaşar. "Idéologie officielle et réaction populaire: un aperçu général sur les mouvements et les courants socio-religieux à l'époque de Soliman le magnifique." In *Soliman le magnifique et son temps*, edited by Gilles Veinstein, 185–192. Paris: La Documentation Française, 1991.

Öngören, Reşat. "Merkez Efendi." In TDVİA.

Ostling, Michael. "'Poison and Enchantment Rule Ruthenia': Witchcraft, Superstition, and Ethnicity in the Polish-Lithuanian Commonwealth." *Russian History* 40 (2013): 488–507.

Özer, Mustafa. *The Ottoman Imperial Palace in Edirne (Saray-ı Cedîd-i Âmire).* Translated by Catherine Bobbitt. Istanbul: Bahçeşehir University Press, 2014.

Pajewski, Janusz. *Wegierska polityka polski w polowie XVI wieku (1540–1571)* [The
Hungarian Policy of Poland in the Mid-16th c. (1540–1571)]. Krakow: Nakł. Pol-
skiej Akademji Umiejętności, 1932.

Pakalın, Mehmed Zeki. *Tarih deyimleri ve terimleri.* Istanbul: Millî Eğitim Basımevi,
1983.

Peirce, Leslie. *The Imperial Harem: Women and Sovereignty in the Ottoman Empire.*
New York: Oxford University Press, 1993.

———. *Morality Tales: Law and Gender in the Ottoman Court of Aintab.* Berkeley:
University of California Press, 2003.

Plokhy, Serhii. *The Gates of Europe: A History of Ukraine.* New York: Basic Books,
2015.

Raby, Julian. "A Sultan of Paradox: Mehmed the Conqueror as a Patron of the Arts."
Oxford Art Journal 5 (1982): 3–8.

Reindl, Hedda. *II. Bayezid ve çevresi: hükümdarın adamları.* Istanbul: Arvana Yayınları, 2014.

Repp, Richard. "Some Observations on the Development of the Ottoman Learned
Hierarchy." In *Scholars, Saints, and Sufis: Muslim Religious Institutions Since
1500,* edited by Nikki Keddie, 17–32. Berkeley: University of California Press,
1978.

Richardson, Glenn. *Renaissance Monarchy: The Reigns of Henry VIII, Francis I and
Charles V.* London: Arnold, 2002.

Ringrose, Kathryn R. *The Perfect Servant: Eunuchs and the Social Construction of
Gender in Byzantium.* Chicago: University of Chicago Press, 2003.

Rosedale, H. E. *Queen Elizabeth and the Levant Company.* London: H. Frowde, 1904.

Rozen, Minna. *History of the Jewish Community in Istanbul in the Formative Years,
1453–1566.* Boston: Brill, 2010.

Şahin, Kaya. *Empire and Power in the Reign of Suleyman: Narrating the Sixteenth-
Century Ottoman World.* Cambridge, UK: Cambridge University Press, 2013.

Sakaoğlu, Necdet. *Bu mülkin kadın sultanları.* Istanbul: Oğlak Yayıncılık, 2011.

Sariyannis, Marinos. "Of Ottoman Ghosts, Vampires, and Sorcerers: An Old Discussion Disinterred." *Archivum Ottomanicum* 30 (2003): 191–216.

Sayers, David Selim. *Tıfli hikâyeleri.* Istanbul: İstanbul Bilgi Üniversitesi, 2013.

Seng, Yvonne. "Fugitives and Factotums." *Journal of the Economic and Social History
of the Orient* 39, no. 2 (1996): 137–160.

———. "Standing at the Gates of Justice: Women in the Law Courts of Early Sixteenth-
Century Üsküdar, Istanbul." In *Contested States: Law, Hegemony, and Resistance,*
edited by Susan Hirsch and Mindie Lazarus-Black, 184–206. New York: Routledge, 1994.

Sertoğlu, Midhat. *Paşalar şehri Istanbul.* Istanbul: Risale, 1991.

Setton, Kenneth Meyer. *The Papacy and the Levant, 1204–1571.* Vol. 3. Philadelphia:
American Philosophical Society, 1976.

Singer, Amy. *Constructing Ottoman Beneficence: An Imperial Soup Kitchen in Jerusalem.* Albany: State University of New York Press, 2002.

———. "Enter, Riding on an Elephant: How to Approach Early Ottoman Edirne."
Journal of the Ottoman and Turkish Studies Association 3, no. 1 (2016): 189–209.

Skilliter, Susan. "Catherine de' Medici's Turkish Ladies-in-Waiting: A Dilemma in
Franco-Ottoman Diplomatic Relations." *Turcica* 7 (1975): 188–204.

———. "Three Letters from the Ottoman 'Sultana' Safiye to Queen Elizabeth I." In
Documents from Islamic Chanceries, edited by S. M. Stern, 119–157. Cambridge,
MA: Harvard University Press, 1965.

Sokolniki, Michel. "La sultane ruthène." *Belleten* 23 (1959): 220–239.

Spagni, E. "Una sultana veneziana." *Nuovo archivio veneto* 19 (1900): 121–148.

Starkey, David. *The English Court: From the Wars of the Roses to the Civil War.* New
York: Longman, 1987.

Stephan, St. H. "An Endowment Deed of Khasseki Sultan, Dated the 24th May 1552." *Quarterly of the Department of Antiquities in Palestine* 10 (1944): 170–199.

Sumner-Boyd, Hilary, and John Freely. *Strolling Through Istanbul: A Guide to the City.* Istanbul: Redhouse Press, 1972.

Taşkıran, Nimet. *Hasekinin kitabı: Istanbul Haseki Külliyesi.* Istanbul: Yenilik Basımevi, 1972.

Tezcan, Hülya. *Tılsımlı gömlekler.* Istanbul: Timaş, 2011.

Turan, Ebru. "The Marriage of Ibrahim Pasha." *Turcica* 41 (2009): 3–36.

Turan, Şerafettin. *Kanuni'nin oğlu Şehzade Bayezid vakası.* Ankara: Türk Tarih Kurumu Basımevi, 1961.

———. "Şehzade Bayezid." In TDVİA.

Uçtum, Nejat R. "Hürrem ve Mihrümah sultanların Polonya kıralı II. Zigsmund'a yazdıkları mektuplar." *Belleten* 44 (1980): 697–715.

Uluçay, M. Çağatay. *Haremden mektuplar.* Istanbul: Vakıt Matbaası, 1956.

———. *Manisa'daki Saray-ı Amire ve Şehzadeler Türbesi.* Istanbul: Resimli Ay Matbaası, 1941.

———. "Notlar ve vesikalar." In *Kanuni armağanı*, 227–258. Ankara: Türk Tarih Kurumu Basımevi, 1970.

———. *Osmanlı sultanlarına aşk mektupları.* Istanbul: Ufuk Kitapları, 1950.

———. *Padişahların kadınları ve kızları.* Ankara: Türk Tarih Kurumu Basımevi, 1980.

Uzunçarşılı, Ismail Hakkı. "Kanuni Sultan Suleyman's Grand Vizier . . . Ibrahim Pasha Was Not His Son-in-Law" [in Turkish]. *Belleten* 29 (1965): 227–288.

———. *Osmanlı Tarihi.* Vol. 2. 4th ed. Ankara: Türk Tarih Kurumu Yayınları, 1983.

Valensi, Lucette. *The Birth of the Despot: Venice and the Sublime Porte.* Ithaca, NY: Cornell University Press, 1993.

Varlık, Nükhet. "Conquest, Urbanization and Plague Networks in the Ottoman Empire, 1453–1600." In *The Ottoman World*, edited by Christine Woodhead, 251–263. London and New York: Routledge, 2011.

Vatan, Nicolas, and Gilles Veinstein. *Le sérail ébranle: Essai sur les morts, dépositions et avènements des sultans ottomans XIVe–XIXe siècle.* Paris: Fayard, 2003.

Veinstein, Gilles. "Sokollu Mehmed Pasha." In EI2.

———. "Süleyman." In EI2.

Weil, Rachel. "The Crown Has Fallen to the Distaff: Gender and Politics in the Age of Catherine de Medici." *Critical Matrix* 1, no. 1 (1985): 1–38.

Wolper, Ethel Sara. "Khidr and the Changing Frontiers of the Medieval World." *Medieval Encounters* 17 (2001): 120–146.

———. "Princess Safwat al-Dunya wa al-Din and the Production of Sufi Buildings and Hagiographies in Pre-Ottoman Anatolia." In *Women, Patronage, and Self-Representation in Islamic Societies*, edited by D. Fairchild Ruggles, 35–52. Albany: State University of New York Press, 2000.

Yelçe, Zeynep. "Evaluating Three Imperial Festivals." In *Celebration, Entertainment, and Theater in the Ottoman World*, edited by Suraiya Faroqhi and Arzu Öztürkmen, 71–109. London: Seagull Books, 2104.

Yermolenko, Galina. "Roxolana: 'The Greatest Empresse of the East.'" *Muslim World* 95 (2005): 231–248.

———. "Roxolana in Europe." In *Roxolana in European Literature, History, and Culture*, edited by Galina Yermolenko, 21–55. Burlington, VT: Ashgate, 2010.

Yıldız, Sara Nur. "Aydınid Court Literature in the Formation of Islamic Identity in Fourteenth-Century Western Anatolia." In *Islamic Literature and Intellectual Life in Fourteenth- and Fifteenth-Century Anatolia*, edited by A. C. S. Peacock and Sara Nur Yıldız. Würtsburg: Ergon Verlag in Kommission, 2016.

Young, George. *Constantinople.* London: Methuen, n.d.

Index

abduction, Roxelana's, 14–15
Abdullah (son), 58, 72, 111, 235
abortion, 112
Adrianople, (Edirne) Thrace, 83, 101,
    196, 222
    Bayezid as lieutenant, 275, 283–285
    hospital, 266
    Pseudo Mustafa's uprising, 288, 298
    Selim (son)'s deputyship, 257–258,
        262
    strategic placement of, 101
    Suleyman's health, 247, 300–301
Aisha (Mihrumah's daughter), 244, 263,
    282, 300, 309
Akkoyunlu dynasty, 104, 107
Alemshah (Suleyman's uncle), 85
Aleppo, 211, 246, 260–263, 280–283,
    285, 287, 290
Alexander the Great, 167, 216
Alqas Mirza, 254–256, 258, 261, 263,305
Amasya, 84, 87, 117, 201, 215–216, 222,
    269, 278, 296–287
Anatolia
    history and range of the Ottoman
        Empire, 17–19
    Mehmed's provincial post, 201
    Mustafa's provincial government
        post, 215
    persecution of Safavid partisans,
        220
    Roxelana's travels through, 226–
        227, 230–235, 237–238
    Selim I's provincial post, 65–66
    See also Amasya; Bozdağ; Konya;
        Manisa
Angiolello, Giovanni Maria, 39, 40, 49,
    55, 85, 124–125
antipathy toward Roxelana, 147–151
architecture
    Haseki Avrat, 172–175, 177–178
    historical debate over Roxelana's
        mosque, 186

Ibrahim's largesse, 156
New Palace, 128–131, 130(fig.),
    131–133, 132(fig.), 134–135
Persian Ali, 186–187
Roxelana's patronage, 147
Sinan, 177, 180,187, 264, 281, 309
the history of royal philanthropy,
    185–186
Armenians, 169, 214, 305
Avrat Pazar (women's market), 172–176,
    173(fig.), 178(fig.), 187, 192–193

background and origins, Roxelana's, 4–6,
    14–16, 24–26, 43–44, 193
Baghdad, 16, 112, 149, 221, 296
    capture of, 145–146
bath (hamam), 9, 47, 88, 122, 126, 134,
    142, 156, 174, 187, 231, 312–313
Bayezid (son), 304–307
    birth of, 58, 111
    circumcision celebration, 204–205
    childhood residence, 210–211
    Iranian campaign, 260–261
    provincial post in Konya, 241
    public career, 247–248
    question of succession, 297–299
Bayezid I, 43, 117, 198–199
Bayezid II, 45, 85, 86(fig.), 185, 215, 220,
    231, 233, 239, 253, 254, 276, 302
    Byzantine forum project, 174–175
    concubines' philanthropic works,
        87–88
    empire building, 10
    family and tragedies, 87
    hospital construction, 266
    overthrow of, 63, 236, 276
Beyhan (Suleyman's sister), 38, 168, 193,
    208, 250, 307
Blue Mosque, 313
Bodin, Jean, 163–164
Boleyn, Anne, 8, 41,171
Bona Sforza, 224–225, 251

Bozdağ, 226, 230–231
Branković, Mara (stepmother of Mehmed
    II), 199–200
Bursa, 85–87, 196, 198, 230–231,
    237–239, 271, 305–306, 310
Busbecq, Ogier Ghiselin de, 118–119,
    147, 199, 245–246, 274, 287–288,
    298–299, 306–307
Byzantine empire, 10, 14, 18, 71, 124,
    133,174, 194, 214, 231, 291, 313

Caesar, Julius, 153
Cairo, 10, 66, 86, 96, 154, 203, 207, 262
caravanserai, 47, 88, 231, 239, 289
Catherine of Aragon, 8
Celalzade Mustafa, 113, 161, 206, 280,
    293
charitable foundations, 4, 9, 11. *See also*
    philanthropy
Charles V (Holy Roman Emperor), 73,
    103, 159–160, 163, 167, 218–219,
    224, 292
charter deeds, 178–179, 189–190, 267
children
    concubinage traditions of, 6, 44–45
    death of Suleyman's, 53, 60–61
    ending reproductive responsibilities,
        111–113
    importance of multiple children, 61
    of Christian captive females, 4–5
    royal concubines' responsibility in
        bearing, 32–33
    Suleyman's, 35–36, 72
    See also Bayezid (son); Cihangir
        (son); Mehmed (son);
        Mihrumah (daughter); Mustafa
        (Suleyman's son); Roxelana,
        children of; Selim (son)
Chinggis Khan (Genghis), 17–18, 215
Christianity, 9, 24, 43, 48, 78, 158, 199,
    213, 227, 238, 267, 290
    Hagia Eirene, 49(fig.), 50, 266
    Hagia Sophia, 48–50, 94, 194, 266,
        313
    Roxelana's background, 4–5
    royal philanthropy and, 185,
        289–294
    Suleyman's religious policy, 292
    and Roxelana, 192, 229, 292
Cihangir (son), 280–281
    birth of, 72, 111, 113

circumcision celebration, 204–205
    concerns over Suleyman's health,
        247
    death of, 281, 285, 287
    domestic arrangements, 210–211
    ill health of, 141–142, 267, 276
    political responsibilities, 243–244
    question of succession, 276, 297
    travels through Anatolia, 238
circumcision of the princes, 102–108,
    112–113, 204–205
civil war among the princes, 167,
    276–278
Cleopatra, 8
clothing, 56(fig.), 56–57, 75, 75(fig.)
Column of Constantine, 47–48
concubines
    emancipation of concubine mothers,
        119
    foreign fascination with the
        Ottoman court, 40–41
    justifying serial concubinage, 60
    mental and physical characteristics
        of, 32–33
    origins of, 14–15
    philanthropic works, 86–87
    physical and intellectual
        requirements, 6–7
    separate apartments for chosen
        women, 45–46
    Suleyman's household, 36
    See also Hafsa (Suleyman's mother);
        harem, imperial; Mahidevran
        (concubine); slaves
Constantine I, 47–48, 174, 290–291
Constantine XI, 48, 200
contraception, 58–59, 111–112
correspondence between Suleyman and
    Roxelana, 283(fig.)
    news from the war front, 282–284
Crimean Khanate, 16–17, 20–21, 25, 34,
    65, 107, 219
Cromwell, Thomas, 153
*Customs of the Janissaries of the
    Imperial Household,* 240

death
    of Hafsa, 113
    of Mehmed, 233–237
    of Roxelana's children, 72, 305–306
    of Selim I, 93–94

death *(continued)*
  of Suleyman, 309–310
  of Suleyman's children, 53–54, 94,
    111, 271–272, 281
  of princes, 85–87
  Roxelana's concerns over internal
    dissent, 275–276
  Roxelana's declining health and, 12,
    281–282, 299–300, 302–304,
    315
  visiting shrines and tombs, 227–229
  See also executions
Dernschwam, Hans, 162, 184, 186, 299
dervishes, 47, 144, 152, 187, 194, 215,
  228(fig.), 230, 280
  See also sufis
diplomacy
  Franco-Spanish conflict, 221–222
  Gritti's contribution of service,
    158–159
  Safavid peace with the Ottomans,
    295–296
  treaties with Iran and the
    Hapsburgs, 286–287
  with Poland, 253–254
  women's role in, 11, 251–252
Divan Hall, New Palace, 131–133, 190,
  255
Divan. *See* Imperial Council
Diyarbakır, 149–150, 200, 206, 222–223,
  250, 259, 274, 285–286
domestic life, Roxelana's, 10–11,
  210–211, 225–226, 307–309
Dulkadir dynasty, 107, 198
dynastic security
  educating the princes, 218–219
  mothers' role in, 315–317
  multiple children securing, 60–61
  See also succession

Ebu Suud, 126–127, 192, 302
education
  benefits of Roxelana's foundation,
    173
  boys' seminary at the New Palace,
    135
  choosing the mothers of princes, 20
  Haseki Avrat, 174–175, 190–191
  of concubines in the Old Palace,
    39, 41
  of imperial princes, 84–85, 218–219
  of Mustafa, 95

  of Roxelana after Mehmed's birth,
    58
  of Roxelana's children, 11, 78,
    82–83, 204
  of slave women, 31–32
  Roxelana's conversion to Islam, 33
  teachers at the Haseki Avrat,
    180–181
Egypt, 8, 10, 19, 66–68, 71, 86, 96, 107,
  135, 155, 219, 262, 294
England, 38
  Anglo-French alliance, 102–103
  foreign fascination with the
    Ottoman court, 40–41
  Roxelana's diplomatic relations
    with, 251–252
  securing the dynasty, 61
  women's diplomacy between the
    Ottomans and, 296–297
epidemics, 36, 53–54, 82, 90, 209, 233
Ertugrul, 18–19
eunuchs, 28–29, 47, 124–125, 124(fig.),
  125, 183, 315
Evliya Çelebi, 22–23, 172
executions
  Bayezid (son)
  Ferhad
  Ibrahim, 150–154, 160–163
  Iskender, 160–161
  Kara Ahmed, 294–295
  Mustafa, 271–279
expansion of the Ottoman Empire, 10–11,
  145, 163–164

family planning, 111–112
Fatima (daughter of Prophet
  Muhammad), 113, 293
Fatma (Selim I's daughter), 207–208
Ferdinand (archduke), 73, 101, 162–164,
  184, 205, 218, 222–224, 286–287
Ferhad (Suleyman's brother-in-law), 38,
  71, 168, 193, 208, 250
Festival of the Sacrifice, 139
Field of the Cloth of Gold, 102–103
finances
  bathing facilities, 142
  charter for the Haseki foundation,
    178–181
  concubine mothers' philanthropic
    roles, 86–87
  costs of the Imperial Council home,
    131

mapping the princely household, 84
 revealing court practices, 88–90
 Roxelana's daily stipend, 77–78, 242
 Rustem Pasha's frugality, 251,
  268–269
 the vizier's income, 155–156
fire, 121, 203, 212–213, 258
Forum of the Bull, 174
foundations. *See* philanthropy
France
 conflict on multiple fronts, 221–222
 marriage connections to the
  Ottomans, 14
 foreign fascination with the
  Ottoman court, 40–41
 French ambassadors, 14, 129, 140,
  210, 221, 261, 300
 French-Ottoman alliance, 221
Francis (king of France), 14, 40, 102, 196,
 213, 221
fratricide, 7, 64, 304

Genoa, 3–4, 16, 24, 39, 45, 146, 197
Giray Tatars. *See* Tatars
gout, Suleyman's, 246, 282, 300
governance
 Divan days, 130–131
 domestic effect of strong empire
  building, 304
 Egyptian revolt, 71
 female monarchs, 315–316
 intelligence gathering, 11
 in Suleyman's absence, 117, 138–139
 Mustafa's governorship, 108–109
 Nurbanu's contributions to Selim II
  and Murad's reigns, 312–313
 overseeing the management of a
  prince, 84–85
 peace treaties: Safavid empire,
  295–296
 public initiation of the princes,
  108–109
 quasi-constitutional sovereignty,
  314–315
 religious policy, 291–292
 Roxelana's marriage giving women
  a voice in, 122–123
 Seljuk influence on Ottomans, 18–19
 state building within the Ottoman
  Empire, 164
 under Selim II, 304
 under Suleyman, 67–68

Gritti, Alvise, 158–160, 162
Gulfem, 35, 75–77, 142, 260, 300
Gurji Khatun, 229

Hadice (Suleyman's sister), 156–157
Hafsa (Suleyman's mother)
 background and tenure of, 20–21,
  34–35, 114
 care of the royal family, 85–86
 correspondence with Suleyman, 79
 death of, 11–12, 113, 127
 female entrepreneurs, 39
 Ferhad's execution, 38
 gift of Roxelana to Suleyman, 34,
  69–71
 harem hierarchy, 36
 informational networks, 140
 philanthropic projects, 88, 171–172,
  187
 Roxelana's rise in status threatening
  Mahidevran, 94–95
 Selim I's aspirations to the throne,
  69–70
 stipend, 90
 succession concerns, 64–65
 Suleyman's relationship with, 32
 Sultaniye complex, 232
 upgrading the New Palace, 123
Hagia Eirene (St. Irene), 49(fig.), 50,
 129
Hagia Sophia, 48–50, 94, 194, 266, 313
Hall of the Maidens, 45, 46, 51, 53, 119,
 121–122
Hammer, J. von, 68, 220
Hapsburg, House of, 72–73, 101, 108–
 109, 145–146, 158–160, 162–163,
 184, 205, 224, 237, 254, 287, 307
harem, imperial, 136–138
 financial management, 77–78
 Hafsa's position in, 34–35
 hierarchy of the Old Palace, 27–29,
  34–36
 New Palace, 11–12, 27–29, 35–37,
  43, 45–47
 Roxelana's daily life during
  Suleyman's military absences,
  75–77
 Roxelana's royal responsibilities
  for, 11
 See also concubines, New Palace;
  Old Palace
Harun al-Rashid, 165, 194, 292–293

Haseki foundation, 178(fig.)
  choosing a site, 172–176
  controversy connected to, 184
  daily life and personnel, 181–184
  following imperial traditions,
    266–267
  healing services provided by, 268
  madrasa, 180–181
  planning the mosque, 176–177
  political significance of, 172
  services and amenities, 177
  staff requirements, 179–180, 268
  Suleyman's endorsement and
    financial support, 189–191,
    193
Hatuniye foundation, 231
Hayreddin Barbarossa, 140–141, 201,
  219, 312
Helena (mother of Constantine I),
  290–291
Henry VIII, 8, 61, 104, 153, 167
hierarchy of the Old Palace, 27–28
hippodrome, 50, 104–105(fig.), 108, 137,
  146, 204, 258, 313
Holy Roman Empire, 14, 73, 103, 159,
  292
honeymoon of Roxelana and Suleyman,
  71–72
hospitals, 9, 47, 88, 112, 170, 184, 187,
  232, 264–268, 300
Huma Shah (Mehmed's daughter), 232,
  235–236, 241–242, 244, 260, 262,
  282, 300
Hungary, 72–73, 82–83, 162–163, 223
Hurrem (Ottoman name of Roxelana), 4,
  30, 52, 144, 303, 319
Husnushah (concubine of Bayezid II), 86,
  88, 231

Ibn Battuta, 19–20
Ibrahim (Suleyman's grand vizier), 90,
  197
  background and career, 154–157
  blame for Suleyman's errors,
    161–162
  conflicting descriptions of his
    virtues, 161–163
  conversion, 161–162
  execution of, 150–154, 160–161, 163
  Mustafa's jealousy, 95–96
  Roxelana as gift from, 32

Roxelana's relationship with,
    165–166
  Suleyman's relationship with,
    167–168
Imperial Council (Divan), 37, 77, 105,
  109, 130(fig.), 140, 155, 226, 237,
  250, 263, 294
interregnum rule, 7, 285, 309, 312–314
Iraq, 17, 116, 145–146, 149, 286, 296
Isabella (queen of Hungary), 223–224,
  254
Iskender (treasurer), 156, 160–161
Islam, 111, 116. 133. 265(fig.), 278
  calendar, 111, 139, 164, 208, 237,
    249, 289
  conversion of slaves, 4–5, 42–44,
    83, 185, 224
  emancipation of slaves, 24, 35, 54,
    113–114, 118–119, 184–186,
    212, 223
  holy men, 75, 284
  Ibrahim and Islam, 156
  Istanbul's built landscape, 46–50
  and law, 35, 54, 58, 78, 85, 113, 115,
    176, 207
  pilgrimage, 118, 262, 265, 290–293
  and philanthropy, 9, 170–171, 192
  Roxelana's charitable actions, 9,
    289–294
  Roxelana's conversion, 33, 192,-193,
    291–292
  shi`i and sunni, 107, 161, 164, 172,
    228, 255, 296
  status of non-Muslims in, 42,
    47,126, 215, 296
  teachers at the Haseki Avrat, 179
  women's chastity through seclusion,
    126–127, 213, 251
  See also dervish; madrasa;
    philanthropy; sufi
Ismail, Shah, 65, 66, 146, 261
Istanbul
  Blue Mosque, 313
  built landscape and attractions,
    46–50
  Haseki Avrat, 173–174
  Kagithane, 264

Janissaries
  antipathy towards Roxelana,
    148–149

engagement in Anatolia, 117
infantry corps, 10, 60
Iranian campaign, 269
Mustafa's popularity, 73
refusal to obey Selim II, 310
revolt of 1525, 96, 162, 258
Roxelana's generosity toward,
    240–241
Jerusalem, 137, 170, 194, 261
rebuilding, 164–165
Roxelana's foundation, 288–293
Suleyman's project, 288–293
jewels and ornaments, 57, 96–97, 158,
    159(fig.), 189, 213, 263
John VI Kantakuzenos, 198
Judaism and Jews, 9, 60, 126, 140, 158,
    213, 223, 227, 238, 289, 292, 312
tradeswomen, 39, 114, 140, 158, 213
Justinian I, 48, 194

Ka`aba (Mecca), 265, 265(fig.)
Karaman, 214–215
Khadija (first wife of Prophet
    Muhammad), 293
Khosraw (Chosroes), 168–169, 216
Knox, John, 315
Konya
    Bayezid's post, 241, 243
    family reunion at, 226–227
    history of a royal presence, 201
    Selim (son)'s post, 214–216,
        226–227
Korkud (Suleyman's uncle), 65–66, 86,
    92, 216
Kosem (dowager queen), 315–316
Kutbeddin el-Mekki, 301–303

lalas (tutors), 84–85, 110, 202, 217, 233,
    308
literature, educational and entertainment
    value of, 169
Lituanus, Michalon, 24–25
loyalty to the dynasty, 42–44, 272, 286
Lutfi, 189, 193–194, 204–208, 230

madrasas, 46–47, 170, 173.180–181,
    190–191, 266
Mahidevran (concubine, mother of
    Mustafa)
    arrival in Istanbul after Selim I's
        death, 93–94

as role model for Roxelana, 57
background and training, 84,
    88–89
circumcision of the princes, 106
eligibility of sons to succeed their
    father, 249
emergence into politics, 101–102
harem hierarchy, 36
Haseki foundation, 188
increasing power at court, 90
life in Manisa, 90–92, 109
Mustafa's execution, 270–272
Mustafa's harmony with Roxelana,
    83
Mustafa's provincial government,
    216–217
public opinion, 7–8, 83, 150,
    270–271, 310
retirement, 310
rivalries among the princes, 10, 62,
    79
rivalry with Roxelana, 90–91,
    94–99, 148–149
Mahmud (Suleyman's son), 35–36,
    54–55, 64, 67
Mamluk dynasty, 10, 66, 104, 107, 157,
    160, 262
Manisa, 82–85
    family reunion, 237–238
    Hafsa's foundation, 88, 113,
        148–149, 165, 186–187
    Mahidevran's life in, 90–92, 109
    Mehmed's post, 214–216, 226
    Roxelana's travels to, 231, 231–232
    royal presence, 201
    Suleyman's post, 34–36, 52, 65–66
Marlowe, Christopher, 198–199
marriage
    arranged, 37–38, 91, 115
    French-Ottoman alliances, 14
    Ibrahim's lavish wedding,
        156–157
    Mihrumah and Rustem, 205–208
    of harem women following palace
        service, 11–12, 138, 211–212
    of Sigismund Augustus, 224–225
Mecca, 10, 66, 75, 137, 170, 188, 247,
    264–265, 265(fig.), 289, 301
de Medici, Catherine, 251, 296, 312
Medina, 10, 170, 264–265, 289, 301
Mehmed (Mustafa's son), 201–202, 286

Mehmed (son), 105(fig.), 203(fig.)
    as intermediary for his mother,
        140–141
    birth of, 53–56, 72
    circumcision of, 102–108, 112–113
    combat experience, 202–203,
        208–209
    competition among princes, 7
    death of, 233–237
    Mehmed's education and service,
        204
    emergence into politics, 110–111
    memorial mosque, 238–240
    preparation for governing, 122
    provincial goverment posting, 214,
        216, 218, 226
Mehmed II "the Conqueror," 86(fig.)
    administration, 43
    architecture of the New Palace,
        131–132
    Christian art and relics, 192–193
    construction of the harem, 136–137
    crisis of succession, 60–61
    ending the Karaman-Ottoman wars,
        215
    financing military expansion, 87
    Franco-Ottoman connection, 14
    fratricide and violence, 63
    hospital construction, 266
    marriage of, 198
    mosque construction, 239
    execution of Mahmud (grand vizier)
    New Palace, 12
    Old Palace, 27–28
    philanthropy, 47, 170–171
    remodeling the New Palace, 134
    Roman successorship, 160
    soldiers' revolt, 59–60
    upgrading the New Palace, 133–134
Menavino Giovanni Antonio, 39, 40, 45,
    100, 115, 204
Mengli Giray, 65
Merkez Efendi, 230, 232
Mevlevi order, 228(fig), 228–229
Mihri Hatun, 215
Mihrumah (daughter), 96, 205(fig.)
    as female companion, 301
    Bayezid's execution, 306–307
    birth of, 58–59, 72, 94, 110
    devotion to Bayezid, 309–310
    emergence of female patronage, 188
    festivities in Adrianople, 261

    inherited wealth, 243
    marriage of, 205–208
    needlework and correspondence, 79
    political service, 223, 225, 250,
        253–254
    relations with Selim, 306–307, 310
    upbringing, 11
military campaigns
    capture of Rhodes, 58
    central Europe, 101
    circumcision celebration as display
        of power, 103–104
    construction of the Suleymaniye
        with the spoils of war, 263–264
    Egyptian revolt, 71
    German campaign, 101, 163, 219
    governance in Suleyman's absence,
        117
    governance without, 314
    Hafsa following the news of,
        113–114
    Iranian campaigns, 108–109,
        116, 138, 257–258, 260–263,
        269–271, 270(fig.), 274, 280,
        285–288
    maintaining family life during,
        141–144
    Mehmed's death cooling Suleyman's
        desire for, 237
    mock battle to celebrate Egyptian
        conquest, 107
    Mustafa's education, 82–83
    return from Iran (1536), 145
    rivalry between Suleyman's sons,
        304–305
    Roxelana's correspondence and
        counsel, 282–285
    Selim I, 63–66
    Suleyman's hiatus from, 71,
        219–220
    Suleyman's inherited empire, 10–11
    taking and losing Buda, 72–73,
        82–83
    the princes' combat experience,
        202–203, 222, 275–279
Mongols, 16–19, 60, 63, 77, 117, 146, 215,
    227
monogamy, 208
    Roxelana's growing political power,
        79–80
    Roxelana's rise as Suleyman's
        favorite, 59–60

Selim II's succession to Suleyman, 311–312
Suleyman's desire to secure the dynasty, 61–62
Suleyman's succession of his father, 68
Mosque of the Prince, 238–239
mosques
    Hafsa's mosque (Sultaniye) 113–114
    Haseki Avrat, 172–174, 176–177, 182–187, 192
    historical debate, 186
    Istanbul foundation, 170–171
    Istanbul's built landscape, 46–47
    Manisa, 231–232
    Ka'aba, 265, 265(fig.)
    Mehmed's memorial mosque, 238–240
    Roxelana's design for, 164–165
    sufi spirituality, 228
    Suleymaniye, 95, 295(fig.)
    Turhan's mosque, 316(fig.)
motherhood
    birth control, 111–112
    care of a royal household, 85–86
    concerns for the children's futures, 92
    death and difficulties, 72
    elevation of status through, 55–57
    identity formation through, 91
    in the event of a prince's death, 85–87
    issues of succession, 297–299
    learning to raise a child, 57–58
    professionalizing the offspring, 101
muhaddere (chaste behavior), 126–127
Murad (Suleyman's son), 35–36, 53–55, 64
Murad II, 14, 60–61, 87, 199–200, 271
Murad III, 238, 296, 309–312, 314
Muscovy, 24, 25, 38
Mustafa 'Ali, 152, 239, 308
Mustafa (Suleyman's son), 105(fig.)
    age of provincial service, 57
    arrival in Istanbul after Selim I's death, 93–94
    as political threat, 285–286
    charge of treason, 269–270
    circumcision of the princes, 102–108, 112–113
    emergence into politics, 101–103, 108–110

    execution, 271–280, 297
    formal education, 82–83
    harmony with Roxelana, 82
    Ibrahim's part in the rivalry with Roxelana's sons, 165–166
    Iranian campaign, 270–271, 270(fig.)
    Janissaries' admiration for, 240
    Mahidevran's privilege, 83–84
    Mehmed's birth, 55
    military and political service, 149–150
    mother and status, 35–36
    palace criticism of Roxelana, 148–149
    provincial government, 208, 222–223
    public opinion, 7–8, 271–272, 275, 290
    relationships with Suleyman, 95
    rivalries among the princes, 10, 62, 73

naval forces, 73, 219
    See also Hayreddin Barbarossa
nedim (boon companion of the sultan), 167–168
needlework, 39–40, 79, 252, 255
New Palace
    architecture of, 128–131, 130(fig.), 131–133, 132(fig.), 134–135
    female quarters, 45–46, 136–137
    illustration, 49(fig.), 130(fig.), 132(fig.)
    kitchens, 132–133
    queen mother's apartments, 311(fig.)
    reflecting the power of the empire, 133–134
    residents and offices, 29–30
    Roxelana's domestic responsibilities, 241–242
    Roxelana's residence in, 114–115, 121–125, 127–128, 136
Novosiltsov, Ivan, 26
nuclear family, Roxelana's, 6, 72
Nurbanu (Selim II's concubine), 238, 295–296, 311–313

Oghuz Khan, 17
Oliviera Despina, 198–199
Old Palace
    education of the women, 41
    fire in, 212–213

Old Palace *(continued)*
  Hafsa's status, 34–36
  hierarchy of, 27–29
  history of, 27–28
  princes' education, 45–46
  role of princesses, 37–38
  Roxelana's arrival, 34
  Roxelana's domestic responsibilities,
    241–242

pages (sultan's), 78, 89, 129, 135, 138,
    202, 247
Palestine, philanthropic endowment in,
    288–294
patronage, political and personal,
    155–156
patronage, royal, 171–172, 185–189,
    191, 231, 267, 292. *See also*
    philanthropy
Peçevi, Ibrahim, 108, 113, 157, 161, 178,
    204, 211, 234, 255, 270, 294, 308
philanthropy
  in Aleppo, 261–262
  as obligation for Muslims,
    170–171
  emergence of female patronage,
    187–188
  for sufi piety, 229–230
  Hafsa's foundation, 187, 232
  Hatuniye foundation, 231
  history of royal building, 194
  hospital construction, 264–269
  in religious sites, 264–265
  Manisa, 232–233
  personal meaning of, 191–192
  Roxelana's concern for Janissary
    welfare, 240–241
  Roxelana's endeavors in Palestine,
    288–294
  Roxelana's imperial affairs, 127
  Roxelana's Istanbul foundation,
    146–147, 171–172
  Roxelana's political and personal
    status, 188–189
  See also Haseki foundation
Pilak Mustafa, 203, 211–212
pilgrimages, 188, 261–262, 264–265
poetry and poets, 8, 74, 143–144,
    147–148, 162, 168, 215, 278,
    305
  elegies for Mustafa, 278–279

Poland, 14, 40, 79, 296,
  capture of Roxelana, 16
  diplomatic correspondence with,
    251–255
  Poland-Lithuania, 24–25, 26, 223,
    251
  See also Bona Sforza; Isabella;
    Sigismund I; Sigismund;
    Augustus
power, political and personal
  architecture reflecting, 128
  Central Asia as source of, 17–18
  circumcision celebration as display
    of, 103–104
  domestic politics during Suleyman's
    absences, 77–78
  hierarchy of the New Palace, 29–30
  hierarchy of the Old Palace, 27–29
  innovation under Suleyman, 67–68
  intimate friendship among males,
    168
  Mustafa's awareness of his own,
    95–96
  of Ibrahim, the grand vizier,
    155–156, 160–161
  overriding family bonds, 37–38
  perception of Ottoman power after
    the war with Iran, 287–288
  royal philanthropy and, 185–187
  within the harem, 5–6
  See also governance; Roxelana,
    personal and political power
pretenders, 288, 305, 307
primogeniture, 6–7, 313–314
princes
  death of, 85–87
  education and management of,
    84–85
  management training, 220–221
  political careers, 214–215
  provincial duties, 217
  royal architectural philanthropy,
    185–186
  See also specific individuals
princesses
  foreign, 14, 20, 43, 103, 115,
    198–200
  function and status of, 37–38
  Ibrahim's marriage, 157
  marriage of, 157, 185, 205
  political role of, 36

stipends and status, 241–243
See also Beyhan; Mihrumah
(daughter); Shah Sultan
Privy Chamber terrace, New Palace, 134
procurator of the Sultana, 125
provincial authorities, 77–78
Pseudo Mustafa, 288, 305, 307

raids, abduction of slaves and, 16–17,
21–22
religion. *See* Christianity; Islam; Judaism
rivalries
among the royal princes, 91–92,
165–166, 281–282, 297
Mahidevran and Roxelana, 90–91,
94–99, 148–149, 165–166,
274–275
Rustem and Ibrahim, 249–250
Rohatyn, Ukraine, 15, 21, 26
Roman empire, 10–11, 14, 48, 66, 73, 103,
159–160, 216, 292
Roxelana, background and origins of
arrival at the Old Palace, 34
as gift to Suleyman, 34, 69–71
capture in Poland, 16, 24–25
Christian background, 4–5
conversion to Islam, 26, 33, 43–44,
291–292
debate over, 4–5, 8–9, 14–16, 25–26
difficulties in, 5–8
Roxelana's personality and
character, 9, 53–54
Roxelana's philanthropy stemming
from slavery, 193
slave trade, 14–15, 21–22
Roxelana, children of
Abdullah, 58, 72, 111, 235
celebrating the circumcision of the
princes, 102–106
changing Roxelana's status at court,
54–57
death of, 72, 305–306
education of, 11, 78, 82–83, 204
marriage of Mihrumah, 205–208
nuclear family, 6, 72
report of, 96–97
Roxelana's custodial responsibilities,
78
Roxelana's later pregnancies, 58–59
Roxelana's presentation to
Suleyman, 51–53

Suleyman securing Selim II's
political future, 308–309
See also Bayezid (son); Cihangir
(son); Mehmed (son);
Mihrumah (daughter); Selim
(son)
Roxelana, correspondence
domestic arrangements, 209–210
gifts and messages from well-
wishers, 75
historical value of, 8–9
maintaining contact during military
campaigns, 141–144, 282–285
pleas for Rustem Pasha's
reinstatement, 284–285
rising standards of living, 262
Roxelana's improving literacy, 209
Roxelana's life in the harem, 75–76
Roxelana's yearning for Suleyman,
73–75
Suleyman and, 283(fig.)
Suleyman's declining health,
246–248, 259–260
Roxelana, daily life of
declining health and death, 12,
281–282, 299–300, 302–304,
315
domestic responsibilities in the Old
Palace, 210–211, 241–242
during Suleyman's military
absences, 75–77
income and daily stipend, 55–57,
77–78, 242
Mahidevran as role model, 57
raising children in Suleyman's
absence, 10–11
residence and domestic
responsibilities in the New
Palace, 114–115, 121–125,
127–128, 136, 241–242
Roxelana's quarters in the New
Palace, 122–123
Roxelana's rise in status threatening
Mahidevran, 94–95
televising Roxelana's life, 26
travels through Anatolia, 225–227,
231
Roxelana, early relationship with
Suleyman
conceiving her second child, 58–59
Roxelana's first summons, 52–53

Roxelana, early relationship with
Suleyman *(continued)*
Suleyman's choice of a concubine,
44–46
Suleyman's partners after Roxelana,
70–71
Roxelana, marriage to Suleyman
as source of historical debate,
199–200
controversy surrounding, 184–185
domestic conflict, 248
giving women a voice in
governance, 122–123
Hafsa's death, 116–117
honeymoon, 71–72
increasing Roxelana's status and
power, 27–28, 79–80, 100–101,
118–120, 189, 197–198
instigation of, 118–120
intimacy replacing sexual relations,
244–245
precedents for succession, 12–13
private nature of, 115–116
public announcement of, 145–147
Roxelana's imperial seclusion
following, 123–125
Roxelana's lack of a coronation,
171
Roxelana's new life in the New
Palace, 114–115, 125–126,
128–129
Roxelana's rise as Suleyman's
favorite, 59–60
securing Selim II's political future,
308–309
speculation on Suleyman's affection
for Roxelana, 245–246
Roxelana, personal and political power of
Bayezid's downfall, 307–309
children changing Roxelana's status
at court, 55–57
diplomatic relations with Britain,
251–252
Roxelana's counsel during
Suleyman's campaigns,
284–285
Roxelana's exposure to Istanbul,
46–50
Roxelana's marriage expanding her
power, 27–28, 79–80, 100–101,
118–120, 197–198
Roxelana's part in Ibrahim's

execution, 150–152
Roxelana's part in Mustafa's
execution, 272–275
Roxelana's plea for Rustem's
reinstatement, 294–297
Roxelana's aggrandizement of the
royal harem as a political force,
3–4, 12
training in social behavior, 33–34
Roxelana, personal and political
relationships
Ibrahim, 32
Ibrahim's part in Mustafa's rivalry
with Roxelana's sons, 165–166
Janissaries' antipathy, 148–149
Mahidevran, 90–91, 94–99,
148–149, 165–166, 274–275
Mustafa, 82–83, 148–149, 275–276
Roxelana, philanthropy of
charitable actions, 9, 289–294
charitable work with slaves, 193
educational benefits of Roxelana's
foundation, 173
endeavors in Palestine, 288–294
historical debate over Roxelana's
mosque, 186
imperial affairs, 127
interest in the training of slaves, 173,
211–212
mosque design, 164–165, 186
political and personal status,
188–189
Roxelana's concerns with the
Janissaries, 240–241
Rumi, Jalal ad-Din, 215, 227–229
Rustem (Mihrumah's husband), 206–207,
223, 249–251, 258, 268–272, 284,
294–297, 301–302
Ruthenia, 4, 10, 14–16, 21, 22, 25, 26, 31,
83, 96, 134, 147–148, 199, 224, 252,
291, 304

saadet (good fortune), 133
sacred places, 264–265
Safavid state, Iran, 65
peace treaty, 295–296
Selim I's concerns over the threat
of, 65
shi`i Islam, 228
territorial losses, 149–150
the princes' circumcision, 107
See also Alqas Mirza; Diplomacy;

Ismail, Shah; military campaigns; Tahmasp Shah
Safiye (Murad III's favor), 295–296
Şemseddin Sami, 151
Sandys, George, 184–185
seclusion
  Roxelana's, 107, 123–126
  sultan's, 126, 133
Selim I, 10, 34, 63–68, 86(fig.), 93, 107, 113, 123, 157, 160, 190–191, 207, 239, 242–243, 255, 261, 290
Selim II (son), 75(fig.)
  arrival in Aleppo, 280–281
  ascension to the throne, 304
  birth of, 58, 94
  circumcision celebration, 103, 107–108
  disavowing his family, 307
  Iranian campaign, 261
  Janissaries' refusal to acknowledge succession, 310
  military campaigns, 201–203
  Poland-Lithuania relations and, 26
  provincial government at Konya, 214, 216, 226–227
  question of succession, 297–299
  selection of pages, 135
  succeding Mehmed in Manisa, 237–238
  Suleyman's deputy, 258
Seljuk empire, 17–19, 214–216
serial concubinage, 61–64
The Seven Beauties, 169
sexual relationship of Roxelana and Suleyman
  conceiving her second child, 58–59
  intimacy replacing, 244–245
  Roxelana's first summons, 52–53
sexual responsibilities: the role of the sultan and the women of the harem, 6
Shah Sultan (Suleyman's sister), 187–188, 193–194, 207, 230, 242–243
Shahnameh (epic poem), 263
shi'i Islam, 107, 111, 228
Sigismund Augustus, 224–225, 252, 256, 296
Sigismund I "the Old," 25, 223–225, 251–254, 256
Sinan (royal architect), 177, 181, 187, 264, 281, 309
Sitti Khatun, 198

slave trade
  European attitude, 24
  fates and destinations of the slaves, 22–24
  history and control of, 16–17
  market locations and practices, 31–32
  Roxelana's origins, 14–15, 21–22
  Suleyman's familiarity with, 21
  sultans' complicity in, 25–26
slaves
  arranged marriages of, 211–212
  conversion to Islam, 42–44
  gift to Suleyman of two Russian slaves, 98
  hierarchy of the Old Palace, 28–29
  instruction of, 15
  Mustafa's pride and arrogance, 95
  physical and mental requisites for concubines, 32–33
  rights and protections of mothers, 54
  Roxelana's charitable work, 193
  Roxelana's interest in the training of, 211–212
  Suleyman's concubines after Roxelana, 70–71
  See also concubines
social behavior
  decline in public prominence of women, 19–20
  education and training of concubines, 39–42
  imperial seclusion, 46, 123–124, 126–127, 133, 213, 251
  Roxelana's training in, 33–34
Sokollu Mehmed, 269, 305, 308–309, 312
Solakzade Mehmed, 161, 204, 269, 295, 308
sorcery, talk of, 59, 147
spectacles and celebrations, 102–106, 262–263, 280–281
stipends, harem, 88–90, 242
Strongila, 39, 140, 158, 213
succession
  Archduke Ferdinand challenging Suleyman's claim to Hungary, 162–163
  Bayezid II and Selim I, 65
  Bayezid and Selim (sons), 297–299, 304–309
  celebration of coronations, 103
  choosing the mothers of princes, 20

succession *(continued)*
    concerns over civil war among the
        princes, 277–278
    death of Suleyman, 309–310
    death of Suleyman's children,
        54–55
    eligibility of sons to succeed their
        father, 248–249
    Mehmed's claim to Roman
        successorship, 160
    Mustafa's emergence into politics,
        109–110
    primogeniture, 6–7, 313–314
    Pseudo Mustafa, 287–288
    Roxelana and Suleyman's
        precedents for, 12–13
    serial concubinage and, 60–63
    sovereignty: eligibility of sons to
        succeed their father, 248–249
    Suleyman succeeding his father,
        63–64, 67–68
    Suleyman's accession to the throne,
        63–67
    Suleyman's concerns over Mustafa,
        276
sufis, 9, 144, 149, 170, 194, 215, 228–230,
    233, 290. *See also* dervishes
Suleyman I "the Magnificent," 159(fig),
    190(fig.), 203(fig.), 236(fig.),
    245(fig.), 270(fig.), 295(fig.)
    appointment to Caffa, 93
    apprenticeship, 92–93
    arrival in Aleppo, 280–281
    choosing Roxelana, 44–46, 51–53
    Damascus foundation, 290
    death of his children, 53–55,
        236(fig.)
    declining health, 246–247, 258–259
    execution of the grand vizier,
        10–154
    foreign fascination with the
        Ottoman court, 40–41
    fortieth birthday, 111, 208–209
    Ibrahim's history with, 154–157
    inherited command, 10
    love life, 30
    luxury purchases, 24
    military hiatus, 219–220
    mother of, 20–21, 34–35
    need for trusted favorites,
        166–169

potential for partners after
    Roxelana, 70–71
public opinion of Suleyman's
    monogamy, 59–60
rivalry between his sons, 304–309
siblings, 37–38
slave women, 98
spectacles and celebrations, 102–106
state building within the Ottoman
    Empire, 164
succession, 63–68, 297–299
See also correspondence between
        Suleyman and Roxelana; Hafsa;
        military campaigns
Suleymaniye mosque, 263–264, 268, 295,
    295(fig.)
Sultaniye complex, 232. *See also* Hafsa
Sunullah Efendi, 315
syncretic religion, 192–193

Tahmasp Shah, 116, 146, 254, 258, 262,
    269, 281, 284, 286, 295, 305
Talikizade Mehmed, 293–294
Tamburlaine the Great (Marlowe),
    198–199
Tatars, 16–17, 19–22, 24–25, 219,
Tavernier, Jean-Baptiste, 126
television, Roxelana's life on, 26
Theodora (Justinian's wife), 194
Theodora (Orhan's wife), 198
Theodosius I, 174
Theodosius II, 174
titles, 4, 242–243
Topkapi Palace, 12, 129, 189
    See also New Palace
Trabzon (Trebizond), 34, 57, 65, 92–93
treason charge against Mustafa,
    269–270
tughra (Suleyman's emblem), 190
Turhan (queen mother), 315–316
Twardowski, Samuel, 26

Ukraine, 14–15, 22–24, 26
ulema, 190–191
urban development, Haseki Avrat as,
    177–178

Venice, 69, 97, 157, 160, 196, 257, 275,
    312
    control of Black Sea slave trade by,
        16–17

Venetian ambassadors, 15, 59, 69, 70(fig.),
  83, 148, 156, 274
  Bragadin, 15, 32, 34, 38, 57, 95–96,
    98, 100, 113, 153–158, 165, 168
  de'Ludovici, 100, 110, 114, 118–119,
    158, 162, 245
  Navagero, 72, 83, 97–99, 166, 207,
    239, 246–247, 261, 270, 277
  Trevisano, 239, 275, 278, 287
  Zen, 59, 109, 154, 158–159
Vienna, military campaign, 101–102, 218
virginity, importance of, 32–33, 200,
  207

wealth
  business interests of wealthy
    women, 127
  income, Roxelana's, 55–57
  inherited wealth, 6–7, 243
widowhood, 37–38
Wolsey, Cardinal Thomas, 153
women
  building as consequential gesture,
    171
  business interests of wealthy
    women, 127
  diplomacy work, 223–224, 251–252
  emergence of female patronage,
    187–188
  entrepreneurs, female, 39, 140
  escaping the Old Palace fire, 213
  female monarchs, 315–316
  informational networks, 139–140
  poets, 215 (Mihri Hatun), 278
    (Nisayi)
  political involvement, 139–140
  public prominence of, 19–20
  role models for Suleyman, 193–194
  Roxelana's memorial in Palestine,
    290–291
  Roxelana's transformation of the
    harem into a political power,
    3–4, 12
  Rumi's spiritual biography,
    228–229
  seclusion as a mark of distinction,
    126
  slave market locations and practices,
    31–32
  Suleyman's love life, 30
  the princes' circumcision, 106
  See also concubines; Hafsa
    (Suleyman's mother);
    Mahidevran (concubine);
    motherhood

Zapata, Luis de, 167
Zapolya, John, 223
Ziadi (witch), 147–148
Zubaida, 165, 194, 292–293

Credit: Lara Heimert

LESLIE PEIRCE has been interested in Turkish and Ottoman history ever since she joined the Peace Corps in Turkey. She has taught at Cornell University; the University of California, Berkeley; and New York University. The award-winning author of two previous books, Peirce lives in New York City.